Library of
The University of Michigan
from
The Directors of
The New York Mercantile Library

S. Hastings Grant,
Lib.

Feb 10, 1857

SUPPLEMENT

TO THE

CATALOGUE

OF THE

MERCANTILE LIBRARY

OF THE

CITY OF NEW YORK.

CONTAINING THE

ADDITIONS MADE TO AUGUST, 1856.

NEW YORK:
BAKER & GODWIN, PRINTERS,
CORNER OF NASSAU AND SPRUCE STREETS,
1856.

SUPPLEMENT

TO THE

MERCANTILE LIBRARY CATALOGUE.

A B B——A C T

Abbott, Rich.—Principles and Practice of Linear Perspective .	8vo.	Lond.	1853
——— Jacob—Corner Stone.	12o.	N. Y.	1852
——— ——— Young Christian	12o.	N. Y.	1851
——— ——— History of Cleopatra	16o.	N. Y.	1851
——— ——— " Nero	16o.	N. Y.	1853
——— ——— " Pyrrhus	16o.	N. Y.	1854
——— J. S. C.—Child at Home.	16o.	N. Y.	1852
——— ——— History of Josephine	16o.	N. Y.	1850
——— ——— " Madame Roland	16o.	N. Y.	1851
——— ——— " Napoleon Bonaparte. 2v. . . .	8vo.	N. Y.	1855
——— ——— Mother at Home; or, Maternal Duty . . .	16o.	N. Y.	1852
Abel, F. A. and Bloxam (C. L.)—Hand Book of Chemistry. (Fr. Ger.)	8vo.	Phil.	1854
Abernethy, Jno.—Memoirs of, by Geo. Macilwain	12o.	N. Y.	1853
Abrantes, Duchess d'(Mde. Junot)—Memoirs of Celebrated Women. 2v.	12o.	Phil.	1835
——— ——— Memoirs of Napoleon	8vo.	N. Y.	1854
——— ——— The Same. 2v.	8vo.	N. Y.	1855
Abstract of Evidence in 1790–1 as to the Slave Trade . . .	8vo.	Lond.	1791
Achilli, Giacinto—Dealings with the Inquisition . . .	12o.	N. Y.	1851
Account of Several late Voyages and Discoveries	8vo.	Lond.	1711
——— the Centennial Celebration in Danvers, Mass., June 16, 1852	8vo.	Bost.	1852
——— Free School Society of New York	8vo.	N. Y.	1814
——— Pilgrim Celebration at Plymouth, Aug. 1, 1853	8vo.	Bost.	1853
Acosta, Jos.—History of the East and West Indies (Fr. Span.) .	4to.	Lond.	1604
Across the Atlantic	12o.	Lond.	1851
Actes des Apôtres	8vo.	Paris.	1789
——— et Mem. concern. les Negociat'n entre France et les Etats Unis, 3v.	12o.	Lond.	1807
Acts of Assembly, passed in Barbadoes 1648–1718 . . .	Fol.	Lond.	1721
——— of the Province of New York, 1691–1731 .	Fol.	N. Y.	1726–31

Adair, Robt.—Negotiations for Peace of Dardanelles in 1808–9. 2 v. 8vo. Lond. 1845
Adam, Wm. P.—Thoughts on the Policy of Retaliation . . . 12o. Lond 1852
Adams, Chas.—Women of the Bible . . . . . 12o. N. Y. 1851
——— C. W.—A Spring in the Canterbury Settlement. . . 12o. Lond. 1853
——— Jno.—Letters addressed to his Wife. 2v. . . 12o. Bost. 1841
——— —— Doctrine of Equity . . . . . . 8vo. Phil. 1852
——— —— On Action of Ejectment . . . . . 8vo. N. Y. 1854
——— —— Works, with Life and Notes, by C. F. Adams. Vols. 2–9 8vo. Bost. 1850–54
——— —— See *Selection of Eulogies*, and *Webster, D.*
——— John Q.—Lectures on Rhetoric and Oratory. Vol. 2. . 8vo. Camb. 1810
——— —— Letters on Silesia, during a Tour in 1800–1 . 8vo. Lond. 1804
——— Neh.—Friends of Christ in the New Testament . . 8vo. Bost. 1853
——— —— Life of John Eliot . . . . . 12o. Bost. 1847
——— —— South-Side View of Slavery . . . . . 12o. Bost. 1854
——— Sam.—Oration, delivered Aug. 1, in Phil. . . 8vo. Phil. 1776
Addison, Jos.—Dialogues on the Usefulness of Ancient Medals . 12o. Lond. 1726
——— —— Miscellaneous Works. 3 v. . . . . 12o. N. Y. 1853
Adventures of Hunters and Travellers, and other Narratives . 12o. Phil. 1852
————— Signor Gaudentio di Lucca . . . . 16o. Lond. 1850
Æschylus.—Tragedies (Fr. Grk., by Buckley.) . . . 16o. Lond. 1849
———— See *Scriptorum Græcorum Bibliotheca;* Vol. 13
Æsop.—Fables (Fr. Grk., by Thos James) . . . . . 8vo. N. Y. no date
Agassiz, L.—Bibliographia Zoologiæ et Geologiæ. Vol. 3 . 8vo. Lond. 1852
Agnel, H. R.—The Book of Chess . . . . . . 12o. N. Y. 1854
Aguilar, Grace—Essays and Miscellanies . . . . 12o. Phil. 1853
——— —— Women of Israel. 2 v. . . . . . 12o. N. Y. 1851
Ahn—Introductory Course to the French Language . . 8vo. Phil. 1854
Aide-Mémoire to the Military Sciences. Vol. 3. . . 8vo. Lond. 1851
Aikin, Lucy—Memoirs of the Court of James I. 2 v. . . 8vo. Lond. 1822
Ainslie, Hen.—Scottish Songs, Ballads and Poems . . . 12o. N. Y. 1855
——— John.—Treatise on Land Surveying. 8vo., and Atlas. . 4to. Lond. 1849
Ainsworth's Magazine. Vols. 18–24. [*Continued.*] . . . 8vo. Lond. 1850–3
Ackerman, J. Y.—Coins of the Romans relating to Britain . 8vo. Lond. 1844
———— —— Catalogue of Rare and Unedited Rom. Coins. 2 v. 8vo. Lond. 1834
*Albany Business Directory for 1852 . . . . . 12o. Albany. 1852
*——— Directory for 1813, '15, '18, '20–25, '27–54. 36 v. . 12o. Albany. 1813–54
*Albion, The Vols 1–4. . . . . Fol. N. Y. 1833–6
*——— The Same. Vols. 28–33. (N. S. 8–13). [*Continued.*] . Fol. N. Y. 1850–54
Albro, Jno. A.—Life of Thomas Shepard, ... 12o. Bost. 1847
Alcott, Dr. Wm. A.—Gift-Book for Young Ladies . . . 12o. Buffalo. 1852
——— —— Lectures on Life and Health . . . . 12o. Bost. 1853
——— —— Tea and Coffee . . . . 16o. Bost. 1839
Alden and Hancock's British Mollusca. See *Ray Society Pub'ns.*
Alexander, Arch.—History of the Israelitish Nation . . 8vo. Phil. 1853
———— —— Outlines of Moral Science . . . . 16o. N. Y. 1852
———— —— Life, by his Son . . . . . 8vo. N. Y. 1854
———— Emperor of Russia. See *Lee, Robt.*
———— J. H.—Universal Dictionary of Weights and Measures 8vo. Phil. 1850
———— Jas. W.—American Mechanic and Workingman . 18o. Phil. 1847
———— —— Consolation: in Discourses on Select Topics . 8vo. N. Y. 1853

Title	Size	Place	Date
Alexander, Jas. W.—Life of Archibald Alexander	8vo.	N. Y.	1854
——— —— Christ and Christianity	12o.	N. Y.	1854
*Alfonce, J. E. d'—Instructions in Gymnastics	4to.	N. Y.	1851
Alfred, King, Life of, by Reinhold Pauli. (Fr. Ger.)	8vo.	Lond.	1852
Alison, Arch.—History of Europe, 1789–1815. Vol. 1	12o.	Edin.	1853
——— —— History of Europe, from the Fall of Napoleon. Vols. 1–3	8vo.	Edin.	1853
——— —— The Same. Vol. 1	8vo.	N. Y.	1853
——— —— The Future; or, Science of Politics	12o.	Lond.	1852
Allah, R. E.—The Thistle and the Cedar of Lebanon	12o.	Lond.	1853
Allen, C. B.—Cottage Building for the Laboring Classes	12o.	Lond.	1849–50
——— Dav. O.—India, Ancient and Modern	8vo.	Bost.	1856
——— Jos.—Battles of the British Navy. 2 v.; vol. 1	16o.	Lond.	1852
——— —— Life of Nelson	16o.	Lond.	1853
——— Julian—Autocracy in Poland and Russia	12o.	N. Y.	1854
——— J. N.—March through Scinde and Affghanistan in 1842	8vo.	Lond.	1843
——— Lewis F.—Rural Architecture	12o.	N. Y.	1852
——— Nathan—Opium Trade in India and China	8vo.	Lowell.	1853
——— Wm.—Memoir of John Codman	8vo.	Bost.	1853
——— Z.—Philosophy of the Mechanics of Nature	8vo.	N. Y.	1852
Allin, Abby—Home Ballads	16o.	Bost.	1850
Allgemeine Zeitung (Augsb.), July, 1851–Sept., 1854. 13 v. [*Cont'd*]	Fol.	Augsburg.	1851–4
Alliance des Jacobins de France avec le Ministre Anglais	8vo.	Paris.	1804
Allston, Wash.—Works and Genius of, by Wm. Ware	16o.	Bost.	1852
Allyn, Avery—Ritual of Freemasonry	12o.	N. Y.	1850
Alston, J. W.—Hints to Young Practitioners in Landscape Painting	8vo.	Edin.	1804
*Almanach de Gotha, from 1853–6. 4 v.	64o.	Gotha.	1852–5
Almeyda, Teodoro de—El Feliz Independente del Mundo. 4 v.	16o.	Madrid.	1799
Alms-House—Fourth Annual Report of the Governors of	8vo.	N. Y.	1853
*Alphabetical and Analytical Catalogue of the Amer. Institute Lib.	8vo.	N. Y.	1852
*——— Index to the Astor Library	8vo.	N. Y.	1851
Amari, M.—History of the War of the Sicilian Vespers. 3 v.	12o.	Lond.	1850
America Discovered. A Poem	12o.	N. Y.	1850
*American Agriculturist. Vols. 6–13. [*Continued*]	8vo.	N. Y.	1847–55
*——— Almanac, for 1851	12o.	Bost.	1850
*——— ——— for 1852	12o.	Bost.	1851
*——— ——— " 1854–56. 3v.	12o.	Bost.	1853–55
——— Art Union. See *Bulletin*, and *Transactions*.			
——— Baptist Register, for 1852. Edited by J. L. Burrows	8vo.	Phil.	1853
*——— Biblical Repository. Index to vols. 1–24 (1831–44)	8vo.	N. Y.	1845
*——— Ephemeris and Nautical Almanac for 1855	8vo.	Wash.	1852
——— Jour. of Med. Science, Ed. by Hays. Vols. 23–28 [*Cont'd*]	8vo.	Phil.	1852–4
——— ——— Science and Arts. Vols. 47–49	8vo.	N. Haven.	1844–5
——— ——— The Same; New Series. Vols. 1–11 [*Continued*]	8vo.	N. Hav.	1846–54
——— ——— The Same; Index to Vols. 1–49	8vo.	N. Hav.	no date.
*——— Medical Monthly. Vols. 1 and 2	8vo.	N. Y.	1854–5
——— Missionary Register, by Z. Lewis. Vol. 1	8vo.	N. Y.	1821
*——— Phrenological Journal. Vol. 12	8vo.	N. Y.	1850
*——— Polytechnic Journal. Vols. 1–4	8vo.	N. Y.	1853–4
*——— Pioneer. Vols. 1 and 2	8vo.	Cincin.	1842–3
——— Print Works *vs.* Cornelius W. Lawrence	8vo	N. Y.	1852

Title	Size	Place	Date
American Quarterly Register; Edited by Stryker. Vols. 2–6	8vo.	N. Y.	1849–51
——— Rail Road Journal, N. S. Vols. 6–7 [*Continued*]	4to.	N. Y.	1850–51
——— Rose Culturist. See *Saxton's Rural Hand-Books.*			
——— State Papers. See *Washington, George.*			
*——— ——— and U. S. Public Documents. 12 v.	8vo.	Bost.	1819
*——— Statistical Annual for 1854	12o.	N. Y.	1854
*——— Text for Letters	Obl.	Bost.	n. d.
——— Whig Review. Vols. 11–16	8vo.	N. Y.	1850–52
Ames, Fisher—Works, 2 v.	8vo.	Bost.	1854
Andersen, Hans C.—Gesammelte Märchen	16o.	Leipzig.	1850
——— ——— Pictures of Sweden	8vo.	Lond.	1850
——— ——— Poet's Day-Dreams	16o.	Lond.	1853
Anderson, C.—Eight Weeks in Norway	12o.	Lond.	1853
——— Dav.—Canada	8vo.	Lond.	1814
——— Jas.—Course of Creation	8vo.	Lond.	1850
——— ——— Ladies of the Covenant	16o.	Glasgow.	1851
——— Jno.—Reminiscences of Thomas Chalmers, D. D.	12o.	Edin.	1851
——— Wm.—Practical Mercantile Correspondence	12o.	N. Y.	1851
Andree, Karl—Nord Amerika	8vo.	Braunsch'g.	1851
*Andrews, E. A.—Latin-English Lexicon	8vo.	N. Y.	1851
——— G. H.—Agricultural Engineering. Vol. 1, Buildings	16o.	Lond.	1852
——— J. D.—Trade and Commerce of British N. Amer. Col. 2 v.	8vo.	Wash.	1853
——— J. R.—Four Months' Tour in the East	8vo.	Dublin.	1853
——— Stephen P.—Discoveries in Chinese	12o.	N. Y.	1854
Anecdotes for the Steamboat and the Railroad	12o.	Phil.	1853
Angell, Jos. K.—Law of Fire and Life Insurance	8vo.	Bost.	1854
Angus, Jos.—Bible Hand-Book	12o.	Lond.	1854
Annals and Magazine of Nat. Hist., New Series. Vols. 6–14. [*Cont'd.*]	8vo.	Lond.	1850–54
——— of Congress. *See Debates and Proceedings.*			
——— Electricity, Magnetism and Chemistry; Vol. 2	8vo.	Lond.	1838
——— San Francisco (The), by Soulé, Gihon and Nésbet	8vo.	N. Y.	1855
——— the Georgetown College Astronomical Observatory. No. 1	4to.	N. Y.	1852
Annuaire de Bureau des Longitudes; 1852, 1853. 2 v.	18o.	Paris.	1851–2
——— l'Economie Politique, et de la Statistique	24o.	Paris.	1853
——— l'Instruction Publique, pour 1852	16o.	Paris.	n. d.
*——— des Deux Mondes; 1850–54; 4 v. [*Continued*]	8vo.	Paris.	1850–4
*——— Général du Commerce, &c., pour 1813, 1847 and 1850	8vo.	Paris.	1843–55
*——— Historique Universel; ou, Histoire Politique pour 1853	8vo.	Paris.	1855
*Annual Register, 1849–1851. 3 v. [*Continued.*]	8vo.	Lond.	1849–51
Ansley, E. A.—Elements of Literature	12o.	Phil.	1849
Anselm, Archb'p.—Life of, by F. R. Hasse. (Fr. Ger.)	8vo.	Lond.	1850
Anspach, F. R.—Sepulchres of the Departed	12o.	Phil.	1854
Answer to the Declaration of the American Congress	8vo.	Lond.	1776
Anthon, Chas.—Manual of Greek Literature	8vo.	N. Y.	1853
Antigua and the Antiguans. 2 v.	8vo.	Lond.	1844
Anzeiger für. Bibliographie; by Petzholdt; für 1851–2; 2 v. [*Cont'd*].	8vo.	Halle.	1851–2
Apocalypse Unveiled. 2 v.	12o.	N. Y.	1853
Apologie des Projets des Chefs de la Révolution Française	8vo.	Lond.	1793
Appeal to the Justice and Interests of the People of Great Britain	8vo.	Lond.	1775
Appianus, Alexandrinus—See *Scriptorum Græcorum Bibliotheca*, Vol. 5.			

*Appleton's Dictionary of Machines, Mechanics, Engineering, &c. 2 v. 8vo. N. Y. 1851–2
——— Mechanics' Mag. Vols 1–3. . . . . 8vo. 4to. N. Y. 1851–3
——— New Catalogue of American and English Books . . 8vo. N. Y. 1855
——— Northern and Eastern Traveller's Guide . . 18o. N. Y. 1853
——— Southern and Western Traveller's Guide. . . 18o. N. Y. 1853
Apuleius, Lucius—Metamorphoses. (Fr Lat. by Head.) . . 12o. Lond. 1852
——— —— Opera. 7 v. See *Valpy's Delphin Classics.*
Arago, Fran.—Astronomie Populaire . . . . . 8vo. Leipz. 1855
——— —— Popular Lectures on Astronomy. . . . 16o. Lond. 1854
——— —— Sämmtliche Werke. Vols. 1–3. . . . 8vo. Leipz. 1854–5
——— J.—Narrative of a Voyage round the World . . . 4to. Lond. 1823
Archdale, Jno.—Description of Carolina . . . . . 4to. Lond. 1707
Archer—Tours in Upper India and Himalaya Mountains. 2 v. . 8vo. Lond. 1833
Arfwedson, C. D.—United States and Canada in 1831–2. . 8vo. Lond. 1834
Aristophanes. See *Script. Græc. Bibliotheca*, Vol. 2, Pt. 2, and Vol. 15.
Aristotle. Opera—See *Scriptorum Græcorum Bibliotheca*, Vols. 30, 35.
——— Nicomachean Ethics—(Fr. Gr'k by Browne.) . . 16o. Lond. 1850
Arlincourt, Vicomte—L'Italie Rouge . . . . . 12o. Paris. 1850
Arminius, Jas.—Works, (Fr. Latin). 3 v. . . . . . 8vo. Auburn. 1853
Armstrong, John—History of the Island of Minorca. . . 8vo. Lond. 1756
——— Wm. J.—Memoir and Sermons, Ed. by Rev. M. Reed . 12o. N. Y. 1853
Arnauld, Antoine—Logique de Port Royal . . . . 16o. Paris. 1846
Arnold, Aug. C. L.—Philosophical History of Freemasonry . 12o. N. Y. 1854
——— Thos.—Travelling Journals . . . . . 16o. Lond. 1852
——— —— Christian Life . . . . 12o Phil. 1856
Arnot Wm.—Race for Riches . . . . . . 12o. Phil. 1853
Arrianus—See *Scriptorum Græcorum Bibliotheca*, Vol. 26. .
Arrowsmith, Jas.—Paper-Hanger's Companion. . . . . 16o. Phil. 1852
*Art Journal, N. S. Vols. 2–6. [*Continued.*] . . . 4to. Lond. 1850–54
*———Illustrated Catalogue of the Great Exhibition . 4to. Lond. no date.
Art and Industry, as represented in the Crystal Palace Exhibition. 12o. N. Y. 1853
——— Nature, under an Italian King . . . . . 8vo. Edin. 1852
Artis E. T.—Antediluvian Phytology . . . . . 4to. Lond. 1838
Arthur, T. S. and Carpenter, (W. H.)—History of Georgia . . 16o. Phil. 1852
——— " Kentucky . 16o. Phil. 1852
——— " Virginia . 16o. Phil. 1852
——— Wm.—The Successful Merchant; a Life of Sam'l Budget 12o. N. Y. 1853
Arvine, Kazlitt—Cyclopædia of Anecdotes of Lit. and the Fine Arts 8vo. Bost. 1835
*Ash, John—Dictionary of the English Language. 2 v. . . 8vo. Lond. 1755
Ashburnham, John—Narrative of his Attendance on Charles I. . 8vo. Lond. 1830
Ashmun, Jehudi—Life of, by Ralph R. Gurley . . . 8vo. Wash. 1852
Ashton, Mrs. S. G.—The Mothers of the Bible . . . . 12o. Bost. 1855
Assassinats comm. sur 81 Prisonniers. [B'd with *Alliance des Jacobins*] Title wanting. n. d.
Assurance Magazine. Vols. 2–4. [*Continued.*] . . . . 8vo. Lond. 1852–53
*Astronomical Observations made during the year 1846, Vol. 2. . 4to. Wash. 1851
Atcheson, Nath.—American Encroachments of British Rights . 8vo. Lond. 1808
*Athenæum; a Weekly Journal, 1850–53. [*Continued*] . . 4to. Lond. 1850–53
——— Français—Vols. 1–2. [*Continued.*] . . 4to. Paris. 1852–5
Atkins, Jno.—Voyage to Guiana, Brazil and the West Indies 8vo. Lond. 1735
Atkinson, H. G., and Martineau, Harriet—Man's Nature & Developm't. 8vo. Lond. 1851

Atlas Geographus for America	4to. Lond.	1717
*—— (The.)—A Literary and Historical Journal. Vol. 4. .	Fol. N. Y.	1831–2
Attaché in Madrid; or, Court of Isabella II. (Fr. Ger.) . .	12o. N. Y.	1856
Aubigné, J. H. Merle d'—History of the Reformation, Vols. 4–5. .	12o. N. Y	1853
Aubuisson de Voivins (J. F. d')—Treatise on Hydraulics . .	8vo. Bost.	1852
Auckland, The Capital of New Zealand, &c.	16o. Lond.	1853
Auerbach, Berth.—Schwarzwälder Dorfgeschichten. 4 v. . .	16o. Mannheim.	1850
Augustine, St.—Life and Labors of, by Rev. P. Schaff . .	12o. N. Y.	1854
Augustinus, Leonardus—Gemmæ et Sculpturæ Antiquæ . .	4to. s. l.	1694
Auldjo, John—Ascent of Mont Blanc, in 1827 . . .	8vo. Lond.	1830
Ausonius Decimus Magnus—Opera. 3 v. See *Valpy's Delphin Classics.*		
Austin, Mrs. Sarah—Germany from 1760 to 1814 . .	8vo. Lond.	1854
——— W. S. and Ralph (Jno.)—Lives of the Poets Laureate .	8vo. Lond	1853
Auteroche, Chappe d'—Voyages to California, Newfoundland, &c.	8vo. Lond.	1778
Autobiography of an English Soldier in the U. S. Army. 2 v. .	12o. Lond.	1853
——————— a New Churchman, or, Life of Jno. A. Little .	12o. Phil.	1852
——————— an Indian Army Surgeon	12o. Lond.	1854
Autographs for Freedom—Edit. by Julia Griffiths . . .	12o. N. Y.	1854
Azara, Felix d'—Quadrupèdes du Paraguay (Fr. Span.) 2 v. .	8vo. Paris.	1801
Bache, A. D.—Report on Education in Europe . . .	8vo. Phil.	1839
——— —— Reports on the Coast Survey. See *United States.*		
Bacon, Francis (Lord)—Moral and Historical Works . .	16o. Lond.	1852
——— —— and Sir W. Raleigh, by M. Napier . . .	8vo. Camb. (E.)	1853
——— Leonard—Thirteen Historical Discourses . .	8vo. N. Haven.	1839
*Backer, Aug. et Alois de—Ecrivains de la Comp. Jesus. 2 v. .	8vo. Liege.	1853–4
Badger, A. G.—Illustrated History of the Flute . . .	8vo. N. Y.	1853
——— Cath. N.—The Teacher's Last Lesson: a Memoir of M. Whiting	12o. Bost.	1855
——— Geo. P.—The Nestorians and their Rituals. 2 v. . .	8vo. Lond.	1852
Bailey, J. T.—Historical Sketches of Brooklyn and its Neighborhood	12o. Brooklyn.	1840
——— Phil. J.—Festus. A Poem	12o. Bost.	1853
——— —— Mystic, and other poems	16o. Bost.	1856
——— Sam.—Discourses on Various Subjects . . .	8vo. Lond.	1852
——— —— Theory of Reasoning	8vo. Lond.	1851
Baillie, Joanna—Dramatic and Poetical Works . . .	8vo. Lond.	1851
——— N. B. E.—The Land-Tax of India	8vo. Lond.	1853
Baily, John—Central America	8vo. Lond.	1850
Baird, Jas. J. J. (Compiler.)—The Classical Manual . .	16o. Lond.	1852
——— Robt.—Christian Retrospect and Register for 1801–51 .	12o. N. Y.	1851
——— —— The Same to 1855	12o. N. Y.	1855
——— Robt. H.—American Cotton Spinner and Managers' Guide	12o. Phil.	1851
Bajon, Mons.—Histoire de Cayenne. 2 v.	8vo. Paris.	1777
Baker, T.—Elements of Mechanism	16o. Lond.	1852
Bakewell, F. C.—Electric Science; its History, &c. . . .	12o. Lond.	1853
Balbirnie, Jno.—Philosophy of the Water-Cure	12o. N. Y.	1852
Balbo, Cesare—Life and Times of Dante Alighieri. (Fr. Ital.) 2 v.	12o. Lond.	1852
Balder, —Part the First; by the author of "The Roman." .	12o. Lond.	1854
*Baldwin, A. C.—Traveler's Vade-mecum; or, Instantaneous Let. Writer	16o. N. Y.	1853
——— Geo. C.—Representative Women	12o. N. Y.	1855
——— J. G.—Sketches of Party Leaders	12o. N. Y.	1855

Baldwin, Thos.—Baptism of Believers and Close Commu'on Vindicated 12o. Bost. 1806
*———— ——Pronouncing Gazetteer . . . . . 12o. Phil. 1851
*———— —— and Thomas, (J.)—Gazetteer of U. S. . . 8vo. Phil. 1854
Balfour, Clara L.—Sketches of English Literature . . 16o. Lond. 1852
——— J. H.—Class Book of Botany . . . . . 8vo. Edin. 1852
——— Walt.—Memoir of, by Thomas Whittemore . . 16o. Bost. 1852
Ball, B. L.—Rambles in Eastern Asia . . . . . 12o. Bost. 1855
Balleydier, A.—Histoire de la Guerre de Hongrie, 1848–9 . 8vo. Brux. 1853
———— —— Révolutions de l'Empire d'Autriche 1848–9 . 8vo. Brux. 1853
Ballou, Hosea—Miscellaneous Poems . . . . . 12o. Bost. 1852
———— —— Life of, by Thos. Whittemore. Vol. 1. . . 12o. Bost. 1854
——— Maturin M.—History of Cuba . . . . . .12o. Bost. 1854
——— Moses—Divine Character Vindicated . . . 12o. N. Y. 1854
Balmes, Jac.—Philosophie Fondamentale. (Fr. Span.) 2v. . 16o. Paris. 1852
———— —— Protestantism and Catholicity Compared. (Fr. Span.) 8vo. Balt. 1851
*Baltimore Directory, for 1845, 1847–51, 53–4. 5 v. . . 8vo. Balt. 1845–53
Balzac, H. de—Maximes et Penseés . . . . . . 16o. Paris 1852
———— —— Pierrette . . . . 12o. Paris 1854
Bancroft, Edw.—Natural History of Guyana . . . . 8vo. Lond. 1769
———— Geo.—History of the United States. Vols. 4–6 . 8vo. Bost. 1852–5
———— —— Literary and Historical Miscellanies . . 8vo. N. Y. 1855
Banfield, T. C.—Statistical Companion for 1852 . . 16o. Lond. 1852
———— —— and Weld, C. R.—Statistical Companion for 1850 . 12o. Lond. 1850
Bangs, S. R.—Memoir of, by W. H. U. Magruder . . 16o. N. Y. 1853
Banker's Almanac for 1851 . . . . 8vo. Bost. 1851
———— Common-Place Book . . . . 18o. Bost. 1851
———— Magazine and State Financial Register. Vols. 3–8. [*Continued.*] 8vo. N. Y. 1848–54
*———— and Journal of Money. Vol. 13, [*Continued.*] 8vo. Lond. 1853
*Banks, T. C.—Dormant and Extinct Baronage of England. 4 v. . 4to. Lond. 1807–37
Banning, E. P.—Common Sense on Pathology of Chronic Diseases 12o. N. Y. no date
Banvard, Jos.—The American Statesman—Life of Webster . 16o. Bost. 1853
———— —— Novelties of the New World . . . . 16o. Bost. 1852
———— —— Plymouth and the Pilgrims . . . . 16o. Bost. 1851
———— —— Wisdom, Wit, and Whims of Ancient Philosophers 12o. N. Y. 1855
Barante, A. G. P. B. de—Ducs de Burgogne. 1364–1477. 8 v. . 8vo. Paris. 1842
———— —— Histoire de la Convent'n Nationale. Vols. 1 & 4 16o. Brux. 1851–2
Barclay, Robt.—Apology for the Quakers . . . . 8vo. N. Y. 1826
Bard, Sam. A.—Waikna : Adventures of the Mosquito Shore . 12o. N. Y. 1855
Bardwell, Wm.—Healthy Hours and how to make them . 8vo. Lond. no date
Barham, Hen.—Hortus Americanus . . . . . 8vo. Kings'n (J.) 1794
Barhydt, D. P.—Life :—A Poem . . . . . 16o. N. Y. 1851
Barker, Jacob (of New Orleans)—Incidents in the Life of . . 8vo. Wash. 1855
——— W. B.—Lares and Penates ; or Cilicia and its Governors 8vo. Lond. 1853
Barnard, Hen.—National Education in Europe . . . 8vo. N. Y. 1854
———— —— School Architecture . . . . . 8vo. Hartf. 1854
———— —— Tribute to Gallaudet; a Discourse . . . 8vo. Hartf. 1852
Barnes, Alb.—Miscellaneous Essays and Reviews. 2 v. . . 12o. N. Y. 1855
———— ——Way of Salvation and Defence of the Same . . 12o. N. Y. 1836
——— W.—Anglo-Saxon Delectus, or First Class Book . 12o. Lond. 1849
Barni, Jules—Philosophie de Kant . . . . . . 8vo. Paris. 1857

Barnum, P. T.—Life of, by himself . . . . . 12o. N. Y. 1855
Barré, Rich.—Genealogical Memoirs of the Royal House of France Fol. Lond. 1825
Barrell, Geo. Jr.—Pedestrian Tour in France and Switzerland . 12o. N. Y. 1853
Barrere, Pierre—L'Histoire Naturelle de la France Equinoxiale . 16o. Paris 1741
Barrett, B. F.—Beauty for Ashes; or, Death of Little Children . 12o. N. Y. 1855
Barrington, A.—Physical Geography . . . . . 12o. N. Y. 1851
——— Sir J.—Personal Sketches of his own Times . 12o. N. Y. 1853
Barrows, E. P., Jr.—Memoir of Everton Judson . . . . 12o. Bost. 1852
——— John—Memoirs of Naval Worthies . . . . 8vo. Lond. 1845
——— ——— Travels into the Interior of Southern Africa. 2 v. . 4to. Lond. 1806
Barruel, Abbé—Memoirs of History of Jacobinism (Fr. Fren.) 3 v. 8vo. Lond. 1797–8
Barter, Chas.—The Dorf and the Veld; or, Six Months in Natal . 12o. Lond. 1852
Bartholomèss, C.—Hist. Philosophique de l' Academie de Prusse. 2v. 8vo. Paris 1850
Bartlett, D. W.—Life of Gen. Frank. Pierce . . . . . 12o. Auburn. 1852
——— ——— " " Joan of Arc . . . . . 12o. Auburn. 1854
——— ——— " " Lady Jane Grey . . . . 12o. Auburn. 1853
——— ——— Modern Agitators; or Pen-Portraits . . 12o. N. Y. 1855
——— ——— What I saw in London . . . . . 12o. Auburn. 1852
——— J. R.—Explorations & Incidents in Texas & N. Mexico, &c. 2 v. 8vo. N. Y. 1854
*——— R. M.—Commercial and Banking Tables . . . . 4to. Cincin. 1853
——— W. H.—Elements of Natural Philosophy. Sect. 1; Mechanics 8vo. N. Y. 1850
Bartol, C. A.—Pictures of Europe, framed in Ideas . . . 12o. Bost. 1855
Barton, E. N.—Cause and Prevention of Yellow Fever . . 8vo. Phil. 1855
——— Manuel de la Danse. (De l'Ang.) . . . . . 18o. Paris. 1830
Bascom, Hen. B.—Life of, by Rev. M. M. Henkle . . 12o. Louisv. 1854
Bassnett, T.—Mechanical Theory of Storms . . . . . 12o. N. Y. 1854
Baucher, F.—Method of Horsemanship. (Fr. Fren.) . . 12o. Phil. 1851
Bauer, Anton—Gerichtsverfassung des Königreichs Westphalen . 8vo. Marburg. 1811
Bayard, F. M.—Voyage dans l'Interieur des Etats Unis, en 1795 8vo. Paris. 1795
Baylee, Jos.—Verbal Inspiration . . . . . . 16o. Lond. 1854
Bayley, F. W. N.—New Tale of a Tub . . . . . 12o. N. Y. 1854
——— Rev. J. R.—Catholic Church on N. Y. Island . . 16o. N. Y. 1853
——— Jno.—Confessions of a Converted Infidel . . . 12o. N. Y. 1854
Bayly, Thos. Haynes—Songs, Ballads, and other Poems. 2 v. . 12o. Lond. 1844
Bayne, Peter—Christian Life; Social and Individual . . 12o. Bost. 1855
Bazin, A.—Histoire de France sous Louis XIII. 1610–61. 4 v. 16o. Paris. 1846
Beadle, D. W.—American Lawyer, and Business Man's Form-Book 12o. N. Y. 1851
Beale, L. J.—Laws of Health in Relation to Mind and Body . 12o. Phil. 1851
——— Lionel—The Microscope applied to Clinical Medicine . . 12o. Lond. 1854
——— Thos.—Natural History of the Sperm Whale . . 12o. Lond. 1839
Beames, Thos.—The Rookeries of London . . . . . 8vo. Lond. 1852
Beans, E. W.—A Manual for Practical Surveyors . . 16o. Phil. 1854
Beard, J. R.—Life of Toussaint l'Ouverture . . . . . 12o. Lond. 1853
Beardmore, Nath.—Hydraulic Tables and Tide Tables . . 12o. Lond. 1852
Beardsley, Levi—Reminiscences; Personal and other Incidents . 8vo. N. Y. 1852
Beasley, Hen.—Pocket-Formulary, and Synopsis of Pharmacopœias 12o. Phil. 1851
Beauchamp, Alp. de—Histoire de Brésil, 1800–1810; 3 v. . 8vo. Paris. 1815
Beauchesne, A. de—Louis XVII; His Life, &c., (Fr. Fren.) 2 v. . 12o. N. Y. 1853
*Beaumont, Fran. and Fletcher, John—Works; Ed. by A. Dyce. 11v. 8vo. Lond. 1843
Beatty, Adam.—Southern Agriculture . . . . . 12o. N. Y. 1843

Beaufoy, Mark—Mexican Illustrations	8vo. Lond.	1824
Beaujour, Fel. de—Sketch of the U. States for 1800–10, (Fr. Fren.)	8vo. Lond.	1841
Bechstein, J. M.—Cage and Chamber Birds	16o. Lond.	1853
Beck, T. R. & J. B.—Elements of Medical Jurisprudence. 2 v. .	8vo. Albany.	1850
*Becker, Geo.—Ornamental Penmanship	Obl. Phil.	1855
Beckett, And.—Dramatic and Prose Miscellanies . . .	12o. Lond.	1883
——— G. A.—Comic History of Rome	8vo. Lond.	n. d.
——— S. B.—Guide-Book to the White Mountains . .	12o. Portland.	1853
Beckford, Wm.—Account of the Island of Jamaica . .	8vo. Lond.	1790
Beecher, Cath. E.—Letters to the People, on Health, &c. . .	12o. N. Y.	1855
——— —— Truth Stranger than Fiction	12o. N. Y.	1850
——— —— True Remedy for the Wrongs of Women . .	12o. Bost.	1851
——— Chas.—Pen-Pictures of the Bible	18o. N. Y.	1855
——— —— Review of the Spiritual Manifestations . .	12o. N. Y.	1853
——— Edw.—The Conflict of Ages	12o. Bost.	1853
——— —— Narrative of Riots at Alton	12o. Alton.	1838
——— H. W.—Star Papers	12o. N. Y.	1855
——— Lyman.—Works	12o. Bost.	1852–3
Belcher, Jos.—The Clergy of America. Anecdotes . .	12o. Phil.	1855
*——— —— Religious Denominations of the U. States . .	8vo. Phil.	1856
Belden, A. R. (Ed'r)—Thrilling Incidents and Narrative . .	12o. Auburn.	1852
——— E. P.—New York; Past, Present, and Future . .	12o. N. Y.	1851
Belfast, Earl of—Poets and Poetry of the Nineteenth Century .	16o. Lond.	1852
Bell, Jno.—Mineral and Thermal Springs of U. S. . . .	12o. Phil.	1855
—— —— and Charles—Anatomy of the Human Body. 4 v. .	8vo. Edin.	1793–1794
—— Wm. C.—Analysis of Pope's Essay on Man . . .	16o. Lexington.	1836
Bellini, V.—I Puritani. (An Opera.)	8vo. Paris.	no date.
Bellisle, O. S.—The Archbishop; or, Romanism in the U. States .	12o. Phil.	1855
Belorimo, Paul—Histoire d'un Coup d'Etat. (Dec. 1851.) .	8vo. Paris.	1851
Beltrami, J. C.—Pilgrimage in Europe and America; 1821–3. 2 v.	8vo. Lond.	1828
Beman, Sam.—The Nightingale; or, Jenny Lind Songster .	12o. N. Y.	1850
Bemis, Geo.—Report of the Case of John W. Webster . .	8vo. Bost.	1850
Bengel, Jno. A.—Gnomon Novi Testamenti. 2 v. . . .	8vo. Lond.	1850
——— —— Memoir of, by J. C. F. Burk	8vo. Lond.	1842
Benger, Miss.—Life of Anne Boleyn	12o. Phil.	1850
——— —— ——— Mary, Queen of Scots. 2 v.	12o. Phil.	1851
Benjamin, A.—Rudiments of Architecture	8vo. Bost.	1814
Bennett, Jas. G.—Memoirs of; and his Times . . .	12o. N. Y.	1855
Benthamiana; or, Select Extracts from the Works of J. Bentham	8vo. Lond.	1843
Bentley's Miscellany. Vol. 1. 1837	8vo. Lond.	1837
——— ——— Vols. 28–36. [*Continued.*] . . .	8vo. Lond.	1850–54
Benton, Thos. H.—Thirty Years' View. Vol. 1	8vo. N. Y.	1854
Béranger, P. J. de—Two Hundred of his Pieces. (Fr. Fren.) .	12o. N. Y.	1850
Berghaus, H—Geographisches Jahrbuch. 1850–1. 2 v. . .	4to. Gotha.	1850–1
Berkeley, Ever.—The World's Laconics	12o. N. Y.	1853
Berkenhout, John—Biographia Literaria. Vol. 1. [All Published.]	4to. Lond.	1777
Bernard, Claude, and Robin, Chas.—On the Blood. (Fr. Fren.) .	12o. Phil.	1854
——— Gov.—Trade and Government of America, in 1763–8 .	8vo. Lond.	1774
——— Pierre—La Bourse et la Vie	12o. Paris.	1855
Bernhard, Wm.—Book of One Hundred Beverages . . .	16o. N. Y.	1853

Berridge, Jno.—The Christian World Unmasked . .	16o.	Bost.	1853
Bertal, A.—Les Etablissements Philanthropiques aux Etats Unis .	12o.	Paris.	1855
Bescherelle Frères—Manuel des Conjugaisons	16o.	Paris.	1852
——— Jeune—Cours Complet de Langue Français. Vols. 1–6	16o.	Paris.	1851
Besse, Alf. de—The Turkish Empire. (Fr. Fren.) . .	12o.	Phil.	1854
Beverley, Robt.—History and Present State of Virginia . .	8vo.	Lond.	1705
——— The Same; Edited by Campbell . . .	8vo.	Richmond.	1855
Bezzi, G. A.—Readings in Italian Prose Literature . . .	16o.	Lond.	1852
*Bezout, E.—Suite de Cours de Mathématiques . . .	8vo.	Paris.	1769
*Bible.—The Holy Bible, in Greek and Latin. 3 v. . . .	8vo.	Paris.	1839
*——— The Same in Greek, 2 v.	8vo.	Lond.	no date.
*——— The Same, Douay Version	8vo.	N. Y.	1851
*——— The Same, with Com. and Notes by D'Oyley and Mant. 3 v.	8vo.	Lond.	1850
——— New Testament, fm. the Syriac Peshito Vers'n, by Murdoch	8vo.	N. Y.	1851
*——— The Same	8vo.	N. Y.	1855
*——— New Test. on the basis of Abp. Newcome's Trans. .	8vo.	Bost.	1809
*——— Three Epistles of St. John, in Delaware Indian . .	18o.	N. Y.	1818
——— Companion	18o.	N. Y.	1853
*——— of Every Land.—A History of the Sacred Scriptures .	4to.	Lond.	no date.
Biblical Repertory and Princeton Rev. Vols. 16–19, 22–26. [*Cont'd.*]	8vo.	Phil.	1844–54
Bibliotheca Sacra and Amer. Bibl. Repos. Vols. 7–16. [*Continued.*].	8vo.	N. Y.	1850–4
Bickell, R.—The West Indies as they are . . .	8vo.	Lond.	1825
Bickersteth, Edw.—Memoir of, by Rev. T. R. Birks . . .	12o.	N. Y.	1851
Bigelow, Jac.—Nature in Disease; and other Essays . .	12o.	Bost.	1854
——— John—Jamaica in 1850	12o.	N. Y.	1851
*Billings, Rob't W.—Baronial and Eccles. Antiquities of Scotland. 4 v.	4to.	Edin.	1845–52
——— ——— Power of Form applied to Geometric Tracery .	8vo.	Lond.	1851
Bingham, H.—Twenty-one Years in the Sandwich Islands .	8vo.	Hartf.	1847
Binns, John—Recollections of his Life, written by himself . .	12o.	Phil.	1854
Binney, Thos.—Is it possible to make the Best of both Worlds .	16o.	Lond.	1853
Biographical Magazine, Vols. 1, 3–5	8vo.	Lond.	1851–4
*Biographie Universelle, Ancienne et Moderne. Vol. 82 .	8vo.	Paris.	1849
Birkbeck, Morris—Journey from Virginia to Illinois . .	8vo.	Lond.	1818
——— ——— Letters from Illinois	8vo.	Lond.	1818
Birks, T. R.—Horæ Evangelicæ; or the Internal Evidence of the Gospel	12o.	Lond.	1852
——— ——— Memoir of Rev. Edward Bickersteth. 2 v. . .	12o.	N. Y.	1851
——— ——— Modern Rationalism and the Scriptures . .	16o.	Lond.	1853
Birt, Wm. R.—Table Moving popularly explained . .	12o.	Lond.	1853
——— ——— Hand-book of the Law of Storms . . .	8vo.	Liverpool.	1853
Bishop, Joel P.—Law of Marriage and Divorce . . .	8vo.	Bost.	1852
Black's Picturesque Tourist of Scotland	16o.	Edin.	1850
——— ——— Through England and Wales .	12o.	Edin.	1850
Blacker, Lt. Col.—The British Army in India, (1817–19.) 2 v. .	4to.	Lond.	1821
*Blackie, W. Y.(Ed'r.)— The Imperial Gazetteer. Vol. 1 .	8vo.	Glasg.	1852
Blackstone, Wm.(Ed'r.)— The Great Charter, and Charter of the Forest	4to.	Oxford.	1759
Blackwater Chronicle—A Narrative of a Virginia Expedition .	12o.	N. Y.	1853
Blackwell, Anna—Poems	16o.	Lond.	1853
——— Eliz.— The Laws of Life	12o.	N. Y.	1852
Blackwood's Edinburgh Magazine. Vols. 68–75. [*Continued.*] .	8vo.	Lond.	1850–54
——— The Same. Vols. 68–73. [*Continued.*]	8vo.	N. Y.	1850–53

Blair, Adam—History of the Waldenses. 2 v.	8vo Edin.	1832
—— Hugh—Lectures on Rhetoric. Ed. by A. Mills . .	12o. N. Y.	1853
—— Robt.—The Grave. A Poem	12o. Phil.	1851
Blake, Jno. L.—Every-day Stripture Readings . . .	12o. N. Y.	1853
——— ——— Farm and the Fireside	12o. Auburn.	1852
——— ——— The Same	12o. Auburn.	1854
——— ——— Farmer's Every-day Book	8vo. Auburn.	1854
——— —— Lessons in Modern Farming; or Agriculture for Schools	12o. N. Y.	1851
——— Robt. (Admiral); Life, by H. Dixon	12o. Lond.	1852
Blakely, Robert—Historical Sketch of Logic	8vo. Lond.	1851
Blakeman, Ruf.—Credulity and Superstition; and Animal Mag.	12o. N. Y.	1849
Blanc, Louis—Hist. de la Révolution Française. 2 v. . .	12o. Brux.	1847
——— ——— The Same. Vol. 3.	8vo. Paris.	1852
Bland, Theod.—Present State of Chili	8vo. Lond.	1820
——— W.—Principles to regulate the Form of Ships and Boats	16o. Lond.	1852
Blanquart, Evrard—Traité de Photographie sur Papier . .	8vo. Paris.	1851
*Blatchford, Sam. (Edr.)—Statutes of the State of N. Y. . .	8vo. Auburn.	1852
Blaze, Henri—Ecrivains et Poètes de l'Allemagne . . .	16o. Paris.	1851
Blenkinsop, (Dr.)—Memoirs of, Written by Himself, 2 v. .	12o. Lond.	1852
Blennerhasset, H.—Life of, by Wm. H. Safford . . .	12o. Cincin.	1853
Blood, Benj.—Philosophy of Justice between God and Man .	12o. N. Y.	1851
Bloomfield, Robt.—Rural Tales, Ballads, and Songs . . .	4to. Lond.	1802
*Blue-Book—for 1839, ...	12o. Wash.	1839
*——— ——— — 1851	12o. Wash.	1851
*——— ——— — 1853	12o. Wash.	1853
Blunt, Edm. M.—The American Coast Pilot	8vo. N. Y.	1850
Boardman, Geo. D.—Memoir of, by Alonzo King . .	12o. Bost.	1852
——— H. A.—Bible in the Counting House . . .	12o. Phil.	1853
——— ——— Bible in the Family: Hints on Domestic Happiness	12o. Phil.	1851
Boccacio, Giov.—Tales from; with other Poems . . .	16o. Lond.	1840
Bodenstedt, Fried.—The Morning-Land, or Days in the East. 2 v.	12o. Lond.	1851
Boethius, A. M. S. S.—Opera, See *Valpy's Delphin Classics.*		
Bogart, W. H.—Daniel Boone and the Kentucky Hunters .	12o. Auburn.	1854
Bogue's Guides for Travellers. 2 v.	18o. Lond.	1852
1. Belgium and the Rhine, with a Map. 2 Switzerland and Savoy, with a Map.		
Bohn's New Hand Book of Games	12o. Phil.	1850
Boieldieu—La Dame Blanche. (A Comic Opera.) . . .	8vo. Paris.	no date.
Boileau Despréaux (Nich.)—Satires. (Fr. Fren.) . .	8vo. Lond.	1808
Boismont, A. B. de—Hallucinations	8vo. Phil.	1853
Boker, Geo. H.—Podesta's Daughter, and other Poems . .	12o. Phil.	1852
Boleyn, Anne—Life of, by Miss Benger . . .	12o. Phil.	1850
Bolingbroke, Hen.—Voyage to the Demarary . . .	4to. Lond.	1807
Bolton, Hannah—Drawing from Objects	8vo. Lond.	1850
*——— Jas.—Nat. Hist. of British Song Birds. 2 vols. in one .	Fol. Lond.	1794–6
——— W. J.—Evidences of Christianity	12o. Bost.	1854
Bonar, Hor.—The Eternal Day	18o. N. Y.	1854
Boucher, Jona.—Causes and Consequences of the Amer. Revolution	8vo. Lond.	1797
Bond, J. W.—Minnesota and its Resources	12o. N. Y.	1853
Bond, Thos. E.—Dental Medicine and Surgery	8vo. Phil.	1852

Bonelli, L. Hugh de.—Travels in Bolivia. 2 v. . . . . 12o. Lond. 1853
Boner, Chas.—Chamois Hunting in Bavaria . . . . . 8vo. Lond. 1853
Bonnefoux, Baron de—Vie de Christophe Colomb. . . . 8vo. Paris. no date.
Bonomi, Jos.—Nineveh and its Palaces . . . . . 8vo. Lond. n. d. [1852]
Bonner, Jno.—Child's History of the U. States. 2 v. . . . 16o. N. Y. 1855
Bonynge, Fran.—The Future Wealth of America . . . . 12o. N. Y. 1852
Book (The) and its Story . . . . , 12o. Lond. 1853
—— of English Songs, From the 16th to the 19th Century . 8vo. Lond. no date.
——— Mottoes, borne by Nobility, Gentry, &c. . . . 16o. Lond. 1851
——— The Telegraph . . . . 12o. Bost. 1851
Boone, Dan.—and the Kentucky Hunters, by W. H. Bogart . 12o. Auburn. 1854
Booth, James C.—See *Smithsonian Report* . . . . . .
—— J. C and Morfit. C.—Recent Improvements in Chemical Arts 8vo. Wash. 1852
Borden, Sim.—Useful Formulæ for Railroad Making . . . 8vo. Bost. 1851
Borrow, Geo.—Lavengro; The Scholar, the Gipsy, The Priest . 12o. N. Y. 1851
Bossuet, Jas. B.—Variations of the Protestant Churches. 2 v. . 8vo. Dubl. 1829
*Boston Directory, 1842–45. 4 v. . . . . . . 16o. Bost. 1842–5
*——— ——— 1846–51; 4 v. . . . . . . 8vo. Bost. 1846–51
*——— ——— 1852–54. 3 v. . . . . . . 8vo. Bost. 1852–54
Bostwick, Homer—Causes of Death from Old Age . . . 12o. N. Y. 1851
Boswell, Jas.—Life of Samuel Johnson, 4 v. . . . . . 12o. Lond. no date.
Bouchette, Jas.—British Dominions in North America . . 4to. Lond. 1837
Boué, Ami.—La Turquie d'Europe, 4 v. . . . . . . 8vo. Paris. 1840
Bougeault, Alf—Principes de Composition et de Style . . 16o. Paris. 1851
Boulden, Jas. E. P.—An American among the Orientals . . 12o. N. Y. 1855
Bourbon, Prince (The); or, The Royal Dauphin, Louis XVII. . 16o. N. Y. 1853
Bourne, B. F.—The Captive in Patagonia . . . . . 12o. Bost. 1853
——— Jno.—Treatise on the Screw Propeller . . . . 4to. Lond. 1852
Bouterwek, Fred.—Hist. de la Littérature Espagnole. (De l'Allemand.) 8vo. Paris. 1812
Bowditch, Nath.—New American Practical Navigator . . . 8vo. N. Y. 1852
*Bowen, Eli—United States Post-Office Guide . . . . 8vo. N. Y. 1851
——— Fran. (Ed'r.)—Documents of the Constitution . . . 8vo. Camb. 1854
Bowyer, Geo.—Commentaries on Universal Public Law . . 8vo. Phil. 1854
Boyhood of Great Men . . . . 12o. Lond. 1853
——— The Same . . . . 16o. N. Y. 1853
Boy's Own Book—Exercises and Diversions . . . . . 16o. Bost. 1851
Boys, John—Expos'n of the Several Offices; adapted for Pub. Wor'p. 8vo. N. Y. 1850
——— ——— Official Calendar of the Church . . . . 8vo. Phil. 1849
Bracciolini, Fran.—Lo Scherno degli dei Poema Piacevole . 16o. Livorno. 1821–2
Brace, C. L.—Home Life in Germany . . . . . . 12o. N. Y. 1853
—— —— Hungary in 1851 . . . . 12o. N. Y. 1852
—— Jona.—Scripture Portraits . . . . 12o. N. Y. 1854
Brackenridge, H. M.—Voyage up the River Missouri in 1811 . 12o. Balt. 1815
Bradford, Alden—Distinguished Men in New England . . . 12o. Bost. 1842
——— Wm. (Ed'r.)—Correspondence of Chas. V. and his Amb'dors 8vo. Lond. 1850
*Bradley, C. W.—Connecticut Register for 1847 . . . . 16o. Hartford. no date.
Braid, Jno. G.—Poems . . . . 8vo. Bost. 1850
Brainerd, Rev. Dr.—Memoirs of, by Sereno E. Dwight . . . 8vo. N. Haven. 1822
Braithwaite, Jos. B.—Memoirs of Jos. Jno. Gurney. 2 v. . . 8vo. Phil. 1854
——— Wm. (Ed.)—Retrospect of Med. Vols. 21–26. 6 v. [*Cont'd.*] 12o. Lond. 1850–52

Brand, Chas.—Voyage to Peru . . . . . . 8vo. Lond. 1828
Brayman, Jas. O. (Ed'r.)—Daring Deeds of American Heroes . 12o. Buffalo. 1852
Breen, Hen. H.—St. Lucia; Historical, Statistical, &c. . . 8vo. Lond. 1844
Brenan, Justin—Composition and Punctuation . . . 24o. Lond. 1849
Bremer, Freder. (Miss)—The Homes of the New World. 3 v. . 12o. Lond. 1853
——— —— The Same. 2 v. . . . . . . 12o. N. Y. 1853
Brewer, E. C.—Guide to English Composition . . . 16o. Lond. 1852
Brewster, Dav.—Memoirs of Sir Isaac Newton. 2 v. . . 8vo. Edin. 1855
——— —— More Worlds than One . . . . . 16o. Lond. 1854
——— Fran. E.—Philosophy of Human Nature . . . 12o. Phil. 1851
Brickell, Jno.—Natural History of North Carolina . . 8vo. Dublin. 1737
Bridges, Geo. W.—Annals of Jamaica . . . . . 8vo. Lond. 1828
Briefe über Humboldts Kosmos. Vols. 1–3 . . . 8vo. Leip. 1848–52
Briggs, Caroline A.—Utterance; a Collection of Poems . . 12o. Bost. 1852
Brigham, Amariah—Influence of Religion on Health . . 8vo. Bost. 1835
Brightwell, Lucy C.—Memorials of Amelia Opie . . . 8vo. Norwich (E) 1854
Bristed, Chas. A.—Five Years in an English University. 2 v. . 12o. N. Y. 1852
*Bristol County Almanac, for 1852 . . . . . . 16o. Bost. 1852
Britain; Its Earliest History and Connections with other Nations 8vo. Lond. 1851
British Almanac and Companion, for 1851–4. 4 v. . . . . 12o. Lond. 1851–4
——— and Foreign Evangelical Review. Vol. 1 . . . . 8vo. Edin. 1852
——— and Foreign Medical Review. Vols. 23–24 . . . 8vo. Lond. 1847
——— and Foreign Medico-Chirurgical Review. Vols. 6–15. [*Cont'd.*] 8vo. Lond. 1850–55
——— Cabinet, for 1853 . . . . 18o. Phil. 1853
——— Catalogue of Books; Oct. '37—Dec. '52. Vol. 1 . 8vo. Lond. 1853
——— Museum, Historical and Descriptive . . . . 16o. Edin. 1850
——— Quarterly Review. Vols. 17 20 . . . . . 8vo. Lond. 1853–4
Brittan, S. B., and Richmond, B. W.—Spiritualism . . 8vo. N. Y. 1853
Broaddus, And.—Sermons and other Writings; with Memoir . 12o. N. Y. 1855
Broadway Journal, (The) Vol. 1 . . . . . . Fol. N. Y. 1845
Brocklesby, John—Views of the Microscopic World . . 8vo. N. Y. 1851
Broderip, W. J.—Leaves from the Note-Book of a Naturalist . 12o. Lond. 1852
Brodhead, J. R.—History of New York State. Vol. 1. 1609–1664 8vo. N. Y. 1853
Brooke, Jas.—Private Letters. 3 v. . . . . . . 12o. Lond. 1853
*Brooklyn Directory, for 1842-3, '48–'56. 8 v. . . . . 12o. Br'klyn. 1842–55
*——— City and King's County Record, for 1855–6 . . 12o. Brooklyn. 1855
Brooks, Chas. T.—German Lyrics . . . . . . 12o. Bost. 1853
——— L.—Short and Easy Method for Averaging Acc'ts, at 6 per ct. 8vo. Gt. Fls. N. H. 1851
——— — Short and Easy Method for Averaging Acc'ts, at 7 per ct. 8vo. Gt. Fls. N. H. 1851
Broom, Herbert—Selection of Legal Maxims . . . . 8vo. Phil. 1852
Brossard, Alf. de—Considérations sur les Républiques de la Plata 8vo. Paris. 1850
*Brother Jonathan. Vols. 1–6 . . . . Fol. N. Y. 1842–43
Brown, And.—The Philosophy of Physics . . . . 8vo. N. Y. 1854
——— Jno.—Discourses and Sayings of our Lord. 2 v. . . 8vo. N. Y. 1854
——— Goold—The Grammar of English Grammars . . . 8vo. N. Y. 1851
*——— S. (Ed'r.)—Citizen and Strangers' Directory of New York . 12o. N. Y. 1853
——— J. N., & Taylor, Wm. B.—Obligation of the Sabbath. A Discus'n. 12o. Phil. 1853
——— Thos.—History of the Shakers . . . . . 12o. Troy. 1812
——— Wm. W.—Sketches of Places and People Abroad . 12o. Bost. 1855
Browne's Bird Fancier. See *Saxton's Rural Hand Books.*

Browne, Chas. T.—Life of Robert Southey . . . . . 16o. Lond. 1854
——— J. R.—Debates in Conv'n of California on the Constitution 8vo. Wash. 1850
——— —— Yusef; or, the Journey of the Frangi . . 12o. N. Y. 1853
——— Pat.—Civil and Natural History of Jamaica . . Fol. Lond. 1789
——— R. W.—History of Greek Classical Literature. 2v. . 8vo. Lond. 1851
——— —— History of Roman Classical Literature . . 8vo. Lond. 1853
——— —— Selection from the Examina'n Papers of King's College 16o. Lond. 1850
——— W. G.—Travels in Africa, Egypt, and Syria, 1792–8 . 4to. Lond. 1799
Brownell, C. de W.—Indian Races of North and South America . 8vo. N. Y. 1853
——— H. H.—Discoverers, Pioneers, and Settlers of N. & S. America 8vo. Bost. 1853
Browning, Eliz. Barrett—Casa Guidi Windows; a Poem . . 16o. Lond. 1851
——— —— Prometheus Bound, and other Poems . . 12o. N Y. 1851
——— Robt.—Men and Women . . . . . . 12o. Bost. 1856
Brownlee, Wm. C.—Tendency of the Religious Principles of the Quakers 8vo. Phil. 1824
Brownson, O. A.—Essays and Reviews . . . . . 12o N. Y. 1852
Brownson's Quarterly Review. 3 v. . . . . . 8vo. Bost. 1844–6
——— ——— New Series. 6 v. . . . . 8vo. Bost. 1847–52
——— ——— Third Series. Vols. 1–2. [*Continued.*] . 8vo. Bost. 1853–4
Bruce, Jas.—Classic and Historic Portraits . . . . 12o. N. Y. 1854
Brushwood picked up on the Continent . . . . . 12o. Phil. 1855
Bryan, Th.—Praktische Englische Grammatik . . . . 12o. N. Y. 1853
Bryant, Alfred—Attractions of the World to come . . . . 12o. N. Y. 1853
——— —— Millenarian Views . . . . . 12o. N. Y. 1852
——— Jac.—Analysis of Ancient Mythology. 6 v. . . . 8vo. Lond. 1807
——— S.—Pocket Manual; or, Repertory of Homœopathic Medicine 12o. N. Y. 1851
———Wm. C.—Poems. 2v. . . . . 12o. N. Y. 1855
Buchanan, Jos. R.—Neurological System of Anthropology . 8vo. Cincin. 1854
Buckingham, Duke of—Mem's of the Court and Cabinet of Geo. III. 2 v. 8vo. Lond. 1853
——— Jos. T.—Personal Memoirs of Editorial Life . 16o. Bost. 1852
——— —— Specimens of Newspaper Literature. 2 v. . 12o. Bost. 1850
Buckler, Thos. H.—Fibro-Bronchitis and Rheumatic Pneumonia 8vo. Phil. 1853
Buckley, Theo. A.—Great Cities of the Ancient World . . 16o. Lond. 1852
——— —— *See Catechism of the Council of Trent.*
Budge, Edw.—Mirror of History; or, Lives of Great Men . . 12o. Lond. 1851
Buff, Hen.—Familiar Letters on the Physics of the Earth . 16o. Lond. 1852
*Buffalo Directory, 1842 . . . . 12o. Buffalo. 1842
Bugeaud, Gen.—L'Algérie . . . . . . 8vo. Paris. 1842
*Builder, The. Vols. 1, 3–4, 8- 9. [*Continued.*] . . . Fol. Lond. 1843–51
Bulkeley, Jno. and Cummins, Jno.—Voyage to the South Seas, 1700–1 8vo. Lond. 1743
Bull, Thos.—Maternal Management of Children in Health, &c. . 12o. Phil. 1853
Bullard, Mrs. A. T. J.—Lights and Scenes in Europe in 1850 . 12o. St. Louis. 1852
Bulletin de la Société de Geographie. Vols. 1–7. [*Continued.*] . 8vo. Paris. 1851–4
*——— of the American Art Union. 1849 . . . . 8vo. N. Y. 1849
*——— ——— for 1851 . . . . 4to. N. Y. 1851–3
——— ——— Geographical and Statistical Society. Vol. 1 8vo. N. Y. 1852
Bullock, Jno.—American Cottage Builder . . . . . 12o. N. Y. 1854
——— —— (Edr.)—Rudiments of the Art of Building . 12o. N. Y. 1853
Bulwer, Edw. L.—Letter to John Bull, on his Landed Property, &c. 8vo. Lond. 1851
——— —— King Arthur . . . . 12o. Lond. 1849
——— —— Poetical and Dramatic Works. Vol. 1 . . . 12o. Lond. 1852

Bunbury, Miss S.—The Star of the Court—Anne Boleyn	16o. Lond.	1844
Bungay, Geo. W.—Off-Hand Sketches of Noticeable Men	12o. N. Y.	1854
Bungener, L. F.—History of the Council of Trent	12o. Lond.	1852
——— —— The Same	12o. N. Y.	1855
——— —— Preacher and the King; Bourdaloue and Louis XIV.	12o. Bost.	1853
Bunkley, J. M.—Testimony of an Escaped Novice	12o. N. Y.	1855
Bunn, Alf.—Old England and New England	12o. Lond.	1853
Bunner, E.—History of Louisiana. (H. F. L.)	18o. N. Y.	1846
Bunsen, C. C. J.—Christianity and Mankind. 7 v.	8vo. Lond.	1854
——— —— Egypt's Place in Universal History. Vol. 2	8vo. Lond.	1854
——— —— Hippolytus and his Age. 4 v.	12o. Lond.	1852
Buonaparte, Louis Nap.—Œuvres. Vols. 1 and 2	8vo. Paris.	1854
——— —— Political and Historical Works. 2 v.	8vo. Lond.	1852
——— —— and his Times by H. W. Dupuy	12o. Buffalo.	1852
——— —— Memoir of, by A. de Le Guérroniere	12o. Lond.	1853
——— —— See *Poetic Works.*		
——— Napoleon—Confiden'l Corespond. with his bro. Joseph. 2 v.	12o. N. Y.	1856
——— —— History of, by Jno. S. C. Abbott. 2 v.	8vo. N. Y.	1855
——— —— Histoire de, par P. M. Laurent	8vo. Paris.	1840
——— —— at St. Helena, by Wm. Forsyth. 3 v.	8vo. Lond.	1853
——— —— The Same. 2 v.	12o. N. Y.	1853
——— —— Life and Exile of, by Las Casas. 4 v.	12o. N. Y.	1855
——— —— Memoirs, of by Duchess d'Abrantes. 2 v.	8vo. N. Y.	1855
——— —— in Exile, by B. E. O'Meara. 2 v.	12o. N. Y.	1853
——— —— Exile of—See *Island Empire.*		
——— —— See *Napoleon Dynasty.*		
Burgess, T. M.—Climate of Italy and Pulmonary Consumption	8vo. Lond.	1852
Buried City of the East	8vo. Lond.	no date.
Burk, Jno. C. F.—Memoir of Jno. A. Bengel, of Würtenburg	8vo. Lond.	1842
Burke, Edm. (Compiler.)—List of Patents issued by U. S. fm 1790–1847	8vo. Wash.	1847
——— Edm. Life of, by Jas. Prior. 2 v.	12o. Bost.	1854
——— —— Works and Correspondence. 8 v.	8vo. Lond.	1852
——— J. B.—Family Romance. 2 v.	12o. Lond.	1853
——— Pet.—Celebrated Trials of the Aristocracy	8vo. Lond.	1849
——— —— International Copy Right Law bet. England and France	12o. Lond.	1852
——— —— Life of the Rt. Hon. Edmund Burke	12o. Lond.	1853
——— —— The Romance of the Forum. 2 v.	8vo. Lond.	1852
——— Wm.—Mineral Springs of Virginia, and their Use	12o. Rich.	1851
Burleigh, Jos. C.—The Legislative Guide	8vo. Phil.	1852
Burmeister, Herm.—Reise nach Brazilien	8vo. Berlin.	1853
*Burn, Lt. Col.—Naval and Military French Technical Dictionary	12o. Lond.	1852
——— R. S.—Illustrated London Drawing-Book	8vo. Lond.	1852
——— —— Illustrated London Practical Geometry	8vo. Lond.	1853
*Burnet, Jno.—Progress of a Painter in the 19th Century	12o. Lond.	1854
——— —— Turner and his Works, Illustrated	4to. Lond.	1852
Burnham, Geo. P.—The History of the Hen Fever	12o. Bost.	1855
Burns, Robt.—Life and Works of, by R. Chambers. 4 v.	12o. N. Y.	1852
*Burr, Dav. H.—Atlas of the State of N. Y. and Counties	Fol. N. Y.	1829
*Burrill, Alex. M.—Law Dictionary and Glossary. 2 v.	8vo. N. Y.	1851
Burritt, Elihu—Thoughts and Things at Home and Abroad	12o. Bost.	1854

Burton, Jno. N.—History of Scotland, 1689–1748. 2 v.	8vo.	Lond.	1853
——— ——— Narratives from Criminal Trials in Scotland. 2 v.	8vo.	Lond.	1852
——— Rich. F.—Falconry in the Valley of the Indus	12o.	Lond.	1852
——— ——— Goa and the Blue Mountains	8vo.	Lond.	1851
——— ——— Scinde; or, The Unhappy Valley. 2 v.	12o.	Lond.	1851
——— ——— Sindh, and the Races in the Valley of the Indus	8vo.	Lond.	1851
——— Robt.—Anatomy of Melancholy	8vo.	Lond.	1849
Bury, Blaze de—Germania; its Courts, Camps and People. 2 v.	8vo.	Lond.	1850
——— ——— Souvenirs des Campagnes d'Autriche	12o.	Paris.	1854
——— ——— Memoirs of the Princess of Bohemia	12o.	Lond.	1853
——— T. T.—Rudimentary Architecture	16o.	Lond.	1853
Bushnan, J. S.—Homœopathy and the Homœopaths	16o.	Lond.	1852
Bushnell, Horace—Christ in Theology; a Vindication of God in Christ	12o.	Hartf.	1851
Butler, Bish.—Analogy of Religion, with Analysis, and Life	12o.	N. Y.	1852
——— Fran.—Spanish Teacher and Colloquial Phrase Book	24o.	N. Y.	1849
——— Geo.—Principles of Imitative Art	8vo.	Lond.	1852
——— Sam.—Geographia Classica and Atlas	8vo.	Phila.	1835–6
Butts, J. R.—Laws of the Sea. The Seaman's Assistant	12o.	Bost.	1850
Buzot, F. N. L.—Mémoires sur la Révolution Française	8vo.	Paris.	1823
By-Laws and Ordinances of the Mayor, &c., of N. Y.	8vo.	N. Y.	1845
Byrd, Wm.—The Westover MSS.	8vo.	Petersburg.	1841
Byrn, M. L.—Adulteration of Food and Drink	12o.	Phila.	1852
——— ——— Artist and Tradesman's Companion	16o.	N. Y.	1853
——— ——— Complete Practical Brewer	16o.	Phila.	1852
——— ——— Practical Distiller	16o.	Phila.	1853
Byrne, Oliver—Amer. Engineer, Draftsman and Machinist's Assistant	4to.	Phila.	1853
——— ——— Artisan, Mechanic and Engineer's Hand Book	8vo.	Phila.	1853
——— ——— Calculator's Constant Companion	16o.	Phila.	1854
——— ——— Mechanics: their Principles and Application	12o.	N. Y.	no date.
——— ——— Practical Metal Worker's Assistant	8vo.	Phila.	1851
——— ——— Practical Model Calculator	8vo.	Phila.	1852
Byron, Lord.—Works	8vo.	Phila.	1852
——— ——— The Same	8vo.	Bost.	1853

Cabinet Lawyer; a Popular Digest of the Laws of England	16o.	Lond.	1850
Cabot, Sebastian—Memoir of, and Review of Maritime Discovery	8vo.	Lond.	1832
Cæsar, Caius Julius—Commentaries, Literally Translated	16o.	Lond.	1851
——— ——— Opera Omnia. 4 v. See *Valpy's Delphin Classics.*			
Cahagnet, S. A.—The Celestial Telegraph	12o.	N. Y.	1851
——— ——— Magnétisme. Vol. 3.	12o.	Paris.	1854
Caird, Jas.—English Agriculture in 1850–51	8vo.	Lond.	1852
Calderon de la Barca, P.—Dramas. (Fr. Span.) 2 v.	16o.		1853
——— ——— Théatre. 3 v.	16o.	Paris.	1845
Caldcleugh, Alex.—Travels in South America in 1819–21, 2 v.	8vo.	Lond.	1852
Caldwell, Chas.—Autobiography; Notes by H. W. Warner	8vo.	Phila.	1855
——— D.—Life and Character of, by E. W. Caruthers	8vo.	Greensb'g.	1842
——— Jas. S.—Law of Arbitration	8vo.	Burl.	1853
——— Jno.—Life of, by John S. Jenkins	12o.	Auburn.	1850
——— Chas.—Thoughts on the Original Unity of the Human Race	12o.	Cincin.	1852
Calhoun, Jno. C.—Works. Vol. 1. On Government	8vo.	Columbia.	1851

Calhoun, Jno. C.—Works. Vols. 1-4.	8vo. N. Y.	1853-4
California, Illustrated	8vo. N. Y.	1852
Callander, Jno.—Terra Australis Cognita; or Voyages. 3 v. .	8vo. Edin.	1766-8
Callery, and Yvan. (M. M.)—Insurrection in China. (Fr. Fren.) .	12o. Lond.	1853
———— ———— The Same	12o. N. Y.	1853
*Callicot, T. C. (Ed'r.)— Hand-Book of Universal Geography .	12o. N. Y.	1853
Calling and Responsibilities of a Governess	12o. Lond.	1852
Calmet, Aug.—Phantom World. (Fr. Fren.)	12o. Phil.	1850
Calvert, Geo. H.—Scenes and Thoughts in Europe. 2d Series. .	12o. N. Y.	1852
Cambridge Directory and Almanac, for 1854	18o. Camb.	1854
Camden Society Publications. Vols. 38-43.	4to. Lond.	1848

Ellis's Obituary of Wm. Smith.
Twysden's Considerations upon the Government of England, Edit. by Kemble.
Visitation of Huntingdon, under Wm. Camden, . . " Ellis.
Letters of Queen Elizabeth, and James VI. of Scotland, . " Bruce.
Cronicon Petroburgense.
Chron. of Q'n Jane; Two Years of Q'n Mary; Rebellion of Wyat, " Nichols.

Campaigns and Cruises in Venezuela and New Grenada, 1817-30. 3 v.	12o. Lond.	1831
Campbell, Geo.—India as it may be	8vo. Lond.	1853
———— —— Modern India	8vo. Lond.	1852
———— Jno.—Concise History of Spanish America . .	8vo. Lond.	1741
———— —— Political Survey of Britain. 2 v.	4to. Lond.	1774
———— —— Negro-Mania	12o. Phil.	1851
———— Thos.—Poetical Works. Ed. by Sargent	8vo. Bost.	1854
———— Thos.—Specimens of the British Poets. . . .	8vo. Phil.	1853
———— Walter—Old Forest Ranger	8vo. N. Y.	1853
———— Wm. W.—Sketch of Robin Hood and Capt. Kidd .	12o. N. Y.	1853
*Canada Directory, by R. W. J. Mackay	8vo. Montreal.	1851
Candlish, Robt. S.—Examination of Maurice's Theological Essays.	12o. Lond.	1854
Canfield, Hen. J.—Breeds, Management, &c. of Sheep . .	12o. Salem. (O.)	1848
*Canina, Cav. Luigi—L'Architettura Antica. 6 v. . . .	Fol. Rome.	1839-44
Canning, Jos. D.—The Harp and Plow. By the Peasant Bard .	12o. Greenf.	1852
Cannon, Jas. S.—Lectures on Pastoral Theology	8vo. N. Y.	1853
Canons and Decrees of the Council of Trent. (Fr. Lat. by Buckley) .	16o. Lond.	1851
*Canova, Antonio—Opere Seleti	Fol. Naples.	1842
Cantu, C.—Histoire de Cent Ans de 1750 à 1850. 2 v. . .	12o. Paris.	1842
Capefigue, B. H. R.—La Ligue et Henri IV.	12o. Paris.	1843
———— ——— Philippe d'Orléans, Regent de France, 1715-23.	12o. Paris.	1845
———— ——— La Réforme et Henri IV.	12o. Paris.	1843
———— ——— Richelieu, Mazarin et la Fronde. 2 v. . .	12o. Paris.	1844
———— ——— Histoire de la Restauration, 4 v. . .	16o. Paris.	1848
———— ——— L'Eglise pendant les Quatre Derniers Siècles. 2 v.	8vo. Paris.	1854
Capper, Jno.—Emigrant's Guide to Australia	12o. Liverpool.	1853
Capron, E. J.—History of California, with Maps . . .	12o. Bost.	1854
——— E. W. Modern Spiritualism. Its Facts, &c. . . .	12o. Bost.	1855
Carey's American Pocket Atlas	12o. Phil.	1796
Carey, Alice—Lyra and other Poems	12o. N. Y.	1852
——— —— Poems	16o. Bost.	1855
——— H. C.—Credit System in France, Gt. Britain, and the U. S.	8vo. Lond.	1838
——— —— The Slave Trade, Domestic and Foreign . .	12o. Phil.	1853
——— —— On Currency	8vo. Phil.	1840

Carey, M.—Nine Letters to Dr. Adam Seybert	8vo.	Phil.	1810
——— Phœbe—Poems and Parodies	16o.	Bost.	1854
Caribbeana—Relating chiefly to Barbadoes. 2 v.	4to.	Lond.	1741
Carlile Jas.—Anatomy and Physiology of the Human Mind	16o.	Lond.	1851
——— Warrand—Short Introduction to Practical Mathematics	12o.	Phil.	1854
Carlisle, Earl of—Diary in Turkish and Greek Waters	12o.	Bost.	1855
Carlyle, Thos.—Latter Day Pamphlets	12o.	Bost.	1850
——— —— Life of John Sterling	12o.	Bost.	1851
Carnes, J. A.—Journal of a Voyage to West Africa	12o.	Bost.	1852
Carpenter, Mary—Reformatory Schools for Children	8vo.	Lond.	1851
——— Wm. B.—Principles of Physiology, General and Comparative.	8vo.	Phil.	1851
——— —— Principles of Human Physiology	8vo.	Phil.	1853
——— W. H.—The History of Massachusetts	18o.	Phil.	1853
——— —— and Arthur (T. S.)—History of New Jersey.	18o.	Phil.	1853
——— ——————— " Vermont	16o.	Phil.	1853
——— ——————— " New York	16o.	Phil.	1853
——— W. W.—Travels and Adventures in Mexico	12o.	Lond.	1851
*Carpmael, Wm.—Law of Patents for Inventions, Familiarly Explained.	8vo.	Lond.	1846
——— —— Law Reports of Patent Cases. Vol. 2.	8vo.	Lond.	1851
Carr, D. C.—Life of Linnæus, the Swedish Naturalist	12o.	Holt.	1837
Carson, Alex.—History of Providence, as Manifested in Scripture	12o.	N. Y.	1852
——— —— Principles of Biblical Interpretation	12o.	N. Y.	1855
*Carstensen, Geo. and Gildermeister, (Chs.)—New York Crystal Palace.	4to.	N. Y.	1854
Carter, Pet.—Crumbs from the Land o' Cakes	12o.	Bost.	1851
——— Sarah C.—Lexicon of Ladies' names, with Floral Emblems.	16o.	Bost.	1852
Caruthers, E. W.—Life and Character of Rev. D. Caldwell	8vo.	Greensbor'h.	1842
Carver, Jno.—Travels in North America, 1766–8	8vo.	Lond.	1781
Case W.—Revolutionary Memorials, Poems, &c.	12o.	N. Y.	1852
Cases Relating to the Law of Railways. Vols. 1–2	8vo.	Bost.	1854–6
Cassagnac, A. G. de—The Bonaparte Plot	16o.	Lond.	1851
——— —— Causes de la Révolution Française. 3 v.	8vo.	Paris.	1850
——— —— The Same. 2 v.	8vo.	Brux.	1851
——— —— Histoire du Directoire. Vol. 1.	8vo.	Paris.	1851
——— —— Voyage aux Antilles. 2 v.	8vo.	Paris.	1844
Castellane, Count P. de—Military Life in Algeria. 2 v.	12o.	Lond.	1853
Castriot, Geo., King of Albania, Memoir of, by C. C. Moore	12o.	N. Y.	1850
Castro, A. de—Spanish Prots., their Persecution by Ph. II. (Fr. Spn.)	16o.	Lond.	1851
Caswall, Hen.—America and the American Church	12o.	Lond.	1851
——— —— Scotland and the Scottish Church	16o.	Oxford	1853
Castanis, C. P.—The Greek Exile; his Captivity and Escape	12o.	Phil.	1851
Catacombs of Rome	12o.	Phil.	1854
———The Same.	12o.	N. Y.	1854
*Catalogue of Books on the Masonic Institution	8vo.	Bost.	1852
*——— in the Library of the American Bible Society	8vo.	N. Y.	1855
*——— Albany Young Men's Library Association	8vo.	Albany	1853
*——— Andover Theol. Sem. Library	8vo	Andover.	1838
*——— Baltimore Mercantile Library	8vo.	Balt.	1851
*——— Boston Mercantile Library	8vo	Bost.	1850
*——— The Same	8vo.	Bost.	1854
*——— Boston Public Library	8vo.	Bost.	1854

*Catalogue of the Brothers in Unity Society Library . . .	8vo. N. Haven.	1851
*——— Cincinnati Mercantile Library . .	8vo. Cincin.	1846–8
*——— The Same	8vo. Cincin.	1855
*——— London Library, by J. G. Cochrane . .	8vo. Lond.	1847–52
*——— Massachusetts Historical Society Library .	8vo. Bost.	1811
*——— New Haven Young Men's Institute Library	8vo. N. Haven	1851
*——— New York Apprentices' and Demilt Libraries . .	12o. N. Y.	1855
*——— New York Society Library (a Supplement).	8vo. N. Y.	1825
*——— New York State Library . . .	8vo. Albany.	1850
*——— Paucatuck Library Association, Westerly, R. I.	8vo. Prov.	1849
*——— Peabody Institute, South Danvers, Mass. .	8vo. Bost.	1855
*——— Philadelphia Mercantile Library Company .	8vo. Phil.	1828
*——— The Same, with a Supplement . .	8vo. Phil.	1828–32
*——— Providence Athenæum Library . .	8vo. Prov.	1853
*——— St. Louis Mercantile Library Association .	8vo. St. Louis.	1850
*——— San Francisco Mercantile Library . . .	8vo. San Fran.	1854
*——— Library of Dr. Kloss (Frankfort o. M.) . .	8vo. Lond.	1835
*——— Officers and Students of Harvard College. 2 v.	12o. Camb.	1852
*——— Cabinet of Natural History, &c., of New York State	8vo. Albany.	1853
*——— Shells in the Cabinet of J. C. Jay . .	4to. N. Y.	1850
Catechism of the Council of Trent. Translated by T. A. Buckley .	16o. Lond.	1852
*Catesby, Mark—Natural History of Carolina, &c. 2 v. .	Fol. Lond.	1754
Catharine II. of Russia, Court and Reign of, by S. M. Smucker .	12o. N. Y.	1855
Catlow, Agnes—Drops of Water; their Marvellous and Beautiful Inhab's	18o. Lond.	1851
Catullus, C. P.—Opera Omnia. 2 v. See *Valpy's Delphin Classics.*		
Cavendish Society Publications	8vo. Lond.	1851–2
Gmelin's Hand-Book of Chemistry. Vol. 6 Life of Hon. Henry Cavendish.		
Cayley, Geo. J.—Las Alforjas. 2 v.	12o. Lond.	1853
Cazenave, Diseases of the Human Hair. (Fr. Fren.) . .	16o. Lond.	1851
Cellini, Benv.—Memoirs of, by Himself. (Fr. Ital.) . .	16o. Lond.	1850
Celsius, Olof—Histoire d'Eric XVI., Roi de Suède. (Fr. Swed.)	12o. Paris.	1777
*Census of Great Britain, 1851	Fol. Lond.	1851
Cervantes Saavedra, Miguel de—Don Quijote de la Mancha .	8vo. Paris.	1845
Chabert, Mons. de—Voyage en 1750–1 dans l'Amerique Septentrionale	4to. Paris.	1753
Chadwick, Mrs. J.—Home Cookery; or, Tried Receipts .	16o. Bost.	1853
Chaldee Reading Lessons, with Translations . . .	12o. Lond.	no date
Chalmeriana, See *Gurney, J. J.*		
*Chalmers, Alex. (Ed'r.)—General Biographical Dictionary. 16 v.	8vo. Lond.	1812–7
——— ——— History of the University of Oxford. 2 v. .	8vo. Oxford.	1810
——— Thos.—Memoir of, by Wm. Hanna. 4 v. . .	12o. N. Y.	1850–1–2
——— ——— Memoir of, by Jas. C. Moffat . . .	12o. Cincin.	1853
——— ——— Reminiscences of, by John Anderson .	12o. Edin.	1851
——— ——— Select Correspondence. Edited by Hanna .	8vo. Edin.	1853
——— ——— The Same	12o. N. Y.	1853
Chambers' Edinburgh Journal. Vols. 14–19. [*Continued.*] .	8vo. Edin.	1850–53
——— Papers for the People. 10 v.	8vo. Edin.	1850
——— Pocket Miscellany. Vols. 1 and 2	18o. Bost.	1852
——— Repository of Instructive and Amusing Papers. Vol. 1	12o. Bost.	1853
Chambers, Robt. (Ed'r.)—Life and Works of Robert Burns. 4 v.	12o. N. Y.	1852

Chambers, Wm.—Things as they are in America . . . . 12o. Phil. 1854
Champfleury—Bourgeois de Molinchart . . . . . 12o. Paris. 1855
———— Contes Domestiques . . . . 12o. Paris. 1852
———— Contes d'Automne . . . . . 12o. Paris. 1854
———— Contes Vieux et Nouveaux . . . . . 12o. Paris. 1852
Champion, Rich.—Present Situation of Great Britain and the U. States 8vo. Lond. 1784
Champlain, S. de—Voyage ; ou, Découvertes de la Nouvelle France. 2 v. 8vo. Paris. 1830
Champlin, J. T.—Short and Comprehensive Greek Grammar . 12o. N. Y. 1852
Chandler, T. B.—Life of S. Johnson, of King's College . . 8vo. Lond. 1824
———— —— The Same. . . . . 8vo. N. Y. 1824
Channing, Wm. H. (Ed'r.)—Mem. and Writings of Jas. H. Perkins. 2 v. 12o. Bost. 1851
Chanvalon, Thib. de—Voyage à La Martinique et Barbadoes en 1751 4to. Paris. 1763
Chapin, E. H.—Characters in the Gospels . . . . 12o. N. Y. 1852
———— —— Christianity, the true Manliness . . . . 12o. N. Y. 1854
———— —— Discourses on the Beatitudes . . . . 16o. Bost. 1853
———— —— Duties of Young Men . . . . . . 16o. Bost. 1853
———— —— Moral Aspects of City Life . . . . 16o. N. Y. 1853
———— —— The Same. . . . . 16o. N. Y. 1854
Chapman, Isaac A.—Sketch of the History of Wyoming . 12o. Wilkesb. 1830
———— Jno.—Cheap Books, and how to get them . . 8vo. Lond. 1852
———— John—Cotton and Commerce of India . . 8vo. Lond. 1851
———— J. G.—The American Drawing-Book, parts 1, 2 and 3 . 4to. N. Y. 1847
Chapus, Eug.—Les Soirées de Chantilly . . . 16o. Paris. 1855
Charity and the Clergy . . . . 12o. Phil. 1853
*Charivari (Le) ;—July 1850—Dec. 1852 . . . . Fol. Paris. 1850–2
Charles V.—Cloister Life of, by Wm. Sterling . . . . 12o. Lond. 1853
———— Correspondence of, and his Ambassadors. Ed. by Bradford 8vo. Lond. 1850
———— Vie. Par M. Mignet. . . . . . . 8vo. Paris. 1854
———— de son Abdication, par Am. Pichot . . . 8vo. Paris. 1854
*Charlestown (Mass) Directory. 1852 . . . . . 16o. Charlestn. 1852
Charlevoix, P. F. X. de—Histoire de St. Domingue. 4 v. . 16o. Amsterdam 1733
———— —— History of Paraguay. (Fr. Fren.) 2 v. . 8vo. Lond. 1769
———— —— The Same. 2 v. . . . . . 8vo. Dubl. 1769
———— —— Voyage to North America. (Fr. Fren.) 2 v. . 8vo. Lond. 1761
Charters and General Laws of Massachusetts Bay Colony . 8vo. Bost. 1814
Chase, L. B.—English Serfdom and American Slavery. . . 12o. N. Y. no date
———— Mary M. and her Writings. Edited by H. Fowler . 12o. Bost. 1855
Chasles, Philar.—Anglo-American Literature and Manners. (Fr. Fren.) 12o. N. Y. 1852
———— —— Le Dix-Huitiéme Siécle en Angleterre. 2 v. . 16o. Paris. 1846
———— —— Etudes de la Littérature des Anglo-Americains . 16o. Paris. no date
———— —— Etudes sur l'Espagne et la Littérature Espagnole, 16o. Paris. no date
———— —— Etudes sur W. Shakspeare, M. Stuart, &c. . . 16o. Paris. no date
———— —— Les Hommes et les Mœurs au XIX. Siècle . 16o. Paris. no date
———— —— Mœurs et Voyages ; ou, Recits du Monde Nouveau . 12o. Paris. 1855
———— —— Notabilities in France and England. (Fr. Fren.) . 12o. N. Y. 1853
———— —— Scènes des Camps et des Bivouacs Hungrois. 1848–9 12o. Paris. 1855
Chateaubriand, F. A. de—Attala ; Réné ; les Abencerrages, etc. 12o. Paris. 1847
———— ———— Mémoires d'outre Tombe. Vols. 9–12 . 8vo. Paris. 1850
Chatto, Wm. A.—Origin and History of Playing Cards . . 8vo. Lond. 1838
Cheever, Geo. B.—Bible in Common Schools . . . . 16o. N. Y. 1854

Title	Size	Place	Year
Cheever, Geo. B.—Powers of the World to Come . . .	12o.	N. Y.	1853
——— Hen. T.—Autobiography and Memoirs of Capt. Obad Congar.	16o.	N. Y.	1851
——— ——— Island World of the Pacific . . .	12o.	N. Y.	1851
——— ——— Life in the Sandwich Islands . . .	12o.	N. Y.	1851
——— ——— (Ed'r.) Voices of Nature to her Foster-Child .	12o.	N. Y.	1852
Chemical Gazette Vol. 8. [*Continued*]	8vo.	Lond.	1850–53
Chemist, N. S. Vols. 1–3. [*Continued*]	8vo.	Lond.	1849–52
Chenier, André—Œuvres en Prose	16o.	Paris.	1850
——— ——— Poésies	16o.	Paris.	1850
——— ——— Poésies Diverses	8vo.	Paris.	1818
Chesney, Col.—Past and Present State of Fire Arms . .	8vo.	Lond.	1852
——— ——— Russo-Turkish Campaigns. 1828 9 . .	12o.	Lond.	1854
——— ——— The Same	12o.	N. Y.	1854
——— ——— Survey of the Euphrates and Tigris, 1835–7. Vols 1, 2.	8vo.	Lond.	1850
Chesterfield, Earl of—Letters and Works, edit. by Lord Mahon. 5 v.	8vo.	Lond.	1847–53
Chesterfield Travesti; or, School for Modern Manners . .	12o.	Phil.	1812
Chess-Player's Chronicle, ed. by H. Staunton. Vols. 1–12 .	8vo.	Lond.	1841–52
Chesterton, Geo. L.—Peace, War, and Adventure, 2 v. . .	12o.	Lond.	1853
——— ——— Proceedings in Venezuela. S. A. 1819–20 . .	8vo.	Lond.	1820
Chevalier, Mons.—Les Maladies, Plantes, etc., de St. Domingue, 2 v.	8vo.	Paris.	1820
*Chevallier, Lamy, et Robiquet, Dict. rais. des Dénom. Chim. &c. Vol. 1	8vo.	Paris.	1853
*Chicago Directory, 1844	12o.	Chicago.	1844
Child, L. M.—Isaac T. Hopper; A true Life	12o.	Bost.	1853
——— ——— Progress of Religious Ideas, 3 v	12o.	N. Y.	1855
Chinese Repository, Vols. 1- 3.	8vo.	Canton.	1833–5
Chipman, Sam.—Reports of Examination of Poor Houses, &c., .	8vo.	Albany.	1835
Chivers, T. H.—Virginalia; or, Songs of my Summer Nights .	12o.	Phil.	1853
*Choice Examples of Art Workmanship, Selected . . .	Fol.	Lond.	1851
Chorlton, Wm.—The Cold Grapery	12o.	N. Y.	1853
Choules, Jno. O.—Cruise of the Yacht North Star . . .	12o.	Bost.	1854
——— ——— Christ our Passover	12o.	Phil.	1854
Christian Examiner and Review, Vols. 1–9	8vo.	Bost.	1824–32
——— ——— The Same. Vols. 49–57. [*Continued.*]	8vo.	Bost.	1850–54
——— Observer. Vols. 13–17. [*Continued.*]	8vo.	Lond.	1850–54
——— Parlor Book, 5 v.	8vo.	N. Y.	1850–54
——— Remembrancer. Vols. 19–27. [*Continued.*] . .	8vo.	Lond.	1850–54
——— Review. Vols. 15–19. [*Continued.*]	8vo.	N. Y.	1850–54
——— Spectator, (Monthly.) Vols. 1–3	8vo.	N. Hav.	1819–21
Christmas, Hen.—Concise History of the Hampden Controversy.	8vo.	Lond.	1848
——— ——— Echoes of the Universe	12o.	Phil.	185–
——— ——— Nicholas I., his Life and Reign . . .	16o.	Lond.	1854
——— ——— Shores and Islands of the Mediterranean, 3 v. .	12o.	Lond.	1851
——— ——— The Sultan of Turkey	16o.	Lond.	1854
——— Miss (Ed'r.)—Blots on the Escutcheon of Rome. .	12o.	Lond.	1851
*Christmas with the Poets. A Collection of Songs, Carols, &c., .	8vo.	Lond.	1851
Chronicles of Cooperstown	12o.	Cooperst.	1838
Chrysostom, J.—Life of, by F. M. Perthes, (Fr. Ger.) . .	12o.	Bost.	1854
Church, A. E.—Elements of Differential and Integral Calculus .	8vo.	N. Y.	1850
Church of England Quarterly, Vol. 36. [*Continued.*] . .	8vo.	Lond.	1854
——— Review. Vols. 1–7. [*Continued.*]	8vo.	N. Hav.	1848–55

Churchman, Jno.—Account of his Gospel Labors, &c., . . 8vo. Lond. 1781
Cicero, Marcus, Tullius—Immortality of the Soul; Notes by Chace . 12o. Camb. 1851
——— —— Offices; Cato; Lælius, &c., (Fr. Lat. by Edmonds.) 16o. Lond. 1850
——— —— Opera Omnia. 12 v. See *Valpy's Delphin Classics.*
——— —— Orations, Literally Trans. by Yonge. 2 v. . . 16o. Lond. 1851–2
——— —— Tusculan Disputations, with Notes . . . 12o. N. Y. 1852
Cieza, Peter de—Seventeen Years' Travel in Peru, &c., (Fr. Span.) 4to. Lond. 1709
*Cincinnati Directory for 1849–55. 4 v. . . . . . 8vo. Cincin. 1849–55
Cist, Chas.—Cincinnati in 1841; Its Early Annals and Prospects. 12o. Cincin. 1841
—— —— Sketches and Statistics of Cincinnati in 1851 . . 12o. Cincin. 1851
*Civil Engineer (The) and Architect's Journal, Vols. 2–3 . 4to. Lond. 1839–40
—— —— The Same, Vols. 13–16. [*Continued.*] . . . 4to. Lond. 1850–53
—— War in Portugal, and the Siege of Oporto . . 8vo. Lond. 1836
Clapp, Wm. W.—Record of the Boston Stage . . . 12o. Bost. 1853
Clark, D. W.—Life and Times of Rev. E. Hedding, D. D. . 12o. N. Y. 1855
—— Jas. F.—Eleven Weeks in Europe . . . . . 12o. Bost. 1852
—— J. V. H.—Lights and Lines of Indian Character . . 12o. Syracuse. 1854
—— R. W.—Lectures on the Formation of Character, &c. . 12o. Bost. 1853
—— —— Life-Scenes of the Messiah . . . . . 12o. Bost. 1855
—— W.—Concise History of England . . . . . 12o. Cincin. 1852
—— —— The Same. . . . . 12o. N. Y. 1853
*Clarke, B.—The British Gazetteer . . . . . 8vo. Lond. 1852
——— Jas. S.—Progress of Maritime Discovery . . . 4to. Lond. 1803
——— Jas. T.—Christian Doctrine of Forgiveness of Sin . 12o. Bost. 1852
——— Sara T. ("Grace Greenwood.")—Greenwood Leaves . 8vo. Bost. 1850–2
——— —— Poems. . . . . 12o. Bost. 1851
——— —— See *Lippincott, Mrs. J. B.*
Clarkson, Thos.—Essay on Slavery, particularly the African . 8vo. Lond. 1786
*Classed Catalogue of the Library of Cambridge High School . 8vo. Camb. 1853
Claude, Jno.—Essay on the Composition of a Sermon . . 12o. Lond. 1849
Claudianus, C.—Opera Omnia. 4 v. See *Valpy's Delphin Classics.*
Clay, Hen.—Life and Public Services of, by E. Sargent . 12o. Auburn. 1852
—— —— Private Correspondence. Edited by C. Colton . 8vo. N. Y. 1855
Clayton, G. Jr.—Angelology; or, Agency and Ministry of Holy Angels 12o. N. Y. 1851
Cleaveland, W. H., and Others—Village and Farm Cottages . 8vo. N. Y. 1856
Clegg, Sam. Jr.—Manufacture and Distribution of Coal Gas . 4to. Lond. 1853
Clements, Geo.—Customs Guide, for 1850–51 and 1853. 2 v. . 12o. Lond. 1850–3
Clement, J.—Memoir of Adoniram Judson . . . . . 12o. Auburn. 1851
——— —— (Ed'r.)—Noble Deeds of American Women . 12o. Buffalo. 1851
——— Pierre—Portraits Historiques . . . . . 12o. Paris. 1855
Cleopatra, (Queen of Egypt)—History of, by Jacob Abbott . 16o. N. Y. 1851
Cleveland, C. D.—English Literature of the Nineteenth Century . 12o. Phil. 1851
Clinton, Hen. F.—Epitome of the Chronology of Greece . 8vo. Lond. 1851
Coale, Wm. Ed.—Hints on Health . . . . . . 16o. Bost. 1852
Cobden, Jno. C.—The White Slaves of England . . 12o. Auburn. 1853
Cochrane, Chas. S.—Residence and Travels in Columbia. 1823–4 2 v. 8vo. Lond. 1825
Cockburn, Lord,—Life of Lord Jeffrey. 2 v. . . . . 8vo. Lond. 1852
——— —— The Same. 2 v. . . . . 8vo. Phil. 1852
Cocks, J.—Sea-Weed Collector's Guide . . . . . 16o. Lond. 1853
Code Napoleon (The.) (Fr. Fren.) . . . . . . 8vo. N. Y. 1841

*Code of Procedure of New York State, as amended, April, 1852	8vo. N. Y.	1852
*———————— Supplement to the Same . . .	8vo. N. Y.	1853
Codman, Jno.—Memoir of, by Wm. Allen . . .	8vo. Bost.	1853
Coe, Benj. H.—Drawing for Schools. Part Second . .	Fol. N. Y.	1852
Coggeshall, Geo. Voyages to various Parts of the World .	8vo. N. Y.	1851
———— —— The Same. Second Series . . .	8vo. N. Y.	1852
Cohen, M. M.—Notices of Florida and the Campaigns . .	12. Charleston.	1836
Coke, Hen. J.—A Ride over the Rocky Mountains . .	8vo. Lond.	1852
Colburn, Zerah—The Locomotive Engine . . .	16o. Phil.	1853
Colburn's United Service Journal. Vols. 66–78. [*Continued.*] .	8vo. Lond.	1850–4
Cole, Alf. W.—The Cape and the Kafirs; or, Notes in South Africa	8vo. Lond.	1852
—— J. W.—Russia and the Russians	16o. Lond.	1854
Coleccion de Obras relativas a la Historia Antigua, &c. 6 v. .	Fol. B. Ayres.	1836–7
Coleman, Lyman—Ancient Christianity Exemplified . .	8vo. Phil.	1852
———— —— Apostolical and Primitive Church . .	12o. Phil.	1853
———— —— Historical Geography of the Bible . .	12o. Phil.	1850
———— —— Historical Text-Book and Atlas of Biblical Geography	4to. Phil.	1844
———— Wm. (Ed'r.)—Death of Maj. Gen. Alexander Hamilton .	8vo. N. Y.	1804
Coleridge, Hartley—Essays and Marginalia. 2 v. . .	16o. Lond.	1851
———— ——— Poems; with a Memoir by his brother. 2 v. .	16o. Lond.	1851
———— L. T.— Notes on English Divines. 2 v. . . .	16o. Lond.	1853
———— —— Notes; Theological, Political, &c. . .	16o. Lond.	1853
———— —— Works. 7 v.	12o. N. Y.	1853–4
Coles, Elisha—Discourse of God's Sovereignty . . .	12o. Phil.	1854
——— L. B.—Beauties and Deformities of Tobacco Using . .	12o. Bost.	1851
——— ——— Philosophy of Health	16o. Bost.	1851
Collection of College Words and Customs	12o. Camb.	1851
*————— Drawings of American Machinery . . .	Fol. N. Y.	1852
————— Familiar Quotations	12o. Camb.	1855
————— Papers relative to the dispute between G. Britain and Am.	8vo. Lond.	1777
————— Statutes relating to Shipping, Commerce, &c. .	4to. Lond.	1818
————— the Constitution of the Thirteen United States of America	16o. Phil.	1783
————— Voyages of Dutch E. I. Company . . .	8vo. Lond.	1703
*Collections of the Maine Historical Society. Vols. 1, 2 . .	8vo Portland.	1831
*—————————Mass. Historical Society. Second & Third Series. 20 v.	8vo. Bost.	1838–49
*————————— Mass. Historical Society. Fourth Series. Vol. 1	8vo. Bost.	1852
*————————— New Jersey Historical Society. Vol. 4 .	8vo. N. Y.	1852
————————— Protestant Episcopal Historical Society. 2 v.	8vo. N. Y.	1851–3
*————————— Rhode Island Historical Society. Vols. 1 and 5	8vo. Prov.	1827–43
————— Topographical, &c. relating to New Hampshire. 3 v. .	8vo. Conc.	1823–41
Colloquies (The) of Edward Osborne, Citizen and Clothworker .	12o. Lond.	1852
Colombia: A Geographical, &c. account of that Country. 2 v. .	8vo. Lond.	1822
Colonial Policy of Great Britain	8vo. Lond.	1816
———— and Asiatic Review. Vol. 2	8vo. Lond.	1853
Colton's Traveler and Tourist's Guide Book. Northern States .	16o. N. Y.	1852
——— Calvin—Protestant Episcopal Church in United States .	12o. N. Y.	1853
——— —— History and Character of American Revivals .	12o. Lond.	1832
——— —— Tour of the American Lakes in 1830. 2 v. . .	8vo. Lond	1833
——— —— See *Clay, Henry.*		
——— Chas.—Poetical Works	12o. Lond.	1834

Colton, C. C.—Lacon	12o. N. Y.	1849
*—— Geo. W.—Colton's Atlas of the World. 2 v.	Fol. N. Y.	1855
—— Walter—Land and Sea in the Bosphorus and Ægean	12o. N. Y.	1851
—— —— Sea and the Sailor; Notes on France, Italy, &c.	12o. N. Y.	1851
—— —— Three Years in California	12o. N. Y.	1850
Columbus, C.—Memorials of, with Memoir	8vo. Lond	1823
—— —— Vie de, par Le Baron de Bonnefoux	8vo. Paris.	no date.
Colvocoressis, Geo. M.—Four Years in a Government Exploring Expe'n	12o. N. Y.	1852
Colwell, Steph.—Christianity and Unpolitical Institutions	8vo. Phil.	1854
Combe, Geo. (Ed'r.)—Life and Correspondence of Andrew Combe	12o. Phil.	1850
—— —— (and Others)—Moral and Intellectual Science	8vo. N. Y.	1850
Coming, B. N.—Preservation of Health	12o. N. Y.	1854
Comfield, A. S.—Alida. With Poems	12o. N. Y.	1849
*Commercial Tariffs and Regulations of Europe and America. 6 v.	Fol. Lond.	1841–50

Vol. 1 Austria. Belgium.
Denmark. France.
Germanic States. Hanse Towns.
Holland. Italian States.
Vol. 2 Ottoman Empire. Greece.
African States. Russian Empire.
Spain. Portugal.
Sweden. Norway.
Vol. 3 United States of America.
Vol. 4 Spanish American Republics.
Hayti, and Foreign West Indies.
Empire of Brazil.
Vol. 5 India, Ceylon, and other Oriental Countries.
Vol. 6 States of Mexico. Appendices.

Common School Journal. Edit. by Mann. Vols. 1–6	8vo. Bost.	1839–44
Compendium of the Writings of Swedenborg	8vo. Bost.	1853
*Complete Collection of State Trials from Richard II. to George III. 11 v.	Fol. Lond.	1742–81
—— Guide to Ornamental Leather Work	16o. Bost.	1854
*Comptes Rendus des Séances de l'Acad. France. Vols. 8–10	4to. Paris.	1839–40
*—— The Same. Vols. 24–27, 32–4, 36–7. [*Continued.*]	4to. Paris.	1847–53
*—— Index to the Same. Vols. 1–31	4to. Paris.	1853
Comstock, J. L.—Readings in Zoology. Pt. 1	12o. N. Y.	1853
Comte, Aug.—Catéchisme Positiviste	12o. Paris.	1852
—— —— Cours de Philosophie Positive. 6 v.	8vo. Paris.	1830–42
—— —— Discours sur l'Ensemble de Positivisme	8vo. Paris.	1848
—— —— Philosophy of Mathematics. (Fr Fren. by Gillespie)	8vo. N. Y.	1851
—— —— Philosophy of the Sciences, by Lewes	16o. Lond.	1853
—— —— Positive Philosophy. (Trans. by Martineau.) 2 v.	8vo. Lond.	1853
—— —— Système de Politique Positive. 4 v.	8vo. Paris.	1851–4
Concise account of British Colonies in North America	8vo. Lond.	1775
—— History of the Eastern Penitentiary of Pennsylvania	8vo. Phil.	1835
Condamine—Voyage à l'Equateur	4to. Paris.	1751
Conductor to Attractive Places in Boston and Vicinity	18o. Bost.	no date.
Confucius, Four Books of. (Fr. Chin.)	8vo.	Title wanting.
Congar, Obad.—Autobiography and Memoirs of, by Rev. H. T. Cheever	12o. N. Y.	1851
*Congress at Rastadt. Official Correspondence	8vo. Lond.	1800
*Congressional Globe, 31st to 33rd Congress. Vols. 21–22, 24–31. 14 pts.	4to. Wash.	1850–55
Conkling, M. C.—Memoirs of the Mother and Wife of Washington	12o. Paris.	1850
Connaissance des Temps, ou des Mouvements Célestes, pour 1856	8vo. Paris.	1853

Conrad, Robt. T.—Aylmere; or, the Bondman of Kent. .	12o.	Phil.	1852
Conscience, H.—La Guerre des Paysans. (Fr. Flem.) . .	12o.	Paris.	1855
——— —— Les Veillées Flamandes. (Fr. Flem.) .	12o.	Paris.	1855
——— —— Scènes de la Vie Flamande. (Fr. Flem.) 2 v. .	12o.	Paris.	1854–5
Considerations on some Recent Social Theories . . .	12o.	Bost.	1853
——— the Propriety of imposing Taxes in the Brit. Colonies	8vo.	Lond.	1766
Constancio, F. S.—Grammaire Portugaise, à l'Usage des Français	12o.	Paris.	1832
Constant, Benj.—Adolphe; Anecdote; et Tragédie de Wallstein .	24o.	Paris.	1849
Constitution and By-Laws of the National Academy of Design .	8vo.	N. Y.	1839
Constitutional Text-Book	12o.	N. Y.	1854
Constitutions of the Several States and the United States .	8vo.	N. Y.	1852
Conybeare, W. J., and Howson, J. S.—Life and Epistles of St. Paul. 2 v.	8vo.	N. Y.	1842
Cooke, Edw.—Voyage to the S. Sea and round the World. 1708–11. 2 v.	8vo.	Lond.	1712
——— J. E.—On the Invalidity of Presbyterian Ordination .	8vo.	Lexington.	1829
——— Wm.—Commentary on Medical and Moral Life . .	8vo.	Lond.	1852
——— —— The Same.	12o.	Phil.	1853
Cooley, A. S.—Cyclopædia of Six Thousand Receipts . .	8vo.	N. Y.	1851
——— Wm. D.—Inner Africa laid open	8vo.	Lond.	1852
Cooper, J. F.—History of the United States Navy . . .	8vo.	N. Y.	1853
——— —— Memorial of	8vo.	N. Y.	1852
——— Miss—Rhyme and Reason of Country Life . . .	8vo.	N. Y.	1854
——— —— Rural Hours	12o.	N. Y.	1850
Copway, Geo.—Running Sketches of Men and Places in Europe	12o.	N. Y.	1851
——— —— Traditional History of the Ojibway Nation .	12o.	Bost.	1851
Corderius, M.—Colloquiorum Centuria Selecta . . .	16o.	Edin.	1818
Cormenin, L. de—Préceptes et Portraits Parlementaires . .	24o.	Brux.	1839
Cornelius Nepos—Opera Omnia. 2 v. See *Valpy's Delphin Classics.*			
Corner, Julia—English Envoy at Court of Nicholas I. . .	12o.	N. Y.	1854
Cornwall; its Mines and Miners	12o.	Lond.	1855
Cornwall, N. E.—Music as It Was, and as It Is . . .	12o.	N. Y.	1851
Correspondence relative to the Affairs of Hungary, 1847–9 .	Fol.	Lond.	no date.
Correspondance entre Mirabeau et La Marck. 1789–91. 3 v. .	8vo.	Paris.	1851
——— Originale des Emigrés	8vo.	Paris.	1793
Cosas de España; or, Going to Madrid via Barcelona . .	12o.	N. Y.	1855
Costa, Eman.—Caput "Si Pater," De Testament. Lib. Sexto .	Fol.	Salaman.	1584
Costello, Louisa S.—Rose Garden of Persia . . .	8vo.	Lond.	1845
——— —— Memoirs of Mary, Duchess of Burgundy . .	8vo.	Lond.	1853
Cotta, Bernh.—See *Briefe über Humbolt's Cosmos.*			
Cottin, Mme.—Elizabeth, ou les Exiles de Sibérie . . .	18o.	Paris.	1832
Cotton, A.—Public Works in India	12o.	Lond.	1854
——— Robt.—Divers Choice Pieces of that Antiquary .	12o.	Lond.	1651
Coues, Sam. E.—Outlines of Mechanical Philosophy . . .	12o.	Bost.	1851
Courcillon, Eug. de—Le Curé Manqué; or, Customs of France .	8vo.	N. Y.	1855
Cousin, Victor—Course of History of Modern Philosophy. 2 v.	8vo.	N. Y.	1852
——— —— Cours de l'Histoire de la Philosophie Moderne. 7 v.	16o.	Paris.	1846–7
——— —— Fragments de Philosophie Cartésienne . .	12o.	Paris.	1845
——— —— Fragments Philosophiques. 4 v.	16o.	Paris.	1847
——— —— Instruction Publique. 2 v.	16o.	Paris.	1850
——— —— Lectures on the True, Beautiful and Good. (Fr. Fren.)	12o.	N. Y.	1854
——— —— Œuvres de Littérature, et Fragments Littéraires. 3 v.	16o.	Paris.	1849

Cousin, Victor—Premiers Essais de Philosophie	8vo.	Paris.	1855
——— —— Madame de Longueville	12o.	Brux.	1853
——— —— Youth of Madame de Longueville. (Fr. Fren.) .	12o.	N. Y.	1854
Coutinho, J. J.—Commerce Portuguese Col. in S. America (Fr. Portug.)	8vo.	Lond.	1807
Cowper, Wm.—Poems. Edited by J. R. Boyd . . .	12o.	N. Y.	1853
Cox, F. A.—Biblical Antiquities	12o.	Lond.	1852
—— Robt.—Sabbath Laws and Sabbath Duties . .	8vo.	Edin.	1853
—— S. H.—Interviews, Memorable and Useful . . .	12o.	N. Y.	1853
—— Sam. S.—A Buckeye Abroad	12o.	N. Y.	1852
Coxe, Wm.—Life and Administration of Sir Robert Walpole. 3 v.	8vo.	Lond.	1800
Coyer, Abbé—Relation of Travellers concerning the Patagonians .	16o.	Lond.	1768
Crabb, Geo.—Technical Dictionary	16o.	Lond.	1851
Craig, N. B.—History of Pittsburg	12o.	Pittsburg.	1851
Craik, Geo. L.—Romance of the Peerage. Vol. 4. . . .	12o.	Lond.	1850
——— —— Outlines of the History of the English Language .	16o.	Lond.	1851
Crawfurd, Jno.—Embassy from Gov. Gen. of India to Court of Ava, 2 v.	8vo.	Lond.	1834
Creasy, E. S.—Fifteen Decisive Battles of the World . .	12o.	Lond.	1851
——— —— The Same	12o.	N. Y.	1851
——— —— Invasions and Projected Invasions of England .	12o.	Lond.	1852
——— —— Memoirs of Eminent Etonians	8vo.	Lond.	1850
——— —— Rise and Progress of English Constitution . .	12o.	Lond.	1853
Creation and the Deluge—a New Theory	8vo.	Phil.	1854
Creagh, Alf.—Masonry and Anti-Masonry in Pennsylvania . .	12o.	Phil.	1854
Crétineau, J. J.—Histoire du Sonderbund, 2 v.	8vo.	Paris.	1850
Cricket Field; or the History and Science of Cricket. . .	16o.	Lond.	1851
Criswell, Robt.—"Uncle Tom's Cabin" Contrasted . .	12o.	N. Y.	1852
Critic, The—London Literary Journal. Vol. 12 [*Continued.*] .	Fol.	Lond.	1853
Critical Essay upon the Writings of T. Carlyle	16o.	Lond.	1853
Crittenden, S. W.—Book Keeping, by Single and Double Entry .	8vo.	Phil.	1853
Crofton, Denis—Genesis and Geology	12o.	Bost.	1853
Croly, George—Scenes from Scripture, with other Poems . .	8vo.	Lond.	1851
Cromwell, Oliver—History of, by F. Guizot. 2 v. . . .	12o.	Phil.	1854
——— —— The Same 2 v.	8vo.	Lond.	1854
——— —— Life of; Edited by F. L. Hawks	16o.	N. Y.	1856
Croncher, J. H. and Le Gray, Gustave—Photography . .	16o.	Phil.	1853
Cronicon Petroburgense. See *Camden Soc. Publications*			
Crosby, Howard—Lands of the Moslem; a Narr. of Oriental Travel	8vo.	N. Y.	1851
Crosland, Mrs. H.—Memorable Women	12o.	Bost.	1854
Crossley, Jas.—Sir Philip Sidney and the Arcadia . .	16o.	Lond.	1853
Crowe, Cath.—The Night-Side of Nature	12o.	N. Y.	1850
Cruickshank, Brodie—Eighteen Years on the African Gold Coast, 2 v.	12o.	Lond.	1853
Cruise, Wm.—Digest of the Law of Real Property . .	8vo.	Bost.	1849
Cruvillier, Fleury—Portraits Politiques et Révolutionnaires, 2 v. .	16o.	Paris.	1852
Cubitz, F. W.—Deutscher Volkskalendar für 1854 . .	16o.	Leipzig.	1853
Culpepper, Mich.—British Herbal and Family Physician . .	16o.	Halifax.	1848
*Cultivator—The Vols. 1–10	Fol.	Albany.	1834–43
——— The Same, N. S. Vols. 7–9	8vo.	N. Y.	1850–2
——— The Same, 3d Series. Vols. 1, 2. [*Continued.*] .	8vo.	Albany.	1853–4
*Cummings, Sam.—The Western Navigator. Vol. 1. . .	Fol.	Phil.	1822
Cumming, Jno.—Apocalyptic Sketches, First Series . .	12o.	Phil.	1854

Entry	Size	Place	Date
Cumming, Jno.—Benedictions; or, the Blessed Life . .	16o.	Bost.	1854
——— ——— Comforter	12o.	Phil.	1854
——— ——— Daily Life	12o.	Bost.	1854
——— ——— Finger of God	12o.	Phil.	1855
——— ——— Is Christianity from God?	12o.	N. Y.	1854
——— ——— Lectures on our Lord's Miracles . .	12o.	Phil.	1854
——— ——— Lectures on our Lord's Parables . . .	12o.	Phil.	1854
——— ——— Minor Works. Second Series . . .	12o.	Phil.	1854
——— ——— Prophetic Studies. Lectures on Daniel	12o.	Phil.	1854
——— ——— Readings on Leviticus	12o.	Bost.	1855
——— ——— ——— Exodus . - . .	12o.	Bost.	1854
——— ——— ——— St. Matthew	12o.	Bost.	1855
——— ——— ——— St. Mark	12o.	Bost.	1855
——— ——— Signs of the Times	12o.	Phil.	1855
——— ——— Voices of the Day	12o.	Bost.	1854
——— ——— Voices of the Night	12o.	Bost.	1854
——— ——— Wellington; A Lecture.	16o.	Lond.	1853
——— R G.—Five Years of a Hunter's Life in South Africa, 2 v.	12o.	N. Y.	1850
——— ——— The Same. 2 v.	12o.	N. Y.	1852
Cummings, Maria—Der Lampenputzer. 2 vols. in one . .	12o.	Leipzig.	1854
——— P.—Dictionary of Congregational Usages, &c., . .	12o.	Bost.	1853
Cunningham, Alex.—The Bhilsa Topes, or Buddhist Monuments.	8vo.	Lond.	1854
——— Pet.—Life of Miss Jones. See *Shakspeare Soc. Pub.* Vol. 38			
——— ——— London in 1853	16o.	Lond.	no date
——— ——— Story of Nell Gwyn	12o.	Lond.	1852
Curran and his Contemporaries, by Charles Phillips . .	12o.	N. Y.	1851
——— Wm. H. Life of Jno. Philpot Curran	12o.	N. Y.	1855
Curtis, Geo. T.—Com. on the Practice, &c., of the U. S. Supreme Court.	8vo.	Phil.	1854
——— ——— Inventor's Manual of Legal Principles	12o.	Bost.	1851
——— ——— Origin of the U. S. Constitution. Vol. 1 . .	8vo.	N. Y.	1854
——— ——— On the Law of Patents in the United States . .	8vo.	Bost.	1849
——— Geo. W.—Howadji in Syria	12o.	N. Y.	1852
——— ——— Lotus Eating; a Summer Book	12o.	N. Y.	1852
——— ——— Nile Notes of a Howadji	12o.	N. Y.	1851
Curtiss, Dan. S.—Western Portraiture and Emigrant's Guide .	12o.	N. Y.	1852
Curtius, Quintus—Opera Omnia, 3 v. See *Valpy's Delphin Classics.*			
Curzon, Robt.—Armenia: A Year at Erzeroum	12o.	N. Y.	1854
Cushing, Caleb—History and Present State of Newburyport .	12o.	Newb'yport.	1826
Cussy, F. de—Réglements Consulaires des Principaux Etats Maritimes.	8vo.	Leipz.	1851
Custine, Marg. de—Russia. (Fr. Fren.)	12o.	N. Y.	1854
Cutts, Mary—Autobiography of a Clock, and other Poems . .	16o.	Bost.	1852
Daguerreian Journal. Vols. 1, 2. [*Continued.*]	8vo.	N. Y.	1851–2
Dalcho, Fred.—Prot. Episcopal Church in South Carolina .	8vo.	Charleston.	1820
Dallas, E. S.—Poetics; An Essay on Poetry	8vo.	Lond.	1852
Damberger, C. T.—Travels through the interior of Africa, in 1781–91.	8vo.	Charl'stown.	1801
Dana's Essay on Manures. See *Saxton's Rur. H. B.*			
——— Jas. D.—Manual of Mineralogy	12o.	N. Hav.	1851
——— ——— On Coral Reefs and Islands	8vo.	N. Y.	1853
Daniel, W. B.—Rural Sports. 3 v.	8vo.	Lond.	1807

Dante, Alighieri, Life and Times of, by C. Balbo. (Fr. Ital.) 2 v.	12o.	Lond.	1851
——— —— Purgatory. (Fr. Ital. by C. B. Cayley.) . . .	16o.	Lond.	1853
Darby, P.—The Fruit Garden	12o.	N. Y.	1851
Dares Phrygius—Opera Omnia. See *Valpy's Delphin Classics*			
*Darling, Jas.—Cyclopædia Bibliographica.	8vo.	Lond.	1854
Darwin, Chas.—Monograph on the Sub-Class Cirripedia . .	8vo.	Lond.	1851
Daumont, Al.—L'Ile de Cuba	8vo.	Paris.	1837
Davidson, B.—Analytical Hebrew and Chaldee Lexicon . .	4to.	Lond.	1848
——— —— Syriac Reading Lessons, Translated . .	12o.	Lond.	no date
——— Sam.—Introduction to the New Testament. 3 v. .	8vo.	Lond.	1848
——— ——Treatise on Biblical Criticism. 2 v. . .	8vo.	Edin.	1852
Davie, Jno. C.—Letters from Paraguay	8vo.	Lond.	1805
Davies, Chas.—Arithmetic	16o.	N. Y.	1855
——— —— Logic and Utility of Mathematics . . .	8vo.	N. Y.	1850
*——— Hen. E.—Laws Relating to the City of New York . .	8vo.	N. Y.	1855
Davis, A.—History of New Amsterdam	16o.	N. Y.	1854
—— A. J.—Approaching Crisis	8vo.	N. Y.	1852
—— —— Great Harmonia. Vol. 2. The Teacher . .	12o.	Bost.	1851
—— —— The Great Harmonia. Vol. 3	12o.	Bost.	1852
—— —— Present Age and Inner Life	8vo.	N. Y.	1853
—— Emerson—The Half Century; or, Changes, &c., from 1800–50	12o.	Bost.	1851
—— Hen. W.—War of Ormuzd and Ahrinam in the 19th Century	8vo.	Balt.	1852
—— Jno. T.—China during the War and since the Peace. 2 v. .	12o.	Lond.	1852
—— Mrs. T.—General History of the Sabbatarian Churches .	12o.	Phil.	1851
Davy, Sir Humphrey—Salmonia; or, Days of Fly Fishing .	16o.	Lond.	1851
Dawson, Jno. W.—Acadian Geology	12o.	Edin.	1855
Day, Chas. W.—Five Years' Residence in the West Indies. 2 v.	12o.	Lond.	1852
—— Hen. M.—Elements of the Art of Rhetoric	12o.	N. Y.	1853
—— Thos.—Four Tracts on the Present State of America .	8vo.	Lond.	1785
Debary, Thos.—Residence in the Canary Islands, South of Spain .	12o.	Lond.	1851
*Debates and Proceedings of U. S. Cong. from 1st to 16th Sess. 37 v.	8vo.	Wash.	1834–55
De Bow's Commercial Review. Vols. 1—17. [*Continued.*] .	8vo.	N. Orl'ns.	1846–54
——— J. D. B.—Industr. Resources of the Sout. & Wes. States. 3 v.	8vo.	N. Orleans.	1852
*——— —— (Compiler.)—Seventh Census of the U. States. 1850	4to.	Wash.	1853
——— —— Statistical View of the United States . .	8vo.	Wash.	1854
*Debrett—Baronetage of England.	8vo.	Lond.	1840
*——— Genealogical Peerage of Great Britain and Ireland	8vo.	Lond.	1849
Decanver, H. C. (Compiler)—Catalogue of Works on Methodism .	8vo.	Phil.	1846
Dedication of Antioch College, with H. Mann's Address . .	16o.	Y. Springs.	1854
Deed of Settlement of the Rock Life Assurance Company . .	8vo.	Lond.	1834
——— ——————— Society for Life Assurance, &c. .	8vo.	Lond.	1833
Defence of Ignorance	16o.	Lond.	1851
———— The Eclipse of Faith	12o.	Lond.	1854
———— The Same, with Newman's Reply	12o.	Bost.	1854
Defoe, Dan.—Works. 20 v.	16o.	Oxford.	1840
De Graff, Sim.—Modern Geometrical Stair Builders' Guide, .	8vo.	N. Y.	1851
De Haas, W.—Early Settlement and Indian Wars of Western Va.	8vo.	Wheeling.	1851
De la Beche, Sir H.—Geological Observer	8vo.	Lond.	1851
Delano, A.—Life on the Plains and in the Diggings . .	12o.	Auburn.	1854
Delectus Sententiarum Græcarum	12o.	Camb.	1819

Delessert, E.—Six Semaines dans l'Ile de Sardaigne . . 12o. Paris. 1855
D'Leina, Wil.—Spring Wild Flowers. Poems . . . . 32o. Lond. 1849
Deleuze, M.—Royal Museum of Natural History, Paris. (Fr. Fren.) 8vo. Paris. 1823
*Delisser, R. L.—Interest and Average Tables . . . . Obl. N. Y. 1854
Dellon, Mons.—Neue Reise-Beschreibung nach Ost-Indien . 12o. Dresden. 1700
De Marguerite, Julie—The Ins and Outs of Paris . . . . 12o. Phil. 1855
Demerara after Fifteen Years of Freedom . . . . 8vo. Lond. 1853
Democratic Review. Vol. 31. (N. S. Vol. 2) . . . . 8vo. N. Y. 1852
*De Morgan, Aug.—Book of Almanacs . . . . 8vo. Lond. 1851
Demosthenes—Opera Omnia. See *Scriptorum Græcorum Bibliotheca*, Vol. 16.
Denison, E. B.—Rudimentary Treatise on Clock and Watch Making 16o. Lond. 1850
Dennistoun, James—Memoirs of the Dukes of Urbino. 3 v. . 8vo. Lond. 1851
Déon, H.—Conservation et Restauration des Tableaux . . 16o. Paris. 1851
Depping, G. B.—Wayland Smith: a Dissertation. (Fr. Fren.) . 16o. Lond. 1847
De Pui, Jas.—Exposition of the Apocalypse . . . 12o. Phil. 1853
De Puy, Hen. W.—Ethan Allen and the Green Mountain Heroes . 12o. Buffalo. 1853
——— —— Louis Napoleon and his Times . . . 12o. Buffalo. 1852
De Quincy, Thos.—Works. 15 v. . . . . . 16o. Bost. 1850–4

Autobiographic Sketches.
Biographical Essays.
Cæsars (The).
Confessions of an English Opium-Eater.
Essays on Philosophical Writers. 2 v.
Essays on the Poets, &c.
Historical and Critical Essays. 2 v.
Letters to a Young Man, &c.
Miscellaneous Essays.
Narrative and Miscellaneous Papers. 2 v.
Theological Papers and other Essays. 2 v.

*Des Barres, J. F. W.—The Atlantic Neptune, Nova Scotia. 2 v. . Fol. Lond. 1777
Descartes, Réné—Method of Rightly Conducting the Reason. (Fr. Fren.) 16o. Edin. 1850
——— —— The Same . . . . 16o. Edin. 1853
——— —— Meditations and Selections fr. Philosophical Writings 16o. Edin. 1853
Descourtilz, M. E.—Voyages d'un Naturaliste. 3 v. . . 8vo. Paris. 1809
Desnos, J. C.—Tableau Hist. de l'Industrie et du Commerce . 16o. Paris. 1829
*—— L. R.—Atlas Général . . . . . .

Fol. Paris. 1769
Desplaces, Aug.—Galérie des Poëtes Vivants . . . 12o. Paris. 1848
Deumier, J. Le F.—Oehlenschläger, le Poete National du Danemark 12o. Paris 1854
Deutsches Museum, 1851–53. 6 v. . . . . . 8vo. Leipzig. 1851–53
Deutsche Monatschrifte. 2 v. . . . . . . 8vo. Bremen. 1851
——— Vierteljahrs Schrift, 1851 4. 7 v. . . . . 8vo. Stuttg. 1851–54
Deutscher Volks-Kalender für 1855 . . . . . 8vo. Leipzig. 1854
De Vere, Aubrey—Picturesque Sketches of Greece and Turkey 12o. Phil. 1850
——— Schele—Outlines of Comparative Philology . . 12o. N. Y. 1853
——— —— Stray Leaves from the Book of Nature . . 12o. N. Y. 1855
Dew, Thos.—Digest of the Laws of Ancient and Modern Nations . 8vo. N. Y. 1853
D'Ewes, Sir S.—Autobiography and Correspondence. 2 v. . 8vo. Lond. 1845
De Witt, C.—Histoire de Washington . . . . . 8vo. Paris. 1855
Diary Illustrative of the Times of George IV. 4 v. . . 8vo. Lond. 1838–9
Dibdin, Thos. F.—Bibliomania; or, Book Madness . . . 8vo. Lond. 1809
Dickens, Charles—American Notes for General Circulation. 2 v. 8vo. Lond. 1842
——— —— Child's History of England. 2 v. . . 16o. N. Y. 1853–4
——— —— See *Home and Social Philosophy*.

Dickens, Chas. (Ed'r)—See *Household Words and Household Narrative.*
Dickinson, And.—My First Visit to Europe . . . 12o. N. Y. 1851
——— Jno.—India: Its Government under a Bureaucracy . 8vo. Lond. 1853
——— Jno.—Political Writings. 2 v. . . . . 8vo. Wilmingtn. 1801
Dickson, Sam. H.—Essays on Life, Sleep, Pain, etc. . . 12o. Phil. 1852
*Dictionnaire Bibliographique des Livres Rares, Precieux, etc. 4 v. 8vo. Paris. 1802
*——— de l' Economie Politique. 2 v. . . . . 8vo. Paris. 1854
Dictionary of Shakspearian Quotations . . . . . 12o. Phil. 1851
Dictys Cretensis—Opera Omnia. See *Valpy's Delphin Classics.*
Didron, M.—Christian Iconography; or, Chr. Art in Middle Ages. V. 1 16o. Lond. 1851
Digby, K. H.—Broad Stone of Honour. 3 v. . . . . 8vo. Lond. 1844–6
Digest of Commer'l Regula'ns of U. States with Foreign Countries. 3 v. 8vo. Wash. 1833–6
Dillon, J. B.—History of Indiana, to 1816. Vol. 1. [All published.] 8vo. Indianap. 1843
Diodorus Siculus.—See *Scriptorum Græcorum Bibliotheca,* Vols. 14–17
Diogène de Laerte—Vies et Doctrines des Philosophes de l'Antiq. 2 v. 12o. Paris. 1847
Diogenes Laertius. See *Scriptorum Græcorum Bibliotheca,* Vol. 34.
*Diogenes. Vol. 1 . . . . 4to. Lond. 1853
Disraeli, Benjamin, M. P.:—A Literary and Political Biography . 8vo. Lond. 1854
Dissertation on a Congress of Nations . . . . . 12o. N. Y. 1837
Disturnell's Guide through the Middle, Northern, and Eastern States 16o. N. Y. 1847
*——— Northern Traveller . . . . . . 16o. N. Y.
*——— Railroad, Steamboat, and Telegraph Book, 1850–53. 4 v. 16o. N. Y. 1850–53
*Divers Ecrits sur la Revolution de Juillet . . . . . 8vo. Various.
Dix, John A.—Winter in Madeira and Summer in Spain and Florence 12o. N. Y. 1850
—— Jno. R.—Hand-Book of Newport and Rhode Island . . 12o. Newp. 1852
—— —— Pulpit Portraits of American Divines . . 12o. Bost. 1854
—— Wm. G.—Deck of the Crescent City . . . . . 12o. N. Y. 1853
—— —— The Unholy Alliance . . . . . 12o. N. Y. 1855
Dixon, Edw. H.—The Scalpel: A Journal of Health. 6 v. . . 8vo. N. Y. 1853
——— E. S.—Hist. and Manage't of Ornamental and Domestic Poultry 12o. Phil. 1851
——— Hepw.—Robert Blake, Admiral and General at Sea . 12o. Lond. 1852
——— W. E.—William Penn: An Historical Biography . . 12o. Phil. 1851
Dobbs, Arthur—Account of Countries near Hudson's Bay . 4to. Lond. 1744
Dobson, Edw.—Plates to Masonry and Stone Cutting . . 4to. Lond. 1849
Docharty, Gerard B.—Practical and Commercial Arithmetic . 12o. N. Y. 1854
——— —— Institutes of Algebra . . . . . 12o. N. Y. 1852
Documents containing Statistics of Virginia . . . . 8vo. Richmd. 1851
——— in Relation to the European and North American Railway 12o. Portland. 1851
*——— of Board of Education of New York City. 1842–52. 2 v. 8vo. N. Y. 1842–52
*——————————— for 1854 . 8vo. N. Y. 1855
*——————— relating to the Free Academy . . 1847–52
*——— relative to Colonial Hist. of New York State. Vols. 3, 4, 5 & 9 4to. Albany. 1853–55
——————— Manufactures in the United States. 2 v. . 8vo. Wash. 1833
*Dod, Chas. R.—Electoral Facts from 1832–53 . . . . 16o. Lond. 1853
*—— —— Peerage, Baronetage, and Knightage of Great Britain, &c. 16o. Lond. no date.
Dodd, Geo.—Curiosities of Industry and the Applied Sciences, . 8vo. Lond. 1852
—— Jas. B.—Algebra . . . . 12o. N. Y. 1854
Doddridge, Phil.—His Life and Labors, by J. Stoughton . 16o. Lond. 1851
Dods, J. B.—Philosophy of Intellectual Psychology . . 12o. N. Y. 1851
Dodsley, J. (Pub'r)—Collection of Poems by Several Hands. 6 v. 16o. Lond. 1775

Dodsley, Robt.—The Œconomy of Human Life	12o.	Lond.	1798
Dollar Magazine. Vols. 7-8	8vo.	N. Y.	1851
Domat, Jean—Civil Law. (Fr. Fren.) 2 v.	8vo.	Bost.	1850
Donaldson, P.—Review of Present Systems of Medicine and Chirurgery	8vo.	N. Y.	1821
——— Prof.—Treatise of Clay Sands, and Loamy Soils	16o.	Lond.	1852
Donizetti, G.—La Figlia del Regimento. (An Opera.)	8vo.	Paris.	no date
Don Pedro I., Roi de Castille. Histoire de, par P. Mérimée	8vo.	Paris.	1848
Doran (Dr.)—Habits and Men	12o.	N. Y.	1855
——— ——— Lives of Queens of England, of House of Hanover. 2 v.	12o.	N. Y.	1855
——— ——— Table Traits; with Something on them	12o.	N. Y.	1855
Dorr, F. O.—Inventor's Assistant, concerning the Patent Laws	12o.	N. Y.	1851
Doubleday, Thos.—Mundane Moral Government	8vo.	Edin.	1852
Douglas, Jas.—Dissertation on the Antiquity of the Earth	4to.	Lond.	1785
Douglass, Fred.—My Bondage and My Freedom	12o.	N. Y.	1855
——— Mrs.—Life of Prof. Gellert. 3 v.	8vo.	Kelso.	1805
Dove and the Eagle—A Poem	12o.	Bost.	1851
——— Pat. Ed.—Elements of Political Science	8vo.	Edinb.	1854
——— ——— Theory of Human Progression	8vo.	Lond.	1850
Dowling, Jno.—History of Romanism	8vo.	N. Y.	1853
Downing, A. J.—Architecture of Country Houses	8vo.	N. Y.	1850
——— ——— The Same	8vo.	N. Y.	1852
——— ——— Cottage Residences	8vo.	N. Y.	1852
——— ——— Landscape Gardening	8vo.	N. Y.	1853
——— ——— Rural Essays. Ed. by G. W. Curtis	8vo.	N. Y.	1853
——— ——— (Ed'r.) See *Horticulturist.*			
Doyle, Martin, (Ed'r.)—Illustrated Book of Domestic Poultry	8vo.	Lond.	1854
Drake, Chas. D.—Law of Suits by Attachment	8vo.	Bost.	1854
——— Fran.—Memoir of a Metaphysician	12o.	Lond.	1853
——— Sam. G.—Indian Captivities; or Life in the Wigwam.	12o.	Auburn.	1850
Drayton, Jno.—View of South Carolina	8vo.	Charleston.	1802
Dreams and Realities in the Life of a Pastor and Teacher	12o.	N. Y.	1856
Drew, Benj.—The Refugee, or Narr. of Fugitive Slaves in Canada.	12o.	Bost.	1856
——— S.—Remarks on the First Part of the Age of Reason	12o.	N. Y.	1831
——— Wm. A.—Glimpses and Gatherings in London in 1851.	12o.	Augusta.	1852
Drummond, Mrs.—Emily Vernon.	16o.	N. Y	1855
Dreyss, Ch.—Chronologie Universelle	16o.	Paris.	1853
Dryden, John—Poetical Works. Notes by Warton and others	8vo.	Lond.	1851
——— ——— Selections from the poetry of	16o.	Lond.	1852
Dublin Review. Vols. 29-36. [*Continued.*]	8vo.	Dublin.	1850-54
——— University Magazine. Vols. 36-44. [*Continued.*]	8vo.	Dublin.	1850-54
Du Casse, A.—Memoirs et Correspondance du Roi Joseph. 2 v.	8vo.	Paris.	1853
Duche, Jacob—Caspipina's Letters on a variety of subjects	12o.	Bath.	1777
Dudley, J. G.—Cotton, its Growth, Trade and Manufacture	8vo.	N. Y.	1853
Dufau, P. A.—La Republique et la Monarchie dans les Temps Modernes	12o.	Paris.	1852
Duffield, Jno. T. (Ed'r.)—The Princeton Pulpit	8vo.	N. Y.	1852
Duffin, Felix—Perspective. A Treatise of Self Instruction	Fol.	Lond.	1852
Dugdale, Thos., and Bennett, Wm.—Eng. and Wales Delineated	8vo.	Lond.	no date
Du Hausset (Md'e.)—Private Memoirs	12o.	N. Y.	1827
Dumas, Alex.—Amaury	16o.	Paris.	1848
——— ——— Capitaine Paul.	16o.	Paris.	1850

Dumas, Alex.—Catherine Blum . . . . . . 16o. Brux. 1854
—— —— Cecile . . . . 16o. Paris. 1848
—— —— Chevalier de Maison Rouge . . . . 16o. Paris. 1850
—— —— Comte de Monte Cristo, 6 v. . . . . . 12o. Paris. 1850
—— —— Comtesse de Charny. 4 v. . . . . 18o. Brux. 1852
—— —— Fernande . . . . 16o. Paris. 1848
—— —— Frère Corses . . . . 16o. Paris 1851
—— —— Georges . . . . 16o. Paris. 1848
—— —— Impressions de Voyage . . . . 12o. Paris. 1851
—— —— Isabel de Bavière . . . . . . 16o. Paris. 1848
—— —— Jaques Ortis . . . . 16o. Paris. 1847
—— —— Pauline et Pascal Bruno . . . . . 16o. Paris. 1848
—— —— Pictures of Travel in the South of France . . 12o. Lond. no date
—— —— Reine Margot . . . . 16o. Paris. 1851
—— —— Souvenirs d'Antony . . . . . . 16o. Paris. 1848
—— —— Vicomte de Bragelonne. 6 v. . . . . 12o. Paris. 1851
—— —— Vie à Vingt Ans . . . . 16o. Paris. 1854
—— —— Vingt Ans après, ... 12o. Paris. 1849
—— ——(Fils) Dame aux Camélias . . . . . 16o. Paris. 1852
—— —— —— Roman d'une Femme . . . . . 16o. Paris. 1855
Dummer, Jer.—Defence of the New England Charters . . 8vo. Lond. s. a.
Dumont, Mons.—Mémoires Historiques sur la Louisiane. 2. v. . 12o. Paris. 1753
—— P. J.—Histoire de l'Esclavage en Afrique . . 8vo. Paris. 1819
Duncan, And.—Practical Surveyor's Guide . . . 16o. Phil. 1854
—— Jas. F.—God in Disease. . . . . . . 16o. Phil. 1852
—— Mrs.—America as I Found It . . . . . 16o. N. Y. 1852
—— Wm. C.—Life and Acts of John the Baptist . . 12o. N. Y. 1853
Duncker, M.—Geschichte des Alterthums. Vol. 1. . . . 8vo. Berlin. 1855
Duncombe, Chas.—Free Banking; an Essay . . . . 12o. Cleveland. 1841
Dunshee, Hen. W.—Hist. of the School of the Ref. Prot. Dut. Ch., N. Y. 12o. N. Y. 1853
Dupuis, C. F.—Abrégé de l'Origine de tous les Cultes . . 18mo. Paris. 1833
Durdent, R. J.—Cent dix Jours du Règne de Louis XVIII. . 8vo. Paris. 1815
Duruy, V.—Chronologie de l'Atlas Historique de la France . 8vo. Paris. 1849
*Düsseldorfer Kunstler Album, 1851–52. 2 v. . . . . 4to. Düsseldorf. 1851–2
Drexelio, R. P. H.—Joseph Ægypti Prorex Descriptus . 24o. Antwerp. 1642
*Duyckinck, E. A. & G. L. (Ed'rs.)—Encyc. American Literature. 2 v. 8vo. N. Y. 1855
Dwight, H. G. O.—Christ'ty Revived in the East among the Armenians 12o. N. Y. 1850
—— Sereno E.—Memoirs of the Rev. D. Brainerd . . 8vo. N. Haven. 1822
—— Theo.—The Roman Republic of 1849 . . . . 18o. N. Y. no date
Dyce, Alex—A Few Notes on Shakspeare . . . . . 8vo. Lond. 1853
Dyer, G.—History of the University of Cambridge. 2 v. . 8vo. Lond. 1814

Eadie, John. (Ed'r.)—Early Oriental History . . . 16o. Lond. 1852
Eager, Sam. W.—Outline History of Orange County . . 8vo. Newb'g. 1846–7
Earle, Pliny—Foreign Institutions for the Insane . . . 8vo. N. Y. 1854
Early Travels in Palestine, Edit. by Thomas Wright . . 16o. Lond. 1848
Earp, G. B.—Gold Colonies of Australia . . . . . 12o. Lond. 1852
*Eastman, Mrs. Mary H.—American Aboriginal Portfolio . 4to. Phil. 1854
—— —— Aunt Phillis' Cabin . . . . . 12o. Phil. 1852
—— Geo. W.—Book-Keeping by Single and Double Entry 12o. N. Y. 1851

Eaton, Charlotte A.—Rome in the 19th Century. 2 v.	16o.	Lond.	1852
Eckfeldt, J. R., & Du Bois (W. E.)—New Varieties of Gold & Silver Coins	8vo.	N. Y.	1851
Eclaireur (The)—A Military Journal. Vol. 2.	8vo.	P'keepsie.	1854–5
Eclectic Magazine of Foreign Literature. Vols. 20—32. [*Continued.*]	8vo.	N. Y.	1850–54
——— Museum, Edited by J. H. Agnew. Vols. 1 & 2.	8vo.	N. Y.	1843
——— Review. Vols. 28, 29.	8vo.	Lond.	1850
——— The Same, Third Series. Vols. 1-8. [*Continued.*]	8vo.	Lond.	1851–4
Eclipse of Faith; or, Visit to a Religious Skeptic	8vo.	Lond.	1852
——— The Same	12o.	Bost.	1852
*Economist (The.) Vol. 11. [*Continued.*]	4to.	Lond.	1853
Edgar, John G.—Footprints of Famous Men	16o.	N. Y.	1854
——— ——— History of Modern Europe, for Boys	16o.	N. Y.	1855
Edinburgh—New Philosophical Journal. Vols. 49–57. [*Continued.*]	8vo.	Edin.	1850–54
——— Review. Vols. 92–99. [*Continued.*]	8vo.	Edin.	1850–54
*——— ——— Index to Vols. 51–79.	8vo.	Lond.	1850
*——— and Leith Directory, 1852–5. 2 v.	8vo.	Edin.	1852–4
Edleston, Jno. (Ed'r.)—Corres. of Sir I. Newton, Prof. Cotes, and others	8vo.	Lond.	1850
Edmonds, John W., & Dexter (Geo. T.)—Spiritualism. 2 v.	8vo.	N. Y.	1853–5
Educational Documents of Connecticut for 1853	8vo.	Hartford.	1853
Edwards, B. B.—Writings, with Memoir, by E. A. Park. 2 v.	12o.	Bost.	1853
——— C.—History and Poetry of Finger Rings	12o.	N. Y.	1855
——— C. R.—John Milton, a Biography	16o.	Lond.	1851
——— Jona.—Charity and its Fruits	16o.	N. Y.	1852
——— Thos.—The Canons of Criticism, and Glossary	8vo.	Lond.	1850
Eglert, Fred.—Characteristic Traits and Dom. Life of Fred. Wm. III.	8vo.	Lond.	1845
Egerton, Fran.—Journal of a Winter's Tour in India. 2 v.	12o.	Lond.	1852
*Ehninger, J. W.—Etchings Illustrative of Hood's Bridge of Sighs	Fol.	N. Y.	no date
——— ——— Illustrations of Irving's Ralph Heyliger	Fol.	N. Y.	1851
Eliot, John—Life of, by Rev. Neh. Adams	12o.	Bost.	1847
——— Sam'l—History of Liberty, Part I. The Ancient Romans. 2 v.	8vo.	Bost.	1853
——— Wm. G., Jr.—Lectures to Young Men	16o.	Bost.	1854
——— ——— Lectures to Young Women	16o.	Bost.	1854
Elizabeth, Queen—Letters of. See *Camden Society Publications.*			
——— ——— Memoirs of. By Agnes Strickland	8vo.	Phil.	1853
Ellet, Chas., Jr.—Laws of Trade in Reference to Internal Improvements	8vo.	Richmond.	1839
——— ——— The Mississippi and Ohio Rivers	8vo.	Phil.	1853
——— Eliz. F.—Domestic History of the American Revolution	12o.	N. Y.	1850
——— ——— Poems, Translated and Original	12o.	Phil.	1835
——— ——— Nouvellettes of the Musicians	8vo.	N. Y.	1851
——— ——— Pioneer Women of the West	12o.	N. Y.	1852
——— ——— Summer Rambles in the West	12o.	N. Y.	1853
——— ——— Watching Spirits	8vo.	N. Y.	1851
*Elliot, Jona. (Comp'r.)—State Debates on the Adop. of the Cons. 4 v.	8vo.	Wash.	1836
Elliott, Eben.—Memoirs of, by J. Searle	8vo.	Lond.	1852
——— ——— Poems.	16o.	N. Y.	1853
——— F. R.—American Fruit Grower's Guide	12o.	N. Y.	1854
——— Chas. W.—St. Domingo and Toussaint l'Ouverture	12o.	N. Y.	1855
——— ——— Mysteries; or, Glimpses of the Supernatural	12o.	N. Y.	1852
——— Wm.—Carolina Sports by Land and Water	12o.	Charleston.	1846
Ellis' Obituary of William Smith. See *Camden Society Publications.*			

Ellis, Aar.—Bible vs. Tradition	12o. N. Y.	1853
—— Benj.—The Medical Formulary Revised	8vo. Phil.	1854
—— Geo.—Irish Ethnology Socially and Politically Considered .	16o. Dublin.	1852
—— Mrs. Sarah. (Sarah Stickney)—Poetry of Life. 2 v. .	12o. Phil.	1835
—— —— Summer and Winter in the Pyrenees . .	16o. Lond.	no date
Elmes, Jas.—Horæ Vacivæ. A Thought Book of the Wise Spirits, &c.	12o. Bost.	1851
—— —— Sir Christopher Wren and his Times . . .	8vo. Lond.	1852
Elton, R.—Life of Roger Williams	16o. Prov.	1853
Elwes, Alfred—Grammar of the Spanish Language . . .	16o. Lond.	1852
Elwood, Jas. L.—Elwood's Grain Tables	12o. Phil.	1852
Emmanuel, Chas.—Astronomie Nouvelle	16o. Paris.	1851
Emerson, Jas., and others—A Picture of Greece in 1825. 2 v. .	12o. N. Y.	1826
Empis, M.—Les Six Femmes de Henri VIII. 2 v. . .	12o. Brux.	1854
English Encyclopædia, Conducted by Chas. Knight.		
Geography. Vol. 1.	4to. Lond.	1854
Natural History. Vol. 1.	4to. Lond.	1854
English, Hen. (Comp'r)—Mining Manual and Almanac for 1851	12o. Lond.	1851
English Review. Vols. 16–18. [*Continued.*] . . .	8vo. Lond.	1852–3
Englishwoman in Russia; or, Impressions of Society . .	12o. Lond.	1855
—————— The Same	12o. N. Y.	1855
Ennemoser, Jos.—History of Magic. (Fr. Ger.) v. . .	12o. Lond.	1854
Enumeration of the Inhabitants of Scotland, 1801, '11, '21 . .	8vo. Glasgow.	1823
Eolopoesis—American Rejected Addresses	12o. N. Y.	[1855]
Episodes of Insect Life. 3 v.	8vo. N. Y.	1851
Eric XIV.—Histoire d', Roi de Suède, by O. Celsius . .	12o. Paris.	1777
Erskine, Jno. E.—Cruise among the Islands of the Western Pacific	8vo. Lond.	1853
Esherolles, Alex. des—Priv. Trials and Pub. Calamities. (Fr. Fren.) 2 v.	12o. Lond.	1853
Essays from the London Times. 2 v.	16o. N. Y.	1852
——— The Same. Second Series	16o. Lond.	1854
Estienne, Hen.—Conformité du Langage François avec le Grec .	12o. Paris.	1852
Estrada, A. F.—Dispute bet. Spain and her Amer. Colonies. (Fr. Span.)	8vo. Lond.	1812
Ethnological Journal. Vol. 1. June, 1848—Apr. 1849. [*All Published*]	8vo. Lond.	1848–9
Etrangers à Paris, par MM. Desnoyes, Janin, &c. . .	R. 8vo. Paris.	no date
Euclid—First Six Books of	8vo. Lond.	1853
Eunapius Sardianus. See *Scriptorum Græcorum Bibliotheca.* Vol. 32.		
Euripides. See *Scriptorum Græcorum Bibliotheca.* Vols. 18–25.		
Europe and the Allies of the Past and of To-day . .	12o. N. Y.	1855
European Magazine. Vols. 25, 27, 28, and 32 . . .	8vo. Lond.	1794–7
Eutropius—Opera Omnia. See *Valpy's Delphin Classics.*		
Evans, R. W.—Treatise on Versification	12o. Lond.	1852
Evelyn, John—History of Religion. 2 v.	8vo. Lond.	1850
——— —— Miscellaneous Writings	4to. Lond.	1825
*Evening Post, for 1850–54. 8 v. [*Continued.*] . . .	Fol. N. Y.	1850–4
Every-Day Wonders; or, Facts in Physiology which all should know	18o. Lowell.	1851
Every Lady her own Gardener. See *Saxton's Rural H. B.*		
Ewbank, Thos.—On Hydraulic Machines, &c.	8vo. N. Y.	1851
——— —— The World a Workshop	12o. N. Y.	1855
*Examiner; a Weekly Paper for 1851–3. 3 v. [*Continued.*] .	Fol. Lond.	1851–3
Excellent Woman, as described in the Book of Proverbs. . .	12o. Bost.	1851
Excelsior; or, The Realms of Poesie, by Alastor . . .	8vo. Lond.	1852

Excelsior. Vol. 1. . . . . 12o. N. Y. 1854
*Exhibition of the Works of Industry of All Nations, 1851 . R. 8vo. Lond. 1852
Explanation; a Sequel to the "Vestiges of the Natural Hist. of Creation." 8vo. Lond. 1845
Exposition of the Weakness, &c., of the Government of the U. States. 12o. N. Y. 1845
——— Universelle de 1851. Commissions Française. Vols. 4–6 8vo. Paris. 1854
Extracts from Papers of the House of Commons relative to the W. I. 8vo. Lond. 1840

Fabens, J. W.—The Camel Hunt . . . . . . 12o. N. Y. 1853
——— —— Story of Life on the Isthmus of Panama . . 12o. N. Y. 1853
Faber, Geo. S.—Difficulties of Infidelity . . . . . 12o. N. Y. 1853
——— —— Predicted Downfall of the Turkish Power . 16o. Lond. 1853
——— —— Revival of the French Emperorship anticipated . 16o. Lond. 1853
Fabian, B.—Australia . . . . 8vo. N. Y. 1852
Fairbairn, Pat.—Typology of Scrip.; or, Doctrines of Types Investig. 8vo. Phil. 1852
——— Wm.—Cast and Wrought Iron applied to Building . 8vo. N. Y. 1854
Fairfield, Sumner L.—Last Night of Pompeii; a Poem . 8vo. N. Y. 1832
Falkener, Edw.—Description of Important Theatres & Remains in Crete 8vo. Lond. 1854
*——— —— Museum of Classical Antiquities . . 8vo. Lond. 1855
Falkner, Thos.—Patagonia, and the Adjoining Parts of S. America 4to. Hereford. 1774
Family Almanack, and Educational Register for 1853 . . 12o. Lond. 1852
Fancourt, Chas. St. John—History of Yucatan . . 8vo. Lond. 1854
Faraday, Mich.—Six Lectures on the Non-Metallic Elements, &c. 16o. Lond. 1853
Farini, L. C.—The Roman State from 1815 to 1850. (Fr. Ital.) 4 v. 8vo. Lond. 1854
Farquhar, Geo.—Works. 3 v. . . . . 16o. Dublin. 1775
*Fasquelle, S.—New Method of Learning French . . . 12o. N. Y. 1851
Fay, T. S.—Ulric; or, The Voices. A Poem . . . . 12o. N. Y. 1851
Featherstonaugh, G. W.—Geology of Country bet. Mis. & Red River, &c. 8vo. Wash. 1835
Federalist: Essays in Favor of the Constitution. 2 v. . . 12o. N. Y. 1788
Fée, A. L. A.—Etudes Philos. sur l'Instinct et l'Intellig. des Animaux 12o. Paris. 1853
Félice, G. de—History of the Protestants of France. (Fr. Fren.) 2 v. 12o. Lond. 1853
Fellows, Chas.—Travels and Researches in Asia Minor . . 12o. Lond. 1852
Felton, C. C. (Ed'r.)—Memorial of Rev. John S. Popkin, D.D. . 12o. Camb. 1852
Female Life among the Mormons . . . . 12o. N. Y. 1855
Fénélon, Abp.—Les Aventures de Télémaque . . . . 12o. N. Y. 1852
Fergusson, Jas.—Palaces of Nineveh and Persepolis Restored . 8vo. Lond. 1851
——— —— The Peril of Portsmouth . . . . 8vo. Lond. 1852
——— Robt.—Poems: in Two Parts . . . . . 12o. Phil. 1851
Fermin, Phil.—Description de la Colonie de Surinam. 2 v. . 8vo. Amsterdm. 1769
Ferrier, Jas. F.—Institutes of Metaphysics . . . . . 12o. Edin. 1854
Ferris, Benj. G.—Utah and the Mormons . . . . 12o. N. Y. 1854
Fessenden, Thos. G.—Amer. Kitchen Gardener. See *Saxton's Rural H. B.*
——— —— Complete Farmer and Rural Economist . 12o. N. Y. 1851
——— —— Democracy Unveiled . . . . . 12o. N. Y. 1806
Festival of the Sons of New Hampshire. Boston, Nov. 7, 1849 8vo. Bost. 1850
Feuchtersleben, E. von—Dietetics of the Soul . . . . 16o. Lond. 1852
Feuerbach, Ludw.—Essence of Christianity . . . . 8vo. Lond. 1854
Fichte, J. G.—Vocation of Man. (Fr. Ger.) . . . . 12o. Lond. 1848
——— —— Way towards the Blessed Life. (Fr. Ger.) . 8vo. Lond. 1849
Ficquelmont, Compte de—Le Côté Religieux de la Question d'Orient 8vo. Paris. 1854
Field, Hen. M.—Irish Confederates, and the Rebellion of 1798 . 12o. N Y. 1851
——— J.—Life of John Howard . . . . . . 8vo. Lond. 1850

Field, M.—City Architecture	8vo. N. Y.	1853
Fielding, Hen.—Life, by F. Lawrence	12o. Lond.	1855
Fields, Jas. T.—Poems	16o. Camb.	1854
——— Wm. (Compiler)—The Scrap Book	8vo. Phila.	1851
Figuier, L.—Principales Découvertes Scientifiques Modernes. 2 v.	12o. Paris.	1851
Finch, M.—An Englishman's Experience in America . .	12o. Lond.	1853
Fincham, Jno.—History of Naval Architecture	R 8vo. Lond.	1851
*Findlay, A. G.—Classical Atlas to Illustrate Ancient Geography	8vo. Lond.	1847
*——— ——— Modern Atlas. A Compendium of Modern Geography	8vo. Lond.	1847
Finlay, B.—Evangelism, Catholicism, Romanism, and Protestantism	12o. N.Y.	1854
——— Geo.—History of Greece from A. D. 1204–1461 . .	8vo. Edin.	1851
——— ——— History of the Byzantine Empire. 716–1453. 2 v.	8vo. Edin.	1853–4
First Thoughts; or, Beginning to Think	12o. N. Y.	1855
Fish, F. W.—The Mind and the Heart; Poems . . .	12o N. Y.	1851
——— Wm. H.—Memoir of Butler Wilmarth, M. D. . .	16o. Bost.	1854
Fisher, Alex.—Voyage to the Arctic Regions, 1819–20 . .	8vo. Lond.	1821
*——— Rich. S.—Statistical Gazetteer of the United States .	8vo. N. Y.	1853
*Fisher's Drawing Room Scrap-Book for 1851–52. 2 v . . .	4to. Lond.	1851–2
Fitch, S. S.—The Functions of the Lungs	8vo. N. Y.	1854
Fitzclarence, (Lieut. Col.)—Jour'l of Route across India to Eng. '17–18	4to. Lond.	1819
Fitzosborne, Thos.—Letters on Several Subjects . .	8vo. Lond.	1844
Flagg, Edm.—Venice; The City of the Sea. 1797–1849. 2 v. .	12o. N. Y.	1853
——— J. F. B.—Ether and Chloroform, and their Employment . .	12o. Phila.	1851
Flanders, Hen.—Lives and Times of Chief Justices Jay and Rutledge	8vo. Phila.	1855
Fleetwood, Jno.—History of the Holy Bible	8vo. N. Y.	1855
Fleming, Fran.—Caffraria and Its Inhabitants . . .	12o. Lond.	1853
Fletcher, Jos.—Education; National, Voluntary, and Free .	8vo. Lond.	1851
Fleury, C.—Nouvelles Etudes Historiques et Littéraires . .	12o. Paris.	1855
——— ——— Portraits Politiques et Revolutionaires. 2 v. .	16o. Paris.	1852
——— Ed.—Saint Just et la Terreur. 2 v.	12o. N. Y.	1852
*Fliegende Blätter. Vols. 10–12, 14, 16–17, 20. [*Continued.*]	4to. Munich.	Various
Flint, Jas.—Sermons	12o. Bost.	1852
Florian, J. P. C. de—Moors in Spain. (Fr. Fren.) (H. F. L.) .	18o. N. Y.	no date
——— ——— Œuvres. 10 v.	24o. Paris.	1820–4

Vol. 1 Estelle; Galatée; Fables.
2 Nouvelles Jeunesse.
3 Gonzalve de Cordoue; ou, Granade Reconquise.
4 Numa Pompilius; G. Tell; Eliezer.
5 Théâtre.
6 Mélanges de Poésie et de Littérature.
7, 8 Traduction de Don Quichotte. 2 v.
9, 10 Œuvres Inédites, Recueillies par R. C. G. de Pixérécourt. 2 v.

Florus, L.—Opera Omnia, 2 v. See *Valpy's Delphin Classics.*

Flourens, P.—Cuvier. Histoire de ses Travaux	16o. Paris.	1845
——— ——— Human Longevity	12o. Lond.	1855
Flower Garden (The); With an Essay on the Poetry of Gardening	16o. Lond.	1852
Foissac, P.—De la Météorologie. 2 v.	8vo. Paris.	1854
Folkard, Hen. C.—The Sailing Boat. English and Foreign .	12o. Lond.	1853
Fontaine, Jas.—Memoirs of a Huguenot Family. (Fr. Fren.) .	12o. N. Y.	1853
Fontenelle, B. L. B. de—Conversations on the Plurality of Worlds	18o. Lond.	1819
——— Julia de—Manuel des Sorciers	18o. Paris.	1830

Foote, And. H.—Africa and the American Flag . . . . 12o. N. Y. 1854
—— A. L. R.—The School of Christ . . . . . 16o. Bost. 1855
Forbes, Fred. E.—Dahomey and the Dahomans. 2 v. . . . 8vo. Lond. 1851
—— Jas. D.—Norway and its Glaciers in 1851 . . . R. 8vo. Edin. 1853
—— John—Happiness in its Relation to Work and Knowledge 16o. Lond. 1850
—— Jno.—Memorandums made in Ireland, in 1852. 2 v. . 12o. Lond. 1853
Force, Pet.—National Calendar, Vols. 1–8 . . . . 12o. Wash. 1820–30
Ford, Thos.—History of Illinois, 1814–1847 . . . . 12o. Chicago. 1854
Foreign Missionary Chronicle. Vols. 1–2, 4, 6–8, 10–17 . 8vo. Pittbg. 1833–47
Forester, Thos. Ed.—Norway and its Scenery . . . . 16o. Lond. 1853
Forfar, Robt.—Analytical Physics, or Trinology . . . 12o. Lond. 1852
—— —— Lectures on a new Philosophy of Physics . . 8vo. Edin. 1853
Form of Government of the Presbyterian Church . . . 18o. Phil. 1845
Forms of Proceedings under the N. Y. Prohibitory Liquor Law 8vo. N. Y. 1855
Forrest, Capt. Thos.—Voyage to New Guinea and the Moluccas . 4to. Lond. 1779
—— Wm. S.—Sketches of Norfolk and its Vicinity . . 8vo. Phil. 1853
Forster, Chas.—The One Primeval Language. 2 v. . . . 8vo. Lond. 1851–2
—— —— Harmony of Primeval Alphabets . . . . 8vo. (In case.)
—— H. K.—Pocket Peerage of Great Britain and Ireland . 16o. Lond. 1851
Forsyth, Wm. Captivity of Napoleon at St. Helena. 3 v. . 8vo. Lond. 1853
—— —— The Same. 2 v. . . . . 12o. N. Y. 1853
—— —— History of Trial by Jury . . . . . 8vo. Lond. 1852
Fortune, Robt.—Journey to the Tea Countries of China . . 8vo. Lond. 1852
Fosbery, T. V.—Hymns and Poems for the Sick and Suffering . 16o. Lond. 1850
Fosbroke, T. D.—British Monachism . . . . . . 8vo. Lond. 1843
—— —— Encyclopædia of Antiquities. 2 v. . . . 8vo. Lond. 1843
—— —— Synopsis of Ancient Costume . . . . 4to. Lond. 1850
Fosdick, W. W.—Ariel and other Poems . . . . 12o. N. Y. 1855
Fosgate, Blanchard—Sleep Physiologically Considered . . 12o. N. Y. 1850
Foster, B. F.—Double Entry Book-Keeping . . . . 8vo. Bost. 1851
—— —— Origin and Progress of Book-Keeping . . 8vo. Lond. 1852
—— J. W. and Whitney (J. D.)—Geology, &c., of Lake Superior 8vo. Wash. 1850–51
—— R. S—Nature and Blessedness of Christian Purity . 12o. N. Y. 1851
Foster's First Principles of Chemistry . . . . . 12o. N. Y. 1855
Four Years' Residence in the West Indies, 1826–9 . . . 8vo. Lond. 1833
Fourier, Chas.—Œuvres Complètes. 6 v. . . . . . 8vo. Paris. 1845–6
—— —— Passions of the Human Soul. (Fr. Fren.) 2 v. . 8vo. Lond. 1851
Fowler, Geo. Lives of the Sovereigns of Russia. Vol. 1 . . 12o. Lond 1852
—— H. (Ed'r).—Mary M. Chase and her Writings . . 12o. Bost. 1855
—— O. S.—A Home for All . . . . 12o. N. Y. 1854
—— Wm. C.—Elements of the English Language . 8vo. N. Y. 1850
—— —— English Grammar and the English Language . . 8vo. N. Y. 1855
Fox, Geo.—Journal. Edit. by W. Armistead. 2 v. . . . 12o. Lond. 1852
—— —— Life of, by Sam. M. Janney . . . . . 8vo. Phil. 1853
—— Chas. J.—Memorials and Correspondence. 2 v. . . . 12o. Phil. 1853
—— Jos. and Harris (C. A.)—Diseases of the Human Teeth . . 8vo. Phil. 1855
Foxton, Fred. J.—Popular Christianity . . . . . 8vo. Lond. 1849
Foy, Le Général—Hist. de la Guerre de la Péninsule. 4 v. . . 8vo. Paris. 1828
Fragmenta Historicorum Græcorum. See *Scriptorum Græc. Bibliotheca.* Vols. 11, 29, 31, 36.
France Littéraire. Vols. 12 and 13 . . . . . . 8vo. Paris. 1843

Franchere, Gabr.—Voyage to N. W. Coast of America, 1811-14.	12o.	N. Y.	1855
Francis, Jno.—Annals and Anecdotes of Life Assurance	12o.	Lond.	1853
——— —— History of the English Railway, 1820–45. 2. v.	8vo.	Lond.	1851
Francis' New Guide to Cities of New York and Brooklyn	16o.	N. Y.	1853
Francœur, L. B.—Compl. Course of Pure Mathematics. (Fr. Fren.) 2 v.	8vo.	Cambridge.	1829
Frankland, B.—Outlines of Literary Culture	16o.	Lond.	1853
Franklin, Benj.—Constitution and Government of Pennsylvania	8vo.	Lond.	1759
——— —— Vie de, par Mons. Mignet	18o.	Paris.	1848
——— —— Select Works and Autobiography	12o.	Bost.	1853
——— Jas.—Philosophical and Political History of the U. States	12o.	Lond.	1784
——— Journal and American Mechanics' Magazine. Vols. 1–12.	8vo.	Phil.	1826–31
Fraser's Magazine. Vols 42–50. [*Continued*]	8vo.	Lond.	1850–54
Frederic Wm. III.—Traits and Domestic Life of, by F. Egbert	8vo.	Lond.	1845
Freedley, Edw. T.—Practical Treatise on Business	8vo.	Phil.	1852
——— —— The Same	8vo.	Phil.	1853
——— —— The Same	12o.	Phil.	1854
Freligh, D. M.—Homœopathic Practice of Medicine	12o.	N. Y.	1853
Freeman, E. A.— Origin and Development of Window Tracery	8vo.	Lond.	1851
——— F.—Africa's Redemption our Country's Salvation	12o.	N. Y.	1852
——— Jno.—Life of the Rev. William Kirby	8vo.	Lond.	1852
——— J. J.—Tour in South Africa	12o.	Lond.	1851
*French, B. F. (Comp'r.)—Hist. Collections of Louisiana. Vols. 2, 3, 5	8vo.	Ph. Y.N.	1850–53
Fresenius, C. R.—Instruction in Quantitative Chemical Analysis	8vo.	Lond.	1854
Frezier, A. F.—Voyage to the South Sea, in 1712–4	4to.	Lond.	1717
Fromberg, Eman. O.—Art of Painting on Glass	16o.	Lond.	1851
Frost, John—Book of the Indians	12o.	N. Y.	1848
—— —— Book of Travels in Africa	12o.	N. Y.	1848
—— —— Border Wars of the West	8vo.	Auburn.	1853
—— —— Heroic Women of the West	12o.	Phil.	1854
—— —— History of the State of California	8vo.	Auburn.	1850
—— —— (Compiler)—Wild Scenes in a Hunter's Life. 2 v.	12o.	Auburn.	1851
Frothingham, N. L.—Sermons in the Order of a Twelvemonth	12o.	Bost.	1852
Fruits of Leisure. See *Helps, Arthur.*			
Fry, Benj. St. Jas.—Lives of Whatcoat, McKendree, and George	18o.	N. Y.	1852
—— W. H. (Ed'r.)—Treatise on Artifical Fish Breeding	12o.	N. Y.	1854
Fryer, John—An Account of East India and Persia, 1672–81	Fol.	Lond.	1698
Fryxell, A.—History of Sweden. (Fr. Swed.) 2 v.	12o.	Lond.	1844
Full Report of the Trial of Matt. F. Ward	8vo.	N. Y.	1854
Fuller, And.—Principal Works and Remains of	16o.	Lond.	1852
—— Meta V., and Francis A.—Poems	12o.	N. Y.	1851
Funnell, Wm.—Voyage round the World	8vo.	Lond.	1707
Furber, Geo. C.—The Twelve Months' Volunteer in Mexico, 1846–7	8vo.	Cincin.	1850
Furniss, Wm.—The Land of the Cæsar and the Doge	12o.	N. Y.	1853
*Galignani's New Paris Guide for 1854	16o.	Paris.	1854
*Gallery of Engravings. Second Series. 4 v.	4to.	Lond.	no date
*——— Nature and Art. 2 v.	8vo.	Lond.	1823
Galloway, Robert—Manual of Qualitative Analysis	12o.	Lond.	1850
Galton, Fran.—An Explorer in Tropical South Africa	8vo.	Lond.	1853
Gan Eden; or, Pictures of Cuba. See *Hurlbut, Wm. H.*			
Gardiner, N. F.—Journey to the Zoolu Country in 1835	8vo.	Lond.	1836

*Gardner, C. K.—Dictionary of U. S. Officers, 1789–1853	12o.	N. Y.	1853
Garland, H. A.—Life of John Randolph. 2 v.	8vo.	N. Y.	1850
——— —— The Same. 2 v.	12o.	N. Y.	1851
Garvey, Mich. A.—The Silent Revolution; or, Steam and Electricity	16o.	Lond.	1852
Gass, Pat.—Voyages and Travels of Capts. Lewis & Clarke	8vo.	Pittsb'g.	1808
Gault, Robert—Popery, the Man of Sin	12o.	N. Y.	1854
Gaussen, S. R. S.—Theopneusty; or, Plenary Inspiration of Scriptures	12o.	N. Y.	1850
Gautier, Theoph.—Caprices et Zigzags	12o.	Paris.	1852
Gavazzi, Alex.—Biography of	12o.	N. Y.	no date
——— —— Lectures	12o.	N. Y.	1854
——— —— Lectures and Life	12o.	N. Y.	1853
Gay, John—Poetical Works. 2 v.	16o.	Bost.	1854
—— Sophie de—Celebrated Saloons, and Parisian Letters. M. Girardin	18o.	Bost.	1851
Gayarré, Chas.—History of Louisiana. The French Domination. 2 v.	8vo.	N. Y.	1854
——— —— ——————— The Spanish Domination. 2 v.	8vo.	Phil.	1854
——— —— Louisiana as a French Colony. Third Series.	8vo.	N. Y.	1852
——— —— School for Politics	12o.	N. Y.	1854
Gazette of the Union. Vols. 10, 11	4to.	N. Y.	1849
Geiger, E. G.—History of the Swedes. (Fr. Swed.)	8vo.	Lond.	no date
Gellius, Aulus.—Opera Omnia. 3 v. See *Valpy's Delphin Classics.*			
Gellert, Prof.—Life of, by Mrs. Douglas. 3 v.	8vo.	Kelso.	1805
Gems of German Verse. Edited by W. H. Furness	12o.	Phil.	no date
——— Spanish Poetry. (Spanish and English.)	12o.	N. Y.	1855
Genealogy of the Ancestry and Posterity of Isaac Lawrence	8vo.	Albany.	1853
General Collection of Portuguese and Spanish Voyages and Discoveries	4to.	Lond.	1789
Genet, Edm. C.—Upward Forces of Fluids	8vo.	Albany.	1825
Genin, Syl.—Selections from his Works, with Memoir	8vo.	N. Y.	1855
Gentleman's Magazine, N. S. Vols. 35–40 [*Continued.*]	8vo.	Lond.	1851–3
Genuine Account of the Trial of Eugene Aram	12o.	Knaresb.	1815
——— Let. & Mem. on the Islands of Cape Breton & St. John. (Fr. Fren.)	8vo.	Lond.	1760
George, Anita.—Annals of the Queens of Spain. Vols. 1 & 2.	12o.	N. Y.	1850
Geral-Milco; or, a Residence in a Brazilian Valley	12o.	N. Y.	1852
Gerard, Gilb.—Institutes of Biblical Criticism	8vo.	Bost.	1823
Gerbard, Edw.—Griechische Mythologie. Vol 1.	8vo.	Berlin.	1854
Gerhardt, Chas.—Aide-Mémoire pour l'Analyse Chimique	16o.	Paris.	1852
German Museum; or, Monthly Repository. Vols. 1 & 2.	8vo.	Lond.	1800
Gerstaecker, F.—Narrative of a Journey round the World. 3 v.	12o.	Lond.	1853
———— —— The Same	12o.	N. Y.	1853
Gervinus, G. G.—Einleitung in die Geschichte des XIX. Jahrhunderts.	8vo.	Leip.	1853
——— ———und seine politischen Ueberzeugungen	8vo.	Leip.	1853
Gesenius' Hebrew Grammar. Edited by Rödiger	sm. 4to.	Lond.	1852
Gessert, M. A.—Art of Painting on Glass, or Glass-Staining	16o.	Lond.	1851
Gibbon, Edw.—Decline and Fall of the Roman Empire. 6 v.	12o.	Bost.	1850–3
——— —— Miscellaneous Works	8vo.	Lond.	1837
——— Lardner—Exploration of Valley of Amazon; & maps. 2 v.	8vo.	Wash.	1854
Gibbs, Montg.—Practical Forms and Precedents	8vo.	N. Y.	1854
Gibson, W. M.—Prison of Weltevreden at the East Indian Archipelago	12o.	N. Y.	1855
Giddings, Major—Campaign in Northern Mexico	8vo.	N. Y.	1853
——— Josh. R.—Speeches in Congress	12o.	Bost.	1853
Giesebrecht, Wil.—Geschichte der Deutschen Kaiserzeit. Vol. 1.	8vo.	Braunschw.	1855

Gilbart, J. W.—Practical Treatise on Banking. 2 v. . . . 8vo. Lond. 1849
——— —— The Same . . . . . . 8vo. N. Y. 1851
——— —— The Same. New edition . . . . . 8vo. Phil. 1855
Gilbert, Davies—Parochial History of Cornwall. 4 v. . . 8vo. Lond. 1838
Giles, Hen.—Christian Thoughts on Life . . . . . 16o. Bost. 1850
——— —— Illustrations of Genius . . . . . 12o. Bost. 1854
Gilfillan, Geo.—Bards of the Bible . . . . . . 12o. N. Y. 1850
——— —— Book of British Poesy, Ancient and Modern . 18o. Lond. 1851
——— —— Scottish Martyrs, Heroes, and Bards . . 16o. N. Y. 1853
——— —— Third Gallery of Portraits . . . . 12o. N. Y. 1855
——— Robt.—Poems and Songs . . . . . 16o. Edin. 1851
Gillespie, Wm. M.—Treatise on Land Surveying . . 8vo. N. Y. 1855
Gillette, A. D.—The Last Gift, from a Pastor's Experience . . 16o. N. Y. 1854
Gillies, R. P.—Memoirs of a Literary Veteran, 1794 to 1849. 3 v. 12o. Lond. 1851
*Gilliss, Lieut. J. M.—U. S. Naval Astron. Exped'n to S. Hemisph. 2 v. 4to. Wash. 1855
*Gillray, Jas.—Works, from the Original Plates . . . Fol. Lond. no date
Gilly, W. O. S.—Shipwrecks of the Royal Navy, from 1793 to 1849 12o. Lond. 1850
Gilson, A.—The Czar and the Sultan . . . . . 16o. N. Y. 1853
Girardin, Mme. E. de—Lettres Parisiennes . . . . . 16o. Paris. 1843
——— —— Marguerite; ou, Deux Amours . . . . 16o. Paris. 1853
——— —— Politique Universelle . . . . . 12o. Paris. 1854
——— —— Parisian Letters. See *Gay, Sophie de.*
Girault Duvivier, Ch. P.—Grammaire des Grammaires . . 8vo. Brux. 1851
Gisborne, Lionel—Isthmus of Darien in 1852 . . . . 8vo. Lond. 1853
——— Thos.—Duties of Man in Higher and Mid. Classes of Eng. 2 v. 8vo. Lond. 1795
*Glasgow Post Office Annual Directory for 1853–5 . . . 8vo. Glasgow. 1853–4
Gleig, G. R.—The Leipsic Campaign . . . . . 12o. Lond. 1852
Glenny, Geo.—Hand-Book to the Fruit and Vegetable Garden. . 8vo. Lond. 1850
Gluck—Iphigenie en Aulide. (An Opera) . . . . 8vo. Paris. no date
Glynn, Jos.—On the Power of Water . . . . . 16o. Lond. 1853
Gmelin's H. B. of Chemistry. See *Cavendish Soc. Publications.*
Gobat, Sam.—Three Years' Residence in Abyssinia . . . . 12o. N. Y. 1850
Goddard, H.—Royal Architectural Society's Prize Model Cottages 4to. Lond. no date
Godley, John R.—Letters from America. 2 v. . . . . 12o. Lond. 1844
*Godwin, Parke—Hand-Book of Universal Biography . . 12o. N. Y. 1852
——— Geo.—History in Ruins, or, Sketch of Architecture . 12o. Lond. 1853
Goethe, J. W.—Faust. (Fr. Ger. by Hayward.) . . . 12o. Bost. 1851
——— —— Dramatic Works . . . . . . 16o. Lond. 1850
——— —— Poems. (Fr. Ger.) by E. A. Bowring . . 16o. Lond. 1853
——— —— Life and Works of, by G. H. Lewes. 2 v. . . 12o. Bost. 1856
Gold and the Gospel . . . . 16o. N. Y. 1854
Golden Dreams and Leaden Realities . . . . . 12o. N. Y. 1853
Goldsmith, Oliver.—History of England. Ed. by Taylor and Pinnock 18o. Lond. 1851
——— —— History of the Earth and Animated Nature . 8vo. Lond. 1852
——— —— Life of, by Wash. Irving. 2 v. . . . 12o. N. Y. 1844
Goodell, Wm.—American Slave Code in Theory and Practice . 12o. N. Y. 1853
——— —— Old and the New; or, Changes in the East . 12o. N. Y. 1853
Goodrich, Chauncey A. (Ed'r.) Select British Eloquence . . 8vo. N. Y. 1853
——— S. G.—Poems . . . . 12o. N. Y. 1851
——— —— Young America; or, Book of Government and Law 12o. N. Y. 1845

Görgei, A.—Mein Leben und Wirten in Ungarn. 2 v.	8vo. Leipz.	1852
——— —— My Life and Acts in Hungary. 2 v.	8vo. Lond.	1852
——— —— The Same	8vo. N. Y.	1852
Gorrie, P. D.—Episcopal Methodism, as it was	12o. Auburn.	1852
——— —— Lives of Eminent Methodist Ministers	12o. Auburn.	1852
*Gorton, John—General Biographical Dictionary. 4 v.	8vo. Lond.	1830
*——— —— Topographical Dictionary of Great Britain. 3 v.	8vo. Lond.	1833
Gosse, Phil. H.—Naturalist's Sojourn in Jamaica	12o. Lond.	1851
——— —— Sacred Streams; or History of the Rivers of the Bible.	12o. N. Y.	1852
Gouge, Wm. M.—Fiscal History of Texas	8vo. Phil.	1852
Gould, Edw. S.—"The Very Age"; a Comedy	12o. N. Y.	1850
—— Miss H. F.—Diosma; a Perennial	12o. Bost.	1851
—— Jno. J.—Report on Food and Diet	8vo. N. Y.	1852
—— Wm. M.—Zephyrs from Italy and Sicily	12o. N. Y.	1852
Grace Greenwood; See *Lippincott, Mrs.*		
Grafton, Hen. D.—Treatise on Camp and March	12o. Bost.	1854
Graham, Maria—Journal of a Residence in Chile in 1822	4to. Lond.	1824
Graham's Magazine. Vols. 37–40, 44–45. [*Continued.*]	8vo. Phil.	1850–55
Grand Pierre, J. H.—A Parisian Pastor's Glance at America	16o. Bost.	1854
Grandville—Petites Misères de la Vie Humaine	8vo. Paris.	1846
Grant, Asahel—Memoir, by Thos. Laurie	12o. Bost.	1853
—— Jas.—Adven. of an Aid-de-Camp; or Campaign in Calabria. 3 v.	8vo. Lond.	1848
——— —— Memoirs and Adventures of Sir J. Hepburn	12o. Edin.	1851
——— —— Run through Continental Countries. 2 v.	12o. Lond.	1853
—— Robt.—History of Physical Astronomy	8vo. Lond.	1852
Grattan, Hen.—Life and Times of Rt. Hon. Henry Grattan. 5 v.	8vo. Lond.	1849
——— Wm.—Adventures of the Connaught Rangers. 2d Series. 2 v.	12o. Lond.	1853
Gray, A., and Adams, C. B.—Elements of Geology	12o. N. Y.	1853
—— Mrs. H.—Emperors of Rome; from Augustus to Constantine	16o. Lond.	1850
—— Thos.—Poetical Works. Edited by Hen. Reed	12o. Phil.	1853
——— —— and Collins, Wm.—Poetical Works	Fol. Glasgow.	1787
——— —— and Mason (Wm.)—Correspondence	8vo. Lond.	1853
*——— —— and Collins, Wm.—Poetical Works of,	Fol. Glasgow.	1787
Grayson, Wm. S.—True Theory of Christianity	12o. N. Y.	1753
Great Exhibition. See *Official Catalogue*		
*Great Gun (The)	Fol. Lond.	1844–5
Greek Anthology—Trans. by Geo. Burger, Bland, Merivale, and others	16o. Lond.	1852
Greeley, Horace—Glances at Europe during the Summer of 1851.	12o. N. Y.	1851
——— —— Life of, by J. Parton	12o. N. Y.	1855
Green, Hor.—Surgical Treatment of Polypi and Œdema Glottidis	8vo. N. Y.	1852
Greene, Geo. W.—History of the Middle Ages	12o. N. Y.	1851
——— Max.—Kanzas Region	12o. N. Y.	1856
Greenleaf, P. H.—Consolatio; or, Comfort for the Afflicted	12o. Bost.	1849
——— Simon—On the Law of Evidence. Vol. 3.	8vo Bost.	1853
——— Jona.—History of the Churches in the City of New York	16o. N. Y.	1850
Greenough, H.—Memorial of, by H. T. Tuckerman	12o. N. Y.	1853
Greenwood, F. W. P.—History of King's Chapel, in Boston	12o. Bost.	1833
——— Jas.—Rudimentary Treatise on Navigation	16o. Lond.	1850
Greg, Wm. R.—Creed of Christendom	8vo. Lond.	1851
——— —— Essays on Political and Social Science. 2 v.	8vo. Lond.	1853

Gregorovius, Ferd.—Corsica, Picturesque, Historical, &c., (Fr. Germ.) 12o. Phil. 1855
Gregory, Jno.—Complete Course of Civil Engineering . . 8vo. Lond. no date
——— Wm.—Hand-Book of Organic Chemistry . . . 12o. Lond. 1852
——— —— Letters to a Candid Inquirer on Animal Magnetism 12o. Lond. 1852
Grenville Papers (The)—Edited by W. J. Smith. Vols. 1–4. . 8vo. Lond. 1852–3
Grenzboten. Vols. 1, and N. S. 1, 3. [*Continued.*] . . 8vo. Leipz. 1851-3
Grey, Earl—Colonial Policy of Lord J. Russell's Administration. 2 v. 8vo. Lond. 1853
—— Lady Jane—Life of, by Dav. W. Bartlett . . . 12o. Auburn. 1853
—— Maria G., and Sherriff, Emily—Thoughts on Self-Cult. for Women 12o. Bost. 1851
Greyhound (The); or, The Art of Breeding, Rearing, &c. . 8vo. Lond. 1853
*Grieb, Chr. Fr.—Dictionary of Eng. and Germ. Languages. 2 v. . 8vo. Phil. 1852
Grier, Mrs. J. R.—Quakerism; or, the Story of My Life . 12o. Dublin. 1852
Griffith, M.—Poems . . . . 12o. N. Y. 1853
Griffiths, John W.—Treatise on Marine and Naval Architecture 4to. N. Y. 1851
——— Thos.—Chemistry of the Crystal Palace . . . 12o. Lond. 1851
Griggs, W. N.—The Celebrated Moon Story . . . 18o. N. Y. 1852
Grimes, J. T.—Phreno-Geology: The Progressive Creation of Man 12o. Bost. 1851
*Grimm, Jac. & W.—Deutsche Wörterbuch. Vol. 1. A–Bi . 4to. Leipz. 1854
Grimshaw, Wm.—History of the U. S. to 1848 . . . 12o. Phil. 1853
Grinfield, E. W.—The Jesuits; an Historical Sketch . . 16o. Lond. 1853
Griswold, C. D.—The Isthmus of Panama, and What I Saw There 12o. N. Y. 1852
*——— Ruf. W.—The Republican Court . . . 4to. N. Y. 1855
Grosh, A. B.—The Odd-Fellow's Manual . . . . . 12o. Phil. 1852
Grosvenor, Robt.—Leaves from my Journal . . . 16o. Lond. 1854
Grote, Geo.—History of Greece. Vols. 1–11 . . . 12o.Bost.&N.Y.1851–3
——— —— The Same. Vols. 9 and 10 . . . 8vo. Lond. 1852
Grotius, Hugo—De Jure Belli et Pacis Libri Tres. 3 v. . . 8vo. Camb. (E.) 1853
——— —— On the Rights of War and Peace, Abridged. (Fr. Lat.) 8vo. Camb. (E.) 1853
——— —— Truth of the Christian Religion. (Fr. Lat.) . 8vo. Lond. 1777
Guéronnière, A. de—Les Hommes d'Etat de l'Angleterre aux XIX Siècle 12o. Paris. 1855
——— —— Napoleon the Third. (Fr. Fren.) . . 12o. Lond. 1853
Guerre de la Vendée et des Chouans . . . . . 8vo Paris. no date
*Guibert, Adrien—Dictionnaire Geographique et Statistique . 8vo. Paris. 1850
Guicciardin, Fran.—History: Containing the Wars of Italy. (Fr. Ital.) Fol. Lond. 1599
*Guide and Directory of the State of Louisiana . . . 12o. N. Orleans. 1838
—— Between Washington and Boston, &c. . . . 16o. N. Y. 1846
—— du Mécanicien des Machines Locomotives. 2 v. . . 8vo. Paris. 1851
*—— to New Rochelle and its Vicinity . . . . . 16o. N. Y. 1842
—— to Northern Archæology, by the Copenhagen Society . 8vo. Lond. 1848
Guizot, M. et Mme.—Abailard et Héloïse; Essai Historique . 8vo. Paris. 1853
——— F.—Corneille and his Times . . . . . . 8vo. Lond. 1852
——— —— The Same . . . . 12o. N. Y. 1852
——— —— Character and Influence of Washington. (Fr. Fren.) 16o. Bost. 1851
——— —— Etudes Biographiques sur la Révolution d'Angleterre 12o. Brux. 1851
——— —— Etudes sur les Beaux Arts en Généraux . . 16o. Paris. 1852
——— —— Fine Arts, their Nature and Relations . . 8vo. Lond. 1853
——— —— Méditations et Etudes Morales . . . 16o. Paris. 1852
——— —— Monk: Chute de la Republique en Angleterre, 1660 8vo. Paris. 1851
——— —— Hist. of Oliver Cromwell and Eng. Commonwealth. 2 v. 8vo. Lond. 1854
——— —— The Same. 2 v. . . . . 12o. Phil. 1854

Author and Title	Size	Place	Date
Guizot, F.—Origines du Gouvernement Représentatif en Europe. 2 v.	12o.	Brux.	1851
——— —— Origin of Representative Gov't in Europe. (Fr. Fren.)	16o.	Lond.	1852
——— —— République d'Angleterre et de Cromwell, 1649–1658. 2 v.	8vo.	Paris.	1854
——— —— Shakspeare and his Times. (Fr. Fren.)	8vo.	Lond.	1852
——— —— The Same	12o.	N. Y.	1852
——— —— Washington. Fondation de la République des Etats Unis	12o.	Brux.	1851
Gurley, Ralph R.—Life of Jehudi Ashmun	8vo.	Wash.	1835
Gurney, Jno. H.—Historical Sketches, 1400–1546	16o.	Lond.	1852
——— J. J.—Chalmeriana; or, Colloquies with Dr. Chalmers	12o.	Lond.	1853
——— Jos. Jno.—Memoirs of, by Jos. B. Braithwaite. 2 v.	8vo.	Phil.	1854
——— —— Observ. on the Views and Prac. of the Soc. of Friends	8vo.	N. Y.	1840
——— T. E.—American School for the Melodeon, Seraphine, &c.	4to.	Bost.	no date
Gurowski, A. de—Russia as it Is.	12o.	N. Y.	1854
——— —— A Year of the War	8vo.	N. Y.	1855
Gustavus Vasa, King of Sweden—History of	8vo.	Lond.	1852
Guy, Jos., Jr.—Illustrated London Geography	8vo.	Lond.	1852
Guynemer, A. M. A.—Dictionnaire d'Astronomie	8vo.	Paris.	1852
Gwilt, Jos.—Elements of Architectural Criticism	8vo.	Lond.	1837
—— —— Rudiments of Architecture	8vo.	Lond.	1839
Hackett, Jas.—Narrative of Expedition from England in 1817	8vo.	Lond.	1818
Hackländer, F. W.—Wachtstubenabenteuer. 3 vols. in one	12o.	Stuttg't.	1845-53
——— —— Das Soldatenleben in Frieden	12o.	Stuttgart.	1846
Hackley, Chas. W.—Trigonometry, Plane and Spherical	8vo.	N. Y.	1851
Hadfield, Wm.—Brazil, the River Plate, &c.	8vo.	Lond.	1854
Hague, Wm.—Christianity and Statesmanship	12o.	N. Y.	1855
——— —— Home Life	12o.	N. Y.	1855
Hahn Hahn, Ida—From Jerusalem	12o.	Lond.	1852
—— ——— —— Letters from the Holy Land	12o.	Lond.	1849
*Hakluyt's Collection of Early Voyages, Travels, &c. 5 v.	4to.	Lond.	1809
Haldane, Alex.—Memoirs of R. and J. A. Haldane	8vo.	N. Y.	1853
——— Robt.—Books of the Bible proved Canonical	16o.	Edinb.	1853
Hale, Edw. E.—Kanzas and Nebraska	12o.	Bost.	1854
—— Sarah J.—Dictionary of Poetical Quotations	8vo.	Phil.	1850
—— —— Ladies' New Book of Cookery	12o.	N. Y.	1852
—— —— New Household Receipt Book	12o.	N. Y.	1853
—— —— Woman's Record	8vo.	N. Y.	1853
—— Wm. A., Cox, F. A., and others—Biog. An. of the Hebrew Nation	16o.	Lond.	1851
Half Hours with Old Humphrey	12o.	N. Y.	1850
Haliburton, T. C.—Rule and Misrule of the English in America	12o.	N. Y.	1851
Hall, A. Oakey—The Manhattaner in New Orleans	12o.	N. Y.	1851
—— Edw. B.—Memoir of Mary L. Ware	12o.	Bost.	1853
—— Mrs. M.—Queens of England before the Norman Conquest. 2 v.	8vo.	Lond.	1854
—— —— The Same.	8vo.	Phil.	1854
—— Newm.—The Land of the Forum and Vatican	16o.	N. Y.	1855
—— Mrs. S. C.—Pilgrimage to English Shrines. Second Series	8vo.	Lond	1853
—— S. T.—The Peak and the Plain	16o.	Lond.	1853
—— Thos.—Floss; or Progress of an Adventurer in Australia	16o.	Lond.	no date
—— W. W.—Bronchitis and Kindred Diseases	12o.	N. Y.	1852
—— —— Throat-Ail, Bronchitis, Consumption, &c.	8vo.	N. Y.	1851

Hallam, A. H.—See *Tennyson, In Memoriam.*
——— Hen.—Europe during the Middle Ages . . . . 8vo. N. Y. 1854
Halleck, Fitz-Greene—Poetical Works . . . . .12o. N. Y. 1852
Halsted, H.—Exposition of Motorpathy . . . . 12o. Rochester. 1853
Ham, Jas.—Elements of Spherical Trigonometry . . 16o. Lond. 1849
Hamerton, P. G.—Observations on Heraldry . . . 8vo. Lond. 1851
Hamilton, Alex.—Death of. Edited by Wm. Coleman . . 8vo. N. Y. 1804
——— —— Works. Edited by J. C. Hamilton. 7 v. . . 8vo. N. Y. 1850–1
——— And.—Sixteen Months in the Danish Isles. 2 v. . 12o. Lond. 1852
——— Jas.—Memoir of Richard Williams . . . 16o. N. Y. 1854
——— —— The Royal Preacher . . . . . 16o. N. Y. 1851
——— J. P.—Travels in Interior Provinces of Columbia. 2 v. . 8vo. Lond. 1827
——— S.—History of the United States' Flag . . 12o. Phil. 1852
——— Wm.—Discussions on Philosophy and Literature . 8vo. Lond. 1852
——— —— The Same . . . . . . 8vo. N. Y. 1853
——— Wm. Jr.—Country and River of the Amazones . . 12o. Lond. 1661
Hamlin, Mrs. H. A. L.—Memoir by M. W. Lawrence . . 12o. Bost. 1854
Hammer, Jas. von—History of the Assassins. (Fr. Ger.) . . 8vo. Lond. 1835
Hammond, C.—Light from the Spirit World . . . 12o. Rochester. 1852
——— S. H.—Hills, Lakes, and Forest Streams . . 12o. N. Y. 1854
——— —— and Mansfield (L. W.)—Country Margins . 12o. N. Y. 1855
Hancock, Thos.—The Principles of Peace . . . . 16o. Prov. 1832
Hand Book for Northern Europe. 2 v. . . . . . 16o. Lond. 1849
——— Northern Germany . . . . . . 12o. Lond. 1854
——— Travellers in Switzerland . . . . 12o. Lond. 1854
——— of Anglo-Saxon Orthography . . . . . 12o. N. Y. 1853
——— Anglo-Saxon Root-Words . . . . 12o. N. Y. 1853
——— Engrafted Words of the English Language . . 12o. Bost. 1853
——— Games . . . . 16o. Lond. 1850
Handel, Geo. F.—The Messiah. (An Oratorio.) . . . . 4to. Lond.
——— —— Samson. (An Oratorio.) . . . . . 4to. Lond.
Handy, Wash. R.—Text-Book of Anatomy and Dissection . . 8vo. Phil. 1854
Hanna, Wm.—Memoirs of Thos. Chalmers. Vols. 2-4 . . 12o. N. Y. 1850–2
Hannay, Jas.—Satire and Satirists . . . . . . 12o. Lond. 1854
——— —— The Same. . . . . 12o. N. Y. 1855
Hannover, A.—On the Microscope. Edited by Jno. Goodsir . 8vo. Edin. 1853
Hanson, Jno. H.—The Lost Prince. [Louis XVII.] . . 12o. N. Y. 1854
Harbaugh, H.—The Heavenly Home . . . . . 12o. Phil. 1853
Harcourt, Robt.—Voyage to Guiana . . . . . sm. 4to. Lond. 1613
Hardee, W. J.—Rifle and Light Infantry Tactics. 2 v. . . 32o. Phil. 1855
Hardemann, H. M.—The Free Flag of Cuba . . . . 12o. N. Y. 1851
*Harding, T. D.—Lessons on Trees . . . . . . Fol. Lond. 1850
Hardman, Fran.—Frontier Life; or, Scenes in the South-West . 12o. Buffalo. 1853
Hardwick, Chas.—History of the Articles of Religion . . 8vo. Phila. 1852
Hardwicke (Lord Chancellor)—Life of, by Geo. Harris . . 8vo. Lond. 1847
Hardy, Thos. D.—Memoirs of Right Hon. H. Lord Langdale. 2 v. 8vo. Lond. 1852
Hare, J. C.—The Contest with Rome . . . . . 8vo. Lond. 1852
—— —— The Mission of the Comforter . . . . . 12o. Bost. 1854
—— Robt.—Experimental Investigation of Spirit Manifestations 8vo. N. Y. 1856
Harmon, Dan. W.—Voyages and Travels in Interior of North America 8vo. Andover. 1820

*Harper and Brothers' Book-List, with Index, &c. . . 12o. N. Y. 1855
Harper's New Monthly. Vols. 1–8 [*Continued.*] . . . 8vo. N. Y. 1850–54
——— New York and Erie Rail-Road Guide Book . . . 12o. N. Y. 1851
Harrington, Jos.—Sermons, by Wm. Whiting . . . 12o. Bost. 1854
Harris, Geo.—Life of Lord Chancellor Hardwicke. 3 v. . 8vo. Lond. 1847
——— Jno.—Patriarchy; or, The Family . . . . . 12o. Bost. 1855
——— Thos. L.—Epic of the Starry Heavens . . . . 12o. N. Y. 1854
Harrison, Gessner—Exposition of the Laws of Latin Grammar . 12o. N. Y. 1852
——— Jno.—On Stricture of the Urethra . . . . 8vo. Lond. 1852
Harsha, Dav. A.—Eminent Statesmen of all Times . . . 8vo. N. Y. 1855
Hart, A. M.—History of the Valley of the Mississippi . . 12o. Cincin. 1853
*—— H. Y.—New Annual Army and Militia List for 1855 . 8vo. Lond. 1855
—— Jno. S.—Epitome of Greek and Roman Mythology . 12o. Phil. 1853
—— —— Female Prose Writers of America . . . 8vo. Phil. 1853
*Hartford Directory, 1842 . . . . 16o. Hartford. 1842
Hartley, R. M.—Intemperance in Cities and Large Towns . . 12o. N. Y. 1851
——— Sherman—Lessons at the Cross . . . . 16o. Bost. 1853
Hartman, F.—Acute Diseases. (Fr. Ger.) Vol. 2. . . . 12o. N. Y. 1848
——— —— Chronic Diseases. (Fr. Ger.) 2 v. . . 12o. N. Y. 1849
*Hartshorn, Jno.—Hartshorn's Commercial Tables . . . Fol. Bost. 1852
Harvestings: Sketches in Prose and Verse . . . . 12o. Bost. 1855
Haskett, Wm. J.—Shakerism Unmasked . . . . . 12o. Pittsfield. 1828
Hasse, F. K.—Life of Anselm, Archb. of Canterbury. (Fr. Ger.) 8vo. Lond. 1850
Hastings, Thos.—Dissertation on Musical Taste . . . 12o. N. Y. 1853
——— —— History of Forty Choirs . . . . 12o. N. Y. 1854
Hatfield, R. G.—The American House Carpenter . . . 8vo. N. Y. 1850
Haupt, Herman—General Theory of Bridge Construction . 8vo. N. Y. 1851
Hawes, Mrs. A. H.—The Grafted Bud; a Memoir of A. J. Hawes . 16o. N. Y. 1853
Hawker, P.—Instructions to Young Sportsmen . . . . 8vo. Phil. 1846
Hawkins' Picture of Quebec; with Historical Recollections . 12o. Quebec. 1834
Hawks, F. L. (Ed'r.)—Life of Oliver Cromwell. . . . 16o. N. Y. 1856
——— —— ——— Richard the Lion-Hearted . . 12o. N. Y. 1855
Hawthorne, Nath.—Life of Franklin Pierce . . . . 12o. Bost. 1852
Hay, D. K.—Geometric Beauty of the Human Figure . . 4to. Edin. 1851
*Hayden, Jos.—Beatson's Political Index. The Book of Dignities 8vo. Lond. 1851
——— Wm. B.—Phenomena of Modern Spiritualism . . 12o. Bost. 1855
Haydon, Ben. C.—Life of, comp. by Tom Taylor. 2 v. . 12o. N. Y. 1853
——— —— The Same. 3 v. . . . . . . 8vo. Lond. 1853
Hayley, Wm.—[Essay on Old Maids.] 3 v. . . . . 12o. Lond. 1786
*Hayward, John—Gazetteer of the United States of America . 8vo. Hartf. 1853
*——— —— New England and New York Law Register for 1835 12o. Bost. 1834
——— Geo.—Surgical Reports and Miscellaneous Papers . 12o. Bost. 1855
*Hazard, Sam.—Annals of Pennsylvania, 1609–82 . . 8vo. Phil. 1850
*——— —— (Ed'r.)—The Register of Pennsylvania. 16 v. . 4to. Phil. 1828–36
*——— —— ——— U. S. Commercial and Statistical Register. 6 v. 4to. 1839–42
Hazlitt, Wm.—Classical Gazetteer . . . . . . 16o. Lond. 1851
——— —— Winterslow Essays and Characters . . 16o. Lond. 1850
Head, F B.—Defenceless State of Great Britain . . . 12o. Lond. 1850
—— —— Faggot of French Sticks . . . . . 12o. N. Y. 1852
—— —— A Fortnight in Ireland . . . . . . 8vo. Lond. 1852

Entry	Size / Place	Year
Head, F. B.—The Same	12o. N. Y.	1853
Headley, P. C.—Historical Descriptive Sketches of Women of the Bible	12o. Auburn.	1850
——— —— Life of Governor Louis Kossuth	12o. Auburn.	1852
——— —— —— The Empress Josephine	12o. Auburn.	1850
——— J. T.—Imperial Guard of Napoleon	12o. N. Y.	1852
——— —— Lives of Winfield Scott and Andrew Jackson	12o. N. N.	1852
——— —— The Power of Beauty	18o. N. Y.	1852
——— —— The Second War with England. 2 v.	12o. N. Y.	1853
Heap, G. H.—Central Route to the Pacific	8vo. Phil.	1854
Hebrew Reading Lessons ; with Translations	12o. Lond.	no date
Hecker, J. T.—Questions of the Soul	12o. N. Y.	1855
Hedley, Jno.—Working and Ventilation of Gold Mines	8vo. Lond.	1851
Hedding, E.—Life and Times of, by Rev. D. W. Clark	12o. N. Y.	1855
Heimann, A.—Materials for Translating from English into German	12o. Lond.	1851
Heighway, O. W. T.—Leila Ada, the Jewish Convert	12o. N. Y.	1854
Heller, Carl B.—Reisen in Mexico in 1845–8	8vo. Leipz.	1853
Helps, Arthur—Fruits of Leisure. Essays in Intervals of Business	12o. N. Y.	1852
Henck, Jno. B.—Field-Book for Railroad Engineers	12o. N. Y.	1854
Henderson, Wm.—Homœopathy fairly Represented	8vo. Phil.	1854
Henfrey, Arthur—The Vegetation of Europe	16o. Lond.	1852
Henkle, M. M.—Life of Bishop Henry B. Bascom, D.D.	12o. Louisville.	1854
Henry, J. J.—Campaign against Quebec	16o. Watertown.	1844
——— Matthew—Miscellaneous Works	8vo. Lond.	1830
——— —— The Same. 2 v.	8vo. N. Y.	1855
——— of Huntingdon's Chronicle	16o. Lond.	1853
——— Paul—Life and Times of John Calvin	8vo. N. Y.	1854
——— V.—Life and Character of, by J. E. Tyler	8vo. Lond.	1838
——— VIII.—Life and Reign of, by Edward Herbert	Fol. Lond.	1672
————— and his Six Wives, by Henry W. Herbert	12o. N. Y.	1855
Hepburn, Sir J.—Memoirs and Adventures of, by J. Grant	12o. Edin.	1855
Herbert, Edw.—Life and Reign of Henry VIII.	Fol. Lond.	1672
——— Geo.—Life and Writings	16o. Bost.	1851
——— Hen. W.—American Game in its Seasons	12o. N. Y.	1853
——— —— Captains of the Old World	12o. N. Y.	1851
——— —— ————— Roman Republic	12o. N. Y.	1854
——— —— Cavaliers of England	12o. N. Y.	1852
——— —— Frank Forester's Field Sports of the United States. 2 v.	8vo. N. Y.	1852
——— —— ————— Fish and Fishing	8vo. N. Y.	1851
——— —— Henry the Eighth and his Six Wives	12o. N. Y.	1855
——— —— The Knights of England, France, and Scotland	12o. N. Y.	1852
——— —— Miscellaneous Poetry. 2 v.	8vo. Lond.	1804
——— —— Persons and Pictures from French and English History	12o. N. Y.	1854
——— —— (Ed'r.)—Sportsman's Vade Mecum	12o. N. Y.	1850
Herndon, Lieut. Wm. L.—Explor. of the Val. of the Amaz. & maps 2 v.	8vo. Wash.	1853
*Hernisz, S.—Conversation in English and Chinese	4to. Bost.	1854
Herodotus Halicarnasseus. See *Scrip. Græcorum Bibliotheca.* Vol. 19.		
Herr Rudolph—Jeweler's Hand-Book	12o. Albany.	1855
Hervey, Geo. W.—Principles of Courtesy	12o. N. Y.	1852
——— —— Rhetoric of Conversation	12o. N. Y.	1853
——— N.—The Memory of Washington	16o. Bost.	1852

Hesiodus Ascræus—Carmina .See *Scriptorum Græcorum, &c.* Vol. 7.			
Hettner—Athens and the Peloponnesus	16o.	Edinb.	1854
Hewitt, Mary E.—Poems	12o.	N. Y.	1854
Heywood, Jas.—Recommendations of Oxford Univ. Commissioners	8vo.	Lond.	1853
Hibernia; or, Comprehensive Sketches of Ireland . . .	12o.	N. Y.	1854
Hickey, W. (Ed'r.)—Constitution of the United States, with Analysis	12o.	Phil.	1854
Hickok, L. P.—Empirical Psychology	12o.	Schen.	1854
——— —— System of Moral Science	8vo.	Schen.	1853
Higgins, Godf.—Anacalypsis; or, the Origin of Languages. 2 v. .	4to.	Lond.	1836
——— W. M.—Researches in the Solar Realms . .	16o.	Lond.	1852
Highton, Edw.—The Electric Telegraph	16o.	Lond.	1852
Hildreth, Rich.—Despotism in America	12o.	Bost.	1854
——— —— Hist. of U. States from the Federal Constitution. 3 v.	8vo.	N. Y.	1849–52
——— —— Japan as it Was and Is	12o.	Bost.	1855
——— —— Lives of Judges Infamous as Tools of Tyrants .	12o.	N. Y.	1856
——— —— Theory of Politics	12o.	N. Y.	1853
Hildyard, Fran.—Principles of Law of Marine Insurances . .	8vo.	Harrisb.	1871
Hill, Fred.—Crime; Its Amount, Causes and Remedies .	8vo.	Lond.	1853
—— Jas.—On the Law relating to Trustees . . .	8vo.	Phil.	1854
—— M., and Cornwallis (C. F.)—Juvenile Delinquency . .	12o.	Lond.	1853
—— S. S.—Travels in Siberia. 2 v.	8vo.	Lond.	1855
—— —— Travels on the Shores of the Baltic . . .	8vo.	Lond.	1854
Hillard, Geo. S.—Dangers and Duties of the Mercantile Profession .	16o.	Bost.	1850
——— —— (Ed'r.)—Selections fr. Writings of Walter Savage Landor	12o.	Bost.	1856
——— —— Six Months in Italy. 2 v.	12o.	Bost.	1853
——— —— The Same. 2 v.	16o.	Bost.	1854
Hilliard, Fran.—American Law of Real Property. 2 v. . . .	8vo.	N. Y.	1855
——— —— Law of Mortgages. 2 v.	8vo.	Bost.	1853
——— Hen. W.—Speeches and Addresses	8vo.	N. Y.	1855
Hillier, Geo.—Attempted Escapes of Chas. I. from Carisbrook Castle	12o.	Lond.	1852
Himerius—Opera. See *Scriptorum Græcorum Bibliotheca.* Vol. 32.			
Hind, J. R.—The Comets; A Descriptive Treatise . .	12o.	Lond.	1852
——— —— The Solar System	16o.	Lond.	no date
Hinds, Wm.—The Harmonics of Physical Science . .	16o.	Lond.	1853
Hinkley, Edw.—Tables of Prime Numbers and Factors fr. 1 to 100,000	8vo.	Balt.	1853
Hines, Gustavus—Oregon; its History, Condition, and Prospects.	12o.	Buffalo	1851
——— Dav. T.—Life, Adventures, and Opinions . . .	12o.	N. Y.	1840
Hinman, Roy. R.—Names of Early Connecticut Settlers. Vol. 1. .	8vo.	Hartf.	1852
——— —— (Comp'r)—Letters from English Kings and Queens.	12o.	Hartf.	1836
Hipsley, W.—Equational Arithmetic, applied	16o.	Lond.	1852
Histoire de Trente Heures, Février, 1848	12o.	Paris.	1848
——— du Cabinet des Tuilleries. Bound with *Alliance des Jacobins*	8vo.	Paris.	1815
——— Naturelle et Morale des Iles Antilles de l'Amérique .	4to.	Rotterdam.	1665
History of America; from the American Cyclopædia . .	12o.	Phil.	1808
——— China	12o.	Lond.	1854
——— England. 4 v.	24o.	Lond.	s. a.
——— England and France under the House of Lancaster .	8vo.	Lond.	1852
——— Greece, Macedonia, and Syria	12o.	Lond.	1852
——— Greek and Roman Philosophy and Science . .	12o.	Lond.	1853
——— Greek Literature. By Talfourd, Blomfield, &c. .	12o.	Lond.	1851

History of New Ipswich, from 1736 to 1852	8vo. Bost.	1852
——— Rome. (L. U. K.)	8vo. Lond.	1830
——— The Buccaneers of America	8vo. Bost.	1853
——— Caribby Islands, Natural and Moral. Trans. by Davis .	Fol. Lond.	1666
——— Mormons; or, Latter-Day Saints . . .	12o. Auburn.	1852
——— Protestant Church in Hungary	12o. Bost.	1854
——— Scottish Wars. From A. D. 85–1746 . .	12o. Edinb.	1825
——— Recent Developments in Spiritual Manifestations .	12o. Phil.	1850
——— Roman Empire from the time of Vespasian . .	12o. Lond.	1853
——— Roman Republic, by Arnold, Pococke, &c., . .	12o. Lond.	1852
Hitchcock, Edw.—Elementary Geology	12o. N. Y.	1854
——— —— Geology of the Globe	8vo. Bost.	1853
——— —— History of a Zoological Temperance Convention	16o. Northamp.	1850
——— —— Religion of Geology, and its Connected Sciences	12o. Bost.	1851
——— —— Religious Lectures on Phenomena of the Four Seasons	12o. Bost.	1853
——— —— (Comp'r.)—Chris. Benevolence; or, Life of Mary Lyon	12o. Northamp.	1852
Hoare, Wm. H.—Outlines of Ecclesiastical History to 1520 .	16o. Lond.	1852
Hoffman—Contes Nocturnes. (Fr. Ger.)	16o. Paris.	1846
——— Murray—Estate and Rights of New York City Corporation	8vo. N. Y.	1853
——— Dav.—Chronicles of Cartaphilus. Vol. 1 . .	R. 8vo. Lond.	1853
Hogan, Wm.—Popery as it Was and Is	12o. Hartf.	1854
Hogg, Jabez—The Microscope; its History, Applications, &c. .	8vo. Lond.	1854
Hogarth, Wm.—Biog. Anecdotes of, by John Nichols . .	8vo. Lond.	1785
Holbrook, J.—Ten Years among the Mail Bags . . .	12o. Phil.	1855
Holgate, Jerome B.—American Genealogy	4to. N. Y.	1851
——— —— The Present Age of the World and Prophecy .	12o. Albany.	1853
Holland, Hen.—Chapters on Mental Physiology . . .	8vo. Lond.	1852
——— J. G.—History of Western Massachusetts. 2 v. .	12o. Springfd.	1855
——— Lady—Memoir of Rev. Sydney Smith. 2 v. . .	12o. N. Y.	1855
——— (Lord)—Foreign Reminiscences	12o. N. Y.	1851
——— —— Memoirs of the Whig Party. Vol. 1 . .	12o. Lond.	1852
Hollard, Hen.—De l'Homme et des Races Humaines . .	12o. Paris.	1853
Holley, O. L. (Ed'r.)—New York State Register, 1843–6. 3 v. .	12o. Albany.	1843–6
Hollis, Thos.—Memoirs of. 2 v.	4to. Lond.	1780
Hollister, G. H.—History of Connecticut. 2 v.	8vo. N. Haven.	1855
*Holmes, A.—Annals of America, 1492–1826. 2 v. . .	8vo. Camb.	1829
——— D.—Pure Gold; or, Truth in its Native Loveliness .	12o. Auburn.	1851
——— —— Wesley Offering; or, Wesley and his Times .	12o. Auburn.	1852
——— Mrs. Marcus H.—Scenes in our Parish . . .	12o. N. Y.	1851
——— Oliver W.—Astræa, the Balance of Illusions . .	12o. Bost.	1850
——— —— Poems	16o. Bost.	1853
Holtzappfel, Chas.—Turning and Mechanical Manipulations. Vol. 3.	8vo. Lond.	1850
Holyoake, G. S.—Rudiments of Public Speaking and Debate .	12o. N. Y.	1853
Homans, J. S.—Banker's Common-Place Book . . .	18o. Bost.	1851
*Home Book of the Picturesque	4to. N. Y.	1852
Home Missionary Magazine. Vols. 22, 23, 25, 26. [*Continued.*]	8vo. N. Y.	1850–3
—— Recreations; a Collection of Perils and Adventures . .	12o. N. Y.	1850
—— and Social Philosophy. From "Household Words" .	12o. N. Y.	1852
Homer's Iliad. See *Scriptorum Græcorum Bibliotheca.* Vol. 1. .		
——— (Fr. Greek, by Buckley.)	16o. Lond.	1851

*Homes of American Authors	8vo. N. Y.	1853
*———— American Statesmen	4to. N. Y.	1854
Honan, Mich. B.—Adventures of "Our own Correspondent" in Italy. 2 v.	12o. Lond.	1852
——— —— The Same	12o. N. Y.	1852
Honey Bee (The.) From the "Quarterly Review" . .	16o. Lond.	1852
Hongrie (La.) Ancienne et Moderne	8vo. Paris.	1851
Honigsberger, John M.—Thirty-five Years in the East. 2 v. .	8vo. Lond.	1852
Hood, Edward P.—The Uses of Biography	16o. Lond.	1852
—— Thomas—Hood's Own: Selected Papers	12o. N. Y.	1852
——— —— Poems. 2 v.	16o. Bost.	1854
——— —— Whimsicalities	12o. N. Y.	1852
——— —— Up the Rhine. 2 v.	12o. N. Y.	1852
—— Visc.—Scripture Female Characters	16o. Lond.	1854
Hook, W. F.—A Church Dictionary	8vo. Lond.	1852
—— Theo.—A Sketch. From the "Quarterly Review" .	16o. Lond.	1852
Hooker, Jos. D.—Himalayan Journals. 2 v.	8vo. Lond.	1854
——— Worth.—Homœopathy, its Doctrines and Evidences .	12o. N. Y.	1852
——— —— Human Physiology	12o. N. Y.	1854
——— —— Lessons from the History of Medical Delusions .	12o. N. Y.	1850
Hopkins, John H.—"The End of Controversy" Controverted. 2 v.	12o. N. Y.	1854
——— —— Novelties which Disturb our Peace . .	12o. Phil.	1844
Hopper, Isaac T.—A True Life, by L. Maria Child . .	12o. Bost.	1853
Hoppin, James M.—Notes of a Theological Student . . .	12o. N. Y.	1854
Horatius, Quintus Flaccus—Opera Omnia. See *Valpy's Delphin Classics.*		
———— —— Odes; translated by F. W. Newman . .	12o. Lond.	1853
———— —— Works. (From Latin, by Smart; revised by Buckley.)	16o. Lond.	1850
Horticulturist (The.)—Vols. 4, 6–9. [*Continued.*] . . .	8vo. Albany.	1849–54
Hoskins, G. A.—Spain as It Is. 2 v.	12o. Lond.	1851
Hosmer, Wm.—The Higher Law and Civil Government . .	12o. Auburn.	1852
——— Wm. H. C.—Poetical Works. 2 v.	12o. N. Y.	1854
Hough, F. B.—History of Jefferson County, N. Y. . . .	8vo. Albany.	1854
——— —— ———— St. Lawrence and Franklin Counties .	8vo. Albany.	1853
*——— —— New York Civil List	12o. Albany.	1855
——— Maj. Wm.—India as It Ought to Be	8vo. Lond.	1853
——— —— Political and Military Events in Br. India, 1756-1849. 2 v.	12o. Lond.	1853
Household Narrative for 1853, Conducted by Charles Dickens. [*Cont'd.*]	8vo. Lond.	1853
———— Words. Vols. 1–10. [*Continued.*] . .	8vo. Lond.	
Housman, Robert F.—Collection of English Sonnets . .	12o. Lond.	no date
Houston, Sam.—Life of	12o. N. Y.	1855
Houssaye, A.—Les Filles d'Eve. Les Trois Sœurs . . .	16o. Paris.	1852
———— —— Men and Women of the Eighteenth Century. 2 v.	12o. N. Y.	1852
———— —— Philosophers and Actresses. 2 v. . .	12o. N. Y.	1852
———— —— Philosophes et Comédiennes. 2 v. . .	16o. Paris.	1851
———— —— Vertu de Rosine. Roman Philosophique . .	24o. Paris.	1852
———— —— Voyage à Ma Fenêtre	8vo. Paris.	no date
How, Thomas G.—Vindication of the Protestant Episcopal Church	8vo. N. Y.	1816
Howard, W. W.—Aids to French Composition	12o. N. Y.	1854
——— John—Life of, by J. Field	8vo. Lond.	1850
——— Insurance Company of New York *ads.* S. Mathews, &c. .	4to. N. Y.	1851
Howitt, Anna M.—Art Student in Munich. 2 v. . .	12o. Lond.	1853

Title	Size. Place.	Date
Howitt, Anna M.—The Same	16o. Bost.	1854
——— Mary (Ed'r.)—Pictorial Calendar of the Seasons .	16o. Lond.	1854
——— Wm.—Boy's Adventure in Wilds of Australia . .	8vo. Bost.	1855
——— —— Country Year Book	12o. N. Y.	1850
——— —— Land, Labor, and Gold. 2 v. . . .	12o. Bost.	1855
——— —— & Mary—Literature and Romance of Modern Europe. 2 v.	8vo. Lond.	1852
Hoyt, Ralph—Sketches of Life and Landscape . . .	8vo. N. Y.	1852
Hubbard, Harvey—Ixion, and other Poems . . .	16o. Bost.	1852
Hübner, Otto—See *Zolltarife.*		
Huc, M.—Journey through the Chinese Empire. 2 v. . .	12o. N. Y.	1855
—— —— Journey through Tartary, Thibet, & China. (Fr. Fren.) 2 v.	16o. N. Y.	1852
Hudson, J. W.—History of Adult Education and Literary Institutions	8vo. Lond.	1851
Hufeland—Art of Prolonging Life. Edited by E. Wilson .	16o. Lond.	1853
Hughes, Edward—Outlines of Scripture Geography and History	12o. Phil.	1853
——— Griffith—Natural History of Barbadoes . . .	Fol. Lond.	1750
——— Wm.—Australian Colonies	12o. Lond.	1852
——— —— Manual of Geography	16o. Lond.	1852
——— Wm. C.—American Miller and Millwright's Assistant .	12o. Phil.	1851
Huguenots in France and America. 2 v.	16o. Bost.	1852
Huidekoper, Fred.—Christ's Mission to the Under World .	16o. Bost.	1854
Humboldt, Alex.—Ansichten der Natur. Two vols. in one. .	8vo. Stuttgart.	1849
——— —— Cosmos. (Fr. Ger., by Otté.) Vols. 3 and 4. .	12o. N. Y.	1851–2
——— —— ——— (Fr. Ger., by Sabine.) Vol. 3, parts 1 & 2.	12o. Lond.	1851–2
——— —— ——— (Fr. Ger., by Otté.) Vol. 4. . .	16o. Lond.	1852
——— —— Essai Polit. sur le Royaume de la Nouv. Espagne. 2 v.	4to. atlas fol. Paris.	1811
——— —— Kleinere Schriften. Vol. 1. . . .	8vo. Stuttgard.	1853
——— —— Kosmos. Vols. 1–3.	8vo. Stuttg't.	1848–50
——— —— Trav. to the Equinoctial Regions of Amer. Vols. 1 & 2.	16o. Lond.	1852
——— —— Umrisse von Vulkanen an den Cordilleren .	Fol. Stuttgart.	1853
——— Alex. & Wm.—Lives of. (Fr. Ger.)	12o. N. Y.	1853
——— Wm.—Letters to a Female Friend. (Fr. Ger.) 2 v. .	12o. Lond.	1849
——— —— Religious Thoughts and Opinions. (Fr. Ger.)	12o. Bost.	1851
Hume, A.—Learned Societies, &c., of the United Kingdom .	12o. Lond.	1853
——— Dav.—History of England. 6 v.	12o. N. Y.	1852
*Humphreys, H. N.—Ten Centuries of Art . . .	4to. Lond.	1852
Hungary and its Revolutions, with Memoir of Kossuth . .	16o. Lond.	1854
Hunt, F. K.—The Rhine; its Scenery and Associations .	4to. Lond.	1845
—— Freeman—Lives of American Merchants. Vol. 1. . .	8vo. N. Y.	1856
*—— F. W.—Pantological System of History. Part I., U. S. .	Fol. N. Y.	1855
—— John W.—Wisconsin Gazetteer	8vo. Madison.	1853
—— Leigh—Book for a Corner	12o. N. Y.	1852
—— —— Table Talk, and Imagin. Conver. between Pope and Swift	16o. Lond.	1851
—— —— Autobiography. 2 v.	12o. N. Y.	1850
—— Robt.—Elementary Physics	16o. Lond.	1851
—— —— Photography	12o. Lond.	1851
—— —— The same	12o. N. Y.	1852
Hunter, Jos.—Protestant Separatists at Scrooby . . .	8vo. Lond.	1854
——— Robt.—Diseases of the Throat and Lungs . . .	16o. N. Y.	1854
——— W. P.—Narr. of Exp. to Syria under Sir R. Stopford. 2 v.	12o. Lond.	1842
Huntington (Lady) and her Friends; Compiled by Mrs. Knight .	12o. N. Y.	no date

Hurlbut, Wm. H.—Gan Eden; or, Pictures of Cuba . . 12o. Bost. 1854
Hurton, Wm.—Voy. fr. Leith to Lapland; or, Scandinavia in 1850. 2 v. 8vo. Lond. 1851
Hutchinson, Thos.—Hist. of Prov. of Mass. Bay, from 1750 to 1774 8vo. Lond. 1848
Hutton, Jas.—Turkey, Past and Present . . . . . 16o. Lond. no date

Ibn Zafer—Solwan; or, Waters of Comfort. 2 v. . . . . 12o. Lond. 1852
*Iconographic Encyclopædia of Science, Literature, and Art. 6 v. 8vo & 4to. N. Y. 1851
Illustrated Hand-Book to London and its Environs . . . 16o. Lond. 1853
*———— London News (The) Vols 1–6. . . . . Fol. Lond. 1842–5
*———— The Same. Vols. 16–26. [*Continued.*] . . Fol. Lond. 1850–55
———— Magazine of Art. Vols. 1–3 . . . . . 8vo. N. Y. 1853–4
*Illustration (L'): Journal Universel. Vols. 15–19, 23–24. [*Cont'd.*] Fol. Paris. 1850–54
*Illustrations of British Paper Manufacture, by T. H. Saunders . Fol. Lond. 1855
Illustrious Personages of the 19th Century . . . . R. 8vo. N. Y. 1853
*Illustrirte Zeitung. 7 Vols. various. [*Continued.*] . . Fol. Leipzig. 1850–54
*Illustrirter Kalender für 1854–56. 3 v. . . . . . 8vo. Leipz. 1853–5
Importance of Literature to Men of Business . . . 16o. Lond. 1852
Incidents in the Life of Jacob Barker, of New Orleans . . 8vo. Wash. 1855
Indiana Annual Register and Manual for 1845–6. 2 v. . . 16o. Indianap. 1844–5
———— Gazetteer . . . . 8vo. Indianap. 1850
Industry of the United States in Machinery, Manufactures, &c., . 16o. Lond. 1854
Information to those having business at the Patent Office . 8vo. Wash. 1852
Ingersoll, Chas. J.—Hist. of Second War bet. U. S. &. Gt. Britain. 2 v. 8vo. Phil. 1852
Ingestre, Visc. (Ed'r.)—Meliora; or, Better Times to Come . 16o. Lond. 1852
Inglefield, E. A.—Summer Search for Sir J. Franklin . . 8vo. Lond.
Institut de France. Annuaire pour 1852 & 1853. 2 v. . . 16o. Paris. 1852 3
International Monthly Magazine. Vols. 1–5 . . . 8vo. N. Y. 1850–2
Introductory Discourse and Lectures before Boston Conv. of Teachers 8vo. Bost. 1831
———— Lectures delivered at the Opening of New College 12o. Lond. 1851
———— Lectures on the Opening of Owen's College . . 8vo. Lond. 1852
Inquiry into the Condition of the Africans in U. S. . . 12o. Phil. 1839
Ireland, W. H.—History of the County of Kent. 4 v. . . 8vo. Lond. 1828
Irish Abroad and at Home . . . . 12o. Bost. 1855
*—— Almanac and Directory for 1855. (Thom's) . . . 8vo. Dublin. 1855
—— Quarterly Review. Vols. 2–3. [*Continued*] . . 8vo. Dublin. 1852–3
Iroquois (The); or, the Bright Side of Indian Character . . 12o. N. Y. 1855
Irrationalism of Infidelity: A Reply to Phases of Faith . 8vo. Lond. 1853
Irving, B. A. Theory and Practice of Caste . . . 12o. Lond. 1853
———— Dav.—Lives of Scottish Writers. 2 Vols. in one . 12o. Edin. 1839
———— Theo.—Conquest of Florida . . . . . . 12o. N. Y. 1851
———— Washington—Alhambra . . . . 12o. N. Y. 1851
———— —— Conquest of Granada . . . . . . 12o. N. Y. 1850
———— —— Life of Goldsmith. 2 v. . . . . . 12o. N. Y. 1844
———— —— Life of George Washington. Vols. 1 & 2 . . 8vo. N. Y. 1855
———— —— Mahomet and his Successors. Vol. 2 . . 12o. N. Y. 1853
Isocrates. See *Scriptorum Græcorum Bibliotheca.* Vol. 23.
Izard, Ralph—Correspondence. 1774–1804. Vol. 1 . . 12o. N. Y. 1844

Jackson, And.—Life of. See *Headley, J. T.*
*———— J. R. (Comp'r)—Index to London Geographical Journal 8vo. Lond. 1844

Entry	Size/Place	Date
*Jackson, R. A.—Views in Affghaunistaun	Fol. Lond.	no date
——— Thos.—Life of Robert Newton, D. D. . . .	12o. N. Y.	1855
Jacob, Wm.—Travels in the South of Spain, 1809–19 . .	4to. Lond.	1838
Jaeger, B.—Life of North American Insects . . .	8vo. Prov.	1854
Jahr's New Manual; or, Symptomen-Codex. V. 3. . .	8vo. N. Y.	1853
James, G. P. R.—Life and Times of Louis XIV. 2 v. . .	16o. Lond.	1851
——— Hen.—Nature of Evil	12o. N. Y.	1855
——— VI. of Scotland—Letters of. See *Camden Soc. Publications.*		
——— Jno. A.—Young Man's Friend	16o. N. Y.	1852
——— —— Cause of Faith; or, the Practical Believer .	16o. N. Y.	1853
——— —— Christian Father's Present to Children . .	16o. N. Y.	1853
——— J. H.—Guide to Benefit Building Societies . .	12o. Lond.	1849
Jameson, Anna—Common-Place Book of Thought, &c., . .	12o. N. Y.	1855
——— —— Legends of the Madonna	8vo. Lond.	1852
——— —— Legends of the Monastic Orders . . .	8vo. Lond.	1850
——— H. G., Sen'r.—Treatise on Epidemic Cholera . .	8vo. Phil.	1855
——— R. G.—Australia and her Gold Regions . . .	12o. N. Y.	1852
Jamieson, Alex.—Mechanics of Fluids, for Practical Men .	8vo. Lond.	1848
Jane, Queen—Chronicle of. See *Camden Soc. Publications.*		
Janin, Jules—Sketches of Genoa, Pisa, Florence, &c., . .	12o. Phil.	1854
Janney, Sam. M.—Life of George Fox	8vo. Phil.	1853
——— ——— Life of Wm. Penn; with Selections fr. his Writings	8vo. Phil.	1852
Jarvis, S. F.—Church of the Redeemed. Vol. 1 . . .	8vo. Bost.	1850
Jaufaet, D.—Travels of Rolando; or, a Tour round the World .	16o. Lond.	1852
Jay, Jno.—Life of. See *Flanders, Hen.*		
—— Wm.—Autobiography. Ed. by Redford and James. 2 v. .	12o. N. Y.	1855
—— —— Lectures on Female Scripture Characters . .	12o. N. Y.	1854
—— —— Mornings with Jesus	12o. Phil.	1855
Jeffers, W. N.—Theory and Practice of Naval Gunnery . .	8vo. N. Y.	1850
Jefferson, Thos.—Manual of Parliamentary Practice . ..	12o. Phil.	1850
——— —— Writings, Edit. by H. A. Washington. 9 v. .	8vo. Wash.	1854
——— —— See *Selection of Eulogies. Webster, D.*		
*Jefferys, Thos.—The American Atlas	Fol. Lond.	1776
Jeffrey, Fran.—Contributions to the Edinburgh Review . .	8vo. Phil.	1854
——— —— Life of, by Lord Cockburn. 2 v. . . .	8vo. Lond.	1852
——— —— The Same	12o. Phil.	1852
Jeffreys, Judge—Life of, by H. W. Woolrych . . .	12o. Phil.	1852
Jenkins, John S.—Heroines of History	12o. Auburn.	1852
——— —— Life of James K. Polk	12o. Auburn.	1850
——— —— Life of John Caldwell	12o. Auburn.	1850
——— —— Lives of the Governors of the State of New York .	8vo. Auburn.	1851
——— —— New Clerk's Assistant	8vo. Auburn.	1851
——— —— United States Explor'g Expedition under Wilkes, &c.	8vo. Auburn.	1850
Jenks, R. W.—The Brachial Telegraph	8vo. N. Y.	1852
*—— Wm. (Ed'r)—Comprehensive Commentary on the Bible. 6 v.	8vo. Phil.	1851
Jerdan, Wm.—Autobiography and Reminiscences. 4 v. .	12o. Lond.	1852–3
Jeremie, Jas. A.—History of the Church, 2d and 3d Centuries .	12o. Lond.	1852
Jervis, J. W.—Manual of Field Operations . . .	12o. Lond.	1852
Jerrmann, Edw.—Pictures from St. Petersburg. (Fr. Ger.) .	12o. N. Y.	1852
——— —— The Same	12o. N. Y.	1855

Jerrold, W. B.—Brage-Breaker with the Swedes . . . 12o. Lond. 1854
Jesse, J. H.—Eng. under the Stuarts and Protectorate, 1603–1661. 4 v. 8vo. Lond. 1840
—— —— George Selwyn and his Cotemporaries. 4 v. . . 8vo. Lond. 1843
—— —— London and its Celebrities. 4 v. . . . . 8vo. Lond. 1850
Jeter, Jere. B.—Campbellism Examined . . . . . 12o. N. Y. 1855
Joan of Arc—Life of, by Dav. W. Bartlett . . . . 12o. Auburn. 1854
Jobson, D. W.—History of the French Revolution . . . 8vo. Lond. 1853
John the Baptist—Life and Acts of, by Wm. C. Duncan . 12o. N. Y. 1853
Johnson, A. B.—The Meaning of Words . . . . . 12o. N. Y. 1854
—— B. P.—Report on the Great Exhibition held in London, 1851 8vo. Albany. 1852
—— Edw. T.—Railroad to the Pacific, Northern Route . 8vo. N. Y. 1854
—— Jas. and J. H.—The Patentee's Manual . . 8vo. Lond. 1853
—— J. E.—Analytical Abridgement of Kent's Commentaries . 8vo. N. Y. 1839
—— M. J.—Astronom. Observa. at the Radcliffe Observat'y, 1847 8vo. Oxford. 1849
—— Sam.—Life of, by Jas. Boswell. 4 v. . . . 12o. Lond. no date
—— —— Lives of the British Poets. Vols. 1 and 3 . 12o. Lond. 1854
*—— —— Works. 11 v. . . . . . . 8vo. Oxford. 1825
—— Sam., of King's College—Life of, by Thos. B. Chandler 8vo. N. Y. 1824
—— Walter K.—Coal Trade of British America . . 8vo. Wash. 1850
*—— Wm. (Ed'r)—Draftsman: Book of Industrial Design . 4to. N. Y. 1854
Johnstone's Edinburgh Mag. Vol. 1. (All pub.; afterwards Tait's Mag.)
*Johnston, Alex. Keith—General Gazetteer . . . . 8vo. Lond. 1850
—— Geo.—Introduction to Conchology . . . 8vo. Lond. 1850
—— Jas. F. W.—Chemistry of Common Life. Vol. 1 . 12o. Edinb. 1854
—— —— The Same. 2 v. . . . . . . 12o. N. Y. 1855
—— —— Lectures on Science and Practical Agriculture 12o. N. Y. 1850
—— —— Notes on North America. 2 v. . . . 12o. Bost. 1851
—— Wm.—England as It Is. 2 v. . . . . 12o. Lond. 1851
Jomini, Baron de—Campaign of Waterloo. (Fr. Fren.) . . 12o. N. Y. 1853
—— —— Summary of the Art of War. (Fr. Fren.) . 12o. N. Y. 1854
Jones, Alex.—Cuba in 1851 . . . . 8vo. N. Y. 1851
—— —— Hist. Sketch of Electric Telegraph . . 8vo. N. Y. 1852
*—— A. D.—Illustrated American Biography. 3 v. . . 4to. N. Y. 1853–5
—— Geo.—History of Ancient America . . . . 8vo. Lond. 1843
—— H. B.—Adventures in Australia in 1852–3 . . . 12o. Lond. 1853
—— —— (Ed'r)—On Animal Electricity . . . 16o. Lond. 1852
—— J. B.—The Monarchist . . . . . . 12o. Phil. 1853
—— Jno. Paul—Life and Character of, by J. H. Sherburne . 8vo. N. Y. 1851
—— Thos.—Book-Keeping . . . . 8vo. N. Y. 1850
—— T. Percy—Firmillian: A "Spasmodic" Tragedy . . 12o. N. Y. 1854
—— Thos. R.—Natural History of Animals. Vol. 2 . . 12o. Lond. 1852
Jonnés, Alex. Moreau de—Eléments de Statistique . . 12o. Paris. 1847
Jopling, Jos.—Practice of Isometrical Perspective . . . 8vo. Lond. 1850
Joseph (Roi)—Memoirs et Correspondence du, par Du Casse. 2 v. 8vo. Paris. 1853
Josephine (Empress)—History of, by J. S. C. Abbott . . 16o. N. Y. 1850
—— —— Life of, by P. C. Headley . . . . . 12o. Auburn. 1850
Josephus, Flavius—Opera. See *Scriptorum Græcorum Bibliotheca.* Vols. 21 and 27.
—— —— Works, by Whiston. 2 v. . . . . 8vo. Phil. 1852
Journal des Débats. [*Continued.*] . . . . . . Fol. Paris. 1851–53
—— Economistes, N. S. Vols. 1, 2 . . . . 8vo. Paris. 1854

Journal de la Cour et de la Ville. Vol. 1	8vo. Paris.	1791
*——— des Travaux, Société Statistique. Vols. 1–20, in 6 v.	4to. & 8vo. Paris.	1830–50
——— of Agriculture, N. S. Vol. 1, July, 1843–March, 1845	8vo. Edin.	1843–5
——————— The Same. Vols. 4, 5, July '49–Mar. '53. [*Cont'd.*]	8vo. Edin.	1849–53
———— American Oriental Society. Vols. 1, 2	8vo B. & N Y	1842–51
———— Assembly of New York State, Seventy-Fourth Session. 2 v.	8vo. Albany.	1851
———————————— Seventy-Sixth Session. 2 v.	8vo. Albany.	1853
———————————— Seventy-Seventh Session	8vo. Albany.	1854
———— a Young Man of Massachusetts, captured in the War of 1813	16o. Bost.	1816
*———— Board of Education. New York, 1854	8vo. N. Y.	1854
———— Commerce (Daily) for 1850–54. 9 v. [*Continued.*]	Fol. N. Y.	1850–54
———— Debates, &c., at Mass. Convention of Constitution Revision	8vo. Bost.	1853
———— Design and Manufactures. 2 v.	8vo. Lond.	1849
———— Franklin Institute. Vols. 1–8	8vo. Phil.	1826–31
———— The Same. Third Series. Vols. 20–28 [*Continued.*]	8vo. Phil.	1850–54
———— Proceedings of a Literary Convention. N. Y., Oct., 1830	8vo. N. Y.	1831
———— Rhode Island Institute of Instruction. 3 v.	8vo. Prov.	1846–9
———— Royal Geographical Society. Vols. 11–23. [*Continued.*]	8vo. Lond.	1841–53
———— The Same. Index to Vols. 1–10, by J. R. Jackson	8vo. Lond.	1844
———— Sacred Literature. New Series. Vols. 3–6. [*Continued.*]	8vo. Lond.	1852–4
———— Senate of New York State. 74th and 77th Sessions. 2 v.	8vo. Albany.	1851–3
——————————— 76th Session	8vo. Albany.	1852
———— Society of Arts. Vol. 1. [*Continued.*]	8vo. Lond.	1852–3
———— Statistical Society of London. Vols. 11–16. [*Continued.*]	8vo. Lond.	1848–53
*Journals of Congress, Sept. 5, 1774–Nov. 3, 1788. 13 v.	8vo. Phil.	1800–1
Jouve, Eug.—Guerre d'Orient	8vo. Paris.	1855
Joy, A.—Pastor's Gift; or, Christian Duty	16o. N. Y.	1854
Judd, Rev. S.—The Church Discourses	12o. Bost.	1854
Judson, Adon.—Memoir of, by Professor F. Wayland. 2 v.	12o. Bost.	1853
——— —— Memoir of, by J. Clement	12o. Auburn.	1851
——— —— Life of [by Rev. Mr. Middleditch]	12o. N. Y.	1854
——— Mrs. A. H. and S. B.—Lives of, by Arabella W. Stuart	12o. Auburn.	1852
——— Emily—The Kathayan Slave, and other Papers	12o. Bost.	1853
——— —— My Two Sisters	16o. Bost.	1854
——— Everton—Memoir of, by E. P. Barrows, Jr.	12o. Bost.	1852
——— J. C.—Biog. of the Signers of the Declaration of Independence	8vo. Phila.	1839
Jukes, J. B.—Popular Physical Geology	16o. Lond.	1853
—— —— Physical Structure of Australia	8vo. Lond.	1850
Junius; Including Letters under other Signatures. 2 v.	16o. Lond.	1850
Justinian; The Institutes of, Edited by T. C. Saunders	8vo. Lond.	1853
Justinus—Opera Omnia. 2 v. See *Valpy's Delphin Classics.*		
Juvenalis—Opera Omnia. 2 v. See *Valpy's Delphin Classics.*		
Kane, E. K.—United States Grinnell Exploring Expedition	8vo. N. Y.	1854
——— Robt.—Elements of Chemistry	8vo. Dublin.	1849
Karr, Alphonse—Histoires Normandes	16o. Paris.	1855
—— —— Les Femmes	16o. Brux.	1853
—— —— Pénélope Normande	16o. Paris.	1855
*Katalog des Commerz-Bibliothek in Hamburg	4to. Hamb.	1847–53
Kavanagh, Julia—Exemplary Women of Christianity	12o. Lond.	1852

Kaye, Jno. W.—Administration of the East India Company	8vo.	Lond.	1853
—— —— Life of H. St. George Tucker	8vo.	Lond.	1854
Keating, Wm. H. (Comp'r.)—Exp. to St. Peter's River, &c., in 1823. 2 v.	8vo.	Lond.	1825
Keble, Jno.—Christian Year	32o.	N. Y.	1854
—— —— Lyra Innocentium	12o.	N. Y.	1850
Keith, Alex.—Harmony of Prophecy	12o.	Edin.	1851
Kelly, W. K.—Life of Wellington, for Boys	16o.	Lond.	1853
Kemp, T. L.—Natural History of Creation	16o.	Lond.	1852
*Kendall, Geo. W.—War between United States and Mexico. Illustrated	Fol.	N. Y.	1851
Kendrick, A. L.—Echoes; or, Hours with German Poets	12o.	Roches.	1855
Kennedy, Jas.—Modern Poets and Poetry of Spain	8vo.	Lond.	1852
——— Wm.—Second Voyage of the Prince Albert	12o.	Lond.	1853
Kennion, Edw.—Essay on Trees in Landscape	Fol.	Lond.	1815
Kenrick, Jno.—Ancient Egypt under the Pharaohs. 2 v.	12o.	N. Y.	1852
Kent, Jas.—Commentaries on American Law. 4 v.	8vo.	N. Y.	1851
Keppel, Hen.—Visit to the Indian Archipelago, in the Mæander. 2 v.	8vo.	Lond.	1853
Kerhallet, C. P. de—Navigation dans la Mer des Antilles, &c. 2 v.	8vo.	Paris.	1853
Keshan, Dan.—Ireland; its Social Condition and Improvement	12o.	Lond.	1853
Kestner, U.—Goethe and Werther	8vo.	Stuttgd.	1854
Kett, Hen.—Elements of General Knowledge. 2 v.	8vo.	Lond.	1806
Kew Gardens; a Sketch: and Tales	12o.	Phila.	1854
Keyser, Rud.—Religion of the Northmen	12o.	N. Y.	1854
Kilbourn, Jno.—Ohio Gazetteer	12o.	Columbus.	1831
Kilbourne, P. K.—Biographical History of Litchfield County, Conn.	8vo.	N. Y.	1851
*Kimball and James' Business Directory	8vo.	Cincin.	1844
*——— J. T. & Co.'s Eastern, Western, and Southern Directory	8vo.	Cin. & N. Y.	1846
——— Rich. B.—Romance of Student Life Abroad	12o.	N. Y.	1853
King, Alonzo—Memoir of Geo. D. Boardman	12o.	Bost.	1852
—— Chas.—Memoir of James G. King	8vo.	N. Y.	1854
—— W. R.—Death of. See *Obituary Addresses.*			
*Kingdom, Wm.—The Secretary's Assistant	12o.	Lond.	1854
Kingsford, W.—Structure and Statistics of Plank Roads	8vo.	Phila.	1851
Kingsley, Chas. Jr.—Alexandria and her Schools	12o.	Camb.	1854
——— —— Glaucus; or, the Wonders of the Shore	16o.	Bost.	1855
——— —— Phaethon; or, Loose Thoughts	12o.	Camb. (E.)	1852
——— —— Saint's Tragedy: a Play	16o.	Lond.	1848
——— —— Sermons on National Subjects	12o.	Lond.	1852
——— —— Twenty-Five Village Sermons	12o.	Phila.	1854
Kingsmill, Jos.—Missions and Missionaries, Historically Viewed	8vo.	Lond.	1853
Kinne, Asa—Kent's Commentaries reduced to Questions	8vo.	N. Y.	1840
Kip, Wm. J.—Catacombs of Rome	12o.	N. Y.	1854
—— —— History, Objects, and Proper Observance of Lent	16o.	Albany.	1853
Kirby, Wm.—Life of, by John Freeman	8vo.	Lond.	1852
*Kirkland, Mrs. C. M.—Book of Home Beauty,	4to.	N. Y.	1852
——— —— Book for the Home Circle	8vo.	N. Y.	1853
——— —— Evening Book	8vo.	N. Y.	1852
——— —— Garden Walks with the Poets	12o.	N. Y.	1852
——— —— The Helping Hand	sm. 4to.	N. Y.	1853
Kirkman, Thos. P.—First Mnemonical Lessons in Geom., Algebra, &c.	16o.	Lond.	1852

Kitto, John—Daily Bible Illustrations. 8 v.	12o. N. Y.	1854
Vol. 1. Antediluvians and Patriarchs. 2. Moses and the Judges. 3. Saul and David. 4. Job and the Poetical Books. 5. Solomon and the Kings. 6. Isaiah and the Prophets. 7. Life of our Lord. 8. The Apostles and Early Church.		
—— —— History of Palestine	12o. Bost.	1852
Klencke, H.—Natur Wissenschaften der letzten Funfzigjahre .	8vo. Leipzig.	1854
—— —— Schöpfungstage	12o. Leipzig.	1854
Knapp, F.—Chemical Technology. Vol. 3.	8vo. Lond.	1851
—— J. L.—Country Rambles in England, edited by Miss Cooper	12o. Buffalo.	1853
—— S. L.—Life of Daniel Webster	12o. Bost.	1831
Knickerbocker (The)—Monthly. Vols. 36–44. [*Continued.*] .	8vo. N. Y.	1850–54
*—— Gallery	4to. N. Y.	1855
*Knight, Chas.—Cyclopædia of the Industry of all Nations .	8vo. N. Y.	1851
—— —— Old Printer and the Modern Press . .	16o. Lond.	1854
—— —— Cyclopædia of London, 1851	8vo. Lond.	no date
—— —— Excursion Companion from London . . .	8vo. Lond.	no date
—— —— Once upon a Time. 2 v.	16o. Lond.	1854
—— Mrs. H. C.—Lady Huntington and her Friends . .	12o. N. Y.	1853
—— —— Memoir of Hannah More	12o. N. Y.	1851
Knighton, Wm.—European Turkey; its People, &c. . .	12o. Lond.	1854
Knowles, Jas. S.—The Idol Demolished by its own Priestcraft .	16o. Edin.	1851
Knox, John—Journal of Campaigns in North America, 1757–60. 2 v.	4to. Lond.	1769
—— John P.—Historical Account of St. Thomas, W. I. .	12o. N. Y.	1852
—— Robt.—Great Artists and Great Anatomists	12o. Lond.	1852
—— —— Historical Relation of the Island of Ceylon .	Fol. Lond.	1681
—— —— Manual of Artistic Anatomy	12o. Lond.	1852
—— —— —— Human Anatomy	16o. Lond.	1853
—— —— The Races of Men	16o. Lond.	1850
—— —— The Same	12o. Phil.	1850
—— V.—Useful Education; or, Methods of Acquiring Learning. 2 v.	12o. Lond.	1795
Koch, Gen.—Mémoires de Masséna. 7 v., . 8vo. and Atlas	4to. Paris.	1848–50
*Koeppen, Adol. L.—The World in the Middle Ages . .	Fol. N. Y.	1854
*Kölnische Zeitung, July 1849—Dec. 1850. 3 v. [*Continued.*] .	Fol. Köln.	1849–50
Kossuth, Louis—In New England, and his Speeches . .	8vo. Bost.	1852
—— —— Life of, by P. C. Headley	12o. Auburn.	1852
—— —— Select Speeches, by Newman	12o. N. Y.	1854
—— —— Sketches of the Life, and some of the Speeches of .	8vo. N. Y.	1851
Kovatski, Rudolph Bardy di—Adventures of	12o. Rochester.	1855
Kraitsir, Chas. V.—The Poles in the United States . . .	12o. Phil.	1837
Krasinski, Valerian—Religious History of the Slavonic Nations	8vo. Edin.	1851
Krider, Jno.—Sporting Anecdotes, Edited by H. M. Knapp .	8vo. Phil.	1855
Krummacher, F. A.—Parables of	12o. Lond.	1854
Kühner, Raph.—Grammar of the Greek Language. (Fr. Ger.)	8vo. N. Y.	1853
—— Latin Grammar. (Fr. Ger.)	12o. Bost.	1851
Kurten, Phil.—Art of Manufacturing Soaps	12o. Phil.	1854
Kurtz, Jno. H.—Manual of Sacred History	12o. Phil.	1855

Labitte, Chas.—Satyre Menippée de la Vertu du Catholicon d'Espagne	16o.	Paris.	1848
Lacombe, Fran.—Histoire de la Monarchie en Europe. Vol. 1	8vo.	Paris.	1853
Lacroix, P. de—Mémoires de la Révolution de St. Domingue. 2 v.	8vo.	Paris.	1820
Lafitau, P.—Mœurs des Sauvages Ameriquains. 2 v.	4to.	Paris.	1824
La Fontaine, J. de—Fables choisies, avec Illustrations. 4 v.	Fol.	Paris.	1755–9
La Gironière, Paul P. de—Twenty Years in the Philipines	12o.	N. Y.	1854
Lagny, G. de—The Knout and the Russians. (Fr. Fren.)	16o.	N. Y.	1854
La Gravière, E. J. de—Guerres Maritimes sous la République. 2 v.	12o.	Paris.	1847
——— ——— Voyage en Chine en 1847–50	12o.	Brux.	no date
Lahontan, Baron—New Voyages to North America. (Fr. Fren.) 2 v.	8vo.	Lond.	1735
Laing, Sam.—Social and Political State of Denmark, &c.	8vo.	Lond.	1852
Lalor, T. M.—Law of Real Property, New York State	8vo.	N. Y.	1855
——— Jno.—Money and Morals	8vo.	Lond.	1852
Lamartine, A. de—1789; Les Constituants. 4 v.	12o.	Brux.	1854–5
——— ——— Histoire de la Restauration. 8 v.	8vo.	Paris.	1851–2
——— ——— The Same. 8 v.	12o.	Paris.	1851–2
——— ——— Restoration of the Monarchy in France. Vols. 1, 2, 4.	16o.	Lond.	1851–3
——— ——— The Same. 4 v.	12o.	N. Y.	1851–3
——— ——— Geneviève: Histoire d'une Servante	8vo.	Paris.	1851
——— ——— Histoire de la Turquie, in 4 vols. Vols. 1 and 2	8vo.	Paris.	1855
——— ——— History of Turkey. Vol. 1.	12o.	N. Y.	1855
——— ——— Memoirs of Celebrated Characters. 2 v.	8vo.	Lond.	1854
——— ——— The Same	12o.	N. Y.	1854
——— ——— Tailleur de Pierres de Saint Point	8vo.	Paris.	1851
——— ——— Toussaint l'Ouverture; une Poëme Dramatique	8vo.	Paris.	1850
Lamb, Chas.—Memoirs and Correspondence of, by J. Q. Leake	8vo.	Albany.	1850
——— ——— Works. 4 v.	16o.	Lond.	1849–50
——— ——— & Mary—Tales from Shakspeare	16o.	N. Y.	1851
Lambe, Wm.—Water and Vegetable Diet in Consumption, &c.	12o.	N. Y.	1850–52
Lambert, Edw. R.—History of Colony of New Haven	12o.	N. Haven.	1838
——— T. S.—Human Anatomy, Physiology, and Hygiene	12o.	Hartford.	1854
Lancelott, F.—Australia as It Is. 2 v.	12o.	Lond.	1852
Lancet for 1851—54. 7 v. [*Continued.*]	8vo.	N. Y.	1851–54
Land we Live in. The British Empire. Vol. 1.	8vo.	Lond.	no date
Lander, E. W.—The Bushman; or, Life in a New Country	8vo.	Lond.	1847
Landis, Robt. W.—Liberty's Triumph; a Poem	12o.	N. Y.	1849
Landor, Walter Sav.—Selections from the Writings of, by G. S. Hillard	12o.	Bost.	1856
Landsborough, D.—Popular History of British Sea-Weeds	16o.	Lond.	1849
*Landseer, Thos.—The Monkeyana	4to.	Lond.	no date
Lane, B. J—Mysteries of Tobacco, and Responses	12o.	N. Y.	1851
Lang, J. D.—Freedom and Independence for Australia	12o.	Lond.	1852
Langdale, H. (Lord)—Memoirs of, by Thos. D. Hardy. 2 v.	8vo.	Lond.	1852
Langford, S. A.—Religion and Education in Relation to the People	16o.	Lond.	1852
Langdon, Wm. B.—Catalogue of the Chinese Collection in London	8vo.	Lond.	1843
Langstroth, L. L.—On the Hive and Honey Bee	12o.	Northam.	1853
Lanman, Chas.—Haw Ho Noo; or, Records of a Tourist	12o.	Phil.	1850
——— ——— Private Life of Daniel Webster	12o.	N. Y.	1852
Lardner, Dion.—The Great Exhibition, and London in 1851	12o.	Lond.	1852
——— ——— Hand Book of Natural Philosophy & Astronomy. 3 v.	12o.	Phil.	1851–4
——— ——— The Same. Vol. 3.	16o.	Lond.	1853

Larkin, Jas.—Practical Brass and Iron Founder's Guide . . 16o. Phil. 1853
Laroche, Benj.—Abolition de l'Esclavage dans les Colonies Françaises 8vo. Paris. 1851
La Rive, Aug. de—Treatise on Electricity in Theory and Practice. Vol. 1 8vo. Lond. 1853
La Rochefoucauld, F., Duc de—Moral Reflect., Sent. and Max. (Fr. Fren.) 12o. N. Y. 1851
Las Casas, Count de—Life and Exile of Napoleon. 4 v. . . 12o. N. Y. 1855
Latham, R. G.—Ethnology of the British Colonies and Dependencies 16o. Lond. 1851
——— —— Man and his Migrations . . . . . 16o. Lond. 1851
——— —— Native Races of the Russian Army . . 8vo. Lond. 1854
——— —— Natural History of the Varieties of Man . . 8vo. Lond. 1850
Laurent, P. M.—Histoire de l'Empereur Napoleon . . R. 8vo. Paris. 1840
Laurie, J.—Elements of Homœopathic Practice . . . 8vo. N. Y. 1853
——— Thos.—Dr. Grant and the Mountain Nestorians . . 12o. Bost. 1853
——— W. F. B.—The Second Burmese War . . . 12o. Lond. 1853
La Vallière, Mad. de—Les Confessions de . . . 16o. Paris. 1854
Lavaysse, M.—Venezuela, Trinidad, Margarita, and Tobago . 8vo. Lond. 1820
Law (The) and the Testimony. [By Miss Warner.] . . 8vo. N. Y. 1853
Lawrence, Amos—Diary and Correspondence . . . 8vo. Bost. 1855
——— —— The Same . . . . . . 12o. Bost. 1856
——— Eugene—Lives of the British Historians. 2 v . . 12o. N. Y. 1855
——— Fred.—Life of Henry Fielding . . . 12o. Lond. 1855
——— Isaác—See *Genealogy.*
——— M. W.—Light on the Dark River. Memoir of Mrs. Hamlin 12o. Bost. 1854
*Laws of New York Colony, 1691–1751 . . . . . Fol. N. Y. 1752
*——————— 1691–1773. 2 vols. in one. . Fol. N. Y. 1774
*——————— State, passed at the 73d, 74th, & 77th Sess. 2 v. 8vo. Albany. 1850–54
*——————— on Canals. 2 v. . . . . . . 8vo. Albany. 1825
Lawton, H. A.—Elodie; a Legend of the Dee, and other Poems 12o. Lond. 1848
Layard, A. H.—Discoveries among the Ruins of Nineveh and Babylon 8vo. N. Y. 1853
——— —— Nineveh and its Remains. 2 v. . . . . 12o. N. Y. 1849–53
——— —— Popular Account of Discoveries at Nineveh . 12o. N. Y.
——— —— Ruins of Babylon and Nineveh—abridged . . 8vo. N. Y. 1853
——— —— The Same—abridged . . . . . 12o. N. Y. 1853
Lazarus, M. E.—Comparative Psychology and Universal Analogy. V. 1 12o. N. Y. 1851
——— —— The Human Trinity; or, Three Aspects of Life . 12o. N. Y. 1851
——— —— The Trinity in its Theological, Scient. & Pract. Aspects 8vo. N. Y. 1851
Leach, Wm. E.—Synopsis of the Mollusca of Great Britain . 8vo. Lond. 1852
Leake, J. Q.—Life and Times of Gen. John Lamb . . 8vo. Albany. 1850
Lear, Edw.—Journals of a Painter in Southern Calabria . . 8vo. Lond. 1852
Lebrun's Manual Complet du Voyageur dans Paris . . 18o. Paris. 1830
Lectures before the Young Men's Christian Association . . 16o. Lond. 1852
——— ——————————— 1853–4 12o. Lond. 1854
——— in connection with the Educational Exhibition . . 12o. Lond. 1855
——— on Evidences of Christianity . . . . . 8vo. N. Y. 1853
——— ——————— by Episcopal Clergymen . 8vo. Phil. 1855
——— on Gold, for the Instruction of Emigrants to Australia 12o. Lond. 1852
——— on the Results of the Great Exhibition of 1851 . . 12o. Lond. 1852
——— The Same . . . . 12o. Phil. 1852
——— The Same. 2d series . . . . . . 12o. Lond. 1853
Ledderhose, Chas. T.—Life of Philip Melancthon. (Fr. Ger.) . 12o. Phil. 1855
Lee, Mrs. R.—Habits and Instincts of Animals . . . 16o. Phil. 1853
—— Alf.—Life of the Apostle Peter . . . . 12o. N. Y. 1852

Lee, Mrs. H. F.—Memoir of Pierre Toussaint . . . . 12o. Bost. 1854
—— —— Sketches of Sculpture and Sculptors. 2 v. . 16o. Bost. 1854
—— Robt.—The Last Days of Alexander and Nicholas . . 16o. Lond. 1854
—— Mrs. R.—Habits and Instincts of Animals . . . 16o. Lond. 1852
—— —— Habits and Instincts of Birds, Reptiles, and Fishes . 16o. Phil. 1853
—— S. P. Cruise of the U. S. Brig Dolphin, and maps. 2 v. . 8vo. Wash. 1854
Legend of the Whirlpool . . . . 16o. Buffalo. 1840
Leger, T.—The Magnetoscope . . . . . . 8vo. Lond. 1852
Le Gray, Gust.—Nouveau Traité de Photographie . . . 8vo. Paris. [1851]
Leighton, W. A.—British Lichens. See *Ray Society Publications.*
Leila Ada, the Jewish Convert, by O. W. T. Heighway . . 12o. N. Y. 1854
Leland, Chas. G.—Meister Karl's Sketch Book . . . 12o. Phil. 1855
—— —— Poetry and Mystery of Dreams . . . 12o. Phil. 1856
*Le Long, Jac.—Bibliothèque Historique de la France . . Fol. Paris. 1719
Lemoinne, Jno.—Etudes Critiques et Biographiques . . 12o. Paris. 1852
—— —— Wellington from a French point of view . 16o. Lond. 1852
Leo X.—Life and Pontificate of, by Wm. Roscoe. 2 v. . . 16o. Lond. 1846
—— Heinr.—Local Nomenclature of the Anglo-Saxons. (Fr. Ger) 8vo. Lond. 1852
Leonard, Peter—The Western Coast of Africa . . . 16o. Phila. 1833
Léouzon, Le Duc, L.—The Russian Question. (Fr. Fren.) . . 16o. Lond. no date
*Le Play, F.—Les Ouvriers Européens . . . . . Fol. Paris. 1855
Lepsius, Rich.—Discoveries in Egypt, Ethiopia, &c. . . 8vo. Lond. 1852
Lerne, Eman. de—Amoureux et Grands Hommes . . 12o. Paris. 1854
Le Sage, A. R.—Gil Blas de Santillane. (In Span.) . . 8vo. Paris. 1847
—— —— Adventuras de Gil Blas de Santillana. 4 v. . 4to. Valen. 1788
Lesdernier, Emily P.—Voices of Life . . . . . 12o. N. Y. 1853
Leslie, Eliza—American Girl's Own Book . . . . 16o. N. Y. 1854
—— Miss—New Receipts for Cooking . . . . . 12o. Phil. 1854
Lessing, G. E.—Laocoon; or, the Limits of Paint'g and Poetry. (Fr. Ger.) 16o. Lond. 1853
Lester, C. Edwards—My Consulship. 2 v. . . . . . 12o. N. Y. 1853
Letters from the Continent . . . . 12o. N. Y. 1851
—— of an American on Russia and Revolution . . . 16o. Lond. 1854
—— —— Englishman on Napoleon. From "The Times" . 16o. Lond. 1852
—— on the Eastern States . . . . 12o. N. Y. 1820
Leuchars, R. B.—Construction, Heating, and Ventilation of Hot Houses 12o. Bost. 1851
Levasseur, V.—Atlas National de la France . . . . Fol. Paris. 1846
Lever, Darcy—Young Sea Officer's Sheet Anchor . . 4to. N. Y. 1843
Levi, Leone—Commercial Laws; its Principles and Administration. V. 1 4to. Lond. 1850–1
—— —— Mercantile Law of Great Britain and Ireland . . 8vo. Phil. 1854
Lewes, G. H.—Life and Works of Goethe and his Contemporaries. 2 v. 12o. Bost. 1856
Lewis, Alonzo—Poems . . . . 12o. Bost. 1831
—— Estelle A.—Myths of the Minstrel . . . . 12o. N. Y. 1852
—— Elisha J.—The American Sportsman . . . . . 8vo. Phil. 1855
—— —— Hints to Sportsmen on Shooting . . . . 12o. Phil. 1851
—— Geo. C.—Methods of Observation and Reasoning in Politics. 2 v. 8vo. Lond. 1852
—— Jno.—History of Translations of the Bible into English . 8vo. Lond. 1818
—— Taylor—Six Days of Creation . . . . . 12o. Schenec. 1855
—— Lady T.—Lives of Friends and Contemporaries of Clarendon. 3 v. 8vo. Lond. 1852
—— Wm. H.—Confession of Christ . . . . . 12o. N. Y. 1852
Leybourn, Thos.—Mathematical Questions, fr. the Ladies' Diary. 4 v. 8vo. Lond. 1817

Title	Size and Place	Date
Library of Useful Knowledge	8vo. Lond.	1851
Waar, G. F. Dynamics, Construction of Machinery, &c.		
Lieber, Fran.—Civil Liberty and Self-Government. 2 v.	12o. Phil.	1853
——— O. M.—The Assayer's Guide	16o. Phil.	1852
Liebig, Justus—Familiar Letters on Chemistry	16o. Lond.	1851
——— —— Hand-Book of Organic Analysis	12o. Lond.	1853
——— —— Principles of Agricultural Chemistry	12o. N. Y.	1855
——— and Kopp—Annual Report on Chemistry. Vols. 1, 2.	8vo. Lond.	1847–8
Life in Bombay and the Neighboring Out-Stations	8vo. Lond.	1852
—— Insurance, its Nature, Origin and Progress	16o. N. Y.	1852
Lights and Shadows of English Life. 2 v.	12o. Phil.	1854
Lilies and Violets; or, Prose and Verse	12o. N. Y.	1855
Lilly, Wm.—Introduction to Astrology	16o. Lond.	1852
Lincoln, Wm. S.—Alton Trials	12o. N. Y.	1838
Lind, Jenny—Life of, by C. G. Rosenberg	8vo. N. Y.	1850
——— —— Memoranda of the Life of, by N. P. Willis	12o. Phil.	1851
Lindley, Thos.—Voyage to Brazil in 1802–3	8vo. Lond.	1808
Lindsay, Robt.—Chronicles of Scotland. 2 v.	8vo. Edin.	1841
Linen, Jas.—Songs of the Seasons and other Poems	12o. N. Y.	no date
Ling, P. H.—Gymnastic Free Exercises	16o. Bost.	1853
Lingard, Jno.—History and Antiq. of the Anglo-Saxon Church. 2 v.	8vo. Lond.	1845
——— —— History of England. Abridged	8vo. Balt.	1855
Linnæus—Life of, by D. C. Carr	12o. Nott.	1837
Linton, Chas.—The Healing of the Nations	8vo. N. Y.	1855
Lippincott, Mrs. J. B.—Haps and Mishaps of a Tour in Europe	12o. Bost.	1854
*Lippincott's Pronouncing Gazetteer, Edited by Thomas & Baldwin	8vo. Phil.	1855
Lisco, F. G.—Parables of Jesus Explained. (Fr. Ger.)	12o. Phil.	1850
List of Persons Assessed in the Providence City Tax	12o. Prov.	1850
——— The Same	12o. Prov.	1852
*——— Persons, Copartnerships, and Corporations in Boston	8vo. Bost.	1846
——— Post Offices and Postmasters in the United States	8vo. Wash.	1855
Litchfield County Centennial Celebration, Aug. 13, 14, 1851	8vo. Hartf.	1851
Literary and Scientific Repository. Vols. 3 & 4.	8vo. N. Y.	1821–2
*——— Gazette (The.) Vols. 1–17.	4to. Lond.	1817–33
*——— The Same, for 1853. [*Continued.*]	4to. Lond.	1853
*——— World. Vols. 7–13	4to. N. Y.	1850–3
Littell's Living Age. Vols. 26, 30, 33, 37, 39–43. [*Continued.*]	8vo. Bost.	1850–54
Littré, E.—Application de la Philosophie Positive	8vo. Paris.	1850
*Liverpool Directory for 1855	8vo. Liverpool.	1855
Lives and Voyages of Drake, Cavendish, and Dampier. (H. F. L.)	18o. N. Y.	1846
——— of the English Saints. 14 vols. in 6.	16o. Lond.	1845
——— Wellington and Peel. From the "London Times"	16o. N. Y.	1852
*Livingston, Jno.—Law Register for 1852–4	8vo. N. Y.	1852–4
——— —— Law Magazine. Vol. 2.	8vo. N. Y.	1854
——— —— Portraits of Eminent Living Americans. 2 v.	8vo. N. Y.	1853
Livius, Titus—Opera Omnia. 20 v. See *Valpy's Delphin Classics.*		
Livre Noir de Messieurs Delevan et Franchet. 4 v.	8vo. Paris.	1829
Locke, Jno.—Essay Concerning Human Understanding	8vo. Lond.	1853
——— Jno. G.—Book of the Lockes, Genealogical and Historical	8vo. Bost.	1853
Lockhart, J. G.—Life of Sir W. Scott	12o. Edinb.	1853

Locock, Wm.—Theory and Practice of Perspective . . .	8vo. Lond.	1852
Locomotive (Die). Vol. 1	4to. Phil.	1853
Loève-Viemars—Histoire des Littératures Anciennes . .	12o. Paris.	1825
Logic; or, the Art of Thinking; being the Port Royal Logic. (Fr. Fren.)	12o. Edin.	1850
—— for the Million; or, the Art of Reasoning . . .	12o. Lond.	1851
London at Table; or How, When, and Where to Dine . .	16o. Lond.	1851
*—— Directory, for 1853 and 1855. (Watkins'.) 2 v. . .	12o. Lond.	1853–5
*—— —— 1855. (Kelly's.)	8vo. Lond.	1855
—— Journal of Arts and Sciences. S. S. Vols. 40–45. [*Continued.*]	8vo. Lond.	1852–54
—— Quarterly Review. Vol. 2.	8vo. Lond.	1854
Long—History of Jamaica. 3 v.	4to. Lond.	1774
—— Geo.—France and its Revolutions	8vo. Lond.	1850
—— S. H.—Expedition to the Rocky Mountains in 1819–20. 3 v.	8vo. Lond.	1823
Longfellow, H. W.—The Golden Legend	16o. Bost.	1852
—— —— Poems. 2 v.	16o. Bost.	1853
*—— —— Poems. Illustrated	8vo. Bost.	1852
—— —— Song of Hiawatha	12o. Bost.	1855
Loomis, Elias—Recent Progress of Astronomy, especially in the U. S.	12o. N. Y.	1850
Lord, Eleazar—Epoch of Creation	12o. N. Y.	1851
—— —— History of N. Y. and Erie Railroad . . .	8vo. N. Y.	1855
—— Jno.—New History of the United States . . .	12o. Phil.	1854
—— John C.—Lectures on the Progress of Civilization and Gov'ment	12o. Buff.	1851
—— Wm. W.—Christ in Hades, a Poem	12o. N. Y.	1851
Lorenzo Benoni—Life of an Italian, by Gio. Ruffini . .	12o. N. Y.	1855
Loring, Jas. S.—The Hundred Boston Orators . . .	8vo. Bost.	1852
Lossing, B. J.—Our Countrymen	12o. Phil.	1855
—— —— Pictorial Description of Ohio	8vo. N. Y.	1850
—— —— Pictorial Field-Book of the Revolution. 2 v. .	8vo. N. Y.	1851
Loud, Mrs. St. Leon—Wayside Flowers	12o. Bost.	1851
Louis XIV.—Life and Times of. 2 v.	16o. Lond.	1851
—— —— his Life, &c., by A. de Beauchesne. (Fr. Fren.) 2 v. .	12o. N. Y.	1853
Louis XVII. (The Dauphin.)—Life of, by Jno. H. Hanson .	12o. N. Y.	1854
Louis-Philippe; Le Roi, par M. de Montalivet . . .	24o. Brux.	1851
*Louisiana Directory	8vo.	1838
Louvet, J. B.—Notices pour l'Histoire de Mes Perils . .	8vo. Paris.	l'an 3
Lovell, Jno. E.—The United States' Speaker . . .	12o. N. Haven.	1847
Lover, M. A.—Chronicles of Battel Abbey, from 1066 to 1176 .	8vo. Lond.	1851
—— —— English Surnames, and Family Nomenclature. 2 v.	12o. Lond.	1849
Lowell, Mrs. A. C.—Thoughts on the Education of Girls .	16o. Bost.	1853
—— Jas.—Poems. 2 v.	12o. Bost.	1853
*—— Directory, 1851	16o. Lowell.	1851
Löwig, Carl—Principles of Organic and Physiological Chemistry	8vo. Phil.	1853
Lowrie, Jno. C.—Manual of Missions	Obl. N. Y.	1854
—— —— Two Years in Upper India	12o. N. Y.	1850
*Lowth, H.—Atlas of European History	Fol. Lond.	no date
*Lubienski, Ed.—Guerres et Révolutions d'Italie en 1848–9 .	8vo. Paris.	1852
Lucianus Samosatensis—Opera. See *Scriptorum Græcorum Bibliotheca.*		
Lucretius, Titus—on the Nature of Things. (Fr. Lat.) Six Books	16o. Lond.	1851
—— —— Opera Omnia. 3 v. See *Valpy's Delphin Classics.*		
Ludlow, Miss.—(Manual of the Fine Arts.) . . .	12o. N. Y.	1851

Ludolphus, Job—Hist. of Ethiopia, and Descrip. of Abyssinia. (Fr. Ger.) Fol. Lond. 1682
Lunt, Geo.—Lyric Poems . . . . 16o. Bost. 1854
Lyell, Chas.—Manual of Elementary Geology . . . 8vo. Lond. 1851
—— —— Principles of Geology . . . . . 8vo. N. Y. 1853
Lyman, Alb.—Journal of a Voyage to California . . . 12o. Hartford. 1852
—— —— Life and Memorials of Daniel Webster. 2 v. . 16o. N. Y. 1853
—— Theo., Jr.—Political State of Italy . . . . . 8vo. Bost. 1820
Lynch, W. F.—Official Report of the U. S. Dead Sea Expedition 4to. Balt. 1852
—— —— Naval Life. The Midshipman . . . . 12o. N. Y. 1851
Lyon, Lucius—Treatise on Lightning Conductors . . 12o. N. Y. 1853
—— Mary—Life of, by Edward Hitchcock . . . . 12o. North'pton. 1852
—— G. F.—Residence and Tour in Mexico in 1826. 2 v. . 8vo. Lond. 1828
Lyrics by the Letter H. . . . . 12o. N. Y. 1854
Lyteria: A Dramatic Poem . . . . . . 16o. Bost. 1854
Lytton, Sir Edward Bulwer. See *Bulwer.*

Macaulay, T. B.—Critical and Historical Essays. 3 v. . . 16o. Lond. 1853
—— —— Critical and Miscellaneous Essays. 5 v. . 12o. Phil. 1851
—— —— Hist. of Eng. from the Accession of James II. Vols. 3–4 12o. N. Y. 1856
—— —— Lays of Ancient Rome . . . . . 8vo. Phil. 1853
—— —— Speeches . . . . 8vo. Lond. 1854
—— —— The Same. 2 v. . . . . . . 12o. N. Y. 1853
Mac Cann, Wm.—Two Thousand Miles Ride thro' Argentine Prov. 2 v. 12o. Lond. 1853
McClintock, Jno., D. D. (Ed'r.)—Eminent Methodist Ministers . 4to. N. Y. 1854
McConnell, J. L.—Western Characters . . . . . 12o. N. Y. 1853
McCord, Louisa S.—Caius Gracchus. A Tragedy . . . 12o. N. Y. 1851
McCormick, Rich. C., Jr.—Visit to the Camp before Sebastopol 12o. N. Y. 1855
McCosh, Jas.—Method of Divine Government, Physical and Moral 8vo. N. Y. 1851
McCulloch, J. R.—Circumstances which Determine the rate of Wages, &c. 16o. Lond. 1851
—— —— Essays on Exchange, Interest, &c. . . 8vo. Bost. 1850
—— —— Essays on Interest, Exchange, Coins, &c. . 8vo. Phil. 1851
—— —— Treatises on Subjects connected with Econom. Policy 8vo. Edin. 1853
McDonald, Jno.—Biographical Sketches . . . . . 12o. Dayton. 1852
Macdonald, Geo., & Allan (Jas.)—Botanist's Word Book . 16o. Lond. 1853
—— J. M.—Credulity, as Illustrated by Imposition in Science, &c. 18o. N. Y. 1843
—— —— Hist. of the Presbyterian Church of Jamaica, L. I. 12o. N. Y. 1847
—— —— Key to the Book of Revelation . . . 12o. N. Lond. 1848
—— —— My Father's House; or, Heaven . . 12o. N. Y. 1855
Macdonall, Jno.—Voyage to Patagonia and Terra del Fuégo, 1826–7 12o. Lond. 1833
McElligott, J. N.—The American Debater . . . . 12o. N. Y. 1855
*McElroy's Philadelphia Directory for 1854 & 5. 2 v. . . . 8vo. Phil. 1854–5
Mac Farlane, Chas.—Catacombs of Rome . . . . 16o. Lond. 1852
—— —— Great Battles of the British Army . . 12o. Lond. 1853
—— —— History of British India . . . . 12o. Lond. 1852
—— —— Japan; an Account, Geographical and Historical 8vo. Lond. 1852
—— —— The Same . . . . 12o. N. Y. 1852
—— —— Kismet; or, The Doom of Turkey . . 16o. Lond. 1853
Macfarlane, Robt.—History of Propellers and Steam Navigation . 12o. N. Y. 1850
McGauley, Jas. W.—Lectures on Natural Philosophy. 2 v. . 8vo. Dublin. 1850
MacGavick, R. W.—A Tennesseean Abroad . . . . 12o. N. Y. 1854

McGee, Thos. d'Arcy—History of the Irish Settlers . . 12o. Bost. 1851
——— —— Protestant Reformation in Ireland, 1540–1830 . 12o. Bost. 1853
Macgillivray, Jno.—Voyage of H. M. S. Rattlesnake. 2 v. . 8vo. Lond. 1852
Macgregor, Jno.—History of Britain from Accession of James I. 2 v. 8vo. Lond. 1852
McGregor, P.—Book-Keeping by Single and Double Entry . . 12o. N. Y. 1850
Machiavelli, N.—Discourses on the first Decade of T. Livius. (Fr. Ital.) 12o. Lond. 1636
McIlvaine, C. P.—The Truth and the Life: Sermons . . 8vo. N. Y. 1855
———— —— A Valedictory Offering . . . . 16o. Lond. 1853
Macilwain, Geo.—Memoirs of John Abernethy . . . 12o. N. Y. 1853
Mackay, Chas.—Egeria; or, The Spirit of Nature, and other Poems 16o. Lond. 1850
——— —— Memoirs of Extraordinary Popular Delusions. 2 v. 12o. Lond. 1852
——— R. W.—Progress of Intellect among Greeks and Hebrews. 2 v. 8vo. Lond. 1852
Mac Kellar, Thos.—Lines for the Gentle and Loving . . 24o. Phil. 1853
McKendree—Life of. See *Fry*, *Benj.*
Mackenzie, Colin—Five Thousand Receipts . . . . . 8vo. Phil. 1852
———— Mrs. C.—Life in the Mission, &c; or, Six Years in India. 2 v. 12o. N. Y. 1853
———— Dav.—Emigrant's Guide to Australia . . . 16o. Lond. 1845
———— D. L.—Practical Dictionary of English Synonyms . 16o. Lond. 1854
———— K. R. H. (Ed'r.)—Schamyl and Circassia . . 16o. Lond. 1854
———— Rod.—Strictures on Col. Tarleton's History . . 8vo. Lond. 1787
Mackey, Alb. G.—Lexicon of Freemasonry . . . 12o. Charleston. 1852
Mac Kinnon, Capt.—Atlantic and Transatlantic . . . 12o. N. Y. 1852
McKinnon, Wm. C.—St. George; or, The Canadian League. 2 v. 12o. Halifax. 1852
Mackintosh, Jas.—Miscellaneous Works. 3 v. . . . 16o. Lond. 1854
Mackness, Jas.—Dysphonia Clericorum; or, Clergyman's Sore Throat 8vo. Lond. 1848
McLees, Arch.—Series of Alphabets for Painters and Engravers . 4to. N. Y. 1855
McLenan—Indian Fairy Book . . . . . 12o. N. Y. 1856
Mac Leod, Donald—Biography of Hon. Fer. Wood, Mayor of N. Y. City 12o. N. Y. 1856
———— —— Life of Sir Walter Scott . . . . 12o. N. Y. 1852
Mac-Micking, R.—Recollections of Manilla and the Philippines, 1848–50 12o. Lond. 1851
McMullen, Thos.—Hand-Book of Wines . . . . . 12o. N. Y. 1852
McMurtrie, H.—Sketches of Louisville and its Environs . . 8vo. Louisville. 1819
McNally, Wm.—Evils and Abuses in the Naval and Merchant Service 12o. Bost. 1839
Macneill, H.—Poetical Works . . . . 12o. Phil. 1815
Macoy, Robt. (Compiler, &c.)—The Masonic Manual . . 32o. N. Y. 1854
——— —— The True Masonic Guide . . . . . 12o. N. Y. 1853
Macpherson, Jas.—Secret History of Great Britain, fr. the Restor. 2 v. 4to. Lond. 1776
McQueen, Hugh—The Orator's Touch Stone . . . . 12o. N. Y. 1854
Macready, Edw. M.—Sketch of Suwarrow and his Campaigns . 12o. Lond. 1851
Macvicar, J. G.—Enquiry into Human Nature . . . . 8vo. Edin. 1853
Mac Walter, J. G.—The Modern Mystery; or, Table Tipping . 16o. Lond. 1854
Madagascar, Past and Present . . . . 8vo. Lond. 1847
Madden, R. R.—Literary Life, &c., of Countess of Blessington. 2 v. 12o. N. Y. 1855
*Madison, Jas.—The Papers of, purchased by Congress. 3 v. . 8vo. Wash. 1840
Magazine of Horticulture. New Series. Vols. 5–7, 10. [*Continued.*] 8vo. Bost. 1849–54
Maginn, Wm.—The Odoherty Papers; Edited by Mackenzie. 2 v. . 12o. N. Y. 1855
Magny, De—Traité des Armoires. Vol. 1. . . . . 4to. Paris.
Magruder, W. H. N.—Memoirs of S. B. Bangs . . . . 16o. N. Y. 1853
Mahan, Asa—Modern Mysteries Explained and Exposed . 12o. Bost. 1855
——— —— System of Intellectual Philosophy . . . . 12o. N. Y. 1854

Mahan, D. H. Elementary Course of Civil Engineering . 8vo. N. Y. 1852
—— —— Industrial Drawing and Drawing Instruments . 8vo. N. Y. 1852
Mayhew, Hen.—London Labor and the London Poor. Vol. 1 . 8vo. N. Y. 1851
Mahogany Tree (The)—Its Botanical Character, Qualities and Uses 8vo. Liverpool. no date
Mahon, Lord—"The Forty-five." Narrative of the Insurrection of 1745 16o. Lond. 1851
—— —— History of England from 1713 to 1783. Vols. 5–7 . 8vo. Lond. 1851–4
—— —— The Same. Vols. 1–7 . . . . . 12o. Bost. 1853–4
Maimburg, Lewis—History of the Crusades. (Fr. Fren.) . . Fol. Lond. 1685
Main, Thos. J., and Brown (Thos.)—The Indicator & Dynamometer 8vo. Lond. no date
—— —— Marine Steam Engine . 8vo. Lond. 1852
Maistre, X. de—Œuvres Complètes . . . . . . 16o. Paris. 1847
—— Jos. de—Du Pape . . . . . . 16o. Paris. 1846
Maitland, S. R.—Eight Essays on various Subjects . . 16o. Lond. 1852
Ma-ka-ta-me-she-kia-kiak; or, Black Hawk . . . 12o. N. Y. 1848
Malan, H.—Family Administration of Homœopathic Medicines . 32o. N. Y. 1853
Mallet, C.—Le Conteur Génévois; Nouvelles, &c. . . 16o. Paris. 1851
—— P. H.—Histoire de Dannemarc. 9 v. . . . 12o. Geneve. 1787–8
Mallet du Pan, J.—Memoirs and Correspondence. 2 v. . . 8vo. Lond. 1852
Malone, R. E.—Cruise in the Australian Colonies . . . 12o. Lond. 1854
*Manchester, [N. H.]—Amoskeag and Piscatagog Directory, 1844 18o. Manch. 1844
*—— Directory for 1846, 1850, & 1852. 3 v. . . 18o. Manch. 1846–52
*—— [Eng.]—Directory for 1855 . . . 8vo. Manch. [E.] 1855
Manilius—Opera Omnia. 2 v. See *Valpy's Delphin Classics.*
Mann, Hor.—The Powers and Duties of Woman . . . 16o. Syracuse. 1853
—— —— Two Lectures on Intemperance . . . 16o. Syracuse. 1852
Manni, D. M.—Observazioni istoriche sopra i Sigilli Antichi. 30 vols. in 8 4to. Florence. 1739
Manning, Jos. A.—Lives of the Speakers of the House of Commons 8vo. Lond. 1850
Mansfield, E. D.—American Education, its Principles and Elements 12o. N. Y. 1851
—— R. B.—Log of the "Water Lily" . . . 16o. Leipzig. 1854
Mantell, G. A.—Petrifactions and their Teachings . . 16o. Lond. 1851
Manual of the Board of Education of N. Y. for 1852–4. 3 v. 18o. N. Y. 1852–4
*—— Corporation of N. Y. City, 1841–2 . . . 18o. N. Y. no date
—— Geographical Science . . . .8vo & Atlas, Folio. Lond. 1852
—— N. Y. State Legislature for 1854–5. 2 v. . . 16o. Albany. 1854–5
—— System of Discipline, &c., N. Y. Public School Society 8vo. N. Y. 1850
Manzoni, Alex.—Les Fiancés, Histoire Milanèse du XVII. Siècle . 16o. Paris. 1850
Mapleson, G. T. W.—Hand-Book of Heraldry . . . 4to. N. Y. no date
*Map of the Valley of Mexico, &c., ... 16o. N. Y.
*—— Railroads from Rome to Albany, &c. . . 16o. 1846
Marcel, G.—Language as a Means of Mental Culture, &c. 2 v. . 12o. Lond. 1853
March, L.—Walk across the French Frontier into Spain . 8vo. Lond. 1852
—— C. W.—Reminiscences of Congress . . . . 12o. N. Y. 1850
Marcou, Jules—Geological Map of U. S. and Brit. Provinces. 2 v. 8vo. Bost. 1853
Marcotte de Quevières (Ch.)—Deux Ans en Afrique . . . 16o. Paris. 1855
Marcy, E. E.—Homœopathy and Allopathy . . . 12o. N. Y. 1852
—— R. B. and McClellan (G. B.)—Explor. of Red River, & Maps. 2 v. 8vo. Wash. 1852
Maretzek, Max.—Crotchets and Quavers . . . . 12o. N. Y. 1855
Marie de Medicis—Queen of France. Life of, by Miss Pardoe. 3 v. 8vo. Lond. 1852
Marie Stuart, Reine d'Ecosse.—Lettres et Mémoires. 7 v. . 8vo. Lond. 1844
Marie Thérèse—Memoirs of, by Mrs. Romer. 2 v. . . . 8vo. Lond. 1852

Margolieuth, Moses—History of the Jews in Great Britain. 3 v.	12o. Lond.	1851
Markham, C. R.—Franklin's Footsteps: a Sketch of Greenland .	16o. Lond.	1853
Marmier, X.—Lettres sur l'Amérique. 3 v.	16o. Brux.	1851
——— ——— Lettres sur l'Adriatique et le Montenegro . .	12o. Brux.	no date
——— ——— Les Voyageurs Nouveaux. 2 v. . .	16o. Paris.	1851
Marriotti, L.—Italy in 1848	12o. Lond.	1851
——— ——— Memoir of Frà Dolcino and his Times . .	12o. Lond.	1853
Marryat, Frank.—Mountains and Molehills	12o. N. Y.	1855
Marsden, Wm.—Grammar of the Malayan Language . .	4to. Lond.	1812
Marsh, Mrs.—History of the Protestant Reformation in France. 2 v.	12o. Phil.	1851
——— C. C.—Science of Double Entry Book-Keeping . .	8vo. N. Y.	1851
——— ——— The Same	8vo. N. Y.	1853
——— ——— Single Entry Book-Keeping	8vo. N. Y.	1853
Marshall, Edw. C.—Book of Oratory	12o. N. Y.	1852
——— ——— First Book of Oratory	12o. N. Y.	1851
——— Jas.—Account of the Population of Gt. Britain, 1801–34 .	4to. Lond.	1833
Martialis, M. Valerius—Opera Omnia. 3 v. See *Valpy's Delphin Classics.*		
Martin, Geo. W.—Equation Tables for averaging accounts .	4to. Rochester.	1853
——— Henry—Journal and Letters	12o. N. Y.	1851
——— Hor.—Pictorial Guide to the Mammoth Cave . .	12o. N. Y.	[1851]
——— Jas. H.—Orthoëpist; or, Words usually pronounced improperly	12o. N. Y.	1851
——— R. M.—Ireland before and after the Union . .	8vo. Lond.	1848
*——— R. M. (Ed'r.)—Tallis' Illustrated Atlas	Fol. Lond.	1851
——— Sam.—The Useful Arts, their Birth and Development .	16o. Lond.	1851
Martineau, A.—Church History in England to the Reformation. .	12o. Lond.	1853
——— Harriet. See *Atkinson, H. G.*		
——— ——— History of England. 1810–1846. 2 v. . .	8vo. Lond.	1850–1
——— Jas.—Miscellanies	12o. Bost.	1851
Mary, Duch. of Burgundy.—Memoirs of, by L. S. Costello . .	8vo. Lond.	1853
——— Queen of Scots.—Life of, by Miss Benger. 2 v. . .	12o. Phil.	1851
——— Queen of England—Two Years of. See *Camden Soc. Publications.*		
Mason, Erskine—A Pastor's Legacy; Sermons on Practical Subjects.	8vo. N. Y.	1853
——— Lowell—Musical Letters from Abroad	12o. N. Y.	1854
——— W.—Correspondence with Horace Walpole. See *Walpole, Horace.*		
——— ——— The English Garden; a Poem	12o. York.	1783
——— ——— Poems. 3 v.	8vo. York.	1773–97
——— ——— Works. 4 v.	8vo. Lond.	1811
Massachusetts Quarterly Review. Vols. 1–3	8vo. Bost.	1848–50
*——— Register. 1826, '29, '30, '33, '35, '37, '42, '44. 9 v.	18o. Bost.	1826–44
*——— The Same. 1852–3. 2 v.	8vo. Bost.	1852–3
——— System of Common Schools. [Hon. H. Mann.] .	8vo. Bost.	1849
Massey, Gerald—Poems and Ballads	12o. N. Y.	1854
Masson, Michel—Celebrated Children of all Ages. (Fr. Fren.) .	16o. Lond.	1853
Mathews, C.—Pen and Ink Panorama of N. Y. City . . .	16o. N. Y.	1853
——— J. M.—The Bible and Civil Government . .	12o. N. Y.	1851
——— T. and Young (Maj.)—Whist and Short Whist . .	18o. N. Y.	1851
——— ——— The Same.	18o. N. Y.	1854
Mathias, Benj.—Rules of Order for conducting Societies, &c. .	16o. Phil.	1851
Mattison, H.—Spirit Rappings Unveiled	12o. N. Y.	1853
Maturin, Edw.—Lyrics of Spain and Erin	12o. Bost.	1850

Maurice, F. D.—Ecclesiastical History of the 1st and 2d Centuries. 8vo. Camb. (E.) 1854
——— —— The Lord's Prayer. Nine Sermons . . . 12o. Phil. 1852
——— —— Moral and Metaphysical Philosophy . . 12o. Lond. 1854
——— —— Prophets and Kings of the Old Testament . . 12o. Bost. 1853
——— —— Religions of the World . . . . . 16o. Bost. 1854
——— —— Theological Essays . . . . 12o. N. Y. 1854
——— —— The Same . . . . 12o. Camb. (E.) 1853
——— Thos.—Indian Antiquities. Vol. 6. . . . . 8vo. Lond. 1796
Maury, M. F.—The Amazon, and the Atlantic Slopes of South America 8vo. Wash. 1853
——— —— Explanation and Sailing Directions . . . 4to. Wash. 1851
——— —— Physical Geography of the Sea. . . . 8vo. N. Y. 1855
——— Sarah M.—Englishwoman in America . . . 12o. Lond. 1848
——— —— Statesmen of America in 1846 . . . 12o. Lond. 1847
Maximilian, Prince of Wied—Trav. into the Interior of N. A. (Fr. Ger.) 4to. & Fol. Lond. 1853
Maxwell, W. H.—Victories of Wellington and British Armies . 16o. Lond. 1852
——— —— History of the Irish Rebellion . . . 8vo. Lond. 1852
May, Caroline (Compiler.)—Treasured Thoughts from Favorite Authors. 12o. Phil. 1850
Mayer, Brantz—Capt. Canot; or, Twenty Years of a Slaver . 12o. N. Y. 1854
Mayhew, Hen.—Story of the Peasant Boy Philosopher . . 16o. N. Y. 1855
Maynard, Félix—Voyage de Paris à Sébastopol . . . 16o. Paris. 1855
Mayo, A. D.—Graces and Powers of the Christian Life . . 12o. Bost. 1852
——— H.—Popular Superstitions . . . . 12o. Phil. 1852
Mazzini, Jos.—Royalty and Republicanism in Italy in 1848 . . 12o. Lond. 1850
Meagher, Thos. F.—Speeches on Irish Independence . . 12o. N. Y. 1853
Mechanic's Magazine. Vols. 53–60. [*Continued.*] . . . 8vo. Lond. 1850–54
Medbery, Mrs. R. B.—Memoir of Mrs. Sarah E. York . . 12o. Bost. 1853
Medway, Jno.—Memoirs of John Pye Smith . . . 8vo. Lond. 1853
Melancthon, Phil.—Life of, by Chas. F. Ledderhose. (Fr. Ger.) 12o. Phil. 1855
Melish, Jno.—Traveller's Directory through the U. States . . 12o. Phil. 1815
Melly, Geo.—Khartoum and the Blue and White Niles. 2 v. . 12o. N. Y. 1851
Melvill, Hen.—Sermons. 2 v. . . . . . . 8vo. N. Y. 1854
Mémoires de Litérature . . . . 16o. La Haye. 1715
——— de l'Abbe Edgeworth de Firmont . . . . 8vo. Paris. 1815
——— Anecdotes à l'Histoire de la Revolution Française. 2 v. 8vo. Paris. 1823
Memorable Accidents and Unheard of Transactions. (Fr. Fren.) . 12o. Glasgow. 1784
Memoranda of the Descendants of Amos Morris . . . 12o. N. Y. 1853
Menander. Fragments. See *Scriptorum Græcorum Bibliotheca.* Vol. ii. Part 2.
Mennechet, Edou.—Histoire de France. 2 v. . . . . 16o. Paris. 1846
Men of the Times in 1852 . . . . 32o. Lond. 1852
——— or, Sketches of Living Notables . . . 16o. Lond. 1853
——— or, Sketches of Living Notables . . . 12o. N. Y. 1852
Menzel, Wolfgang—German Literature. (Fr. Fren.) 4 v. . 12o. Lond. 1840
——— —— History of Germany. (Fr. Ger.) Vols. 2–3 . . 16o. Lond. 1853
Mercein, T. F. R.—Natural Goodness . . . . 12o. N. Y. 1854
Mercersburg Quarterly Review. Vols. 4–6. [*Continued.*] . . 8vo Mercers'b. 1852–4
Merchant's and Banker's Almanac for 1852 . . . . 8vo. Bost. no date
——— The Same for 1853 . . . 8vo. N. Y. 1853
*——— The Same for 1855 . . 8vo. N. Y. 1855
——— Mag. and Com. Rev.—Edit. Hunt. Vols. 23–30. [*Continued.*] 8vo. N. Y. 1850–54
Mercier, Louis Sebastian—Tableau de Paris . . . . 16o. Paris. 1853

Meredith, Mrs. C.—My Home in Tasmania; or, nine Years in Australia. 2 v. 12o. Lond. 1852
——— —— The Same . . . . 12o. N. Y. 1853
Mérimée, P.—Colomba; suivi de la Mosaique, etc., . . 16o. Paris. 1850
——— —— Cronique du Temps de Charles IX. . . 16o. Paris. 1850
——— —— Hist. de Don Pedre I., Roi de Castille . . 8vo. Paris. 1850
——— —— Mélanges Historiques et Littéraires. . . 12o. Paris. 1855
——— —— Nouvelles . . . . . 12o. Paris. 1852
Merivale, Chas.—Fall of the Roman Republic . . . 8vo. Lond. 1853
——— —— History of the Romans under the Empire. Vol. 2 16o. Lond. 1851
Merryweather, F. S.—Glimmerings in the Dark Ages . . 8vo. Lond. 1852
Méry, J.—Nuits Anglaises . . . . 16o. Paris. 1853
——— —— Nuits de l'Orient . . . . 16o. Paris. 1854
——— —— Salons et Souterrains. 3 v. . . . . 16o. Brux. 1851
——— —— Une Nuit du Midi . . . . . . 16o. Paris. 1855
Message of the Governor of the State of Florida, Nov. 22. 1852 . 8vo. Tallahassee. 1852
——— Governor of Maryland on Boundary Line . . 8vo. Wash. 1850
——— President of the U. S. on California and New Mexico 8vo. Wash. 1851
——— President of the U. S. 32d Congress. 3 v. . . 8vo. Wash. 1851–2
——— 33d Congress. 5 v. . 8vo. Wash. 1853–4
Methodist Preacher, Containing 28 Sermons . . . . 8vo. Auburn. 1852
——— Quarterly Review. Vols. 32–36. [*Continued.*] . 8vo. N. Y. 1850–54
Metropolitan Catholic Almanac for 1854 . . . . 12o. Balt. s. a.
Meyerbeer, G.—Roberto il Diavolo. (An Opera) . . . 8vo. Paris. no date
Meyer's Volksbibliothek. Vols. 1 & 2 . . . . . 32o. N. Y. do date
Miall, Edw.—Bases of Belief . . . . . . 8vo. Lond. 1853
—— J. G.—Footsteps of our Forefathers . . . . 16o. Lond. 1851
——— —— The Same . . . . 12o. Bost. 1852
Michaud, J. F.—History of the Crusades. (Fr. Fren.) 3 v . . 16o. Lond. 1852
Michelet, J.—Femmes de la Révolution . . . . . 16o. Paris. 1854
——— —— Histoire de France au Sixième Siècle; Renaissance 8vo. Paris. 1855
——— —— Women of the French Revolution . . 12o. Phil. 1855
Michelsen, Edw. H.—Life of Emperor Nicholas . . . 16o. Lond. 1854
Miers, Jno.—Travels in Chile and La Plata. 2 v. . . 8vo. Lond. 1826
Mignet, F. A.—Charles Quint . . . . . . 8vo. Paris. 1854
——— —— Histoire de Marie Stuart. 2 v. . . . . 8vo. Paris. 1851
——— —— The Same 2 v. . . . . . . 16o. Paris. 1854
——— —— History of Mary, Queen of Scots. (Fr. Fren.) 2 v. 8vo. Lond. 1851
——— —— Notices Historiques. 2 v. . . . . . 8vo. Paris. 1853
——— —— Vie de Franklin . . . . . . 18o. Paris. 1848
Milburn on the Cow. See *Saxton's Rural H. B.*
Miles, Pliny—Nordurfari; or, Rambles in Iceland . . . 12o. N. Y. 1854
——— —— Postal Reform, its Necessity and Practicability . 8vo. N. Y. 1855
Military Journals of two Private Soldiers, 1758–75 . . 8vo. Pok'psie. 1855
Mill, Jno.—The Fossil Spirit: a Boy's Dream of Geology . 12o. N. Y. 1854
Millard, Dav.—Travels in Egypt, Arabia, and Holy Land . . 8vo. N. Y. no date
Miller, Hugh—Geology of the Bass Rock . . . . 12o. N. Y. 1851
——— —— My Schools and Schoolmasters . . . . 12o. Bost. 1854
——— —— The Two Records—Mosaic and Geological . 16o. Bost. 1854
Millevoye—Poesies de, avec une notice, par M. de Pongerville . 16o. Paris. 1851
Mills, A.—Literature and Literary Men of Great Britain & Ireland. 2 v. 8vo. N. Y. 1851

Mills, A.—Outlines of Rhetoric and Belles Lettres	12o.	N. Y.	1854
—— —— Poets and Poetry of the Ancient Greeks	8vo.	Bost.	1854
—— John—Christmas in the Olden Time	18o.	Lond.	no date
—— Lucius—Compendium of Hygiene	12o.	W. Wierst'd.	1855
—— Robt.—Statistics of South Carolina	8vo.	Charleston.	1826
Milman, Hen. H.—History of Latin Christianity. 3 v.	8vo.	Lond.	1854
Milton, Jno.—A Biography, by Cyrus R. Edwards	16o.	Lond.	1851
—— —— Life and Writings of, by H. J. Todd	8vo.	Lond.	1809
—— —— Paradise Lost; Notes by Rev. J. R. Boyd	12o.	N. Y.	1851
—— —— Poetical Works, Edited by C. D. Cleveland	12o.	Phil.	1853
—— —— Works in Verse and Prose. 8 v.	8vo.	Lond.	1851
*Mineral Region of Lake Superior	16o.	N. Y.	1845
*Minerva. Vol. 1.	8vo.	Jena.	1854
*Minutes of the Provincial Council of Pennsylvania. 3 v.	8vo.	Harrisb.	1838–40
Minutoli, J. F.—Alter und Neues aus Spanien	8vo.	Berlin.	1854
Mirabeau, Correspondence with La Marck. See *Correspondence.*			
Missionary Chronicle. See *Foreign Missionary Chronicle.*			
—— Herald. Vol. 17	8vo.	Bost.	1821
—— The Same. Vols. 40–50. [*Continued.*]	8vo.	Bost.	1844–54
*Mitchell's Universal Atlas	4to.	Phil.	1852
Mitchell, C.—Newspaper Press Directory of Great Britain for 1846	16o.	Lond.	1846
—— D. G.—Battle Summer	12o.	N. Y.	1852
—— Jno.—Jail Journal	12o.	N. Y.	1854
—— Thos.—The Gospel Crown of Life	12o.	Albany.	1851
Mitchison, Wm. (Ed'r.)—Hand-Book of the Songs of Scotland	12o.	Glasgow.	1851
Mitford, Mary R.—Our Village. 2 v.	16o.	Bost.	1853
—— —— Recollections of a Literary Life. 3 v.	12o.	Lond.	1852
—— —— The Same	12o.	N. Y.	1852
Modern Standard Drama. Vol. 13	12o.	N. Y.	[1855]
Moffat, Jas. C.—Life of Thos. Chalmers	12o.	Cincin.	1853
Mohammed, Ibn.—Omar El Tounsy. Voyage au Ouaday de l'Arabe	8vo.	Paris.	1851
Moir, D. M. [Δ]—Sketches of the Poet. Liter. of the past Half Century	16o.	Edin.	1851
—— —— Poetical Works, Edited by T. Aird. 2 v.	16o.	Edin.	1852
Molina, Fel.—Bosquejo de la Republica de Costa Rica	8vo.	N. Y.	1851
Moltke, Baron—The Russians in Bulgaria. (Fr. Ger.)	8vo.	Lond.	1854
Monk, C. J.—The Golden Horn, and Sketches in Asia Minor. 2 v.	8vo.	Lond.	1851
Monnard, Chas.—Tableaux d'Histoire de la Suisse au 18 Siècle	12o.	Paris.	1854
Monod, Adolphe—Woman; her Mission and her Life. (Fr. Fren.)	16o.	Lond.	1852
Montagu, Edw. W.—Rise and Fall of Ancient Republics	12o.	Phil.	1806
—— Robt.—Naval Architecture	8vo.	Lond	1852
Montalivet—Louis Philippe et sa Liste Civile	18o.	Brux.	1850
—— The Same	18o.	Brux.	1851
Montgomery, Cora—Eagle Pass	12o.	N. Y.	1852
—— Jas.—Sacred Poems and Hymns	16o.	N. Y.	1854
Monthly Mirror. Vols. 1–20	8vo.	Lond.	1795–1805
Montlosier, Comte de—Mémoires sur la Révolution Française. 2 v.	8vo.	Paris.	1830
*Montreal Directory for 1843–4	12o.	Montreal.	1843
Moodie, Mrs.—Life in the Clearings *vs.* the Bush	12o.	Lond.	1853
—— —— Roughing it in the Bush. 2 v.	12o.	N. Y.	1852
Moral Amusement	12o.	Title Wanting	

Mordaunt, Chas.—Memoir of, by A. Warburton. 2 v. . .	12o. Lond.	1853
Moore, Corn.—The Craftsman and Freemason's Guide . .	16o. Cincin.	1852
——— C. C.—Memoirs of George Castriot, King of Albania .	12o. N. Y.	1850
——— Frank—Songs and Ballads of the American Revolution .	12o. N. Y.	1856
——— Geo.—Health, Disease, and Remedy . . .	12o: N. Y.	1850
——— Jac. B.—Memoirs of American Governors. Vol. 1 .	8vo. N. Y.	1846
——— J. G.—Patent Office and Patent Laws . . .	12o. Phil.	1855
*——— Jno. W.—Complete Encyclopædia of Music . .	8vo. Bost.	1854
*——— Thos.—Irish Melodies	8vo. Phil.	1853
——— ——— Letters to his Music Publisher . . .	12o. N. Y.	1854
——— ——— Memoirs of Rt. Hon. Rich. B. Sheridan. 2 v. .	12o. N. Y.	1853
——— ——— Popular History of British Ferns and Allied Plants	16o. Lond.	1851
Moral Play of Wit and Science. See *Shakspeare Soc. Pub.* Vol. 37.		
Moralistes Grecs: Socrate, Théophraste, Epictete . .	16o. Paris.	1845
Moran, Benj.—Footpath and Highway; or, Great Britain in 1851–2	12o. Phil.	1853
More, Han.—Memoir of, by Mrs. H. C. Knight . . .	12o. N. Y.	1851
Morell, J. D.—Analysis of Sentences Explained and Systematized	8vo. Lond.	no date
——— ——— The Same	12o. Lond.	no date
——— ——— Elements of Psychology. Part 1. . .	12o. Lond.	1853
——— ——— Russia as It Is	16o. Lond.	1854
——— ——— Turkey, Past and Present . . .	16o. Lond.	1854
Morfit, Campbell. See *Smithsonian Report.*		
——— ——— (Ed'r.)—Arts of Tanning, Curry. & Leath. Dres. (Fr. Fren.)	8vo. Phil.	1852
Morgan, L. H.—League of the Ho-De-No-Saw-Nee; or, Iroquois .	8vo. Rochester.	1851
——— ——— Diffusion against Centralization . .	16o. Rochester.	1852
Morier, Jas.—Journey through Persia, Armenia, and Asia Minor .	4to. Lond.	1812
Morin, A.—Leçons de Mécanique Pratique . . .	8vo. Paris.	1853
Morley, Hen.—Life of Bernard Palissy, of Saintes. 2 v. . .	16o. Bost.	1853
Mormons (The); or, Latter-Day Saints	12o. Lond.	no date
Mornand, Félix—La Vie de Paris	16o. Paris.	1855
*Morning Courier and New York Enquirer, 1850–54. 9 v. [*Continued.*]	Fol. N. Y.	1850–4
Morning of Life; a Memoir of Miss A—n, Educated for a Nun .	18o. N. Y.	1851
Morpeth, Lord (Earl of Carlisle)—Trav. in Amer.; the Poetry of Pope	12o. N. Y.	1851
Morris, Amos—See *Memoranda.*		
——— Geo. P.—The Deserted Bride, &c.	8vo. N. Y.	1853
——— Robt.—Lights and Shadows of Freemasonry . .	8vo. Louisville.	1852
*Morrison's Stranger's Guide to Washington . . .	16o. Wash.	1844
Morse, Jed. & Parish, Elijah—History of New England . .	8vo. Lond.	1808
*Mortality Statistics of 7th Census of U. S., 1850, by J. D. De Bow	8vo. Wash.	1855
Mortimer, G. W.—Pyrotechny; or, Recreative Fireworks . .	12o. Lond.	no date
Morton, W. T. G.—Statem. in favor of his Discov. of Anæsthetic Ether.	8vo. Wash.	1853
Moschzisker, F. A.—Guide to German Literature. 2 v. .	16o. Lond.	1850
Moseley, Jos.—Political Elements; or, Modern Legislation . .	12o. Lond.	1852
*Moses, Hen.—Collection of Antique Vases, Altars, &c. . .	4to. Lond.	no date
Mosquera, T. C. de—Physical and Political Geography of N. Granada	8vo. N. Y.	1853
Mossman, Sam. and Thos. B.—Australia Visited and Re-visited .	8vo. Lond.	1853
Most Exact and Accurate Map of the whole World . .	4to. Lond.	1676
Mother's Magazine. Vol. 18	8vo. N. Y.	1850
Motherwell, Wm—Posthumous Poems	16o. Bost.	1851
Motives for Missions	16o. Lond.	1853

Moule, Thos.—English Counties delineated. 2 v.	4to. Lond.	1837
Mowatt, Mrs. A. C.—Autobiography of an Actress	12o. Bost.	1854
Mozart—Don Giovanni. (An Opera.)	Fol. Bologne.	no date
—— Marriage of Figaro, in Vocal Score, &c.	4to. Lond.	no date
—— Noces de Figaro. (An Opera.)	8vo. Paris.	no date
Müffling, Baron—Passages from My Life	8vo. Lond.	1853
Mulchinock, Wm. P.—Ballads and Songs	12o. N. Y.	1851
Mullaly, Jno.—Trip to Newfoundland	12o. N. Y.	1855
Müller, C. O.—Ancient Art, and Its Remains. (Fr. Ger.)	8vo. Lond.	1850
—— J. G.—Geschichte der Americanischen Urreligionen	8vo. Bafel.	1855
—— John—History of the World. (Fr. Ger.) 4 v.	12o. N. Y.	1847
—— Otto—Charlotte Ackermann	8vo. Frankft.	1854
Mundy, G. C.—Our Antipodes; or, Residence in Australia. 3 v.	8vo. Lond.	1852
Municipal Register of the City of Boston, for 1854	8vo. Bost.	1854
Munn, L. C.—The American Orator	12o. Bost.	1853
Munsell, Joel—Annals of Albany, Vols. 1–4 and 6	12o. Albany.	1850–5
—— —— Every-Day Book of History and Phrenology. 2 v.	12o. Albany.	1843
—— —— Typographical Miscellany	8vo. Albany.	1850
Murchison, R. J.—Siluria. The History of the Oldest Rocks	8vo. Lond.	1854
Mure, Wm.—Hist. of the Language and Lit. of Ancient Greece. Vol. 4	8vo. Lond.	1853
Murger, Henri—Les Buveursd' Eau	16o. Brux.	1854
—— —— Scènes de la Bohême	18o. Paris.	1851
—— —— Le Pays Latin	16o. Paris.	1851
*Murphy, Jas. C.—Arabian Antiquities of Spain	Fol. Lond.	1813
*—— John G.—Review of Chemistry for Students	12o. Phil.	1851
Murray's Official Hand-Book of Church and State	16o. Lond.	1852
Murray, Hon. Amelia M.—Letters from the U. States, Cuba, & Canada	12o. N. Y.	1856
—— Hen.—Art of Portrait Painting in Oil Colors	16o. Lond.	1851
—— Hugh—Pictorial History of the United States of America	8vo. Bost.	1851
—— J. F.—Picturesque Tour of the River Thames	8vo. Lond.	1849
—— Lindley—Power of Religion on the Mind in Retirement, &c.	18o. N. Y.	1838
—— Nich.—Men and Things as I saw them in Europe	12o. N. Y.	1853
—— —— Parish and other Pencillings	12o. N. Y.	1854
—— —— Romanism at Home	12o. N. Y.	1852
—— Robt.—Treatise on Marine Engines and Steam Vessels	16o. Lond.	1852
Music, and the Art of Dress. Two Essays	16o. Lond.	1852
Musset, Alf. de—Comédies et Proverbes	16o. Paris.	1851
—— —— Contes	12o. Paris.	1854
—— Paul de—Femmes de la Régence	16o. Paris.	1848
—— —— Originaux du XVII. Siècle	16o. Paris.	1854
Muston, A.—The Israel of the Alps; or, the Waldenses	12o. Lond.	1852
Mutterings and Musings of an Invalid	12o. N. Y.	1851
Muzzey, A. B.—The Young Maiden	16o. Bost.	1851
My Progress in Error, and Recovery to Truth	12o. Bost.	1842
Napier, Jas.—Chemistry applied to Dyeing	12o. Phil.	1853
—— —— Manual of the Art of Dyeing	12o. Glasgow.	1853
—— —— Manual of Electro-Metallurgy	12o. Lond.	1851
—— —— The Same	12o. Phil.	1853
—— Macvey—Lord Bacon and Sir Walter Raleigh	8vo. Camb. (E.)	1853

Napier, Wm.—English Battles and Sieges in the Peninsula	.	12o. Lond	1852
——— —— Sir Charles Napier's Administration of Scinde	.	8vo. Lond.	1851
Napoleon Ballads, By Bon Gaultier		16o. N. Y.	1852
Narrative of the Conquest of Finland by the Russians, in 1809	.	12o. Lond.	1854
Nash, J. A.—The Progressive Farmer; or, Agricultural Chemistry		12o. N. Y.	1853
*Nashua and Nashville Directory, 1850		12o. Nashua.	1850
*National (Le)—May 16, 1849–Dec 31, 1850. 3 v. . . .		Fol. Paris.	1849–50
*National Journal. Vols. 1 and 2		4to Wash.	1823–5
——— Magazine. Vols. 1–5. [*Continued.*] . . .		8vo. N. Y.	1852–4
*——— Portrait Gallery of Distinguished Americans. 4 v. .		8vo. Ph.&N.Y.	1837–9
*Natural History of New York State. Vol. 19 . . .		4to. Albany.	1854
Agriculture of N. Y. By E. Emmons. Vol. 5.			
Nature and Elements of the Material World		8vo. Lond.	1847
*Nautical Almanac and Astronomical Ephemeris for 1855 .	.	8vo. Lond.	1852
*——— The Same for 1854		8vo. Lond.	1851
——— See *United States Ephemeris.*			
——— Magazine. Vol. 19–23. [*Continued.*] . .		8vo. Lond.	1850–53
Naval Temple (The): Battles fought by U. S. Navy .	.	8vo. Bost.	1816
Neal, Erskine—Life of Field Marshal H. R. H. the Duke of Kent		8vo. Lond.	1850
—— Fred. A.—Narrative of a Residence in Siam . .	.	12o. Lond.	1852
Neander, Aug.—Planting and Training of the Christian Church. 2 v.		16o. Lond.	1851
——— —— Hist. of the Christian Religion and Church. Vols. 4 & 5		8vo Bost.	1851–4
——— —— Memorials of Christian Life		16o. Lond.	1852
Neave, Digby—Four Days in Connemara	.	12o. Lond.	1852
Neill, P.—Fruit, Flower, and Vegetable Gardener's Companion	.	12o. N. Y.	1855
Nelligan, J. N.—Treatise on Diseases of the Skin . .	.	12o. Phil.	1852
Nelson—Life of, by Jos. Allen		16o. Lond.	1853
Nero—History of, by Jacob Abbott	.	16o. N. Y.	1853
Newil, Chas.—Contes Eccentriques		12o. Paris.	1855
Netscher, P. M.—Les Hollandais au Brésil	.	R. 8vo. La Haye.	1853
Neumann, C.—Chemical Works, abridged by Lewis . .		4to. Lond.	1759
New Collection of Voyages, Discoveries and Travels. 7 v. .	.	8vo. Lond.	1767
*Newark Directory, 1835–1856. 21 v.		12o. Newark.	1841–53
New Bedford Directory, 1836, '38, '39, '41, '45, '49, '52. 7 v.	.	12o. N. Bedf.	1836–52
New Bond of Love.		16o. N. Y.	1853
*Newcomb, Harvey—Cyclopedia of Missions . . .	.	8vo. N. Y.	1854
Newcombe, S. P.—Pleasant Pages for Young People . .		16o. Bost.	1853
New Dido (The); or, An Honest Laugh at Honest People .	.	12o. N. Y.	1851
New Englander. Vol. 1		8vo. N. Hav.	1843
——— Vols. 8–12. [*Continued.*] . . .	.	8vo. N. Hav.	1850–54
New England—Hist. and Genealog. Reg. Vols. 4–8. [*Continued.*]		8vo. Bost.	1852–4
——— Primer.	.	18o. Bost.	1777
*New Jersey Business Directory. (Kirkbride's.) . .		8vo. Trenton.	1850
Newland, Hen.—The Erne, its Legends and Fly-Fishing .	.	16o. Lond.	1851
Newman, Fra. W.—History of the Hebrew Monarchy . .		8vo. Lond.	1847
——— —— Lectures on Political Economy . .	.	12o. Lond.	1851
——— —— Regal Rome; Introduction to Roman History	.	12o. Lond.	1852
——— —— The Soul, her Sorrows and Aspirations .	.	12o. Lond.	1849
——— —— Reply to Eclipse of Faith. See *Defence*, &c.			
New Mirror for Travellers; and Guide to the Springs .	.	12o. N. Y.	1828

New Monthly Magazine. Vols. 89–101. [*Continued.*] . . 8vo. Lond. 1850–54
*New Navy List and General Record. By J. Allen . . . 8vo. Lond. 1852
Newport Illustrated . . . . 12o. N. Y. 1854
New Quarterly Review. Vols. 1 & 2 . . . . . 8vo. Lond. 1852–3
New Testament. See *Bible.*
New Themes for the Protestant Clergy . . . . . 12o. Phil. 1851
———— Condemned . . . . 12o. Phil. 1853
Newton, Isaac—Memoirs of, by Sir David Brewster . . 8vo. Edin. 1855
——— Robt.—Life of, by Rev. Thos. Jackson . . . 12o. N. Y. 1855
New York and Brooklyn Partnership Directory. By Rode, 1853, '4 8vo. N. Y. 1853
———— as It Is, in 1837 . . . . . . 18o. N. Y. 1851
———— CityBus'n's Direct'y, for 1840–41 ; '48, '51–52, '55–56. 4 v. 12o. N. Y. 1840–55
———— By-Laws and Ordinances of the Mayor, &c. . 8vo. N. Y. 1839
*———— Directory for 1786. (by David Franks.) . . 16o. N. Y. 1851
*———————— 1789, '99, '1806, '10, '11, '14, '15. 8 v. 12o. N. Y. 1789–1815
*———————— 1821–2, '23–25, '32–3, '36–7. 6 v. . 12o. N. Y. 1821–36
*———————— 1852–56. 4 v. . . . . 8vo. N. Y. 1852–5
———— Documents of Board of Aldermen. Vols. 1–4 . . 8vo. N. Y. 1855, '8
———————————— and Assistants. 6 v. 8vo. N. Y. 1835, '9
—————————— Assistants. 4 v. . . 8vo. N. Y. 1837
———— Mayor Lee's Messages to Common Council . 8vo. N. Y. 1834
———— Proceedings of Board of Aldermen. Vols. 1–15 . 8vo. N. Y. 1835–8
———————————— and Assistants. 1831–6 8vo. N. Y. 1836
—————————— Assistants. 10 v. . . 8vo. N. Y. 1837, '8
*———— Street Directory, 1851 . . . . . 8vo. N. Y. 1851
*———— Commercial Advertiser, 1850–54. 9 v. [*Continued.*] . Fol. N. Y. 1850–54
*———— Express, 1854. 2 v. [*Continued.*] . . Fol. N. Y. 1854
*———— Times, Sept. 51–Dec. 1854. 5 v. [*Continued.*] . Fol. N. Y. 1851–4
*———— Daily Tribune, 1850–54. 9 v. [*Continued.*] . Fol. N. Y. 1850–54
———— Ecclesiologist. Vols. 1–5 . . . . . 8vo. N. Y. 1848–53
———— Geol. and Mineralogical Reports, 1837–41. 5 v. 8vo. & Atlas 4to. Albany. 1837–44
*———— Herald, 1848 to 1854. 13 v. [*Continued*] . . Fol. N. Y. 1848–54
———— In a Nut-Shell . . . . 16o. N. Y. 1853
*———— Journal of Commerce for 1852, '3. 4 v. . . Fol. N. Y. 1852–3
———— 1st & 2d Repts. of Comm. on Practice and Pleadings R.8vo. Alb'y. 1838–'9
———— Quarterly. Vol. 1 . . . . 8vo. N. Y. 1852
*———— Mercantile Union Business Directory . . 8vo. N. Y. 1850
*———— State Business Directory . . . . 8vo. N. Y. 1850
Nicander. See *Scriptorum Græcorum Bibliotheca.* Vol. 33.
Nichol, J. P.—The Planetary System . . . . . 8vo. Lond. 1851
Nicholas (Emperor.) See *Lea, Robt.*
——— —— his Life and Reign, by H. Christmas . . 16o. Lond. 1854
——— —— Life of, by E. H. Michelson . . . 16o. Lond. 1854
——— Sir H.—History of the Battle of Agincourt . . 8vo. Lond. 1832
Nicholls, Benj. E.—Help to the Reading of the Bible . . 12o. Lond. 1849
——— —— The Same . . . . 12o. N. Y. 1854
Nichols, Jno.—[Biographical Anecdotes of Wm. Hogarth] . 8vo. Lond. 1785
——— Reb. S—Songs of the Heart and Hearth Stone . . 8vo. Phila. 1851
——— T. L.—Esoteric Anthropology . . . . . 18o. Port Chest. 1853
Nicholson Mrs. A.—Annals of the Famine in Ireland in 1847–9 . 12o. N. Y. 1851

Niebuhr, B. G.—Ancient Ethnography and Geography. 2 v.	8vo.	Bost.	1854
——— — Lectures on Ancient History. 3 v.	8vo.	Lond.	1852
——— — The Same. 3 v.	8vo.	Phil.	1852
——— — Lectures on Roman History. 3 v.	16o.	Lond.	1852
——— — Life and Letters, with Essays. 2 v.	8vo.	Lond.	1852
——— — The Same	12o.	N. Y.	1852
Nieritz, Gustav—Deutscher Volkskalendar für 1854	12o.	Leipz.	1853
Nikkanochee, O.—Narrative of his Early Days	8vo.	Lond.	1841
Nisard, D.—Etudes sur la Renaissance et Réforme	12o.	Paris.	1855
Nixon, Jas.—Rudiments of Book-Keeping	12o.	N. Y.	1854
Noback, Fried.—Systematisches Lehrbuch der Handels-Wissenschaft	8vo.	Leipz.	1851
Noctes Ambrosianæ—By Wilson, Maginn, Lockhart, &c. 5 v.	12o.	N. Y.	1854
Nodier, Chas.—Contes Fantastiques	16o.	Paris.	1850
——— — Souvenirs de la Révolution. 2 v.	16o.	Paris.	1850
——— — Souvenirs de Jeunesse	16o.	Paris.	1850
——— — Souvenirs et Portraits	8vo.	Paris.	1833
Nolte, Vinc.—Fifty Years in Both Hemispheres	12o.	N. Y.	1854
——— — Funfzig Jahre in beiden Hemisphären	8vo.	Hamb.	1854
Normandy, A.—Commercial Hand-Book of Chemical Analysis	12o.	Lond.	1850
*Norrie, J. W.—Marine Atlas; or, Seamen's Complete Pilot. 2 v.	Fol.	Lond.	1821
Norris, Sept.—Norris' Hand-Book for Locomotive Engineers	12o.	Phil.	1852
Northall, R. W.—Before and Behind the Curtain	12o.	N. Y.	1851
North American Miscellany. Vols. 1, 2 & 4,	8vo.	N. Y.	1851–2
——— Review and Miscellaneous Journal. Vols. 3 & 4.	8vo.	Bost.	1816–7
——— Vols. 71–79. [*Continued.*]	8vo.	Bost.	1850–4
*——— The Same. Index to Vols. 1–25	8vo.	Bost.	1829
North British Review. Vols. 13–21. [*Continued.*]	8vo.	Edin.	1850–54
*—— Briton. Vol. 1, Part 2, and Vol. 2. 2 v.	Fol.	Lond.	1768–70
Northend, Chas.—The Teacher and the Parent	12o.	Bost.	1853
Norton, Andrews—Tracts concerning Christianity	8vo.	Camb.	1852
——— Mrs.—The Undying One; and other Poems	16o.	N. Y.	1854
——— Jno. P.—Elements of Scientific Agriculture	12o.	Albany.	1850
Northrup, Sol.—Narrative of, as Twelve Years a Slave	12o.	Auburn.	1853
Notes and Queries. Vols. 1–8. [*Continued.*]	4to.	Lond.	1849–53
——— Respecting the Origin of the District of Columbia	8vo.		no title page
Nott, J. C., & Gliddon (Geo. R.)—Types of Mankind	8vo.	Phil.	1854
Noyes, Eli.—Lectures on the Truth of the Bible	12o.	Bost.	1853
Nunnery for Coquettes	12o.		Title Wanting
Nystrom, J. W.—Treatise on Screw Propellers and Steam Engines	8vo.	Phil.	1852
*Oakes, C. B.—Who's Who in 1854	18o.	Lond.	no date
Oates, Geo.—Tables of Sterling and Federal Exchange	8vo.	N. Y.	1851
Oberkirch, Baroness de—Memoirs, Written by Herself. 3 v.	8vo.	Lond.	1852
Obituary Addresses on the Death of Hon. W. R. King	8vo.	Wash.	1854
——— Webster	8vo.	Wash.	1853
O'Brien, Pat.—Residence in the Danubian Principalities	12o.	Lond.	1854
Observations on the Wisconsin Territory	12o.	Phil.	1838
O'Callaghan, E. B.—Documentary History of New York. Vols. 3 & 4	8vo.	Albany.	1850–1
*——— ——— State. 4 v.	4to.	Albany.	1850–1
O'Connell, Cath. M.—Excursions in Ireland in 1844 and 1850	8vo.	Lond.	1852

O'Connor—Chronicles of Eri; History of the Irish. 2 v. . 8vo. Lond. 1822
Oersted, Hans C.—The Soul in Nature. (Fr. Ger.) . . 16o. Lond.
*Official Catalogue of the Great Exhibition. . . . . 4to. Lond. 1851
*——— Description and Illust. Catalogue of the Great Exhibition. 3 v. 8vo. Lond. 1851
*——— Report of the Mass. Convention to amend Constitution. 3 v. 8vo. Bost. 1853
*Ogilvie, Jno. (Ed'r.)—Imperial Dictionary, Eng., Technological, &c. 2 v. 8vo. Edin. 1850
Oldham's Amusing and Instructive Reader . . . . . 12o. N. Y. 1854
Old Sights with New Eyes, by a Yankee . . . . . 12o. N. Y. 1854
Olin, Steph.—Greece and the Golden Horn . . . . . 16o. N. Y. 1854
—— —— Life and Letters. 2 v. . . . . . . 12o. N. Y. 1853
—— —— Works. 2 v. . . . . 12o. N. Y. 1852
Oliphant, L.—Journey to Katmandu, the Capital of Nepaul . 16o. N. Y. 1852
——— Law.—The Russian Shores of the Black Sea . . 8vo. Lond. 1853
——— —— The Same . . . . 12o. N. Y. 1854
Oliver and Boyd's Scottish Tourist . . . . 16o. Edin. 1852
—— G.—Dictionary of Symbolic Masonry . . . 12o. Lond. 1853
Ollendorff, H. G.—New Method of Learning Italian . . . 12o. N. Y. 1849
——— —— ——————— Spanish . . 12o. N. Y. 1851
——— —— Neue Methode Leren de Englisch . . . 8vo. Frankfort 1850
Olmsted, Den.—Introduction to Astronomy . . . . 8vo. N. Y. 1854
——— Fred. L.—Walks and Talks of an Amer. Farmer in Eng. 2 v. 12o. N. Y. 1852
Olmstead, J. M.—Noah and his Times . . . . . 12o. Bost. 1853
O'Meara, B. E.—Napoleon in Exile; or, a Voice from St. Helena. 2 v. 12o. N. Y. 1853
On the New General Biographical Dictionary . . . . 8vo. Lond. 1839
Onderdonk, Hen. (Jr.)—Barbar. Capture & Death of Gen. N. Woodhull 16o. N. Y. 1848
Opdyke, Geo.—Treatise on Political Economy . . . . 12o. N. Y. 1851
Opie, Amelia—Memorials of, by Lucy Aikin . . . . 8vo. Norwich [E.] 1854
Opinion of Authors on the Bookselling Question . . . . 8vo. Lond. no date
Oppianus, Cilex. See *Scriptorum Græcorum Bibliotheca.* Vol. 33.
Oration and Poem Delivered before the Delta Phi Convention . 8vo. N. Y. 1855
Oratores Atticæ. See *Scriptorum Græcorum Bibliotheca.* Vol. 23.
Orchard, G. H.—Concise History of Foreign Baptists . . 12o. Nashv. no date
Oriental Herald and Colonial Review. Vols. 1–23 . . 8vo. Lond. 1824–9
Original Papers relative to the Disturbances in Bengal, 1759–1764. 2 v. 8vo. Lond. 1765
Origin and Progress of Despotism in Oriental and other Empires . 12o. Amsterd. 1764
Orleans, Duchesse de—Correspondence, complete. 2 v. . 12o. Paris. 1855
Orlich, Leopold von—Travels in India. (Fr. Ger.) 2 v. . . 8vo. Lond. 1845
Orr's Circle of the Sciences. Vol. 1 . . . . . . 8vo. Lond. 1854
Orton, J. R.—Camp Fires of the Red Men . . . . . 12o. N. Y. 1855
Osborn, S.—Stray Leaves from an Arctic Journal . . 12o. N. Y. 1852
——— —— The Same . . . . 12o. Lond. 1852
Osgood, Sam.—God with Men . . . . 12o. Bost. 1853
——— —— Hearth Stone . . . . 12o. N. Y. 1853
——— —— Mile Stones in our Life Journey . . . 12o. N. Y. 1855
Ossoli, Marg. F.—Memoirs. 2 v. . . . . 12o. Bost. 1852
——— —— Woman in the 19th Century . . . . 12o. Bost. 1855
Our Coal and Our Coal-Pits; The People in them, &c. . . 12o. Lond. 1853
Our First Mother . . . . 16o. N. Y. 1852
Outline of the Revolution in Spanish America . . . . 8vo. Lond. 1817
Overman, Fred.—Manufacture of Steel . . . . . 12o. Phil. 1851

Overman, Fred.—Mechanics for the Millwright, Machinist, &c. .	12o. Phil.	1851
——— —— Moulder's and Founder's Pocket Guide . .	12o. Phil.	1851
——— —— Practical Mineralogy, Assaying, and Mining .	18o. Phil.	1851
——— —— Treatise on Metallurgy	8vo. N. Y.	1852
Ouverture, Toussaint l'—Life of, by J. R. Beard . .	12o. Lond.	1853
Ovid, P. Naso—Fasti, Tristia, Epistles, &c.	16o. Lond.	1851
—— —— Heroïdes; or, Epistles of the Heroines . .	16o. Lond.	1852
—— —— Metamorphoses, Translated by Riley . . .	16o. Lond.	1851
—— —— Opera Omnia. 9 v. See *Valpy's Delphin Classics.*		
Owen, D. D.—Geological Survey of Wisconsin, Iowa, and Minnesota	4to. Phil.	1852
—— Mrs. O. F.—Heroines of History	12o. N. Y.	1854
—— Robt. D.—Hints on Public Architecture : . .	4to. N. Y.	1849
Ozaneaux, Geo.—Nouveau Système d'Etudes Philosophiques .	8vo. Paris.	1830
Paddy Land, and the Lakes of Killarney	12o. Lond.	1853
Paganel, C.—Histoire de Scanderbeg	12o. Paris.	1855
Paget, Jas.—Lectures on Surgical Pathology . . .	8vo. Phil.	1854
—— John—Hungary and Transylvania. 2 v. . .	12o. Phil.	1850
Pagitt, E.—Heresiography; or, Hereticks and Sectaries . .	8vo. Lond.	1661
*Paine, Robt. T.—Memoirs of, by his Parents . . .	4to. N. Y.	1852
Painter, Gilder, and Varnisher's Companion . . .	12o. Phil.	1850
Palenzuela y Ramon—Método para apprender el Ingles .	12o. N. Y.	1851
Palfrey, Jno. G.—Judaism and Christianity . . .	8vo. Bost.	1854
——— —— Lectures on the Jewish Script. and Antiq. Vols. 1 & 2	8vo. Bost.	1838–40
Palgrave, Sir F.—History of Normandy and of England. Vol. 1 .	8vo. Lond.	1851
Palissy, Bernard—Life of, by Henry Morley. 2 v. . .	16o. Bost.	1853
Palmer, Jos. H.—First Lessons in Book-Keeping . . .	12o. N. Y.	1852
——— Ray—Closet Hours	12o. Albany.	1851
——— S.—General History of Printing . . .	4to. Lond.	1733
Palmerston, Viscount—Opin. & Policy, with Memoir, by G. H. Francis	8vo. Lond.	1852
Pamphlets. Vols. 26–34. 8vo. Vol. 53, 12mo. . . .	Various.	
*Pamphlets on the Harrisburgh Buckshot War . .	8vo.	
Panegyrici Veteres. 5 v. See *Valpy's Delphin Classics.*		
Panoplist (The). Vols. 1 and 2	8vo. Bost.	1805–7
——— and Missionary Magazine, N. S. Vols. 1 and 2 .	8vo. Bost.	1808–10
Papers on Chemistry, Mineralogy, &c.	8vo. Lond.	1810–43
——— Polite and Fine Arts	8vo. Lond.	1810–43
Pardee, R. G.—Manual for the Cultivation of the Strawberry .	12o. N. Y.	1854
Pardoe, Miss—Life of Marie de Medicis, Queen of France. 3 v.	8vo. Lond.	1852
Paris, E.—Catéchisme du Mécanicién à Vapeur. . . .	8vo. Paris.	no date
—— —— Directory. See *Annuaire General du Commerce.*		
Parisian Sights and French Principles	12o. N. Y.	1852
*Park, Mungo—Mission to the Interior of Africa in 1805 .	4to. Lond.	1815
*—— —— Travels in the Interior of Africa in 1795–7 . .	4to. Lond.	1799
——— Roswell—Hand-Book for Travellers in Europe . .	16o. N. Y.	1853
Parker, Geo.—Life: Painter of Variegated Characters . .	8vo. Lond.	1789
——— Joel—Sermons on Various Subjects . . .	12o. Phil.	1852
——— John A.—Quadrature of the Circle . . .	8vo. N. Y.	1851
——— N. Howe—Iowa as It Is in 1856	12o. Chicago.	1856
——— R. G.—Aids to English Composition . . .	12o. N. Y.	1848

Parker, Theod.—Sermons on Theism, Atheism, &c. . . . 12o. Bost. 1853
——— —— Speeches, Addresses, and Occasional Sermons. 2 v. . 12o. Bost. 1852
——— —— Ten Sermons on Religion . . . . . 12o. Bost. 1853
Parker's Journal; a Weekly Gazette. Vol. 1 . . . . 4to. N. Y. 1850–1
Parkinson, Jas.—Fossil Remains. 3 v. . . . . . 4to. Lond. 1804–11
Parkman, F., (Jr.)—History of the Conspiracy of Pontiac, . 8vo. Bost. 1851
Parkyns, M.—Life in Abyssinia. 2 v. . . . . . 8vo. Lond. 1853
——— —— The Same. 2 v. . . . . 12o. N. Y. 1854
Parliamentary Right Maintained; or, The Hanover Succession Justified 8vo. s. l. 1714
Parnell, Hen.—Penal Laws against Irish Catholics . . . . 8vo. Lond. 1825
——— Thos., and Tickell (Thos.)—Poems . . . . 16o. Bost. 1854
Parsons, C. G.—Inside View of Slavery . . . . . 12o. Bost. 1855
——— Theoph.—The Law of Contracts. 2 v. . . . . 8vo. Bost. 1853–5
——— Thos. W.—Poems . . . . 12o. Bost. 1854
Parton, J.—Life of Horace Greeley . . . . . 12o. N. Y. 1855
Pascal, Jaqueline; or, A Glimpse at Convent Life. (Fr. Fren.) . 12o. N. Y. 1854
Passion Flowers . . . . 16o. Bost. 1854
Patent Laws of the United States . . . . 8vo. Wash. no date
Paterculus, M. V.—Opera Omnia. 1 v. See *Valpy's Delphin Classics.*
Paton, A. A.—The Goth and the Hun; or, Transylvania in 1850 . 8vo. Lond. 1851
*Patria—France Ancienne et Moderne, Morale et Matérialle. 2 v. 12o. Paris. 1847
Patriot Warrior (The); a Sketch of the Duke of Wellington . 16o. Lond. 1853
*Pattison, Wm.—Plans and Elevations of Cottage Villas, &c. . Fol. Lond. 1852
Paul, St.—Life and Epistles, by Conybeare and Howson. 2 v. - 8vo. N. Y. 1854
Paulding, Jas. K.—[New Mirror for Travellers; or, Guide to the Springs] 12o. N. Y. 1828
Pauli, Reinhold—Life of King Alfred. (Fr. Ger.) . . . . 8vo. Lond. 1852
Pausanias—Græciæ Descriptio. See *Scriptorum Græcorum Bibliotheca.* Vol. 20.
Pauthier, G.—Chine; Description Historique . . . . 8vo. Paris. 1837
Payson, Edw.—Memoir, Select Thoughts and Sermons. 3 v. . 8vo. Phil. 1851
Peabody, Elizabeth—Æsthetic Papers . . . . . 8vo. Bost. 1849
——— Eliz. P. (Ed'r.)—Crimes of the House of Austria agt. Mankind 16o. N. Y. 1852
Pearce, R. H.—History of the Inns of Court and Chancery . 8vo. Lond. 1848
——— Robt. R.—Memoirs and Corresp. of Richard Marq. Wellesley. 3 v. 8vo. Lond. 1846
Pearson, John—Exposition of the Creed . . . . . 8vo. N. Y. 1850
——— Thos.—Infidelity; its Aspects, Causes, &c. . . . 8vo. N. Y. 1854
Peck, Geo. W.—Melbourne and the Chincha Islands . . 12o. N. Y. 1854
Pedder, Jas.—Farmer's Vade Mecum . . . . . 16o. N. Y. 1854
Peel, Robt.—Life of. See *Lives.*
——— —— Speeches. 4 v. . . . . 8vo. Lond. 1853
—— W.—A Ride through the Arabian Desert . . . . 12o. Lond. 1852
Peirce, C. H.—Examinations of Drugs, Medicines, &c. . . 12o. Camb. 1852
——— B. K.—Recovery of Jerusalem; or, Wars of the Crusaders 18o. Bost. 1851
Pelouze, J., and Fremy (E.)—Chemistry. (Fr. Fren.) . . 12o. Phil. 1854
Peña, D. M. de la—Manual de Nueva York . . . . 18o. N. Y. 1851
Pencil, Mark—White Sulphur Papers; or, Life at the Springs of Va. 12o. N. Y. 1839
Penn, Wm.—An Historical Biography, by Wm. E. Dixon . . 12o. Phil. 1851
——— —— Life of, by S. M. Janney . . . . . 8vo. Phil. 1852
Pennsylvania State Register for 1831 . . . . . 12o. Phil. 1831
People's Illustrated Journal of Arts, &c. . . . . 4to. Lond. 1852
——— and Howitt's Journal. Vol. 10 . . . . . 8vo. Lond. 1850

Perkins, Geo. R.—Plane Trigonometry and its Applications . 8vo. N. Y. 1852
——— Jas. H.—Annals of the West . . . . . 8vo. Cincin. 1847
——— ——— Mem. and Writings of, by W. H. Channing. 2 v. 12o. Bost. 1851
Perrot, A. M.—Livre de Guerre . . . . . . 8vo. Paris. no date
*Perry, Com.—Naval Expedition to Japan . . . . 8vo. Wash. [1855]
——— G. W.—The Peasantry of England . . . . . 12o. Lond. 1846
Persius, Aulus Flaccus—Opera Omnia. 1 v. *See Valpy's Delphin Classics.*
Personal Narrative of the First Voyage of Columbus. (Fr. Span.) 8vo. Bost. 1827
Perthes, Fred. M.—Life of St. Chrysostom. (Fr. Ger.) . . 12o. Bost. 1854
Pertz, G. H.—Leben der Freiherrn von Stein. Vols. 1–4 & 6 . 8vo. Berlin. 1850–55
Peter the Apostle—Life of, by Alfred Lee . . . . . 12o. N. Y. 1852
Peterson, Edw.—History of Rhode Island . . . . 8vo. N. Y. 1853
——— R. E.—Familiar Science; or, Explanation of Common Things 12o. Phil. 1851
Petit, J. L.—Architectural Studies in France . . . . R. 8vo. Lond. 1854
*Petzholdt, Jul.—Handbuch der Deutscher Bibliotheken . 8vo. Halle. 1853
Pfeiffer, Ida—Visit to Holy Land, Egypt, and Italy . . . 8vo. Lond. 1852
——— ——— Journey to the Holy Land . . . . 12o. Lond. 1852
——— ——— ——— Iceland, Sweden, and Norway . . 12o. N. Y. 1852
——— ——— A Lady's Journey Round the World . . 12o. N. Y. 1852
——— ——— The Same . . . . 12o. Lond. no date
Phædrus—Opera Omnia. 1 v. See *See Valpy's Delphin Classics.*
Pharmacopœia of the United States . . . . . . 8vo. Phil. 1842
——— The Same . . . . 8vo. Phil. 1851
Phelan, Mich.—Billiards without a Master . . . . . 8vo. N. Y. 1850
Phelp's New York City Guide . . . . 18o. N. Y. 1852
——— Mrs. A. C.—The Life of Christ and other Poems . . 12o. Bost. 1852
*Philadelphia Business Directory for 1847 . . . . 8vo. Phila. 1847
*——— Directory and Register, 1820 . . . . 12o. Phila. 1820
*——— ——— 1837, '39–55. 18 v. . . . . 8vo. Phila. 1837–55
Philemon—Fragmenta. See *Scriptorum Græcorum Bibliotheca.* Vol. 2, Part 2.
Philip I.—History of the Reign of, by W. H. Prescott. Vols. 1 & 2 8vo. Bost. 1855
Philippe d'Orléans, Régent de France, par B. H. R. Capefigue . 12o. Paris. 1845
Phillips, Chas.—Curran and his Contemporaries . . . 12o. N. Y. 1851
——— Hen.—Companion for the Orchard . . . . 8vo. Lond. 1831
——— Jno. A.—Gold Mining and Assaying . . . . 16o. Lond. 1852
——— ——— Manual of Metallurgy . . . . . 12o. Lond. 1852
——— Willard—On the Laws of Insurance. 2 v. . . . 8vo. N. Y. 1853
——— Wm.—Elementary Introduction to Mineralogy . . 12o. Lond. 1852
Philosophia Græca. (Græcé.) . . . . 8vo. Oxford. 1834
Philosophical Magazine. Vol. 37. United Series . . . 8vo. Lond. 1850
——— The Same. Fourth Series. Vols. 1–6 [*Continued.*] 8vo. Lond. 1851–3
Philostratus, F. and L.—Opera. See *Scriptorum Græcorum Bibliotheca.* Vol. 32.
Phrenological Journal. Vol. 20 . . . . 8vo. Lond. 1847
Physiology of the Opera . . . . 16o. Phil. 1852
Piatt, Mrs. Donn—Bell Smith Abroad . . . . . 12o. N. Y. 1855
*Picard, H.—English and Dutch Pocket Directory . . . 16o. Zalt-Bonn. 1843
Pichot, Am.—Charles Quint de son Abdication . . . . 8vo. Paris. 1854
Pickering, Chas.—Races of Men and their Geographical Distribution 16o. Lond. 1851
Pickett, A. S.—Hist. of Alabama & Incidentally of Geo. and Miss. 2 v. 8vo Charleston. 1851
Pictorial Hand-Book of London . . . . 16o. Lond. 1854

Title	Format / Place	Date
Pictures from Sicily	R. 8vo. Lond.	1853
Picture of Philadelphia	18o. Phil.	1835
Pierce, Frank—Life of, by D. W. Bartlett	12o. Auburn.	1852
——— ——— ——— by Nath. Hawthorne	12o. Bost.	1852
*Pierer H. A. (Ed'r.)—Universal Lexicon. 17 v., 8vo. and Atlas	Fol. Altenb.	1849–52
*——— ——— Supplement to the Same. Vols. 1-3 . . .	8vo. Altenb.	1851–3
Pierron, A.—Histoire de la Littérature Romaine . .	12o. Paris.	1852
Pierson, H. W. (Ed'r.)—American Missionary Memorial . .	8vo. N. Y.	1853
Piggott, A. S.—Chemistry and Metallurgy as Applied to Dental Surg.	8vo. Phil.	1854
Pillaus, Prof.—The Rationale of Discipline	8vo. Edin.	1852
Pilpay—Fables of	16o. Lond.	1852
Pindar—Odes of, Literally Translated by Turner . .	16o. Lond.	1852
*Pinkerton, John (Ed'r.)—Collection of Voyages and Travels. 17 v.	4to. Lond.	1808–14
Pinkney, Wm.—Life of	8vo. N. Y.	1853
Pinney, N., and Barcelo (J.)—Practical Spanish Teacher .	12o. N. Y.	1855
Piozzi, Hester L.—Anecdotes of Dr. Johnson	16o. Lond.	1786
Piper, R. M.—Operative Surgery Illustrated	12o. Bost.	1852
Piranesi, P.—Bellezze delle Novelle	12o. Paris.	1823
Pitrat—Americans Warned of Jesuitism	12o. N. Y.	1851
*Pittsburgh Directory, 1850 and '52. 2 v.	8vo. Pittsb'g.	1850–2
Pius Ninth, The Last of the Popes	12o. N. Y.	1855
Plan for Shortening the Time of Passage from New York to London	8vo. Portland.	1850
Planche, Gus.—Nouveaux Portraits Littéraires. 2 v. . . .	16o. Paris.	1854
Plato—Opera. See *See Scriptorum Græcorum Bibliotheca.* Vol. 2, Part I.		
—— Phædo; or, The Immortality of the Soul	12o. N. Y.	1854
—— Works. Vol. 2. (Fr. Greek, by Davis.)	16o. Lond.	1849
—— ——— Vol. 3. (Fr. Greek, by Burges.) . . .	16o. Lond.	1850
Plautus—Opera Omnia. 5 v. See *Valpy's Delphin Classics.*		
——— Comedies, Translated by Hen. Riley. 2 v. Vol. 1 .	16o. Lond.	1852
Playfair, Jno.—Elements of Geology.	8vo. Phila.	1854
Plays. 5 v.	8vo. Various.	
Pleasants, Julia, and Bradley (Thos. B.)—Aphelia; Poems .	12o. N. Y.	1854
Plinius, Caius Secundus—Opera Omnia. 12 v. See *Valpy's Delphin Classics.*		
Plint, Thos.—Crime in England as Developed from 1801–48 .	12o. Lond.	1851
Plough, Loom, and Anvil. Vols. 1–6. [*Continued.*] . .	8vo. N. Y.	1848–53
Plurality of Worlds	8vo. Lond.	1853
————— The Same, with an Introduction by E. Hitchcock	12o. Bost.	1854
————— An Argument from Scripture . .	12o. Lond.	1855
Plutarchus Chæronensis—Opera. See *Scriptorum Græcorum Biblio.*	Vols. 24, '28, '6, '12.	
Pococke, E.—India in Greece; or, Truth in Mythology . .	12o. Lond.	1852
Poems. By Meditatus	16o. Phila.	1853
Poesche, T. and Goepp (C.)—The New Rome; or, U. S. of the World	12o. N. Y.	1853
Poetæ Bucolici et Didactici. See *Scriptorum Græcorum Bibliotheca.*	Vol. 22.	
Poetic Works of Louis Napoleon, done into plain English .	24o. Lond.	1852
Poetry of Germany. Trans. by A. Baskerville.	12o. N. Y.	1854
——— The Anti-Jacobin. *Notes by C. Edmonds . .	16o. Lond.	1854
*Poey, Felipe—La Historia Natural de la Isle de Cuba. Vol. 1 .	R. 8vo. Haban.	1851-4
Police de Paris Dévoilée, par P. Manuel. 2 v. . . .	8vo. Paris.	1790
Politics for American Christians	8vo. Phil.	1852
Polk, Jas. K.—Life of, by John S. Jenkins . . .	12o. Auburn.	1850

Pollok, Robt.—Course of Time. Notes by Scott	16o.	N. Y.	1854
Polonius. A Collection of Wise Saws and Modern Instances	16o.	Lond.	1852
Polybius Megalopotamus. See *Scriptorum Græcorum Bibliotheca.* Vol. 4.			
Polytechnisches Journal. (Dingler's). Vols. 115–133. (*Continued.*)	8vo.	Stuttgd.	1850–54
Pompeius Festus—Opera Omnia. 2 v. See *Valpy's Delphin Classics.*			
Ponchet, F. A.—Histoire des Sciences Naturelles au Moyen Age	8vo.	Paris.	1853
Pontmartin, Aren. de—Nouvelles Causeries Littéraires	12o.	Paris.	1855
Poole, R. S.—Horæ Ægyptiacæ; or, Chronology of Ancient Egypt	8vo.	Lond.	1851
—— T. E.—Life, Scen. and Cost. in Sierra Leone, and the Gambia. 2 v.	12o.	Lond.	1850
*—— Wm. F.—Index to Periodical Literature	R. 8vo.	N. Y.	1853
*Pope, Chas.—Yearly Journal of Trade	8vo.	Lond.	1854
—— The Same, for 1837–8	8vo.	Lond.	1837
Popkin, Jno. S.—Memorial of, by C. C. Felton	12o.	Camb.	1852
Popular Introduction to the Study and Practice of Chess	12o.	Lond.	1851
Porter, Chas. L.—Pebbles from the Lake Shore; or, Poems	12o.	Phil.	1855
—— Noah—Educational Systems of the Puritans and Jesuits Comp.	12o.	N. Y.	1851
Port-Royal, Mess. de—Method of Learning Latin. 2 v.	8vo.	Lond.	1758
Potter, A.—Hand-Book for Readers and Students	18o.	N. Y.	no date
*—— E. R.—Reports and Documents on Public Schools, &c. R. Island	8vo.	Prov.	1855
*—— —— Report on Public Schools and Education in R. Island	8vo.	Prov.	1855
—— J. H.—The Consumptive's Guide to Health	12o.	N. Y.	1852
Poussin, G. T.—United States; its Power and Progress. (Fr. Fren.)	8vo.	Phil.	1851
Power, W. T.—Three Years' Residence in China	8vo.	Lond.	1853
Pownall, Thos.—Administration of the British Colonies. 2 v.	8vo.	Lond.	1774
Poyer, Jno.—History of Barbadoes, 1605–1801	4to.	Lond.	1808
Practical Guide to the Greek Testament.	12o.	Lond.	no date
*—— Mechanics' Journal. Vols. 3–4, 6	4to.	Glasgow.	1850–4
—— Hints to Intending Emigrants	12o.	Lond.	1853
Pratz, Le Page du—History of Louisiana	8vo.	Lond.	1774
Pratt, W. T.—Law relating to Benefit Building Societies.	12o.	Lond.	1850
Prentice, A.—Sketches and Recollections of Manchester, 1792–1832	12o.	Lond.	1851
Prentiss, S. S.—Memoir of, Edited by his Brother. 2 v.	12o.	N. Y.	1855
Presbyterian Quarterly. Vols. 1 & 2.	8vo.	Phil.	1852–4
Prescott, Wm. H.—History of the Reign of Philip II. Vols. 1 & 2	8vo.	Bost.	1855
Present State of the Finances in Austria	8vo.	Leipzic.	1853
Present (The.) Vol. 1	8vo.		1843–4
Pridham, Chas.—Kossuth and the Magyar Land	12o.	Lond.	1851
Prime, Sam. I.—Thoughts on the Death of Little Children	16o.	N. Y.	1852
—— —— Travels in Europe and the East. 2 v.	12o.	N. Y.	1855
Princess of Bohemia—Memoirs of, by Baroness Blaze de Bury	12o.	Lond.	1853
Principles of Botany; the Cryptogamia	12o.	Phil.	1853
Prinsep, Hon. T.—Thibet, Tartary, and Mongolia	12o.	Lond.	1851
Print Collector (The); or, Necessary Knowledge	4to.	Lond.	1844
Prior, Jas.—Life of Hon. Edmund Burke. 2 v.	12o.	Bost.	1854
—— —— Life of Oliver Goldsmith. 2 v.	8vo.	Lond.	1837
Pritts, J. (Comp'r.)—Olden Time: Border Life of America	8vo.	Abington.	1849
*Pritzel, G. A.—Thesaurus Literaturæ Botanicæ	4to.	Lipsiæ.	1851
Private Life of an Eastern King	12o.	N. Y.	1855
Procedure Criminelle, Instruite au Chatelet de Paris	8vo.	Paris.	1790
Procedures in de zaak van P. Marcus op en tegen F. A. Kemp	8vo.	Leyden.	1782

Proceedings and Docu. of the Board of Assistant Aldermen. V. 37, 38 8vo. N. Y. 1850–1
——— of Amer. Assoc. for the Advancement of Science 8vo. Various. 1849–51
——— American Association of Science, May, 1851 . 8vo. Wash. 1851
*——— New York Historical Society, for 1843–'8. 3 v. . 8vo. N. Y. 1843–8
Procès Célèbres de la Révolution. 2 v. . . . . 8vo. Paris. 1814
Proctor, B. W.—English Songs and other Small Poems . . 12o. Bost. 1851
——— Maj.—History of the Crusades . . . . . 8vo. Phil. 1854
Propertius, Sex. Aurelius—Opera Om. 2 v. See *Valpy's Delphin Classics.*
Pro-Slavery Argument, as Maintained by Southern Writers . 12o. Phil. 1853
Prospective Review. Vols. 4–9 . . . . . . 8vo. Lond. 1848–53
Protestant in Ireland in 1853 . . . . . 16o. Lond. 1854
Proudhon, P. J.—Idée Générale de la Révolution au XIX Siècle 16o. Paris. 1851
*Providence (R. I.) Directory, for 1841, '44, '47–8, '50–1, 52–3. 5 v. 12o. Prov. 1841–52
Prudentius, Opera Omnia. 3 v. See *Valpy's Delphin Classics.*
Public Documents relating to the New York Canals . . 8vo. N. Y. 1821
——— School Matches, and those who meet there . . . 16o. Lond. 1853
Puffendorf, Baron—Introduction to the History of Europe. 2 v. . 8vo. Lond. 1764
Pugin, A. W.—Floriated Ornament . . . . . 4to. Lond. 1849
Pulte, J.—Homœopathic Domestic Physician . . . 12o. N. Y. 1852
——— ——— Woman's Medical Homœopathic Guide . . 12o. Cincin 1853
Pulszky, Theresa—Tales and Traditions of Hungary . . 12o. N. Y. 1852
——— F. and T.—White, Red, and Black: Sketches of Ame. Soc. 2 v. 12o. N. Y. 1853
*Punch; or, the London Charivari. Vols. 18–28 . . 4to. Lond. 1850–5
*Purchas, Sam.—His Pilgrimage: In Four Parts . . . Fol. Lond. 1613
Purpose of Existence Popularly Considered . . . 12o. Lond. 1850
*Putnam, Geo. P.—World's Progress; or, Dictionary of Dates . 12o. N. Y. 1850
——— ——— Supplement to the World's Progress . . 12o. N. Y. 1852
——— Worthy—Science and Art of Elocution . . . 12o. Auburn. 1854
Putnam's Monthly. Vols. 1–4 . . . . . . 8vo. N. Y. 1853–4
Putz, Wm.—Modern Geography and History. (Fr. Ger.) . . 12o. N. Y. 1851
Puynode, Gustave de—Monnaie du Crédit et de l'Impot. 2 v. . 8vo. Paris. 1853
Pycroft, Jas.—Course of English Reading. Edited by Spencer . . 16o. N. Y. 1854
Pye, Hen. J.—Alfred; an Epic Poem . . . . . 4to. Lond. 1801

Quackenbos, G. P.—Course of Composition and Rhetoric . . 12o. N. Y. 1855
——— ——— First Lessons in Composition . . 12o. N. Y. 1851
Quakerism; or, the Story of my Life . . . . 12o. Phil. 1852
Quarles, Fran.—Emblems; Divine and Moral . . . 16o. N. Y. 1854
Quarterly Journal of Chemical Society, Vols. 1–4 & 6. [*Continued*] 8vo. Lond. 1849–54
——— the London Geological Society. Vols. 2–6 8vo. Lond. 1846–50
——— Review. Vols. 87–94 [*Continued.*] . . . 8vo. Lond. 1850–54
——— Journal of Science and Arts, 32 v. in 16 . . 8vo. Lond. 1816–31
——— of the Meth. Epis. Church South. Vols. 6–8. [*Cont'd.*] 8vo. Richm. 1852–4
Quekett, Jno.—Lectures on Histology: Elementary Tissues . 8vo. Lond. 1852
Quincy, Josiah—History of the Boston Athenæum . . 8vo. Camb. 1850
——— ——— Municipal History of Boston . . . 8vo. Bost. 1852

Radcliffe, J. H.—Fiends, Ghosts, and Sprites . . . 16o. Lond. 1854
Raffenel, Anne—Voyage dans l'Afrique Occidentale en 1843–4 . 8vo. Paris. 1846
Raffinesque, C. S.—Atlantic Journal and Friend of Knowledge . 8vo. Phil. 1852–3

Raikes, Chas.—Notes on North-Western India . . . . 8vo. Lond. 1852
——— H.—The Marriage Contract. 2 v. . . . 12o. Lond. 1849
——— Hen.—Origin and Developm. of the English Constitution. Vol. 1 8vo. Lond. 1851
Raleigh, Sir W.—Life of . . . . 12o. Lond. 1790
——— ——— Life and Times of, by C. Whitehead . . 12o. Lond. 1854
——— ——— Life of. See *Bacon, Lord*
Ramsay, Allan—Works, with Life. 3 v. . . . . . 12o. Lond. 1851
Ramel, J. P.—Journal, Bound with *Salvandy's Paris* . . 8vo. Lond. 1799
Ramsey, J. G. M.—Annals of Tennessee . . . . . 8vo. Phil. 1853
Randall, S. S.—Common School System of N. Y. State . . 8vo. Troy. 1851
Randolph, Jno.—Life of, by H. A. Garland. 2 v. . . . 8vo. N. Y. 1850
——— ——— The Same. 2 v. . . . . . 12o. N. Y. 1851
——— ——— Life of, by F. W. Thomas . . . . 12o. Phil. 1853
Ranke, L.—Civil Wars in France in 16th and 17th Cent's. (Fr. Ger.) 2 v. 12o. Lond. 1852
——— ——— Civil Wars and Monarchy in France . . 12o. N. Y. 1853
——— ——— History of Servia and the Slave Provinces of Turkey 16o. Lond. 1853
Ranking, W. H. (Ed'r)—Half-Yearly Abs. of Medicine. Jan.–Dec. '51 8vo. Phil. 1851–2
*Ranlett, Wm. H.—The Architect; Designs for Cottages, Villas, &c. 2 v. 4to. N. Y. 1849
Rappers, The; or, Their Mysteries, Fallacies, and Absurdities . 12o. N. Y. 1854
Rapport fait des trouvés chez Robespierre et ses complices . . 8vo. Title wanting
Raspail, F. V.—Domestic Medicine . . . . . 16o. Lond. 1853
Rawle, Wm. Hen.—On the Law of Covenants for Title . . 8vo. Phil. 1854
Rawson, Jas.—Dictionary of Synonymical Terms . . 12o. Phil. 1850
Rawstrome, Law.—Gamonia; or, the Preserving of Game . . 8vo. Lond. 1837
Ray Society Publications . . . . 8vo. Lond. 1850–1

British Species of Angiocarpous Lichens. By Rev. W. A. Leighton.
Bibliographia Zoologiæ et Geologiæ. Vols. 2 and 3. By Agassiz.
*Monograph of British Nudibrianchiate Mollusca. By Alden and Hancock. Part 5.
Monograph on Sub-Class Cirripedeia. By C. Darwin.

Reach, Angus B.—Claret and Olives . . . . . 12o. N. Y. 1852
Read, C. R.—What I Heard, &c., at the Australian Gold-fields . 8vo. Lond. 1853
——— T. B.—House by the Sea: a Poem . . . . 12o. Phil. 1855
——— ——— The New Pastoral . . . . . . 16o. Phil. 1855
——— ——— The Onward Age. An Anniversary Poem . 12o. Cincin. 1852
——— ——— Poems . . . . 16o. Phil. 1853
Readings in Poetry. Selections from the best Poets . . 16o. Lond. 1852
Recollections of a Ramble from Sidney to Southamp., *viâ* S. Am. & U. S. 12o. Lond. 1851
Records of the School of Mines and of Science . . . R. 8vo. Lond. 1852
Recreation; a Gift-Book for Young Readers . . . . 16o. Edin. 1844
*Recueil de Piéces. 9 v. . . . . 8vo. various
Red Book—State of New York. 1837 . . . . . 24o. Albany. 1837
Redding, Cyr.—History and Description of Modern Wines. . 16o. Lond. 1851
*Reden, F. F. W.—Deutschland und das Uebrige Europa . . 8vo. Weisbaden. 1854
Redfield, Jas. W.—Comparative Physiognomy . . . 8vo. N. Y. 1852
Reed, Hen.—Lectures on English History and Tragic Poetry . 16o. Phil. 1855
——— ——— Lectures on English Literature . . . . 12o. Phil. 1855
Reese, Jno. J.—Analysis of Physiology . . . . . 12o. Phil. 1852
Reeve, T.—Treatise on the Law of Descents . . . . 8vo. N. Y. 1825
Register of the Commissioned and Warrant Officers of the U. S. Navy 12o. Wash. 1842
——— — The Same . . . . 12o. Wash. 1852
——— — The Same . . . . 12o. Wash. 1853

Entry	Size	Place	Year
Regnault, M. N.—Elements of Chemistry. (Fr. Fren.) 2 v.	8vo.	Phil.	1852
——— Elias—Histoire du Gouvernment-Provisoire . .	8vo.	Paris.	1850
*Regulations for the Uniform and Dress of the U. S. Army .	4to.	Phil.	1851
Reichardt, C. F.—Nicaragua in 1852	8vo.	Braunsch'g.	1854
Reichenbach, C.—Physico-Physiological Researches on Magnetism	12o.	N. Y.	1851
Reid, Thos.—Clock and Watch Making	8vo.	Glasg.	1849
—— —— Essays on the Intellectual Powers of Man. Abridged	12o.	Camb.	1850
Relation of R. M.'s Voyages to Buenos Ayres, &c. . . .	12o.	Lond.	1716
Remarks on the "Natural History of the Vestiges of Creation"	12o.	Phil.	1846
——— ——— Writings and Conduct of J. J. Rousseau . .	16o.	Lond.	1767
*Remembrancer (The;) or, Repository of Public Events. 16 v.	8vo.	Lond.	1775–83
Reminiscences of an Emigrant Milesian. 3 v.	12o.	Lond.	1853
——— Thought and Feeling	12o.	Lond.	1852
——— The Same	16o.	Bost.	1853
Renaudot, Euseb. (Trans.)—Anc't Acc'ts of India and China. (Fr. Arab.)	8vo.	Lond.	1733
Rendell, E. D.—Antediluvian History; and Narrative of the Flood	12o.	Bost.	1851
Repertory of Patent Inventions. Vols. 16–24. [*Continued.*] .	8vo.	Lond.	1850–55
Report, (12th Annual,) of Board of Education, N. Y. . .	8vo.	N. Y.	1854
——— of the Board of Education, N. Y. 1854 . .	8vo.	N. Y.	1855
——— ——— British Association, 20th Meeting . . .	8vo.	Lond.	1851
——— 21st Meeting . . .	8vo.	Lond.	1852
——— 22d Meeting . . .	8vo.	Lond.	1853
——— 23d Meeting . . .	8vo.	Lond.	1854
——— First, of the Commissioners for the Exhibition of 1851 .	R. 8vo.	Lond.	1852
*——— of the Commissioners of Patents for 1844 . .	8vo.	Wash.	1845
*——— for 1845 . . .	8vo.	Wash.	1846
——— for 1849. Pts. 1 and 2	8vo.	Wash.	1850
——— for 1850. Part 1 . . .	8vo.	Wash.	1851
——— for 1851. 2 v. .	8vo.	Wash.	1852
——— for 1852. 2 v. . .	8vo.	Wash.	1853
——— for 1853. 2 v. .	8vo.	Wash.	1854
——— for 1854. 2 v. . .	8vo.	Wash.	1855
——— Committee on Examining Life-Boat Models .	Fol.	Lond.	1850
*——— Invasion of Washington City . .	8vo.	Wash.	1814
*——— Explor. & Sur. for R. R. fr. Miss. R. to Pacific Ocean. V. 1	4to.	Wash.	1855
——— Governors of the Alms-House, N. Y., for 1853 .	8vo.	N. Y.	1854
——— for 1854 .	8vo.	N. Y.	1855
——— Lieut. Col. J. D. Graham, on the Mexican Boundary .	8vo.	Wash.	1852
——— The N. Y. State Engineer and Surveyor on Canals .	8vo.	Albany.	1851
——— on Railroads .	8vo.	Albany.	1851
——— Officers of the Light-House Board . .	8vo.	Wash.	1852
——— Prison Association of New York . . .	8vo.	N. Y.	1847
——— Proceed. at Trial of Am. Print Works *vs.* C. W. Lawrence	8vo.	N. Y.	1852
——— Secretary of State on Commercial Regulations .	8vo.	Wash.	1853
——— Treasury on Com. and Navig. for 1849	8vo.	Wash.	1850
——— &c. for 1850 . .	8vo.	Wash.	1851
——— for 1851 .	8vo.	Wash.	1852
——— for 1852 . .	8vo.	Wash.	1853
——— for 1853 .	8vo.	Wash.	1854
——— for 1854 . .	8vo.	Wash.	1855

Report of the Secretary of Treasury on Finances . .	8vo. Wash.	1853
———————————— the Finances . .	8vo. Wash.	1854
——— Regents of Smithsonian Institute for 1852 .	8vo. Wash.	1852
———————————— for 1853 . .	8vo. Wash.	1854
———————————— for 1854 .	8vo. Wash.	1855
——— Regents of the State University . . .	8vo. Albany.	1852
——— Sanitary Commission of Massachusetts . .	8vo. Bost.	1850
——— Senate Committee on Claims against Mexico . .	8vo. Wash.	1854
———————————— Mortality on Emigrant Ships	8vo. Wash.	1854
——— Superintendent of the Census for Dec. 1, 1851–2 .	8vo. Wash.	1853
———————————— Coast Survey for 1851. 8vo. & atlas	4to. Wash.	1852
———————————— for 1852 . .	4to. Wash.	1852
———————————— for 1853 .	4to. Wash.	1854
———————————— for 1854 . .	4to. Wash.	1855
——— Sup't of N. Y. State Common Schools . .	8vo. Albany.	1845
——— on the Poor and Insane of Rhode Island . . .	8vo. Prov.	1851
——— Principal Fisheries of American Seas . .	8vo. Wash.	1853
——— State of the Finances, Jan. 1, 1853 . . .	8vo. Wash.	1853
——— (Parliamentary) from the Select Com. on Commerce with China	Fol. Lond.	1847
——— ——— of Com. on Laws respecting Friendly Societies	Fol. Lond.	1825
——— ——— on the Eleventh French Exposition of Industry	Fol. Lond.	1849
Reports (7th, 8th, & 9th) of the American Institute, 1849–51 .	8vo. Albany.	1849–51
——— of the New York Deaf and Dumb Institution . .	8vo. N. Y.	1838–46
——— ——— Prot. Epis. Church Missionary Society . .	12o. N. Y.	1845–54
——— (Parliamentary) on Friendly Societies . . .	Fol. Lond.	1848–9–50
——— ——— Printed Papers, 1837 and 1853 . .	Fol. Lond.	1837–53
Restoration of Belief; I. Christianity in Relation to its Antagonists	12o. Phil.	1853
Retrospective Review. Vol. 1	8vo. Lond.	1853
Review, by a Layman, of "New Themes for the Clergy" .	12o. Phil.	1852
——— of Capt. B. Hall's Travels in America . . .	8vo. Lond.	1830
*Revised Statutes of the State of New York. 2 v. . .	8vo. Albany.	1852
Resources of the City of New York Municipal Government .	8vo. N. Y.	1827
Reumont, Alf. de—The Carafas of Maddaloni. (Fr. Ger.) .	16o. Lond.	1854
*Révolutions de Paris. Vols. 1–10, 12–18	8vo. Paris.	1790–3
Revue des Deux Mondes, 1849–53. 20 v. [*Continued.*] .	8vo. Paris.	1849–53
——— de Paris, 1851–4. 7 v. [*Continued.*] . . .	8vo. Paris.	1851–54
——— des Romans des plus Célèbres Romanciers. 2 v. .	8vo. Paris.	1836
Reynolds, E. W.—Our Campaign; or, Thoughts on the Course of Life	12o. Bost.	1851
——— Josh.—Literary Works. 2 v.	16o. Lond.	1852
——— J. H.—Address on Exploring Expedition to the Pacific .	8vo. N. Y.	1836
Rhind, W. G.—Six Days of Creation	12o. Phil.	1855
Rhode Island Educational Magazine. Vol. 1, 1852 . . .	8vo. Prov.	1852
Rice, Geo. E., and Wainwright (J. H.)—Ephemera . .	16o. Bost.	1852
Richard Cœur de Lion. See *Hawks, F. L.*		
Richards, Geo. K.—Population and Capital	8vo. Lond.	1854
——— Maria T.—Life in Judea	12o. Phil.	[1854]
——— Wm. C.—A Day in the Crystal Palace . . .	12o. N. Y.	1853
Richardson on the Horse. See *Saxton's Rural H. B.*		
——— ——— Hog. " " " "		
——— ——— Honey Bee. " " "		

Richardson's Pests of the Farm. See *Saxton's Rural H. B.*
———— Domestic Fowls. " " "
———— Capt.—Horsemanship; or, The Art of Riding, &c. . 8vo. Lond. 1853
———— Jas.—Mission to Central Africa in 1850–1. 2 v. . 8vo. Lond. 1853
———— Sir John—Arctic Searching Expedition. 2 v. . . 8vo. Lond. 1851
———— —— The Same . . . . . . 12o. N. Y. 1852
———— M. A.—Borderer's Table-Book; or, Hist. of the Eng. Bor. 4 v. 8vo. Newcastle. 1846
Richelieu, Card.—Life of, by Wm. Robson . . . . . 16o. Lond. 1854
———— Mazarin et la Fronde, par Capefigue. 2 v. . . 12o. Paris. 1844
Richer, Edw.—The Religion of Good Sense . . . . 16o. Belf. 1852
Rickey, Anna S.—Forest Flowers of the West. Poems . 12o. Phil. 1850
*Ricord, Phil.—Illustrations of Syphilitic Disease. (Fr. Fren.) . 4to. Phil. 1852
———— —— Letters on Syphilis. (Fr. Fren.) . . 8vo. Phil. 1852
———— F. W.—Stories of Ancient Rome . . . . . 16o. N. Y. 1852
Ridgeley, Dav.—Annals of Annapolis, 1649–1812 . . 12o. Balt. 1841
Ridner, John P.—Artist's Chromatic Hand-Book . . . 12o. N. Y. 1850
Rifle, The: Its Uses and Advantages in War . . . 8vo. Lond. 1852
Riker, Jas., Jr.—Annals of Newtown, Queen's County, N. Y. . 8vo. N. Y. 1852
Rimbault, Edw. F.—Biblio. Madrigalia of Eng. in the 16th & 17th Cen. 8vo. Lond. 1847
———— —— Little Book of Songs and Bal. fr. Ancient Music-Books 12o. Lond. 1851
*Ringgold, Cadw.—Charts of the Ports of California . . 4to. Wash. 1852
Ripley, G., and Taylor (Bayard)—Hand-Book of Lit. and the Fine Arts 12o. N. Y. 1852
Ritchie, Leitch—The Wye and its Associations . . . 8vo. Lond. 1841
Rivarol—Œuvres de . . . . 12o. Paris. 1852
Rivero, M. E., & Tschudi (Jno. J.)—Peruvian Antiquities . 8vo. N. Y. 1853
Robb, Jas. B.—On Patent Cases. 2 v. . . . . 8vo. Bost. 1854
Robbins, Chandler—History of the Old North Church, Boston . 8vo. Bost. 1852
Robert du Var—Histoire de la Classe Ouvrière. 4 v. in 2. . 8vo. Paris. 1845
Robert, Cyp.—Die Slawen der Türkei . . . . . 16o. Stuttg. 1851
Roberts, Mary—Popular History of Mollusca . . . 16o. Lond. 1851
Robertson, Jas. C.—History of the Christian Church to 590 . 8vo. Lond. 1854
———— T.—Claves de los Ejercicios conten. el Nuevo Curso de Ingles 8vo. N. Y. 1852
———— —— Nuevo Curso de Idioma Ingles . . . 8vo. N. Y. [1851]
———— Wm.—Historical Works. 6 v. . . . . 8vo. Edin. 1813
———— Wm. P.—Visit to Mexico by the West India Islands. 2 v. 12o. Lond. 1853
*Robinson, C.—Discoveries in the West until 1519 . . 8vo. Richmond. 1848
———— Henrietta—Life of, by D. Wilson . . . 12o. N. Y. 1855
———— H. N.—Mathematical Recreations . . . 8vo. Albany. 1851
———— J. H.—The Religion of Manhood . . . 12o. Bost. 1854
———— Wm. D.—Memoirs of the Mexican Revolution. 2 v. 8vo. Lond. 1821
———— —— The Same . . . . . . 8vo. Phil. 1820
Robson, Wm.—Life of Cardinal Richelieu . . . . 16o. Lond. 1854
Rochau, A. L.—Wanderings through the Cities of Italy in 1850–51. 2 v. 12o. Lond. 1853
*Rochester City Directory for 1841 & 1844–52. 6 v. . . 12o. Roch. 1840–51
Rockingham, Marq. of—Memoirs of, by Geo. Thomas. 2 v. . 8vo. Lond. 1852
Roebuck, Jno. A.—History of the Whig Ministry of 1830. 2 v. . 8vo. Lond. 1852
Roelker, Bern.—Manual for Notaries Public . . . 8vo. N. Y. 1853
Roemer, J.—Dictionary of English and French Idioms . . 12o. N. Y. 1853
———— —— Polyglot Reader. French, German, Spanish and Italian 12o. N. Y. 1855
Roger of Wendover—Flowers of History. (Fr. Lat., by Giles.) 2 v. 16o. Lond. 1849

Rogers, E. C.—Automatic Powers of the Brain	12o. Bost.	1853
—— —— Philosophy of Mysterious Agents	8vo. Bost.	1853
—— Hen.—Reason and Faith, and Miscellanies . .	12o. Bost.	1853
—— Hen. D.—Rept's, 2d, 3d, 4th, & 5th, on the Penn. Geolog. Expl.	8vo. Harrisb.	1838–41
—— Sam.—Complete Poetical Works	12o. Bost.	1854
Roget, Pet. M.—Thesaurus of English Words and Phrases. .	8vo. Lond.	1852
—— —— The Same. Edited by Sears	12o. Bost.	1854
Roland, Mad.—History of, by J. S. C. Abbott	16o. N. Y.	1851
Romance of Modern Travel—New Series	16o. Lond.	1851
Romer, Mrs.—Filia Dolorosa; Memoirs of Marie Thérèse. 2 v.	8vo. Lond.	1852
*Ronalds, Hugh.—Concise Description of Selected Apples . .	Fol. Lond.	1831
—— Edmund, and Richardson, (Thos.)—Chem. Technology. Vol. 1	8vo. Lond.	1855
*Roorbach, O. A. (Comp'r.)—Supplement to Bibliotheca Americana	8vo. N. Y.	1855
Roscoe, Thos.—Continental Tourist, (Italy, Granada, Andalusia.) 3 v.	8vo. Lond.	no date
—— Hen.—Digest of the Laws of Evidence in Criminal Cases .	8vo. Phil.	1852
—— Wm.—Life and Pontificate of Leo X. 2 v. . . .	16o. Lond.	1846
Rosenberg, C. G.—Jenny Lind in America	12o. N. Y.	1851
—— —— Life of Jenny Lind	8vo. N. Y.	1850
Ross, Joel H.—What I saw in New York	12o. Auburn.	1851
—— —— The Spirit World	18o. N. Y.	1852
Rossini, G.—Otello. (An Opera.)	8vo. Paris.	no date
—— ——Semiramide. (A Melo-drama.)	8vo. Paris.	no date
Roussell, Système Physique et Morale de la Femme. . .	16o. Paris.	1845
—— Napol.—Catholic and Protestant Nations Compared .	8vo. Bost.	1855
*Routledge's American Hand-Book through the United States .	16o. Lond.	1854
Rovings in the Pacific from 1837–49. 2 v.	8vo. Lond.	1851
Rowell, Chas. A.—Manual of Dental Economy	12o. N. Y.	1855
Rowley, Thos.—Poems	4to. Lond.	1782
Rowton, Fred.—The Debater; A New Theory of Speaking . .	12o. Lond.	1850
*Roxbury Directory, 1850	16o. Roxbury.	1850
Royle, J. F.—Culture and Commerce of Cotton in India, &c. .	8vo. Lond.	1851
*Ruding, R.—Annals of the Courage of Great Britain. 3 v. .	4to. Lond.	1840
Ruffin, Edm.—Essay on Calcareous Manures	12o. Richmond.	1852
Ruffner, H.—Fathers of the Desert; or, Monkery among Heathens. 2 v.	12o. N. Y.	1850
Ruins of Sacred and Historic Lands	16o. Lond.	1850
Ruskin, Jno.—Lectures on Architecture and Painting . .	12o. Lond.	1854
—— —— Lectures on Painting	12o. N. Y.	1854
*—— —— Stones of Venice. Vol. 1. Foundations . .	8vo. Lond.	1851
—— —— The Same	8vo. N. Y.	1851
*—— —— The Stones of Venice. Vols 2 & 3. . .	8vo. Lond.	1853
Russell, Rachel—Letters	12o. Phil.	1854
—— Wm.—American Elocutionist	18o. Boston.	1851
—— —— Orthophony; or, Cultivation of the Voice . .	12o. Boston.	1849
—— W. H.—The War, to the Death of Lord Raglan .	12o. N. Y.	1855
Russian Empire, Its Resources, &c., by a Looker-on from America .	12o. Cincin.	1856
Rutledge, Jno.—Life of. See *Flanders, Hen.*		
Rutter, J. O. N.—Human Electricity	12o. Lond.	1854
Ryan, Jno.—Preparation of Long-Line, Flax-Cotton, &c. . .	8vo. Lond.	1852
*Ryde, Edw.—Text-Book for Architects, Engineers, &c. .	8vo. Lond.	1854
Ryder, Alf. P.—Treatise on Economy of Fuel . . .	8vo. Lond.	1852

Ryland, Arthur—The Assay of Gold and Silver Wares . . 12o. Lond. 1852
Ryle, J. C.—Home Truths . . . . 16o. N. Y. 1854
Ryves, Burns—Mercurius Rusticus . . . . . 8vo. Lond. 1685

Sabine, L.—Notes on Duels and Duelling . . . . . 8vo. Bost. 1855
——— —— Report on the Principal Fisheries of the American Seas 8vo. Wash. 1853
Sacred Music . . . . 4to. Lond.
Sadler, P.—Art of Correspondence—English and French . 16o. Brux. 1850
Saemund, The Edda of; Trans. by A. S. Cottle . . . . 8vo. Bristol. 1797
Safford, Wm. H.—Life of H. Blennerhassett . . . . 12o. Cincin. 1853
Sage, Ruf. B.—Wild Scenes in Kansas and Nebraska . . 12o. Phil. 1855
Sailors' Magazine. Vols. 22–25. [*Continued.*] . . . . 8vo. N. Y. 1850–3
Saint-Ange—Derniers Guerres de la Russie contre la Turquie . 16o. Brux. 1853
Saint-Beuve, C. A.—Derniers Portraits Littéraires . . 16o. Paris. 1852
Saintine, X. B.—The Solitary of Juan Fernandez. (Fr. Fren.) . 12o. Bost. 1851
St. John, Bayle—Purple Tints of Paris. 2 v. . . . . 12o. Lond. 1854
———— —— The Same . . . . 12o. N. Y. 1854
———— —— The Turks in Europe . . . . . 12o. Lond. 1853
———— —— Village Life in Egypt. 2 v. . . . . 16o. Bost. 1853
———— Ferd.—Rambles in Germany, France, &c. . . . 12o. Lond. 1853
———— Hor.—British Conquests in India. 2 v. . . . . 12o. Lond. 1852
———— —— The Indian Archipelago. 2 v. . . . . 12o. Lond. 1853
———— Jas. A.—The Nemesis of Power . . . . . 12o. Lond. 1854
———— Sam.—Elements of Geology . . . . . 12o. N. Y. 1851
Saints, The; An Example . . . . 16o. Lond. 1852
Sakuntala; ein Indisches Schauspiel von Kalidasa. (Fr. Sanscrit.) . 16o. Stuttg. 1852
*Salem [Mass.] Directory for 1842, '46, '50, '51, '53. 5 v. . . 18o. Salem. 1842–53
Salkeld, Jos.—First Book in Spanish . . . . . 12o. N. Y. 1850
Salles, E. F. de—Histoire Générale des Races Humaines . . 16o. Paris. 1849
Sallust, C. C., Florus (L. A.), and Paterculus (C. V.) (Fr. Latin.) 16o. Lond. 1832
——— —— Opera Omnia. 2 v. See *Valpy's Delphin Classics.*
Salvandy, N. A. de—Paris, Nantes, et la Session . . . 8vo. Paris. 1832
Sampson, Ezra—Brief Remarker on the Ways of Man . . 12o. N. Y. 1855
Sand, Geo.—La Comtesse de Rudolstadt. 4 Vols. in 3 . . 24o. Brux. 1844
Sandeau, Jules—Fernand, Vaillance, Richard . . . . 16o. Paris. 1852
———— —— Madame de Sommerville . . . . 16o. Paris. 1852
———— —— Marianna . . . . 16o. Paris. 1851
Sanders, F. W.—Essays on Uses and Trusts. 2 Vols. in 1. . 8vo. Phil. 1855
Sanderson's Biography of the Signers of the Declaration . . 8vo. Phil. 1852
Sandwich Islands Notes. By a Häole . . . . . 12o. N. Y. 1854
Sandys, Wm.—Christmastide, Its History, Festivities, and Carols 12o. Lond. [1852]
——— Chas.—Consuetudines Kanciæ, Remarkable Customes of Kent 8vo. Lond. 1851
Santarem, Visc.—Americus Vespucius and his Voyages . 16o. Bost. 1850
———— —— Essai sur l'Hist. de la Cosmogra. en Moyen-age. 2 v. 8vo. Paris. 1849–52
Sargent, Epes.—Standard Speaker . . . . . . 8vo. Phil. 1852
———— —— Life and Public Services of Henry Clay . . 12o. Auburn. 1852
———— W. (Ed'r.)—Braddock's Expedition against Fort du Quesne 8vo. Phil. 1855
Sarmiente, D. F.—Civilisation et Barberie . . . . 12o. Paris. 1853
Saroni, H. J.—Musical Vade Mecum . . . . . . 12o. N. Y. 1852
Sarpent, F. S.—Private Journal. 3 v. . . . . . 12o. Lond. 1853

Sauer, M.—Geog'l and Astronom'l Expedition to Nr. Russia, 1785–94	4to. Lond.	1802
Saulcy, F. de—Journey Round the Dead Sea, &c. 2 v. . .	8vo. Lond.	1853
——— —— The Same. 2 v.	12o. Phil.	1854
Saunders, F.—Memories of the Great Metropolis; or, London in 1851	12o. N. Y.	1852
——— —— Salad for the Solitary	12o. N. Y.	1853
Savarin, B.—Physiology of Taste. (Fr. Fren.) . . .	12o. Phil.	1854
Sawyer, Mrs. C. M.—Memoir of Mrs. J. H. Scott, with her Poems .	12o. Bost.	1853
——— L. A.—Elements of Biblical Interpretation . .	12o. N. Haven.	1836
——— —— Organic Christianity	12o. Bost.	1854
——— Thos. J.—Memoir of Rev. Stephen R. Smith . .	12o. Bost.	1852
——— —— and Wescott, Isaac—Discussion on Universalism .	12o. N. Y.	1854
Sayous, A.—Histoire de la Littérature Française. 2 v. . .	8vo. Paris.	1853
Sax, J. B.—The Organic Laws	16o. N. Y.	1851
Saxe, Jno. G.—Poems	12o. Bost.	1852
Saxton, L. C.—Fall of Poland. 2 v.	12o. N. Y.	1851
Saxton's Rural Hand-Books. 1st and 2d Series. 2 v. . .	12o. N. Y.	1852

Vol. 1. Richardson on the Horse.
" " " Hog.
" " " Honey Bee.
" Pests of the Farm.
" Domestic Fowls.
Milburn on the Cow.
Vol. 2. Every Lady her Own Flower Gardener.
Skinner's Elements of Agriculture.
Browne's Bird Fancier.
Dana's Essay on Manures.
Fessenden's American Kitchen Gardener.
American Rose Culturist.

Scalpel, The; Edited by Edw. H. Dixon. Vols. 1–4 in 2 Vols. .	8vo. N. Y.	1849–52
Scenes and Adventures in Spain from 1835–40. 3 v. . .	8vo. Lond.	1845
——— The Same	18o. Phil.	1846
——— From Christian History	12o. Bost.	1852
Schaff, Phil.—Amerika, Politischen, Socialen, etc. . . .	8vo. Berlin.	1854
——— —— America; Political, Social and Religious . .	12o. N. Y.	1855
——— —— History of the Apostolic Church. (Fr. Ger.) . .	8vo. N. Y.	1853
———. —— Life and Labors of St. Augustine. (Fr. Ger.) .	12. N. Y.	1854
Schenck, Pet. A.—Gardener's Text-Book	18o. Bost.	1851
Schiefferdecker, C. C.—Treatment of Children by Water Cure .	12o. Phil.	1852
Schiller, Fred.—Historical Dramas	16o. Lond.	1850
——— —— Philosophic and Æsthetic Letters . .	12o. Lond.	1845
——— —— Poems. (Fr. Ger. by E. A. Bowring.) . .	16o. Lond.	1851
——— —— Works. Vol. 2.	16o. Lond.	1847
Schlegel, Aug. W.—Lectures on Dramatic Art and Literature .	16o. Lond.	1846
Schlesinger, Max—Saunterings in and about London . .	12o. Lond.	1853
——— —— The War in Hungary, 1848–9. 2 v. .	12o. Lond.	1850
Schliermacher, A. A. E.—Bib. Sys. d. gesamm. Wissenchafts Kunde. 2 v.	8vo. Braunsch'g.	1852
——— F.—Outline of the Study of Theology . .	12o. Edin.	1850
Schmitz, Leonh.—Elementary Latin Grammar and Exercises .	16o. Phil.	1852
——— —— History of Greece	12o. Lond.	1851
——— —— The Same	12o. N. Y.	1851
Schnitzler, J. H.—Statistique générale de la France. 4 v. .	8vo. Paris.	1846
Schoedler, Fred.—Book of Nature. 2 v.	8vo. Lond.	1851

Title	Size	Place	Date
Schœlcher, V.—Histoire des Crimes du 2d Décembre . .	8vo.	Lond.	1852
Schonberg, Erich—Travels in India and Kashmir. 2 v. . .	12o.	Lond.	1853
School Journal, and Vermont Agriculturist. Vol. 3. . .	8vo.	Windsor.	1849–50
Schoolcraft, Hen. R.—American Indians; their History, &c. .	8vo.	Buffalo.	1851
——— —— Expedition to the Sources of the Mississippi, renewed	8vo.	Phil.	1855
*——— —— Indian Tribes of the United States. Vols. 1–5 .	4to.	Phil.	1851–5
——— —— Personal Memoirs of a Residence among Indians	8vo.	Phil.	1851
——— —— View of the Lead Mines of Missouri . .	8vo.	N. Y.	1819
Schouw, J. F.—The Earth, Plants, and Man. . . .	16o.	Lond.	1852
Schubert, F.—Quarante Melodies	8vo.	Paris.	no date
Schwarz, Jos.—Geography and Hist. Sketch of Palestine. (Fr. Ger.)	8vo.	Phil.	1850
*Science and Mechanism illustrated in N. Y. Exhibition . .	4to.	N. Y.	1854
——— Revived; or, the Vision of Alfred. A Poem . .	4to.	Lond.	1802
Scoffern, J.—The Chemistry of Gold	16o.	Lond.	no date
——— —— Projectile Weapons and Explosive Compounds .	16o.	Lond.	1852
Scoresby, Wm.—Magnetical Investigations. Vol. 2 . .	8vo.	Lond.	1852
——— —— Records of the Adventurous Life of . .	8vo.	Lond.	1851
Scotia's Bards. Compiled by Peter Carter	8vo.	N. Y.	1854
Scott, Chas.—Analogy of Ancient Craft Masonry to Religion .	8vo.	Phil.	1850
—— Mrs. J. H.—Memoir and Poems of, by Mrs. C. M. Sawyer . .	12o.	Bost.	1853
—— R.—Practical Cotton Spinner and Manufacturer's Companion	8vo.	Lond.	1851
—— Thos. (Trans.)—Articles of the Synod of Dort . .	12o.	Utica.	1831
—— Sir Walter. See *Waverley Poetry.*			
—— —— Lay of the Last Minstrel	16o.	N. Y.	1811
—— —— Life of, by Donald MacLeod	12o.	N. Y.	1852
—— —— ——— by J. Y. Lockhart	12o.	Edinb.	1853
—— —— Poetical Works	8vo.	Phil.	1851
—— Winfield—Infantry Tactics. 3 v.	18o.	N. Y.	1854
—— —— Life of. See *Headley, J. T.*			
—— —— Life and Public Services	12o.	Phil.	1852
—— W. A.—Daniel a Model for Young Men	8vo.	N. Y.	1854
*—— W. B.—Ornamental Designs for Silver and Gold Work .	4to.	Edin.	no date
Scratchley, Arthur—Life Assurance Societies & Sav'gs Banks. Part 1.	8vo.	Lond.	1851
*Scriptorum Græcorum Bibliotheca. Vols. 1–36 . . .	8vo.	Paris.	1839–51

Vol. 1. Homeri Carmina, et Cycli Epici Reliquiæ.
2. Part 1. Platonis Opera.
Part 2. Aristophanis Comœdiæ et Perditarum Fragmenta.
Menandri et Philemonis Fragmenta.
3. Xenophontis Scripta quæ Supersunt.
4. Polybii Historiarum Reliquiæ.
5. Appiani Romanorum Historiarum quæ Supersunt.
6. Plutarchi Chæronensis Scripta Moralia. Vol. 1. (Works, vol. 3.)
7. Hesiodi Carmina.
8. Luciani Samosatensis Opera.
9. Thucydidis Historia Belli Peloponnesiaci
10. Theophrasti Characteres.
11. Fragmenta Historicorum Græcorum. Vol. 1.
12. Plutarchi Scripta Moralia. Vol. 2. (Works, vol. 3.)
13. Æschyli et Sophoclis Tragædiæ et Fragmenta.
14. Diodori Siculi Bibliotheca. Vol. 1.
15. Scholia Græca in Aristophanem.
16. Demosthenis Opera.
17. Diodori Siculi Bibliotheca. Vol. 2.
18. Euripidis Fabulæ.
19. Herodoti Halicarnassensis Historiarum Libri IX.

*Scriptorum Græcorum Bibliotheca (continued).

Vol. 20. Pausaniæ Descriptio Græciæ.
21. Flavii Josephi Opera. Vol. 1.
22. Poetæ Bucolici et Didactici.
23. Oratores Attici; Isocratis Orationes et Epistolæ.
24. Plutarchi Vitæ. Vol. 1. (Works, vol. 1.)
25. Euripidis Perditarum Fabularum Perdita.
26. Arrianus Anabasis et Indica.
27. Flavii Josephi Opera. Vol. 2.
28. Plutarchi Vitæ. Vol. 2. (Works, vol. 3.)
29. Fragmenta Historicorum Græcorum. Vol. 2.
30. Aristotelis Opera Omnia. Vol. 1.
31. Fragmenta Historicorum Græcorum. Vol. 3.
32. Philostratorum, Eunapii, Homerii, Opera.
33. Scholia in Theocritum, Nicandorum, et Oppiannum.
34. Diogenis Lærtii Vitæ Philosophorum.
35. Aristotelis Opera Omnia. Vol. 2.
36. Fragmenta Historicorum Græcorum. Vol. 4.

Scrivinor, Harry—History of the Iron Trade from the Earliest Records 8vo. Lond. 1854
Scudo, P.—Critique et Littérature Musicales . . . . 16o. Paris. 1852
Sealsfield, Chas.—The Cabin-Book; or, National Characteristics 8vo. Lond. 1852
——— —— Gesammelte Werke. 15 vols. in 7. . . 16o. Stuttg't. 1845–7
Seaman, E. C.—Essays on the Progress of Nations . . 8vo. N. Y. 1852
Searle, J.—Memoirs of Ebenezer Elliott . . . . . 8vo. Lond. 1852
Sears, Robt. (Ed'r.)—Pictorial History of China and India . 8vo. N. Y. 1853
*Secret Journal of the Acts and Proceedings of Congress. 4 v. . 8vo. Bost. 1820–1
Sedgwick, Adam—Discourse on the Studies of Cambridge University 8vo. Camb. (E.) 1850
——— Jas.—The Law of Storms . . . . . . 8vo. Lond. 1852
——— Theo.—Treatise on the Measure of Damages . . 8vo. N. Y. 1852
Seeman, B.—Voyage of H. M. S. Herald, 1845–51. 2 v. . . 8vo. Lond. 1853
Ségur, Le Comte de—Histoire Ancienne. 2 v. . . . 16o. Paris. 1847
——— —— Histoire Romaine. 2 v. . . . . . 16o. Paris. 1850
Seixas, Jas.—Manual Hebrew Grammar . . . . 8vo. Phil. 1852
*Seizinger, J. G.—Bibliothekstechnik . . . . . 8vo. Leipzig. 1855
Selections from the Popular Poetry of the Hindoos . . 12o. Lond. 1814
Selection of Eulogies on Adams and Jefferson . . . . 8vo. Hartf. 1826
Selwyn, Geo.—See *Jesse, J. H.*
Semmes, Raphael—Campaign of General Scott . . . 12o. Cincin. 1852
——— —— Service Afloat and Ashore in the Mexican War . 8vo. Cincin. 1851
Senior, N. W.—Four Lectures on Political Economy . . 8vo. Lond. 1852
*Seoane's Neuman & Baretti's Spanish Dictionary, by Velazquez 8vo. N. Y. 1852
*Sermons before the Gospel Propagation Society. 20 v. . . 4to. Lond. 1702–1829
*Seventh Census of the United States . . . . . 4to. Wash. 1853
Seven Wonders of the World and their Associations . . 16o. Lond. 1853
Sévigné, Mdme. de—Letters of, Edited by Mrs. S. J. Hale . 12o. N. Y. 1856
Seward, Wm. H.—Life of, with Selections from his Works . . 12o. N. Y. 1855
——— —— Works, Edited by Geo. E. Baker. 3 v. . . 8vo. N. Y. 1853
Sewell, Jno.—Elementary Treatise on Steam and Locomotion. Vol. 1 16o. Lond. 1852
——— Miss—Journal Kept during a Summer Tour . . 12o. N. Y. 1852
Sexagenary; or, Reminiscences of the American Revolution . 12o. Albany. 1833
Sforza, Frances—Life and Times of, by Wm. P. Urquhart. 2 v. . 8vo. Lond 1852
*Shakspeare, Wm.—Dramatic Works. 10 v. . . . . 18o. Chiswick. 1826
——— —— ——————— Lansdowne Ed. . . 8vo. Lond. 1852
——— —— Dramatische Werke. (Fr. Eng.) 12 v. in 6. 8vo. Berlin. 1843

Title	Size / Place	Date
*Shakspeare, Wm.—Notes and Emendations to, by J. Payne Collier	8vo. Lond.	1853
——— ——— The Same	12o. N. Y.	1853
——— ——— Seven Ages of Man. Illustrated by Mulready	8vo. Lond.	1838
——— ——— Works	8vo. Phil.	1852
——— ——— Works, amended after J. P. Collier's Folio. 8 v.	16o. N. Y.	1853
——— ——— The Same. 2 v.	8vo. N. Y.	1853
——— ——— Works, Edited by H. N. Hudson. Vols. 1–6	12o. Bost.	1852
——— Society Publications. Vols. 37–41 . . .	8vo. Lond.	1848–50

Vol. 37. Moral Play of Wit and Science, and Early Poetical Miscellanies.
" 38. Life of Inigo Jones, by Peter Cunningham; Remarks, by Planché.
" 39. Shakspeare Society's Papers. Vol. 4.
Vols. 40, 41. Works entered at Stationers' Office, from 1577–87. 2 v.

Title	Size / Place	Date
Sharpe's London Journal. Vols. 1–15	8vo. Lond.	1845–51
——— The Same. New Series. Vols. 2–4. [*Continued.*] .	8vo. Lond.	1853–4
Shaw, Thos.—Travels in Barbary and the Levant . . .	Fol. Oxford.	1738
——— Thos. B.—Outlines of English Literature . . .	12o. Phil.	1852
Shea, Jno. G.—Discovery and Exploration of the Mississippi Valley	8vo. N. Y.	1852
Shepard, Thos.—Life of, by Jno. A. Albro	12o. Bost.	1847
Sherburne, J. H.—Life and Character of John Paul Jones . .	8vo. N. Y.	1851
Sherwood, Adiel.—Gazetteer of the State of Georgia . .	16o. Charleston.	1827
Sheridan, Rich. B.—Dramatic Works and Memoir . . .	16o. Lond.	1852
——— ——— Memoirs of, by Thos. Moore. 2 v. . .	12o. N. Y.	1853
——— Thos.—Lectures on the Art of Reading. 2 v. . .	8vo. Lond.	1775
Sherrill, Hunting—Homœopathic Practice of Medicine . .	16o. N. Y.	1854
Shew, Joel—Consumption: Its Prevention and Cure by Water .	8vo. N. Y.	1850
Shier, John—Directions for Testing Cane Juice . . .	12o. Lond.	1851
Shiel, R. L.—Sketches of the Irish Bar. 2 v.	12o. N. Y.	1854
Shillaber, B. P.—Rhymes with Reason and Without . .	16o. Bost.	1853
Shipp, B.—Progress of Freedom, and other Poems . . .	12o. N. Y.	1852
Shoberl, Fred.—Persecutions of Popery. 2 v.	8vo. Lond.	1844
Short Narrative of the Boston Massacre, 1770	8vo. N. Y.	1849
Shortland, Edw.—Southern Districts of New Zealand . .	8vo. Lond.	1851
Shuttleworth, Jas. K.—Public Education and Future Policy .	8vo. Lond.	1853
Sibley, J. L.—History of the Town of Union, Me. . .	12o. Bost.	1851
Sickel, J.—Spectacles; their Uses and Abuses. (Fr. Fren.) .	8vo. Bost.	1850
Sickness and Health of the People of Bleaburn . . .	16o. Bost.	1853
Sidney, Algernon—Life of, by G. Van Santvoord . . .	12o. N. Y.	1851
——— Sam.—Three Colonies of Australia . . .	8vo. Lond.	1852
Sigourney, Mrs. L. H.—Examples of Life and Death . .	12o. N. Y.	1852
——— ——— Olive Leaves	16o. N. Y.	1852
——— ——— Past Meridian	12o. N. Y.	1854
——— ——— The Western Home, and other Poems .	12o. Phil.	1854
Silliman, Benj.—Visit to Europe in 1851. 2 v.	12o. N. Y.	1853
——— ——— The Same. 2 v.	12o. N. Y.	1854
——— ——— (Ed'r.) See *American Journal of Science and Arts.*		
*——— B. Jr., & Goodrich (C. R.)—The World of Science, Art, & Ind'y	4to. N. Y.	1854
Silvestre, J. B.—Universal Palæography. 2 v.	8vo. Lond.	1850
Simmonds, P. S.—Sir John Franklin, and the Arctic Regions .	16o. Lond.	1851
Simmons, Jas. W.—The Greek Girl; a Tale, in two Cantos . .	16o. Bost.	1852
Simms, J. R.—Trappers of New York	12o. Albany.	1851

Simms, Wm. G.—History of South Carolina	12o.	Charleston.	1840
——— Poems. 2 v.	12o.	N. Y.	1853
Simon, Jno.—General Pathology	8vo.	Phil.	1852
——— T. C.—Scientific Certainties of Planetary Life	16o.	Lond.	1855
Simpson, Jas.—Paris after Waterloo	12o.	Edin.	1853
——— Jas. H.—Journal of a Military Reconnaissance in N. Mexico	8vo.	Phil.	1852
——— Jas. Y.—Homœopathy	8vo.	Phil.	1854
——— L. F.—Literature of Italy to the Death of Boccaccio	8vo.	Lond.	1851
Sims, Rich.—Hand-Book to the British Museum Library	16o.	Lond.	1854
——— Index to Pedigrees in the Herald. Visitation of Brit. Mus.	8vo.	Lond.	1849
Sinclair, Catharine—Kaleidoscope of Anecdotes and Aphorisms	8vo.	Lond.	1851
——— Shetland and the Shetlanders	12o.	N. Y.	1840
——— Sir John—Statistical Account of Scotland. 21 v.	8vo.	Edin.	1791–9
Singer, Sam. W.—Text of Shakspeare Vindicated, from J. P. Collier	8vo.	Lond.	1853
Sismondi, J. C. L. S. de—The French under the Merovingians. (Fr. Fren.)	8vo.	Lond.	1850
Sitgreaves, Capt. L.—Expedition down the Zuni and Colorado	8vo.	Wash.	1853
Skelton, John—Poetical Works. 2 v.	8vo.	Lond.	1843
Sketch of Old England, by a New England Man. 2 v.	12o.	N. Y.	1822
Sketches of Boston, Past and Present, and of its Vicinity	16o.	Bost.	1851
——— Canadian Life, Lay and Ecclesiastical	12o.	Lond.	1849
——— Newport and its Vicinity	12o.	N. Y.	1842
Skene, Jas. H.—The Three Eras of Ottoman History	8vo.	Lond.	1851
Sketch of the Resources of the City of New York	8vo.	N. Y.	1827
Skinner's Elements of Agriculture. See *Saxton's Rural Hand-Books.*			
Skinner, J. S. (Ed'r)—Monthly Journal of Agriculture. Vols. 1–3	8vo.	N. Y.	1845–8
Slack, H. J.—Ministry of the Beautiful	12o.	Phil.	1850
Sleigh, Lt. Col.—Pine Forests, and Hacmatack Clearings	8vo.	Lond.	1853
Sloane, Hans—Voyage to and Natural History of Jamaica. 2 v.	Fol.	Lond.	1707–25
*Sloan, Law.—The Model Architect. A Series of Designs. Vol. 1	4to.	Phil.	
Small Books on Great Subjects. Vols. 19–22.	16o.	Lond.	1851–4
State of Man Subsequent to Christianity. Parts 1–4.			
Smeaton, A. C.—Builder's Pocket Companion	12o.	Phil.	1850
Smee, Alf.—Elements of Electro-Metallurgy	12o.	N. Y.	1852
——— Process of Thought, adapted to Words and Language	8vo.	Lond.	1851
Smith, Albert.—Story of Mt. Blanc	12o.	N. Y.	1853
——— Alex.—Poems	16o.	Bost.	1853
——— Chas. H.—Natural History of the Human Species	12o.	Bost.	1851
——— Chas. H. J.—Parks and Pleasure Grounds	12o.	Lond.	1852
——— Chas. M.—Curiosities of London Life	12o.	Lond.	1853
——— Dav.—Dyer's Instructor, and art of Padding	12o.	Phil.	1853
——— Edm. R.—The Araucanians; or, Tribes of Southern Chili	12o.	N. Y.	1855
——— Mrs. E. O.—Old New York. A Tragedy	12o.	N. Y.	1853
——— Woman and her Needs	12o.	N. Y.	1851
——— E. P.—Manual of Political Economy	12o.	N. Y.	1853
——— E. V.—History of Newburyport	8vo.	Nbpt.	1854
——— Fra. G.—Domestic Medicine, Surgery, &c.	8vo.	Phil.	1851
——— Geo.—Lewchew and the Lewchewans	16o.	Lond.	1853
——— Gerrit—Speeches in Congress	12o.	N. Y.	1855
——— Hor. & Jas.—Rejected Addresses	16o.	Bost.	1851
——— J.—Trade and Travels in the Gulph of Guinea	12o.	Lond.	1851

Smith, Jas.—Lights and Shadows of Artist Life . . . 12o. Lond. 1854
——— Jas. E.—Tour on the Continent in 1786–7. 3 v. . 8vo. Lond. 1793
——— Jno.—Fruits and Farinacea the food of Man . . 12o. N. Y. 1854
——— Jno. A.—Functions of the Nervous System . . 8vo. N. Y. 1840
——— —— Prelections on Sub. con. with Moral and Physical Science 12o. N. Y. 1853
——— J. C.—Harper's Statistical Gazetteer of the World . 8vo. N. Y. 1855
——— J. J.—Designs for Monuments and Mural Tablets . . 4to. N. Y. 1846
——— J. P.—Romantic Incidents in the Lives of English Queens 12o. N. Y. 1853
——— Jno. Pye—Memoirs of, by Jno. Medway . . . 8vo. Lond. 1853
——— John Storrs—Social Aspects . . . . . 12o. Lond. 1850
——— Jno. Toulmin—Local Self-Government and Centralization . 8vo. Lond. 1851
——— J. V. C.—Pilgrimage to Egypt . . . . . 12o. Bost. 1852
——— —— Turkey and the Turks . . . . . 12o. Bost. 1854
——— Jno. W.—Compendium of Mercantile Law . . 8vo. N. Y. 1855
——— Jos.—Old Redstone ; or, Western Presbyterianism . . 8vo. Phil. 1854
——— R. A.—Philadelphia as It Is, in 1852 . . . 12o. Phil. 1852
——— R. S.—Manual of Topographical Drawing . . . 8vo. N. Y. 1854
——— Sam. B.—Application of Electro-Magnetism . . 8vo. N. Y. 1850–53
——— Seba.—New Elements of Geometry . . . . . 8vo. N. Y. 1850
——— Steph. R.—Memoir of, by Thos. J. Sawyer . . 12o. Bost. 1852
——— Sydney—Memoir of, by Lady Holland. 2 v. . . 12o. N. Y. 1855
——— —— Selections from his Writings. Vol. 1. . . 16o. Lond. 1854
——— Thos.—Five Years' Residence at Nepaul. 2 v. . . 12o. Lond. 1852
——— Thos. L.—Elements of the Laws in force in the U. S. . 12o. Phil. 1853
——— Wm.—Obituary of, by Ellis. See *Camden Soc. Publications.*
——— —— A History of Greece . . . . . 12o. N. Y. & Bst. 1854
*——— —— New Classical Dictionary of Biography, Mythology, &c. 8vo. Lond. 1850
*——— —— (Ed'r.)—Dictionary of Greek and Roman Geography. 2 v. 8vo. Bost. 1854
——— W. H.—Canada; Past, Present, and Future. 2 v. . . 8vo. Toronto. 1851
——— Wm. R.—Observations on Wisconsin Territory . . 12o. Phil. 1838
*Smithsonian Contributions to Knowledge. Vols. 2–7 . . 4to. Wash. 1851–5
Smucker, S. M.—Court and Reign of Catherine II. of Russia . 12o. N. Y. 1855
Smyth, Thos.—The Unity of the Human Races . . . 12o. Edin. 1851
——— Wm. H.—The Mediterranean . . . . . 8vo. Lond. 1854
——— W. W.—A Year with the Turks . . . . . 12o. Lond. 1854
Snelgrave, Wm.—New Account of Guinea and the Slave Trade. 8vo. Lond. 1734
Snell, D. W.—Manager's Assistant; or Treatise on Cotton Manufacture 16o. Bost. 1850
Société Linnéenne de Paris—Histoire et Mémoires. Vol. 3 . 8vo. Paris. 1825
——— (La) et les Governments de l'Europe. Vol. 4 . . 8vo. Paris. 1849
Solis Ant. de—Historia de la Conquista de Mexico. 5 v. . 16o. Madrid. 1798
——— —— The Same . . . . 8vo. Paris. 1844
Some Account of Domestic Architecture in Eng. fr. Edw. I. to Rich. III. 8vo. Oxford. 1853
Songs, Madrigals, and Sonnets . . . . 16o. Lond. 1849
Sons of the Sires—A History of the American Party . . 16o. Phil. 1855
Sontag, Henriette—Life; with Interesting Sketches . . 8vo. N. Y. 1852
Sophocles. See *Scriptorum Græcorum Bibliotheca.* Vol. 13.
——— Tragedies. Oxford Translation . . . 16o. Lond. 1849
Sotheby, W.—Tour through Parts of Wales; and Sonnets . 4to. Lond. 1794
South, J. F.—Household Surgery . . . . . . 12o. Phil. 1850
Southern Literary Messenger. Vols 16–18. [*Continued.*] . 8vo. Richmd. 1850–52

Southern Presbyterian Review. Vol. 6	8vo.	Colum.	'52 & 53
——— Quarterly Review. Vols. 17–26. [*Continued.*]	8vo.	Cha'stn.	1850–54
Southey, C. C. (Ed'r.)—Life and Correspondence of Robert Southey	8vo.	N. Y.	1850
——— Robert—Common-Place Book. Vol. 2	8vo.	N. Y.	1850
——— —— Letters during a Residence in Spain and Portugal	8vo.	Bristol.	1799
——— —— Life of, by Chas. T. Browne	16o.	Lond.	1854
——— Thos.—Rise, Progress, &c., of Colonial Wools	8vo.	Lond.	1852
Souvestre, Emile—Les Derniers Paysans. 2 v.	16o.	Paris.	1851
Sowerby, Hen.—Popular Mineralogy	16o.	Lond.	1850
Soyer, A.—Pantropheon; or, History of Food	8vo.	Lond.	1853
Spalding, J. W.—Japan and Around the World	12o.	N. Y.	1855
——— Wm.—History of English Literature	12o.	N. Y.	1853
Sparks, Jared—Letters to Lord Mahon	8vo.	Bost.	1852
——— —— Letters on the Protestant Episcopal Church	8vo.	Balt.	1820
——— —— Life of George Washington. Abridged	12o.	Auburn.	1851
——— —— Remarks on a "Reprint of Letters, &c."	8vo.	Bost.	1853
——— —— Reply to the Strictures of Lord Mahon	8vo.	Camb.	1852
——— —— (Ed'r.)—Correspondence of the American Revolution. 4 v.	8vo.	Bost.	1853
Spectator; with Biographical Notice of Contributors	8vo.	Lond.	1852
*——— a Weekly Journal. Vols. 24, 25. [*Continued.*]	Fol.	Lond.	1851–2
Speed, Jno.—Historie of Great Britaine	Fol.	Lond.	1623
Speeches of the Governors of the State of New York, 1777–1825	8vo.	Albany.	1825
Spencer, Capt.—Turkey, Russia, the Black Sea, &c.	12o.	Lond.	1854
——— Chas. C.—Art of Playing the Piano Forte	16o.	Lond.	1851
——— Edmund—Tour of Inquiry through France and Italy. 2 v.	12o.	Lond.	1853
——— Geo.—English Grammar on Synthetical Principles	12o.	N. Y.	1851
——— Herbert—Social Statics; or, Human Happiness	8vo.	Lond.	1851
——— Ich. S.—A Pastor's Sketches	12o.	N. Y.	1850
——— —— The Same	12o.	N. Y.	1852
——— —— The Same. Second Series	12o.	N. Y.	1853
——— —— Sermons. With Life, by Sherwood. 2 v.	12o.	N. Y.	1855
——— Thos.—Conversion; its Theory and Process	12o.	N. Y.	1854
——— T.—Life and Discourses	12o.	N. Y.	1855
Spiers and Surenne's French and English Dictionary	8vo.	N. Y.	1852
Spineto, Marquis—Elements of Hieroglyphics, and Egyptian Antiquities	8vo.	Lond.	1845
Spirit of Missions. Vols. 15–19. [*Continued.*]	8vo.	N. Y.	1850–54
*——— the Times. Vols. 17 and 24. [*Continued.*]	Fol.	N. Y.	1845–55
——— Rappings; or, Life and Times of old Billy McConnel	8vo.	Cincin.	1851
Spiritual Telegraph, Edited by S. B. Brittan. Vols. 1–8	12o.	N. Y.	1853–5
——— Visitors. By the author of "Musings of Invalid"	12o.	N. Y.	1854
Spix, J. B. and Martius (C. F. P.)—Travels in Brazil. 1817–20. 2 v.	8vo.	Lond.	1824
Spon, Isaac—History of the City and State of Geneva	Fol.	Lond.	1687
Spooner, L.—Essay on the Trial by Jury	8vo.	Bost.	1852
——— S.—Anecdotes of Painters, Engravers, Sculptors, &c. 3 v.	16o.	N. Y.	1853
*——— —— Biograph. and Critical Dict. of Painters, Sculptors, &c.	8vo.	N. Y.	1853
*Sporting Magazine, for 1853. [*Continued.*]	8vo.	Lond.	1853
Sportsman and his Dog; or, Hints on Sporting	12o.	Lond.	1850
Spottiswoode, J.—Hist. of the Ch. of Scotl'd, fr. A.D. 203 to Jas. VI. 3 v.	8vo.	Edin.	1851
Sprague, Wm. B.—Visits to European Celebrities	12o.	Bost.	1855
Spring, Gard.—Contrast between Good and Bad Men. 2 v.	8vo.	N. Y.	1855

Title	Size	Place	Date
Spring, Gard.—First Things. 2 v.	8vo.	N. Y.	1851
——— ——— The Glory of Christ. 2 v.	8vo.	N. Y.	1852
Springer, Jno. S.—Forest Life and Forest Trees	12o.	N. Y.	1851
Squier, E. G.—Antiquities of the State of New York	8vo.	Buffalo.	1851
——— ——— Nicaragua ; Its People, Scenery, &c. 2 v.	8vo.	N. Y.	1852
——— ——— Notes on Central America	8vo.	N. Y.	1855
——— ——— Serpent Symbol, and Worship of Nature	8vo.	N. Y.	1851
Stable Practice ; with Hints on Training Horses, &c.	16o.	Lond.	1852
Stackhouse, Thos.—Complete Body of Divinity. 3 v.	8vo.	Dumfries.	1776
Stafford, Thos.—Pacata Hibernia ; or, Warres in Ireland. 2 v.	4to.	Title wanting	
Stagg, Edw.—Poems	12o.	St. Louis.	1852
Stamboul, and the Sea of Gems	8vo.	Lond.	1852
Standish and Noble—On Planting Ornamental Trees	16o.	Lond.	1852
Stanford, Jno.—Discourses Delivered on Public Occasions	8vo.	Various	
Stanislaus, Fran. A.—A Voyage to Saint Domingo, 1788–90. (Fr. Ger.)	8vo.	Lond.	1817
Stansbury, H.—Valley of the Great Salt Lake of Utah. 2 v.	8vo.	Phil.	1852
——— ——— The Same, with Maps. 3 v.	8vo.	Wash.	1853
*State Papers and U. S. Public Documents. Vol. 2	8vo.	Bost.	1819
——— of the Union ; a History of U. S. Public Affairs	8vo.	Wash.	1855
Statius, Publius Papinius.—Opera Omnia. 4 v. See *Valpy's Delphin Classics.*			
Staunton, H.—The Chess Tournament : Games	16o.	Lond.	1852
Stearns, E. J.—Notes on Uncle Tom's Cabin	12o.	Phil.	1853
——— Jona. F.—History of the first Presbyterian Church in Newark	8vo.	Newark.	1853
Steele, J.—On Establishing the Melody of Speech by Symbols	4to.	Lond.	1775
Steffens, Karl—Volks Kalendar für 1854	16o.	Berlin.	1853
Stephens, Sir Jas.—Lectures on the History of France	8vo.	N. Y.	1852
——— Ann S.—Ladies' Guide to Crochet, Knitting, &c.	12o.	N. Y.	no date
——— Hen.—The Book of the Farm. 2 v.	8vo.	N. Y.	1854
Stephen, Jas.—Lectures on the History of France. 2 v.	8vo.	Lond.	1851
Stephenson, Robt.—The Great Exhibition ; its Palace and Contents	16o.	Lond.	1851
Sterling, Jno.—Life of, by Thomas Carlyle	12o.	Bost.	1851
*Sterne, Laurence—Sentimental Journey through France and Italy	8vo.	Lond.	no date
*Stevens, Hen.—Catalogue of My English Library	16o.	Lond.	1853
Stevenson, Alan.—On the Hist'y, Constr'n, and Illum'n of Light Houses	16o.	Lond.	1850
Stewart, Dug.—Collected Works. Ed. by Hamilton. Vols. 1–8	8vo.	Edin.	1854–5
——— ——— Philosophy of the Active and Moral Powers of Man	12o.	Camb.	1851
——— ——— Philosophy of the Human Mind. Ed. by Bowen	12o.	Bost.	1854
——— K. J.—Freemason's Companion	12o.	Phil.	1851
Stiles, Wm. H.—Austria in 1848–9. 2 v.	8vo.	N. Y.	1852
Stilling, J. H. S.—Theory of Pneumatology. (Fr. Ger.)	12o.	N. Y.	1851
Stillingfleet, Edw.—Origines Sacræ ; or, The Grounds of Christ'n Faith	4to.	Lond.	1663
Stirling, O. S.—Australian and Californian Gold Discoveries	12o.	Edinb.	1853
——— Wm.—Cloister Life of Charles the Fifth	12o.	Lond.	1852
——— ——— The Same	12o.	Lond.	1853
——— ——— The Same	8vo.	Bost.	1853
Stith, Wm.—Discovery and Settlement of Virginia	8vo.	Will'ms'bg.	1747
Stöckhardt, J. A.—Principles of Chemistry. (Fr. Fren.)	12o.	Camb.	1850
Stocqueler, J. H.—Life of the Duke of Wellington. 2 v.	8vo.	Lond.	1852
Stoddard, Rich. Hen.—Poems	16o.	Bost.	1852
Stoddart, Jno.—Introduction to the Study of Universal History	12o.	Lond.	1850

Stokes, J.—Cabinet Maker and Upholsterer's Companion . .	12o. Phil.	1850
*Stolle, Ed.—Einheimische und ausländische Patent Gesetzgebung	8vo. Leipzig.	1855
Stone, Thos. T.—Sermons	12o. Bost.	1854
Story of the Madiai	18o. N. Y.	1853
—— Jos.—On Equity Jurisprudence. 2 v.	8vo. Bost.	1848
—— —— On the Law of Agency	8vo. Bost.	1851
—— —— On the Law of Bills of Exchange . . .	8vo. Bost.	1847
—— —— On the Law of Partnership : . .	8vo. Bost.	1850
—— —— On the Law of Promissory Notes . . .	8vo. Bost.	1851
—— —— Exposition of the United States Constitution .	12o. N. Y.	1854
—— —— Life and Letters of, Edited by W. W. Story. 2 v.	8vo. Bost.	1851
—— —— Miscellaneous Writings	8vo. Bost.	1852
—— Wm. W.—Law of Contracts not under Seal . .	8vo. Bost.	1851
—— —— Law of Sales of Personal Property . . .	8vo. Bost.	1847
Stoughton, Jno.—Philip Doddridge; his Life and Labors .	16o. Lond.	1851
Stowe, Harriet B.—A Key to Uncle Tom's Cabin . . .	R. 8vo. Bost.	1853
—— —— Oheim Tom's Hütte	8vo. Bost.	1853
—— —— Onkel Tom's Hütte	12o. Leipzig.	1853
—— —— Sunny Memories of Foreign Lands. 2 v. . .	12o. Bost.	1854
Stowell, Hugh—A Model for Business Men	12o. Lond.	1854
Strachey, Edw.—Hebrew Politics in the Times of Sargon, &c. .	8vo. Lond.	1853
Strada, F.—History of the Low Country Warres. (Fr. Lat.) .	Fol. Lond.	1650
Strain, Isaac G.—Journey in Chili and the Argentine Prov. in 1849	12o. N. Y.	1853
Strang, John—Germany in 1831. 2 v.	8vo. Lond.	1836
Stranger's Guide round New York and Vicinity . . .	18o. N. Y.	no date
Strickland, Agnes—Lives of Queens of England. 6 v. . .	8vo. Phil.	1851
—— —— Lives of Queens of Scotland. Vols. 1–5 .	12o. N. Y.	1851–5
—— —— Lives of Scot. and Eng. Princesses. Vols. 1 & 2 .	12o. N. Y.	1851
—— —— Memoirs of Queen Elizabeth . . .	8vo. Phil.	1853
—— —— Queens of Hen. VIII. [Taken fr. "Queens of Eng."]	8vo. Phil.	1853
—— Maj.—Twenty-seven Years in Canada West. 2 v. .	12o. Lond.	1853
—— W. P.—History of the American Bible Society .	8vo. N. Y.	1849
—— —— Hist. of the Missions of the Method. Epis. Church	12o. Cincin.	1850
Stroud, Wm.—Physical Cause of the Death of Christ . .	12o. Lond.	1847
Struenzée, Count; The Sceptic and Christian. (Fr. Ger.) .	16o. Bost.	1853
Struve, Gustav—Weltgeschichte. Vols. 1–3, in 1 vol. . .	8vo. N. Y.	1852
Stryker, J. (Ed'r.)—See *American Quarterly Register.*		
Stuart, And.—Genealogical History of the Stewarts . .	4to. Lond.	1798
—— Arabella W.—Lives of Mrs. A. H. & Sarah B. Judson .	12o. Auburn.	1852
*—— Chas. B.—The Naval and Mail Steamers of the U. States .	4to. N. Y.	1853
*—— —— Naval Dry Docks of the United States . .	4to. N. Y.	1852
—— Lieut. Col.—Residence in Northern Persia and Turkey .	8vo. Lond.	1854
—— Marie; Hist. de, par F. A. Mignet	8vo. Paris.	1851
—— —— The Same. 2 v.	16o. Paris.	1854
*—— Robt.—Dictionary of Architecture. 3 vols. in 2. .	8vo. Phil.	1851
Student (The); or, The Oxford and Cambridge Miscellany. 2 v. .	8vo. Oxford.	1750–1
—— —— Edited by Calkins. Vols. 1–8. [*Continued.*] .	8vo. N. Y.	1850–4
Sturge, Jos.—Visit to the United States in 1841 . . .	12o. Bost.	1842
—— Wm.—Scientific Researches	4to. Lond.	1852
Sturm, Mathesis—Compendaria, Jure, Tyrocinia Math. Fabulis .	Fol. Altdorf.	1698

Sturt, Chas.—Two Expeditions into South Australia in 1829–31. 2 v. 8vo. Lond. 1834
Sue, Eug.—L'Adventurier; ou, le Barbe-Bleue . . . 18o. Brux. 1847
—— —— Les Septs Péchés Capitaux. Vols. 1–3 . . 12o. Paris. 1851
L'Orgueil; L'Envie; La Colère.
Suetonius Tranquillius—Opera Omnia. 3 v. See *Valpy's Delphin Classics.*
Sullivan, Edw.—Rambles and Scrambles in North and South America 8vo. Lond. 1852
—— Jas.—History of the District of Maine . . 8vo. Bost. 1795
Sumner, Chas.—Orations and Speeches. 2 v. . . . . 12o. Bost. 1850
—— —— White Slavery in the Barbary States . . 16o. Bost. 1853
Summer's Tour (A) in Europe in 1851 . . . . . 12o. Charleston. 1852
Sunderland, L.—Book of Human Nature . . . . 12o. N. Y. 1855
Sunlight upon the Landscape, and other Poems . . . 12o. Cincin. 1853
Sunshine on Daily Paths. From "Household Words" . . 12o. Phil. 1854
*Surenne, Gabriel—French and English Pronouncing Dictionary . 12o. N. Y. 1846
Surville, Mme. (née de Balzac)—Compagnon du Foyer . . 16o. Paris. 1854
Sutcliffe, Thos.—Sixteen Years in Chili and Peru . . . 8vo. Lond. [1841]
Swan, Jos.—The Brain in Relation to the Mind .. . . 8vo. Lond. 1854
Swedenborg, Eman.—Economy of the Animal Kingdom. 2 v. . 8vo. Lond. 1845–6
—— —— The Same . . . . . . 8vo. St. Clairv. 1850
—— —— Gems from, with Memoir . . . . 24o. Lond. 1852
—— —— Heaven and Hell . . . . . 8vo. N. Y. 1854
—— —— Heavenly Arcana. Vols. 5–12, and Index. 9 v. 8vo. Bost. 1843–8
—— —— Writings. See *Compendium.*
Sweetser, Wm.—Mental Hygeine . . . . . . 12o: N. Y. 1850
Swett, Jno. A.—Treatise on Diseases of the Chest . . 8vo. N. Y. 1852
Swift, Jona.—Works. 2 v. . . . . 8vo. Lond. 1851
Swinburne, Hen.—Travels in the Two Sicilies in 1777–80. 2 v. 8vo. Dublin. 1783
Swisshelm, Jane G.—Letters to Country Girls . . . 12o. N. Y. 1853
Sym, Pat.—Tables for Finding the Mean Heights of Cross Sections, &c. 8vo. Phil. 1853
Syme, J. B.—Readings for Railways; or, Anecdotes, &c. . . 16o. Lond. no date
Symons, Jelinga—School Economy . . . . . 16o. Lond. 1852
Szapary, Le Comte de—Magnétisme et Magnéto-thérapie . . 8vo. Paris 1853

Tableau general de l'Empire Ottoman. Tome 1 . . . . Fol. Paris. 1787
—— des Mouvements du Cabotage pour 1848 . 4to. Paris. 1849
—— du Commerce de la France pour 1848 . . Fol. Paris. 1849
*Tableaux, &c., de la Galerie de Florence et du Palais Pitti. 4 v. Fol. Paris. 1804–14
Tables of Commerce and Navigation of the United States for 1851 . 8vo. Wash. 1852
Tacitus, Caius Cornelius—Opera Omnia. 9 v. See *Valpy's Delphin Classics.*
—— —— The Germania of, Notes by Latham . . 8vo. Lond. 1851
Taghconic; or, Letters about our Summer Home . . . 12o. Bost. 1852
Tait's Edinburgh Magazine. Vols. 17–21. [*Continued.*] . 8vo. Edin. 1850–54
Talbot, G. M.—Philosophy of French Pronunciation . . 12o. N. Y. 1854
Tales of the Mountains; or, Sojourns in Eastern Belgium. 2 v. 16o. Lond. 1851
*Tanner's Travelling Map of Michigan, &c. . . . . . 16o. Phil. 1849
Tanner, H. S.—American Traveller; or, Guide through the U. States 12o. Phil. 1839
*—— —— Geographical, &c., View of Central United States . 16o. Phil. 1841
—— T. H.—Manual of Clinical Medicine . . . . 16o. Phil. 1855
Tappan, Hen. P.—A Step from the New World to the Old. 2 v. . 12o. N. Y. 1852
—— —— University Education . . . . . 12o. Phil. 1851
Tasso, Torquato—Jerusalem Delivered. (Fr. Ital., by Smith.) 2 v. 16o. Lond. 1851

Tate, Thos.—Principles of Mechanical Philosophy . . . 8vo. Lond. 1853
Tayler, C. B.—Memorials of the English Martyrs . . 12o. N. Y. 1853
Taylor, Bayard—Book of Romances, Lyrics, and Songs . . 16o. Bost. 1852
——— —— Journey to Central Africa . . . . 12o. N. Y. 1854
——— —— Lands of the Saracen . . . . . . 12o. N. Y. 1855
——— —— Poems of Home and Travel . . . . 16o. Bost. 1855
——— —— Poems of the Orient . . . . . 16o. Bost. 1855
——— —— Visit to India, China, and Japan . . . . 12o. N. Y. 1855
——— E. E. L.—The Christian Sanctuary . . . . . 18o. N. Y. 1853
——— Isaac—Physical Theory of Another Life . . 12o. N. Y. 1852
——— —— Wesley and Methodism . . . . . 12o. Lond. 1851
——— —— The Same 2 v. . . . . 12o. N. Y. 1852
——— Jef.—The Young Islanders . . . . 16o. N. Y. 1854
——— Jeremy—Readings for Every Day in Lent: comp. fr. his Works 16o. N. Y. 1851
——— Jno. E.—Michael Angelo as a Philosophic Poet . . 12o. Lond. 1840
——— Jno. J.—Christian Aspects of Faith and Duty . . 12o. N. Y. 1851
——— John N.—Law of Executors and Administrators . . 12o. N. Y. 1851
——— R. C.—Statistics of Coal, Edited by Haldeman . . 8vo. Phil. 1855
——— Tom—Life of B. R. Haydon. 3 v. . . . . . 8vo. Lond. 1853
——— —— The Same . . . . 12o. N. Y. 1853
Tazewell, L. W.—Commercial Negotiations bet. U. S. & Great Britain 8vo. Lond. 1829
Technologiste, Le. Vols. 12 & 15. [*Continued.*] . . 8vo. Paris. 1850–54
Tefft, B. F.—Hungary and Kossuth . . . . . 12o. Phil. 1852
——— —— Webster and his Master Pieces. 2 v. . . . 12o. Auburn. 1854
*Tegg's Dictionary of Chronology . . . . . . 12o. N. Y. 1854
Temple, Wm.—Introduction to the History of England . 12o. Lond. 1695
——— —— Letters while Ambassador at the Hague . . 12o. Lond. 1699
Templeton's Engineer, Millwright, and Mechanics' Companion . 12o. N. Y. 1852
——— Wm.—Practical Examinator on Steam & Steam Engine . 16o. Phil. 1853
Tennemann, W. G.—Manual of the History of Philosophy . 16o. Lond. 1852
Tennyson, Fred.—Days and Hours . . . . . . 16o. Lond. 1854
——— Alf.—In Memoriam. A. H. H., [Arth. H. Hallam,] obiit 1833 16o. Bost. 1851
——— —— Maud and other Poems . . . . . 12o. Bost. 1855
Terentius, Publius—Opera. 4 v. See *Valpy's Delphin Classics.*
*Ternaux, Campans H.—Bibliothèque Américaine . . 8vo. Paris. 1837
——— —— Voyages, Relations, and Mémoires Originaux. Vols. 1–20 8vo. Paris. 1837–41
Tesoro della Prosa Italiana dai Primi Tempi . . . . . 8vo. Firenze. 1841
Testimony of Christ's Second Appearing. [The Shaker Bible.] 12o. Albany. 1810
*Texier, Edm.—Tableau de Paris. 2 v. . . . . Fol. Paris. 1852
Thackeray, W. M.—Ballads . . . . 12o. Bost. 1855
——— —— English Humorists of the 18th Century . 18o. Leipzig. 1853
——— —— The Same . . . . 12o. N. Y. 1853
Thalatta: a Book for the Sea-Side . . . . . . 16o. Bost. 1853
Thanksgiving Sermons, Preached 1759, '66, '74, '75. See *Pamphlets.* Vol. 53.
Thayer, Wm. W.—Hints for the Household . . . . . 12o. Bost. 1853
——— —— Spots in our Feasts of Charity . . . . 12o. Bost. 1854
Theller, E. A.—Canada in 1837–8. 2 v. . . . . . . 12o. Phil. 1841
Theoc., Bion, & Moschus—Idyls of; & War Songs of Tyrtæus. (Fr. Grk.) 16o. Lond. 1853
Theocritus Syracusius—See *Scriptorum Græcorum Bibliotheca.* Vol. 33.
Theological and Literary Journal. Vol. 5 . . . . 8vo. N. Y. 1852–3

Title	Size	Place	Date
Theologische Studien und Kritiken. Vol. 27. [*Continued.*]	8vo.	Hamb.	1854
Theremin, L. F. F.—The Awaking	32o.	Bost.	1855
Thierry, A.—Essai sur l'Histoire du Tiers Etat	8vo.	Paris.	1853
Thiers, L. A.—Histoire du Consulat et de l'Empire. Vol. 11	8vo.	Paris.	1851
——— —— History of the French Revolution. 5 v.	8vo.	Lond.	1838
——— —— The Same. 2 v.	8vo.	Phil.	1852
Things to be Thought of	18o.	N. Y.	1854
Tholuck, F. A. D.—Guido and Julius	16o.	Bost.	1854
Thomas, F. W.—John Randolph of Roanoke	12o.	Phil.	1853
——— Geo.—Memoirs of Marquis of Rockingham. 2 v.	8vo.	Lond.	1852
——— J.—Travels in Egypt and Palestine	12o.	Phila.	1853
——— Jno. S.—Farm Implements	12o.	N. Y.	1854
Thompson, A. C.—The Better Land	12o.	Bost.	1854
——— Edw. P.—The Passions of Animals	8vo.	Lond.	1851
——— G. A.—Visit to Guatemala from Mexico	16o.	Lond.	1829
——— Jos. P.—The Good Man's Memorial	12o.	N. Y.	1855
——— —— Hints to Employers	32o.	N. Y.	1851
——— —— Topographic Views of Egypt	12o.	Bost.	1854
——— —— Young Men Admonished. Lectures	12o.	Buffalo.	1852
——— Robt. A.—Christian Theism	12o.	N. Y.	1855
——— Theoph.—On Pulmonary Consumption	8vo.	Phil.	1854
——— Thos.—History of the Royal Soc., to end of 18th Century	4to.	Lond.	1812
——— Z.—Geography and Geology of Vermont	16o.	Burlington.	1848
*Thomson's Delaware Mercantile and Professional Directory for 1851 '2	8vo.	Balt.	1851
Thomson, Dav. P.—Stranger's Vade Mecum; or, Liverpool Described	12o.	Liverpool.	1854
——— Jas.—The Seasons. Notes, by Boyd	12o.	N. Y.	1852
——— J. L.—Wars of the United States	8vo.	Phil.	1854
——— Spencer—Wanderings among the Wild Flowers	16o.	Lond.	1854
——— Thos.—Western Himalaya and Tibet	8vo.	Lond.	1852
Thorburn, Grant—Life and Writings. By Himself	12o.	N. Y.	1852
Thoreau, Hen. D.—Walden; or, Life in the Woods	12o.	Bost.	1854
Thornton—Sporting Tour through France. 2 v.	4to.	Lond.	1806
——— Jas. B.—Digest of Conveyancing and Testamentary Laws	8vo.	Bost.	1854
——— T. C.—Inquiry into the History of Slavery	12o.	Wash.	1841
Thornwell, Jas. H.—Discourses on Truth	12o.	N. Y.	1855
Thorpe, Benj. (Comp'r)—Northern Mythology. 3 v.	12o.	Lond.	1851
Thoughts and Stories on Tobacco	18o.	Bost.	1852
——— to Help and Cheer. 2 v.	16o.	Bost.	1854–5
Thrilling Stories of the Forest and Frontier	12o.	Phil.	1852
Thucydides. See *Scriptorum Græcorum Bibliotheca.* Vol. 9.			
——— Hist. of the Peloponnesian War. (Fr. Grk., by Vale.) 2 v.	16o.	Lond.	1849
Tibullus, Albius—Opera. See *Valpy's Delphin Classics.*			
Tiby, Paul—Deux Couvens au Moyen Age	16o.	Paris.	1851
Tilt, E. J.—Elements of Health, and Female Hygiene	12o.	Phil.	1853
——— —— On the Preservation of the Health of Women	24o.	N. Y.	1851
Timbs, John—Year-Book of Facts for the Great Exhibition of 1851	16o.	Lond.	1851
——— —— Year-Book of Facts for 1851–4. 4 v.	16o.	Lond.	1851–4
——— —— The Same, for 1852–3. 2 v.	12o.	Phil.	1852–3
Times, The (London)—July, 1849 to June, 1854. 22 v. [*Continued.*]	Fol.	Lond.	1849–54
Tirabosch, G.—Storia della Litteratura Italiana. 9 Vols. in 14	8vo.	Flor.	1805–13

"To Daimonion;" or, the Spiritual Medium	16o. Bost.	1852
Todd, Hen. J.—Life and Writings of John Milton . .	8vo. Lond.	1809
—— R. B.—Clinical Lectures on Affections of the Nervous System	8vo. Phil.	1855
—— —— and Bowman (Wm.)—Physiological Anatomy, &c. .	8vo. Phil.	1850
Tomes, Robt.—Panama in 1855	16o. N. Y.	1855
*Tomlinson, Chas. (Ed'r)—Cyclopedia of Useful Arts., &c. 2 v.	8vo. Lond.	1854
Töpffer, R.—Nouvelles Genevoises . . . . - .	8vo. Paris.	1851
—— —— Presbytère	16o. Paris.	1852
—— —— Rosa et Gertrude	16o. Paris.	1847
—— —— Voyages en Zigzag	8vo. Paris.	1850
Torrente, Mariano—Slavery in the Island of Cuba . . .	8vo. Lond.	1853
Torrey, Jesse, Jr.—Moral Instructor and Guide to Virtue .	12o. Phil.	1830
—— Wm.—[Account of the State Prison in the City of N. Y.] .	8vo. N. Y.	1801
Toulmin, C.—Lays and Legends of English Life . .	4to. Lond.	1852
Tour through parts of the U. S. and Canada . . .	8vo. Lond.	1828
Tournay, Stewart—Laws of Exchange and Promissory Notes .	12o. Lond.	1851
Toussaint, Pierre—Memoir of, by Mrs. H. F. Lee . . .	12o. Bost.	1854
Townsend, Eliz. W.—The White Dove, and other Poems .	16o. N. Y.	1855
—— Hannah—History of England, in Verse . . .	12o. Phil.	1852
—— W. C.—Memoirs of the House of Commons. 2 v. .	8vo. Lond.	1844
Townshend, C. H.—Sermons, in Sonnets	12o. Edin.	1851
Traces of the Roman and the Moor	12o. N. Y.	1853
Tracy, Stephen—The Mother and her Offspring . . .	12o. N. Y.	1853
Traits of American-Indian Life and Character . . .	12o. Lond.	1853
Trall, R. T.—Hydropathic Encyclopedia. 2 v. . . .	12o. N. Y.	1852
*Transactions of the American Art Union, for 1848 . .	8vo. N. Y.	1849
—— American Institute of N. Y. City. 1853–'54. 2 v.	8vo. Albany.	1854–5
*—— American Philosophical Society. Vols. 1–3 .	4to. Phil.	1786–93
—— Highl'd & Ag. Soc. of Scot. N. S. Vols. 4 & 5. [*Cont'd*]	8vo. Edin.	1849–53
*—— Histor'l & Philosophical Soc. of Ohio. Vol. 1. Pt. 2	8vo. Cincin.	1839
*—— Horticultural Society of London. Vols. 1–6 .	4to. Lond.	1812–26
—— N. Y. State Agricultural Soc. Vols. 2, 4, 5, 8, 13, 14.	8vo. Albany.	1813–15
—— Wisconsin State Agricultural Society. Vol. 2.	8vo. Madison.	1853
Transport Voyage to the Mauritius and back . . .	16o. Lond.	1851
*Traveller's Guide to the Middle and Northern States, &c. .	16o. Sara. Spg's.	1832
*—— Own Book	16o.	
Travels of Anna Bishop in Mexico, 1849	12o. Phil.	no date
Treatise on the Proper Condition for all Horses . . .	16o. Lond.	1852
Treaty of Amity, Commerce, &c., between Gt. Britain and U. S.	16o. Phil.	1795
Tredgold, Thos.—Machinery used in Steam Navigation. 2 v. .	4to. Lond.	1851
—— —— Principles of Warming and Ventilating . .	8vo. Lond.	1836
Tregelles, S. P.—The Jansenists; their Rise, Persecutions, &c. .	12o. Lond.	1851
Tremenheere, Hugh S.—Constitutions of the U. States and England	8vo. Lond.	1854
—— —— Political Experience of the Ancients .	16o. Lond.	1852
Trench, R. C.—English Past and Present	12o. N. Y.	1855
—— —— Hulsean Lectures, for 1845–1846 . . .	12o. Phil.	1854
—— —— On the Lessons in Proverbs	16o. Lond.	1853
—— —— The Same	12o. N. Y.	1853
—— —— On the Study of Words	16o. Lond.	1851
—— —— The Same	12o. N. Y.	1854

Trench, R. C.—Synonyms of the New Test.	16o. Camb.	1854
Trendall, E. W.—Monuments, Cenotaphs, Tombs, &c., with Details	4to. Lond.	1850
Trescot, Wm. H.—Diplomacy of the Revolution	12o. N. Y.	1852
Trial of Wm. Freeman, for the Murder of J. G. Van Nest	8vo. Auburn.	1848
Tri-Colored Sketches in Paris. Illustrated	12o. N. Y.	1855
Triumphs of Perseverance and Enterprise	12o. N. Y.	1854
Troubat, F. J.—Law of Partnership in the United States	8vo. Phil.	1853
*Troy Directory for 1841–2, '48–50, '51–54. 7 v.	16o. Troy.	1841–53
True Inventory of the Effects of Sir John Fellowes. 2 v.	Fol. Lond.	1721
Trumbull, J. H.—Public Records of Connecticut Colony, 1665–78	8vo. Hartford.	1852
Truth of God against the Papacy	16o. Edin.	1851
Truths Illustrated by great Authors	8vo. Lond.	1852
Tucker, Geo.—Laws of Wages, Profit, and Rent	8vo. Phil.	1837
——— —— Life of, by Jno. W. Kaye	8vo. Lond.	1854
——— —— Progress of the U. S. in Population and Wealth	8vo. N. Y.	1855
——— H. St. G.—Lectures on Constitutional Law	12o. Rich'd.	1843
——— —— Lectures on Natural Law	12o. Charlottsv'l.	1844
——— —— Memorials of Indian Government	8vo. Lond.	1853
Tuckerman, Hen. V.—Characteristics of Literature, 2d Series	12o. Phil.	1852
——— —— Memorial of H. Greenough	12o. N. Y.	1853
——— —— A Month in England	12o. N. Y.	1853
——— —— Poems	12o. Bost.	1851
——— —— Sicily; A Pilgrimage	12o. N. Y.	1852
Tuckey, J. H.—Expedition to Explore the River Zaire in 1816	4to. Lond.	1818
Tuner's Guide for the Piano Forte, Organ, &c.	12o. Bost.	no date
Turnbull, Benj.—Plea in Behalf of the Conn. Title to N. Y. Lands	12o. N. Hav.	1774
Turner's Companion	12o. Phil.	1851
Turner, G.—Traits of Indian Character. 2 v.	12o. Phil.	1836
——— S. H.—Thoughts on Prophecy	12o. N. Y.	1852
——— T. H.—Domestic Architecture in England	8vo. Oxford.	1851
——— and Girtins'—Picturesque Views. Edit. by T. Miller	R. 8vo. Lond.	1854
Turnley, Jos.—Popery in Power, or the Spirit of the Vatican	8vo. Lond.	1850
Tupper, M. F.—A Hymn for all Nations, in thirty languages, 1851	8vo. Lond.	[1851]
——— —— Philosophie Proverbiale	16o. Lond.	1851
——— —— Poetical Works [excepting Proverbial Philosophy.]	16o. Lond.	1853
Turnbull, Lawrence—Lectures on the Electro-Magnetic Telegraph	8vo. Phil.	1852
——— —— Electro-Magnetic Telegraph	8vo. Phil.	1853
——— Robt.—Christ in History	12o. Bost.	1854
——— —— The Genius of Italy	12o. N. Y.	1855
Tweedie, W. K.—A Lamp to the Path	16o. Bost.	1854
——— —— Seed-Time and Harvest	16o. Lond.	1852
——— —— The Same	16o. Bost.	1854
Twysden's Considerations on Government of England. See *Camden Soc. Publications.*		
Twelve Lectures before the Young Men's Christian Association, 1850–1	16o. Glasgow.	1851
Twining, Hen.—Elements of Picturesque Scenery	8vo. Lond.	1853
Twiss, Rich.—Travels through Portugal and Spain in 1772–3	4to. Lond.	1775
Tyler, Chas.—Historical Tour in Franconia in 1852	16o. Brighton.	1852
——— J. G.—Life and Character of Henry V. 2 v.	8vo. Lond.	1838
Tyson, Phil. T.—Geology and Industrial Resources of California	8vo. Balt.	1851
——— Jas. L.—Diary of a Physician in California	8vo. N. Y.	1850

Ubiciné, A.—La Question d'Orient	12o. Paris.	1854
——— —— Lettres sur la Turquie	16o. Paris.	1853
Umfreville, Edw.—Present State of Hudson's Bay . . .	8vo. Lond.	1790
Uncle Tom's Cabin in Ruins. A Letter	16o. Bost.	1853
Underhill, E. B.—Struggles and Triumphs of Religious Liberty .	12o. N. Y.	1851
Unconnected Whig's Address to the Public on the Present War	8vo. Lond.	1777
Ungerwitter, F. H.—Europe, Past and Present . . .	12o. N. Y.	1850
Union Magazine. Vols. 7–10	8vo. Phila.	1850–52
*United States Economist. Vol. 3. April '24, to Oct. '53 . .	Fol.	
*————— Almanac for 1845	12o. Phil.	1845
*————— Digest. Vols. 6–16	8vo. Bost.	1849–55

Vol. 6. Table of Cases in Vols. 1–5.
7. Annual Digest for 1847.
8. " " " 1848.
9. " " " 1849.
10. " " " 1850.
11. " " " 1851.
12. " " " 1852.
13 & 14. Decisions in Courts of Equity. Vols. 1 and 2.
15. Annual Digest for 1853.
16. " " " 1854.

United States Digest of Decisions in Common Law and Admiralty. 9 v.	8vo. Bost.	1847–50
————— Law Magazine. Vols. 1–4. [*Continued.*] . .	8vo. N. Y.	1849–51
————— Magazine and Democratic Review. Vols. 27, 28 .	8vo. N. Y.	1850–1
————— The Same. For Continuation, See *Democratic Review.*		
————— Post Office Guide, by Rode	8vo. N. Y.	1853
*————— Statutes at Large. 11 v.	8vo. Bost.	1850–52

Vols. 1–5. Public Statutes at Large.
6. Private Statutes at Large, 1789–1845.
7. Treaties between the U. S. and Indian Tribes.
8. " " " Foreign Nations.
9–10. Statutes at Large and Treaties, 1845–'55.
11. Synoptical Index to Laws and Treaties, 1789–1851.

Universalist Quarterly. Vols. 8–11. [*Continued.*] . . .	8vo Bost.	1851–4
Universe no Desert (The.)	12o. Bost.	1855
Updike, Wilk.—Memoirs of the Rhode Island Bar . . .	8vo. Bost.	1842
Urbino, Dukes of—Memoirs of, by Jas. Dennistoun. 3 v. .	8vo. Lond.	1851
Urcullu, J. de—Gramatica Inglesa	12o. Phil.	1851
*Ure, Andrew—Dictionary of Arts, Manufactures, &c. 2 v. .	8vo. N. Y.	1853
Urquhart, David—Progress of Russia	16o. Lond.	1853
———— Wm. P.—Life and Times of Francesco Sforza. 2 v.	8vo. Edin.	1852
Useful Letter-Writer	32o. N. Y.	no date
*Utica City Directory for 1846–7	12o. Utica.	1846

Varden, Thos. J.—America Vindicated from European Aspersions .	12o. N. Y.	1855
Valentia, Geo.—Travels in India, Abyssinia, and Egypt, 1802–6. 3 v.	4to. Lond.	1809
Valentine, Dav. T.—History of the City of New York . .	8vo. N. Y.	1853
*———— —— New York Corporation Manual, 1841–6. 4 v.	16o. N. Y.	no date
———— —— The Same for 1852–5. 4 v.	12o. N. Y.	1852–5
Valerius Maximus—Opera Omnia. 3 v. See *Valpy's Delphin Classics.*		

*Valpy's Delphin and Variorum Latin Classics. 159 v. 8vo. Lond. 1819-30

Apuleius. 6 v.
Aulus Gellius. 3 v.
Aurelius Victor. 2 v.
Ausonius. 3 v.
Boethius. 1 v.
Cæsar. 4 v.
Catullus. 2 v.
Cicero:
  Epistolæ ad Familiares. 2 v.
  Libri Rhetorici. 3 v.
  Opera Philosophica. 3 v.
  Orationes. 5 v.
  Ernesti Clavis. 1 v.
Claudianus. 3 v.
Cornelius Nepos. 2 v.
Dicty's Cretensis, et Dares Phrygius. 1 v.
Eutropius. 1 v.
Florus. 2 v.
Horatius. 4 v.
Justinus. 2 v.
Juvenalis. 2 v.
Livius. 20 v.
Lucretius. 3 v.
Manilius. 2 v.
Martialis. 3 v.
Ovidius. 9 v.
Panegyrici Veteres. 5 v.
Persius. 1 v.
Phædrus. 1 v.
Plautus. 5 v.
Plinius (Senior.) 12 v.
Pompeius Festus. 2 v.
Propertius. 2 v.
Prudentius. 3 v.
Quintus Curtius. 3 v.
Sallustius. 2 v.
Statius. 4 v.
Seutonius. 3 v.
Tacitus. 10 v.
Terentius. 4 v.
Tibullus. 1 v.
Valerius Maximus. 3 v.
Velleius Paterculus. 1 v.
Virgilius. 8 v.

Vanderkiste, R. W.—Notes and Nar. of a Six Years' Mission in London 16o. Lond. 1852
Van Doren, Wm. H.—Mercantile Morals; or, Thoughts for the Young 16o. N. Y. 1852
Van Santvoord, G.—Life of Algernon Sidney . . . 12o. N. Y. 1851
———— —— Lives of the Chief Justices of United States 8vo. N. Y. 1854
Varnum, Jos. B., Jr.—United States Seat of Government . 8vo. Wash. 1854
Venegas, Mig.—Histoire de Californie. (Fr. Span.) 3 v. . . 12o. Paris. 1767
Vere, Schele de—Grammar of the Spanish Language . . 12o. N. Y. 1854
Vernon, Edw.—History of Jamaica . . . . . . 8vo. Lond. 1740
*Véron, L.—Memoires d'un Bourgeois de Paris. Vols. 1 and 2 8vo. Paris. 1853
Vestiges of the Natural History of Creation . . . 18o. N. Y. 1854
——— The Same . . . . . . 8vo. Cincin. 1852
——— See *Remarks*
Victor, Sextus Aurelius—Opera Omnia. 2 v. See *Valpy's Delphin Classics.*
Vidal, E. E.—Picturesque Views of Buenos Ayres and Monte Video 4to. Lond. 1820
Villemain, A. F.—Histoire de Cromwell . . . . . 16o. Brux. 1851
Vinet, A.—Etudes sur la Littérature Française au 19e Siécle. 3 v. 8vo. Paris. 1849-51
—— —— Homiletics. Translated and Edited by Rev. Dr. Skinner 12o. N. Y. 1854
—— —— Pastoral Theology . . . . . . 12o. N. Y. 1853
Virginia Historical Register, Vols. 1-4, in 2 v. . . . 8vo. Rich. 1848-51
Virgilius, Publius—Opera Omnia. 9 v. See *Valpy's Delphin Classics.*
Visitation of Huntingdon, under Wm. Camden. See *Camden Soc. Publications.*
Vivien, O.—Etudes Administratives. 2 v. . . . 12o. Paris. 1852
Voice to America (A); or, the Model Republic . . . 12o. N. Y. 1855
Volks-Kalender für 1855 . . . . . . 8vo. Leipzig.
Voyage dans la haute Pennsylvanie et l'Etat de New York. 3 v. . 8vo. Paris. 1801
Voyage to Peru; by the Conde of St. Malo, 1745-9 . . 12o. Lond. 1753
*Vries, D. P. de—Voyages from Holland to Amer. 1632-44. (Fr. Dutch.) 4to. N. Y. 1853

Waagen, Dr.—Treasures of Art in Great Britain. 3 v. . . 8vo. Lond. 1854
Waddington, Geo. and Hanbury (B.)—Journal of a Visit to Ethiopia 4to. Lond. 1822
Wagner, Moritz, & Scherzer (Carl)—Reisen in N. A., in 1852 & '3. V. 1-3 12o. Leipzig. 1854
Wailly, Leon de—Stella et Vanessa . . . . . 12o. Paris. 1855

Wainwright, Jona. M.—The Land of Bondage. A Tour in Egypt . 4to. N. Y. 1851
Walker, Alex.—Jackson and New Orleans . . . . 12o. N. Y. 1856
——— Donald—Manly Exercises . . . . . . 12o. Phil. 1856
*——— J.—Rhyming, Spelling, and Pronouncing Dictionary . 12o. Phil. 1852
——— —— Elements of Elocution and Oratory . . . 12o. Phil. 1852
——— Tim.—Introduction to American Laws . . 8vo. Cincin. 1846
——— Wm. S.—Poetical Remains of . . . . . 16o. Lond. 1852
Wallace, Alf. K.—Travels on the Amazon and Rio Negro . 8vo. Lond. 1853
——— Hor. B.—Art, Scenery, and Philosophy in Europe . 12o. Phil. 1855
Wallis, S. T.—Spain; Her Institutions, Politics, and Public Men 16o. Bost. 1853
Walpole, Fred.—The Ausayrii and the Assassins. 3 v. . . 8vo. Lond. 1851
——— Hor.—Anecdotes of Painting in England. 5 v. . 8vo. Lond. 1786
——— Robt.—Life and Administration of, by Wm. Coxe. 3 v. 8vo. Lond. 1800
Walshe, Anthony—Catechism on Regimental Standing Orders . 8vo. Lond. 1852
Walton, H. H.—Operative Ophthalmic Surgery . . 8vo. Phil. 1853
Warburton, A.—Memoir of Charles Mordaunt, Earl. 2 v. . . 12o. Lond. 1853
——— —— Rollo and His Race; or, Footst. of the Normans. 2 v. 8vo. Lond. 1848
——— Eliot—The Crescent and the Cross . . 12o. N. Y. 1850-1
Waring, Geo. E., Jr.—Elements of Agriculture . . . 12o. N. Y. 1854
Ward, F. D. W.—India and the Hindoos . . . . 12o. N. Y. 1850
——— Harriet—The Cape and the Kaffirs . . . . . 16o. Lond. 1851
——— Jas.—The World in its Workshop; or, the Great Exhibition 16o. Lond. no date
——— Jas. W. Woman: A Poem . . . . . . 12o. Cincin. 1852
——— R. P.—Historical Essay on the Revolution of 1688. 2 v. 12o. Lond. 1838
Warden, D. B.—Origin, Nature, &c., of Consular Establishments . 8vo. Paris. 1813
Wardlaw, Ralph—Lectures on Magdalenism . . . 18o. N. Y. 1843
Ware, Hen., Jr.—Memoirs of Rev. Noah Worcester, D. D. . . 12o. Bost. 1844
——— John—Hints to Young Men on the Relation of the Sexes 16o. Bost. 1850
——— Mary L.—Memoir of, by Edward B. Hall . . . . 12o. Bost. 1853
——— Wm.—Sketches of European Capitals . . . . 12o. Bost. 1851
——— —— Works and Genius of Washington Allston . . 16o. Bost. 1832
Warner, Fred.—Ecclesiastical History of England. 2 v. . Fol. Lond. 1765
——— John E.—Notes of an Attaché in Spain, in 1850 . . 8vo. Lond. 1851
——— —— Para; or, Scenes and Adventures on the Amazon 12o. N. Y. 1851
——— H. W.—The Liberties of America . . . . . 12o. N. Y. 1853
——— Maj.—Schamyl; Le Prophète du Caucase . . 16o. Paris. 1854
Warr, G. F.—Dynamics, Construction of Machinery, &c. (L. U. K.) 8vo. Lond. 1851
——— —— Dynamics. See *Library of Useful Knowledge.*
Warren, Jno. C.—Preservation of Health . . . . 18o. Bost. 1854
——— —— Address before the American Medical Association . 8vo. Bost. 1850
——— Sam.—Intellectual and Moral Development of the Present Age 16o. Edin. 1853
——— —— Lily and the Bee; an Apologue of the Crystal Palace 16o. N. Y. 1851
Washburn, Emory—Judicial History of Massachusetts. 1630-1775 8vo. Bost. 1840
*Washington and Georgetown Directory for 1853 . . . 8vo. Wash. 1853
——— Geo.—Character and Influence of, by F. Guizot. (Fr. Fren.) 16o. Bost. 1851
——— —— Histoire de, par C. de Witt . . . 8vo. Paris. 1855
——— —— Life of. By Washington Irving. Vols. 1 and 2 8vo. N. Y. 1855
——— —— Maxims of. Edited by Schroeder . . 12o. N. Y. 1855
——— —— Official Letters to Cong'ss during the Am. Rev. 2 v. 8vo. Lond. 1795
——— —— Reprint of his Letters to Joseph Reed . . 8vo. Phil. 1852

Washington, Geo.—Life of, by Jared Sparks. Abridged . 12o. Aub'n. 1851
———— Mrs.—Memoirs of, by M. C. Conkling . . . . 12o. Aub'n. 1850
Water-Cure Journal. Vols. 9 and 10. [*Continued.*] . . 8vo. N. Y. 1850
Wathen, Geo. H.—Arts, Antiquities, and Chronology of Ancient Egypt 8vo. Lond. 1843
Watson, Hen. C.—Camp Fires of the Revolution . . 8vo. Phil. 1850
——— —— Heroic Women of History . . . . . 8vo. Phil. 1852
Watts, Isaac—Works, with Memoirs. 6 v. . . . . 4to. Lond. 1810
Waverley Poetry; being Poems Scattered through the Waverley Novels 12o. Lond. 1851
Wayland, Fran.—Elements of Intellectual Philosophy . . 12o. Bost. 1854
——— —— Memoir of Rev. A. Judson. 2 v. . . . . 12o. Bost. 1853
Wayte, Sam. C.—Equestrian's Manual; with Advice to Purchasers 12o. Lond. 1850
Weale, John (Ed'r)—London and Its Vicinity—Exhibited in 1851 . 12o. Lond. 1851
——— —— Rudimentary Dictionary of Terms used in the Arts 16o. Lond. 1850
Weaver, G. S.—Hopes and Helps for the Young of Both Sexes . 12o. N. Y. 1853
——— R.—Popery Considered, as to Its Claims, &c. . . 12o. Lond. 1851
Webber, C. W.—Hunter-Naturalist. Vol. 1. Romance of Sporting 8vo. Phil. no date
——— —— Romance of Natural History . . . 8vo. Phil. 1852
——— —— Spiritual Vampirism . . . . . 12o. Phil. 1853
Weber's Volks-Kalendar für 1854-55. 2 v. . . . . 8vo. Leipzig. 1853–4
Weber, Geo.—Outlines of Universal History. (Fr. Ger.) . . 8vo. Lond. 1851
——— Carl Maria—Der Freischutz. (An Opera.) . . Fol. Paris. no date
Webster, Dan.—Eulogy on Adams and Jefferson, and other Speeches 8vo. Rochester. 1853
——— —— Life of . . . . 16o. Phil. 1853
——— —— " By Jos. Banvard . . . . . 16o. Bost. 1853
——— —— " By S. L. Knapp . . . . . 12o. Bost. 1831
——— —— Private Life of. By Chas. Lanman . . 12o. N. Y. 1852
——— —— Life and Memorials of. By S. P. Lyman. 2 v. 16o. N. Y. 1853
——— —— Personal Memoirs of . . . . . 8vo. Phil. 1851–2
——— —— Works. 6 v. . . . . 8vo. Bost. 1851–3
——— —— and his Master-Pieces. By Rev. B. F. Tefft. 2 v. . 12o. Auburn. 1854
——— E.—The Phonographic Teacher . . . . . 16o. N. Y. 1852
——— Pela.—Political Essays on Money, &c. . . . 8vo. Phil. 1791
Weddell, H. A.—Voyage dans le Nord de la Bolivie . . 8vo. Paris. 1853
Weeks, Jno. M.—Easy Method of Managing Bees . . 12o. N. Y. 1854
Weiss, Ch.—Histoire des Réfugées Protestants de France. 2 v. . 16o. Paris. 1853
——— —— French Protestant Refugees. (Fr. Fren.) 2 v. . 12o. N. Y. 1854
Welch, A. S.—Analysis of the English Sentence . . . 12o. N. Y. 1855
Weld, Chas. R.—The Search for Sir John Franklin; a Lecture . 8vo. Lond. 1851
——— H. H.—Dictionary of Sacred Quotations, from the Poets . 12o. Phil. 1851
Wellesley, Rich.—Memoirs and Correspondence, by R. R. Pearce. 3 v. 8vo. Lond. 1846
Wellington, Duke of. See *Patriot Warrior*.
——— —— Life of. See *Lives*.
——— —— " By J. H. Stocqueler. 2 v. . . 8vo. Lond. 1852
——— —— " For Boys, by W. K. Kelly . . 16o. Lond. 1853
——— —— Memoir. From "The Times." . . . 12o. Lond. 1852
——— —— Military and Political Life of . . . 12o. Lond. 1852
——— —— Speeches in Parliament. 2 v. . . . 8vo. Lond. 1854
Wellingtoniana. Selected by John Timbs . . . 12o. Lond. 1852
Wells, A. N.—Picturesque Antiquities of Spain . . . 8vo. Lond. 1846
——— D. A., and Bliss, G., Jr. (Ed'rs)—Annual of Scientif. Discov. for '51 12o. Bost. 1851

Wells, Dav. A. (Ed'r)—Annual of Scientific Discovery for 1852–5. 4 v.	12o.	Bost.	1852–5
Wemyss, Fran. C.—Chronology of the American Stage. 1752–1852	12o.	N. Y.	1852
——— —— Theatrical Biography of Actors and Authors .	12o.	N. Y.	no date
——— —— (Ed'r)—Modern Standard Drama. Vols. 10–12 .	12o.	N. Y.	no date
Wesleyan-Methodist Magazine. Vols. 7 and 8. [*Continued.*] .	8vo.	Lond.	1851–2
West, Jno.—Journal of Residence at Red River Colony . .	8vo.	Lond.	1824
Westgarth, Wm.—Victoria; late Australia Felix . . .	8vo.	Edin.	1853
Westminster and Foreign Quarterly Review. Vols. 54 and 56 .	8vo.	Lond.	1850–1
——— Review. N. S. Vols. 2–6. [*Continued.*] . .	8vo.	Lond.	1852–4
——— Shorter Catechism. Ed. by Boyd . . .	16o.	N. Y.	1854
What to Observe at the Bed-Side, and After Death . . .	12o.	Phil.	1853
Whatcoat—Life of. See *Fry*, *Benj.*			
Whately, Rich.—Easy Lessons on Reasoning . . .	12o.	Bost.	1852
——— —— Elements of Logic	12o.	Bost.	1855
——— —— Elements of Rhetoric	12o.	N. Y.	1854
——— —— Historic Doubts and Certainties . . .	16o.	N. Y.	1853
——— —— Selection of English Synonyms . . .	16o.	Lond.	1852
——— —— View of Scripture Relations Concerning a Future State	12o.	Phil.	1855
Wheat Sheaf; a Suggestive Reader	12o.	Phil.	1853
Wheaton, Hen.—Elements of International Law . . .	8vo.	Bost.	1855
——— Robt.—Memoir of, with Select Writings . .	16o.	Bost.	1854
Wheeler, Gerv.—Homes for the People in Suburb and Country .	12o.	N. Y.	1855
——— —— Rural Homes; or, Houses Suited to Am. Country Life	12o.	N. Y.	1851
——— J. A.—Hand-Book of Anatomy for Students of the Fine Arts	12o.	Lond.	no date
——— J. H.—Historical Sketches of North Carolina, 1584–1851	8vo.	Phil.	1851
——— J. T.—Analysis and Summary of Herodotus . .	16o.	Lond.	1852
Whewell, Wm.—Astronomy and General Physics . . .	16o.	Lond.	1852
——— —— History of Moral Philosophy in England .	8vo.	Lond.	1852
Whipple, E. P.—Washington and the Principles of the Revolution	12o.	Bost.	1850
White, Adam—Popular History of Mammalia . . .	16o.	Lond.	1850
——— Geo.—Historical Collections of Georgia . . .	8vo.	N. Y.	1854
——— Hen.—History of England, for Junior Classes . .	16o.	Edin.	1851
——— —— History of France, to 1850	12o.	Edin.	1850
——— John—Voyage to New South Wales . . .	4to.	Lond.	1790
——— Nath. F.—Voices from the Spirit-Land . . .	12o.	N. Y.	1854
——— Rich. G.—Shakspeare's Scholar	8vo.	N. Y.	1854
——— Wal.—To Mount Blanc and Back Again . . .	16o.	Lond.	1854
——— Wm.—Memoirs of the Protest. Epis. Church in United States	8vo.	Phil.	1820
——— Walt.—Papers on Railway and Electric Communications, &c.	12o.	Edin.	1850–1
Whitehead, Chas.—Life and Times of Sir W. Raleigh . .	12o.	Lond.	1854
Whitefield, Geo.—Twenty-Three Sermons	16o.	Lond.	1745
——— —— Voyage from London to Savannah, Ga. .	8vo.	Lond.	1739
Whiting, H. S.—Pictures of Nurnberg and Rambles in Franconia. 2 v.	12o.	Lond.	1850
Whitman, S. H.—Hours of Life, and other Poems . .	16o.	Prov.	1853
——— Z. G.—Ancient and Honorable Artillery Company .	8vo.	Bost.	1820
——— Walter—Leaves of Grass	8vo.	Brooklyn.	1855
Whitney, J. D.—Metallic Wealth of the United States . .	8vo.	Phil.	1854
Whittemore, Thos.—Commentary on Revelation of St. John .	12o.	Bost.	1848
——— —— Memoir of Rev. Walter Balfour . . .	16o.	Bost.	1852
——— —— Life of Rev. Hosea Ballou, Vol. 1 . .	12o.	Bost.	1854

Whittier, J. G.—Chapel of the Hermits, and other Poems	16o.	Bost.	1853
——— —— Literary Recreations and Miscellanies	12o.	Bost.	1854
——— —— Poems	8vo.	Bost.	1850
——— —— Songs of Labor, and other Poems	12o.	Bost.	1850
Wide-Awake Gift and Know-Nothing Token, for 1855	12o.	N. Y.	1855
Wikoff, Hen.—My Courtship and its Consequences	12o.	N. Y.	1855
Wiggins, Jno.—Practice of Embanking Lands from the Sea	16o.	Lond.	1852
Wight, J.—Mornings at Bow Street	16o.	Lond.	1838
Wild Oats, Sown Abroad	12o.	Phil.	no date
Wilde, Wm. R.—Aural Surgery and Diseases of the Ear	8vo.	Phil.	1853
——— —— Irish Popular Superstitions	16o.	Dublin.	no date
Wilks, G. A. F.—The Popes, from Linus to Pius IX.	8vo.	Lond.	1851
——— Wash.—The Half Century; its History, &c.	12o.	Lond.	1852
Wilkes, Chas.—Voyage Round the World. (The "Narrative" abridged)	8vo.	N. Y.	1851
——— Geo.—Europe in a Hurry	12o.	N. Y.	1852
Wilkinson, J. G.—Popular Account of the Ancient Egyptians. 2 v.	12o.	N. Y.	1854
——— —— The Same. 2 v.	12o.	Lond.	1854
——— J. J. G.—The Human Body, and its Connexion with Man	12o.	Phil.	1851
Will, Hen.—Outlines of Chemical Analysis	8vo.	Bost.	1855
——— —— Outlines of Qualitative Analysis	12o.	Bost.	1847
Willard, Emma—Abridged History of the United States	12o.	N. Y.	1846
——— Jno.—Treatise on Equity Jurisprudence	8vo.	Albany.	1855
——— Jos.—Address in Commem. of the Incorp. of Lancaster, Mass.	8vo.	Bost.	1853
——— Sid.—Memories of Youth and Manhood, 2 v.	12o.	Camb.	1855
Willement, Emily E.—Catechism of Familiar Things	12o.	Phil.	1852
William III. (Late King of England)—Life of	8vo.	Lond.	1703
Williams, A. D.—Rhode Island Freewill Baptist Pulpit	12o.	Bost.	1852
——— B.—Manual for Teaching Model-Drawing	8vo.	Lond.	1852
——— B. B.—Mental Alchemy	12o.	N. Y.	1852
*——— Edwin—New York Annual Register. 1830–40, 6 v.	12o.	N. Y.	1830–39
——— Fred. S.—Our Iron Roads; their History, &c.	8vo.	Lond.	1852
——— Jno.—Redeemed Captive returning to Zion	16o.	Northamp.	1853
——— J. J.—The Isthmus of Tehuantepec. 2 v.	8vo.	N. Y.	1852
——— Rog.—Life of, by R. Elton	16o.	Prov.	1853
——— W.—Appleton's United States Guide-Book	16o.	N. Y.	1850
——— —— Trav's and Tourist's St'mbt. Guide thro' U. S. & Canada	12o.	Phil.	1851
——— Wm. R.—Lectures on the Lord's Prayer	12o.	Bost.	1851
——— —— Religious Progress	12o.	Bost.	1850
——— —— Worship at Work	18o.	N. Y.	1854
Williamson, A.—Jews not the Heirs of the Abrahamic Will	24o.	N. Y.	1852
——— Jno.—Medical Observations on the West Indies. 2 v.	8vo.	Edin.	1817
Willis, N. P.—Famous Persons and Places	12o.	N. Y.	1854
——— —— Health Trip to the Tropics	12o.	N. Y.	1853
——— —— Hurry-Graphs; or, Sketches of Scenery, Celebrities, &c.	12o.	N. Y.	1851
——— —— Life Here and There	12o.	N. Y.	1850
——— —— Memoranda of the Life of Jenny Lind	12o.	Phil.	1851
——— —— Out Doors at Idlewild	12o.	N. Y.	1855
——— —— Pencillings by the Way	12o.	N. Y.	1852
——— —— Poem before the Society of United Brothers	8vo.	N. Y.	1831
——— —— The Rag-Bag: Ephemera	12o.	N. Y.	1855

Willis, N. P.—Rural Letters	12o. N. Y.	1849
——— —— Summer Cruise in the Mediterranean . .	12o. N. Y.	1853
——— —— (Ed'r.)—Trenton Falls, Picturesque and Descriptive .	16o. N. Y.	1851
——— —— and Bartlett (W. H.)—American Scenery, 2 v. .	4to. Lond.	1840
Willson, Marcius—Outlines of History	8vo. N. Y.	1854
Wilmarth, Butler—Memoir of, by Wm. Henry Fish . .	16o. Bost.	1854
Wilme, B. P.—Manual of Writing and Printing Characters .	4to. Lond.	1845
Willmott, Robt. A.—Journal of Summer Time in the Country .	16o. N. Y.	1852
——— —— Pleasures, Objects, &c., of Literature . .	16o. Lond.	1852
——— —— Precious Stones, Aids to Reflection . .	16o. Lond.	1853
Wilson, Dan.—Archæology and Prehistoric Annals of Scotland .	8vo. Edin.	1851
*——— D.—Life of Henrietta Robinson	12o. N. Y.	1855
——— Edw. (Compiler)—Naturalists' Poetical Companion .	16o. Lond.	1852
——— Erasmus—On Syphilis, Constitutional and Hereditary	8vo. Phil.	1851
——— Geo.—Life and Adventures of, by G. Griffith . .	12o. Lond.	1854
——— —— Electricity and the Electric Telegraph . .	16o. Lond.	1852
——— John—Dies Boreales; or, Christopher under Canvass .	12o. Phil.	1850
——— —— Treatise on English Punctuation, &c. . .	12o. Bost.	1850
——— R. A.—Mexico and its Religion	12o. N. Y.	1855
——— Thos.—Parochialia; or, Instructions to the Clergy .	12o. N. Y.	1812
——— Wm.—Little Earnest Book upon a Great Old Subject .	16o. Lond.	1851
Wimmer, Herm.—Die Kirche und Schule in Nord Amerika .	8vo. Leipzig.	1853
Windsor, Lloyd—Inquiry into the Ministerial Commission . .	12o. Claremont.	1844
Wines, E. C.—Commentaries on Ancient Hebrew Laws .	8vo. N. Y.	1853
*Wingfield, W., and Johnson (G. W.)—The Poultry Book . .	4to. Lond.	1853
Winslow, C. F.—Cosmography; or, Philosophical Views of the Univ.	16o. Bost.	1853
Winter, Wm.—Poems	12o. Bost.	1855
Winthrop, Edw.—Characteristics and Laws of Prophetic Symbols	12o. N. Y.	1854
——— Robt. C.—Speeches and Addresses	8vo. Bost.	1852
Wirth, J. G. A.—Geschichte der Deutschen Staaten. Vols. 1–4	8vo Karlsr.	1847–50
Wise, Isaac M.—History of the Israelitish Nation. Vol. 1 . .	8vo. Albany.	1854
Wisner, Wm.—Incidents in the Life of a Pastor . .	12o. N. Y.	1851
Witherspoon, Jno.—Inquiry into the Nature and Effects of the Stage	16o. N. Y.	1812
Wolcott, Jno. (Peter Pindar)—Poetical Works. 2 v. . .	12o. Phil.	1792
Woehler, F.—Analytical Chemist's Assistant. (Fr. Ger.) .	12o. Phil.	1852
Wolff, H. D.—Madrilenia; or, Pictures of Spanish Life . .	8vo. Lond.	1851
——— O. L. B.—Encyclopädie der Deutschen Nat'l Literatur. 8 v. in 4.	4to. Leipzig.	1846–7
Woman's Influence and Woman's Mission	12o. Phil.	1854
——— Mission	12o. N. Y.	1839
Wood, Fernando, Mayor of N. Y.; Biography, by D. Mac Leod	12o. N. Y.	1856
——— J. G.—Sketches of Animal Life	16o. Lond.	1854
——— —— Illustrated Natural History	12o. N. Y.	1853
——— Jno.—Administration of John Adams . . .	12o. Phila.	1846
——— Wm. B.—Personal Recollections of the Stage . .	12o. Phila.	1855
Woods, D. B.—Sixteen Months at the Gold Diggings . .	12o. N. Y.	1851
——— Jos.—Letters of an Architect from France. 2 v. .	4to. Lond.	1828
——— Leonard—Works. 5 v.	8vo. Bost.	1851
Woodbury, Levi—Writings: Political, Judicial, and Literary. 3 v.	8vo. Bost.	1852
Woolrych, H. W.—Life of Judge Jeffreys	12o. Phil.	1852
Woolley, Jos.—Elem. of Descrip. Geom. & Applicat'n to Ship Building	8vo. & 4to. Lond.	1850

Worcester, Noah—Memoirs of, by H. Ware, Jr. . . . 12o. Bost. 1844
——— Sam. M.—Life and Labors of Rev. Sam. Worcester, D.D. 2 v. 12o. Bost. 1852
Words in Earnest to Young Men in Cities . . . . 12o. N. Y. 1851
——— to a Young Man's Conscience . . . . 32o. Albany. 1848
Wordsworth, Chris.—Memoirs of Wm. Wordsworth. 2 v. . 12o. N. Y. 1851
——— Wm.—Complete Poetical Works. . . . 8vo. Phil. 1851
——— ——— The Prelude; an Autobiographical Poem . 12o. N. Y. 1850
Works Entered at the Stationer's Office from 1577–87. 2 v. See *Shakspeare Soc. Publications.*
World, Here and There; or, Notes of Travellers . . . 12o. N. Y. 1852
Worsaae, J. J. A.—Account of the Danes and Norwegians in Britain 12o. Lond. 1852
Worsley, Israel—A View of the American Indians . . 12o. Lond. 1828
Wortley, Emmeline Stuart—&c. . . . . 8vo. Lond. 1853
——— ——— Travels in the United States during 1849–'55 . 12o. N. Y. 1851
——— ——— Visit to Portugal and Madeira . . . 12o. Lond. 1854
Wright, A. S.—Three Thousand Receipts . . . . 8vo. Phil. no date
——— Dav.—Executors', Administrators', and Guardians' Guide 12o. Auburn. 1851
——— Hen. C.—Marriage and Parentage . . . . . 12o. Bost. 1854
——— J.—American Negotiator; or, Currencies of American Colonies 8vo. Lond. 1763
——— Thos.—The Celt, the Roman, and the Saxon . . 12o. Lond. 1852
——— ——— Narrative of Sorcery and Magic. 2 v. . . . 8vo. Lond. 1851
Wronski, H.—Philosophie Absolue de l'Histoire. 2 v. . 8vo. Paris. 1852
Wyatt, Thos.—Memor. of Disting. Amer. Generals & other Officers 8vo. Phil. 1848
Wyckoff, W. H.—The American Bible Society and the Baptists . 12o. N. Y. 1852
Wyld, Robt. S.—The Philosophy of the Senses . . 16o. Edin. 1852
Wylie, J. A.—The Papacy; its History, Dogmas, &c. . . 8vo. Edin. 1852
Wynkoop, W. B.—Song Leaves from the Book of Life and Nature 12o. N. Y. 1852
Wynne—History of the British Empire in America. 2 v. . 8vo. Lond. 1770
——— Jas.—Lives of Eminent Scientific, and Literary Men of America 12o. Bost. 1850
Wythes, Jos. H.—The Microscopist: a Manual for the Use of the Micro. 12o. Phil. 1851

Xenophon, Athen.—Expedition of Cyrus. (Fr. Grk., by Spelman.) 2 v. 8vo. Lond. 1742
——— ——— Scripta. See *Scriptorum Græcorum Bibliotheca.* Vol. 3.

Year Book of the American Congregational Union, for 1854 . 8vo. N. Y. 1854
Yendys, Sydney—The Roman. A Dramatic Poem . . 8vo. Lond. 1852
York, Sar. E.—Memoir of, by Mrs. R. B. Medbery, . . . 12o. Bost. 1853
Youatt, Wm.—The Horse, Edited by Skinner . . . 8vo. Phila. 1851
Young, A. W.—American Statesman . . . . . 8vo. N. Y. 1855
——— Edw.—Night Thoughts on Life, Death and Immortality 12o. N. Y. 1852
——— Americans Abroad; or, Vacation in Europe . . 16o. Bost. 1852
——— Traveller's Tour in North and South America in 1850 . 16o. Lond. 1852
Yriarte, Thos. de—Literary Fables of. (Fr. Span.) . . . 12o. Bost. 1855
Yvan, Dr.—Voyages et Recits. 2 v. . . . . . 12o. Brux. 1853

Zeller, Jules—Histoire de l'Italie . . . . . . 12o. Paris. 1853
Zincke, F. B.—Some Thoughts about the School of the Future 12o. Lond. 1852
*Zolltarife Aller Länder, Gesammelt von Otto Hübner . . 8vo. Leipzig. 1852
Zschokke, Hein.—History of Switzerland . . . . 12o. N. Y. 1855
——— ——— Novellen und Dichtungen. 15 v. . . . 12o. Aarau. 1851
——— J. H. D.—Stunden der Andacht, &c. (Hours of Devotion) 8vo. 1847

NOVELS,

TALES, AND ROMANCES,

IN ENGLISH PROSE.

Part First.

ALPHABETICAL ARRANGEMENT.

Abbess. Mrs. Frances Trollope.
Abbot; Sequel to "Monastery." W. Scott.
Abednego, the Money-Lender. Mrs. Gore.
Abel Allnut. J. Morier.
Abellino; or, Bravo of Venice. M. G. Lewis.
Aben-Hamet. F. A. de la Chateaubriand.
Adam Blair. J. Galt.
Adam Brown. Horace Smith.
Additional Memoirs of my Youth. Lamartine.
Adelaide Lindsay. Mrs. Marsh.
Admiral's Daughter.
Adrian. G. P. R. James & M. B. Field.
Adsonville; or, Marrying Out.
Adventures of an Attorney.
Adven. of a Medical Student. Robt. Douglas.
Adven. of a Younger Son. Capt. Trelawney.
Adventures of Lilly Dawson.
Adventures of my Cousin Smooth.
Adventures of Paul Periwinkle.
Adventures in Fairy Land. R. H. Stoddard.
Afloat and Ashore. J. F. Cooper.
Afraja; or, Life & Love in Norway. F. Mugge.
Agatha Beaufort; or, Family Pride.
Agatha's Husband.
Agathonia. Mrs. Gore.
Agincourt. G. P. R. James.
Agnes; a Franconia Story. Jac. Abbott.
Agnes de Mansfeldt. Thos. C. Grattan.
Agnes Gray. Miss Bronte.
Agnes Morris; or, Heroine of Domestic Life.
Agnes Serle. Ellen Pickering.
Agnes Sorel. G. P. R. James.
Aims and Obstacles. G. P. R. James.
Alamance; or, the Great and Final Experiment.
Alban. Rev. J. V. Huntington.
Albatross. Wm. H. G. Kingston.
Alderbrook. Emily Chubbuck.
Algic Researches. H. R. Schoolcraft.
Alice: or, The Mysteries. E. L. Bulwer.
Alice Paulet. Sequel to "Sydenham."
Alida; or, Town & Country. Mrs. Sedgwick.
Alieford.
Aline; an Old Friend's Story.
Allen Prescott. Mrs. Sedgwick.
All's not Gold that Glitters. Mrs. A. B. Neal.
Alone. "Marion Harland."
Almack's.
Althea Vernon; & Hen. Harrison. Miss Leslie.
Alton Locke. Chas. Kingsley.
Altowan; or, Life in the Rocky Mountains.
Amabel; a Family History. Eliz. Wormeley.
Amadeus. Karl Valman.
Amaury. Alex. Dumas.
Ambrosio de Letinez. A. T. Myrthe.
Amelia. Hen. Fielding.
American Cruiser; Tale of Last War. G. Little.
Amer. Lounger. (Tales, &c.) J. H. Ingraham.
Amy Harrington.
Amy Herbert. Edited by Rev. Wm. Sewell.
Amy Lawrence; or, the Freemason's Daughter.
Amy Lee; or, Without and Within.
Amy Wilton. Emma J. Worboise.
Anastasius; or, Mem. of a Greek. T. Hope.
Ancient Eng. Fictions. W. J. Thoms (Ed'r).

Ancient Régime. G. P. R. James.
Angela. Mrs. Marsh.
Angel's Song. C. B. Tayler.
Anna Clayton; or, The Mother's Trial.
Anna Hammer. Temme.
Annals of Family of McRoy. Mrs. Blackford.
Annals of the Parish. John Galt.
Anne of Geierstein. Walter Scott.
Antidote to the Miseries of Human Life.
Anti-Fanaticism; Tale of the South. M. H.Butt.
Antiquary. W. Scott.
Arabella Stuart. G. P. R. James.
Arabian Night's Entertainments.
Arasmanes; or, The Seeker. E. L. Bulwer.
Archibald Cameron; or, Heart Trials.
Archibald Werner. Chas. Spindler.
Ardent Troughton. Capt. Marryat.
Armenians. Charles Macfarlane.
Arrah Niel. G P. R. James.
Arthur Arundel. Horace Smith.
Arthur Carryl. L. Osborne.
Arthur Conway. Capt. Milman.
Arthur Mervyn. Chas. B. Brown.
Arthur Monteith. Mrs. Blackford.
Artist. Mrs. L. C. Tuthill.
Artist Wife, and other Tales. Mary Howitt.
Ascanio, the Sculptor's Appren. Alex. Dumas.
As Good as a Comedy; or, the Tenn'n's Story.
Asmodeus at Large. E. L. Bulwer.
Aspen Court. Shirley Brooks.
Aspiration. Mrs. Manners.
Atar Gull; or, the Slave's Revenge. E. Sue.
Atherton, and other Tales. Mary R. Mitford.
Atlantic Club-Book. Paulding and others.
Attic Philosopher in Paris. E. Souvestre.
Attila. G. P. R. James.
Aubrey. Mrs. Marsh.
Augustus; or, the Ambitious Student.
Aunt Kitty's Tales. Maria J. McIntosh.
Aunt Patty's Scrap-Bag. Caroline L. Hentz.
Aunt Phillis' Cabin. Mary H. Eastman.
Aurifodina; or, Adventures in Gold Regions.
Aurunzebe, a Tale of Alraschid.
Australian Captive. J. Chamberlayne (Ed'r.)
Authorship.
Author's Daughter. Mary Howitt.
Autobiography of Jack Ketch.
Avillion.
Ayesha, the Maid of Kars. J. Morier.
Ayton Priory. John M. Neale.
Bachelor of the Albany. M. W. Savage.
Bachelor, the; and other Tales S. L. Knapp.
Balloon Travels of R. Merry and his Y'ng Fr'd.
Banking-House. Sam. Phillips.
Barnaby Rudge. C. Dickens.
Bar Sinister; or, Memoirs of an Illegitimate.
Barclays of Boston. Mrs. H. G. Otis.
Barny O'Reirdon; and other Tales. S. Lover.
Basil; a Story of Modern Life. M. W. Collins.
Basket of Chips. John Brougham.
Battle of Life. Chas. Dickens.
Beatrice; or, the Unknown Relat. C. Sinclair.
Beautiful Gate, and other Tales. C. Chesebro'.
Beechcroft. Miss C. M. Yonge
Beechnut: A Franconia Story. Jac. Abbott.
Beauchamp; or, the Error. G. P. R. James.
Beauties of the English Annuals, for 1835.
Behemoth. Cornelius Mathews.
Behind the Curtain.
Behind the Scenes. Lady B. Lytton.
Belford Regis. Mary R. Mitford.
Belinda. Maria Edgeworth.
Bells, The; a Collection of Chimes.
Ben Brace; a Naut. Romance. Capt. Chamier.
Bernardo del Carpio. Jorge Montgomery.
Bertha and Lily. Mrs. E. Oakes Smith.
Bertie; or, Life in the Old Field.
Benjamin, the Jew of Granada. E. Maturin.
Berber. W. S. Mayo.
Berkeley, the Banker. Harriet Martineau.
Betrothed. (I Promessi Sposi.) A. Manzoni.
Bianca. Edw. Maturin.
Big Abel and Little Manhattan. C. Mathews.
Big Bear of Arkansas. W. T. Porter (Ed'r.)
Bishop's Wife. L. Schefer.
Bit o' Writin'; and other Tales. J. Banim.
Bits of Blarney. R. S. Mackenzie.
Bivouac; or, Rival Suitors. W. H. Maxwell.
Blackbeard.
Black Prophet. Wm. Carleton.
Blanche Dearwood; a Tale of Modern Life.
Blanche of Brandywine. G. Lippard.
Bleak House. C. Dickens.
Blind Girl of Wittenberg.
Blithedale Romance. Nath. Hawthorne.
Bloodstone. Donald Mac Leod.
Blue-Stocking Hall. Mrs. Wilmot.
Blue Ribbons. Anna H. Drury.
Boarding Out. Mrs. Sarah J. Hale.
Body and Soul.
Bondman; a Story of the Times of Wat Tyler.
Book of Snobs. W. M. Thackeray.
Book of St. Nicholas. Jas. K. Paulding.
Border Beagles. W. G. Simms.
Bosom Friend. Mrs. Grey.
Boy of Mount Rhigi. Miss Sedgwick.
Boy Trained to be a Clergyman. J. N. Norton.
Boys at Home. Chas. Adams.
Bracebridge Hall. Wash. Irving.
Bragelonne, the Son of Athos. A. Dumas.

Brambletye House. Horace Smith.
Bravo. J. F. Cooper.
Breach of Promise. (By Author of "The Jilt.")
Brian O'Linn. W. H. Maxwell.
Bride of Omberg. (Fr. Swed.) Em. F. Carlen.
Brothers. Wm. Hen. Herbert.
Brothers and Sisters. Frederika Bremer.
Bruno; or, Lessons of Fidelity, &c. J. Abbott.
Bubbles of Fiction. Geo. Barrell, Jr.
Bug Jargal. Victor Hugo.
Budget of the Bubble Family. Lady Bulwer.
Buff and Blue. Chas F. Stirling.
Burrcliffe: Its Sunshine & Clouds. Trowbridge.
Burton; or, The Sieges. J. H. Ingraham.
Bush Rangers of V. Dieman's Land. Rowcroft.
Busy Moments of an Idle Woman. Mrs. King.
Butchers of Ghent. H. H. Weld.
Cabin and Parlor. J. T. Randolph.
Cabin Boy's Story.
Cabinet Minister. Mrs. Gore.
Calavar; a Romance of Mexico. Dr. Bird.
Calderon, the Courtier. Edw. L. Bulwer.
Caleb Field. A Tale of the Puritans.
Caleb Williams. Wm. Godwin.
Camilla; or, Picture of Youth. Miss Burney.
Camperdown; or, News fr. Our Neighborhood.
Canadian Crusoes. Cath. P. Traill.
Canterbury Tales. S. & H. Lee.
Canvassing. J. Banim.
Cap Sheaf. A Fresh Bundle. Lewis Myrtle.
Captain Kyd. J. H. Ingraham.
Captain O'Sullivan. W. H. Maxwell.
Captain Singleton. Dan. De Foe.
Carbonaro. Duke De Levis.
Cardinal's Daughter. Robt. M. Daniel.
Carlington Castle: A Tale of the Jesuits.
Carl Krinken. Miss Warner.
Carlotina, and the Sanfadesti. E. Farrenc.
Caroline: A Franconia Story. Jac. Abbott.
Carl Werner; with other Tales. W. G. Simms.
Carpenter of Rouen. J. S. Jones.
Carrie Emerson. Mrs. C. A. Hayden.
Casper. Miss Warner.
Caste. S. A. Story, Jr.
Castle Avon. Mrs. Marsh.
Castle Builders. Miss C. M. Yonge.
Castle Dismal. W. G. Simms.
Castle of Ehrenstein. G. P. R. James.
Castle of Otranto. Horace Walpole.
Castle Rackrent. Maria Edgeworth.
Castles in the Air. Mrs. Gore.
Catanese; or, the Real and the Ideal. E. Rodman.
Cavaliers of Virginia. Dr. Caruthers.
Caxtons. Edw. L. Bulwer.
Cecil; or, Adven. of a Coxcomb. Mrs. Gore.
Cecil a Peer; Sequel to "Cecil." Mrs. Gore.
Cecil Hyde.
Cecilia Howard. T. S. Arthur.
Cecilia; or, Mem. of an Heiress. Miss Burney.
Celebrated Crimes. Alex. Dumas.
Chainbearer. J. F. Cooper.
Chairolas; and other Tales. Bulwer & others.
Chance Medley of Light Matter. T. C. Grattan.
Chances and Changes.
Chanticleer. C. Mathews.
Charcoal Sketches. J. C. Neal.
Charcoal Sketches. 2d Series. J. C. Neal.
Charles Auchester. E. Berger.
Charles Chesterfield. Mrs. Trollope.
Charles Elwood. O. A. Brownson.
Charles O'Malley, the Irish Dragoon. C. Lever.
Charles Tyrrell. G. P. R. James.
Charles Vincent; or, the Two Clerks.
Charles Westcote.
Charmed Sea. Harriet Martineau.
Charms and Counter Charms. Miss McIntosh.
Chateau d'If. Alex. Dumas.
Chatsworth. R. P. Ward (Ed'r.)
Chestnut Wood.
Chevalier D'Harmental. Alex. Dumas.
Cheveley. Lady Bulwer.
Children of the Abbey. R. M. Roche.
Children of New Forest. Fran. Marryat.
Children's Trials. (Fr. Ger.) Augusta Linden.
Choice Stories, fr. Househ'd Words. Dickens.
Christian Indian; or, Times of First Settlers.
Christie Johnston. Chas. Reade.
Christmas Books. (Carol, &c.) C. Dickens.
Christmas Carol. Chas. Dickens.
Christmas Shadows.
Christmas Stories. (Carol, &c.) C. Dickens.
Christopher Tadpole. Albert Smith.
Chronicles of Clovernook. Douglas Jerrold.
Chronicles of the Canongate. W. Scott.
Chronicles of Pineville.
Chrysal; or, the Adventures of a Guinea.
Chrystalline; a Romance. F. W. Shelton.
Cinq-Mars. Alf. de Vigny.
City Side; or, Passages fr. a Pastor's Portfolio.
Claiborne the Rebel. W. H. Carpenter.
Clarence. Miss C. M. Sedgwick.
Clarrissa Harlowe. S. Richardson.
Claude, the Colporteur.
Clement Falconer.
Clement Lorimer. Angus B. Reach.
Clement Walton. W. Gresley.
Cleve Hall. Wm. Sewell, Ed'r.
Cleveland; a Tale of the Catholic Church.
Clifford Family; a Tale of the Old Dominion.
Clinton (Aimwell Stories.) Wm. Simonds.

Clinton Bradshaw. F. W. Thomas.
Clockmaker. T. C. Haliburton.
Clouded Happiness. (Fr. Fren.) C'ss D'Orsay.
Cloud with Silver Lining. Miss Planché.
Cloudesley. W. Godwin.
Clouds and Sunshine. Chas. Reade.
Clouds and Sunshine.
Clouds and Sunshine in Life of a Village Pastor.
Clovernook. Alice Carey.
Clovernook. 2d Series. Alice Carey.
Club-Book. Tales by Various Authors.
Cœlebs in Search of a Wife. Hannah More.
Collegians, the. Gerald Griffin.
Comic Tales, &c. W. M. Thackeray.
Commander of Malta. Eugene Sue.
Commissioner. G. P. R. James.
Con Cregan. C. Lever.
Cone Cut Corners.
Confession; or, Blind Heart. W. G. Simms.
Confessions of an Attorney.
Confessions of a Housekeeper.
Confess. of an Elderly Gent. Lady Blessington.
Confessions of a Poet.
Confessions of a Pretty Woman. Miss Pardoe.
Confessions of Fitz-Boodle. W. M. Thackeray.
Confidences. A de Lamartine.
Coningsby. B. D'Israeli.
Conquest and Self-Conquest. Miss McIntosh.
Conscript. Alex. Dumas.
Conscious Duplicity.
Conspirator. A. E. Dupuy.
Constance; or, the Debutante. J. H. Mancur.
Consuelo. Geo. Sand.
Contarina Fleming. B. D'Israeli.
Contentment. Mrs. Alice B. Neal.
Conti, the Discarded, &c. Hen. F. Chorley.
Convict. G. P. R. James.
Coquette.
Coquette; or, History of Eliza Wharton.
Cora and her Doctor.
Corinne; or, Italy. Madame de Staël.
Corse de Leon. G. P. R. James.
Cottagers of Glenburnie. Eliz. Hamilton.
Count Julian. W. G. Simms.
Count of Monte-Christo. Alex. Dumas.
Countess Ida. T. S. Fay.
Countess of Morion. Fred. Soulié.
Countess of Rudolstadt. Geo. Sand.
Countess of Salisbury Alex. Dumas.
Country Curate. G. R. Gleig.
Country Quarters. Lady Blessington.
Courtier of the Days of Chas. II. Mrs. Gore.
Courtship and Wedlock.
Cousin Franck's Household.
Cousin Marshall. Harriet Martineau.
Cousin William.
Cousins, the. Maria J. McIntosh.
Cranford. By the Author of "Ruth."
Crater; or, Vulcan's Peak. J. F. Cooper.
Crayon Sketches. By an Amateur.
Creole. J. H. D. Zschokke.
Creole Orphans. Jas. S. Peacocke.
Crichton. Wm. H. Ainsworth.
Cricket on the Hearth. Chas. Dickens.
Crockfords; or, Life in the West.
Crock of Gold. Martin F. Tupper.
Cromwell. H. W. Herbert.
Cruise of the Midge. Capt. Chamier.
Curious Stories about Fairies & Funny People.
Curse of Clifton. Mrs. E. D. E. N. Southworth.
Cyril Thornton. T. Hamilton.
Cyrilla.
Czarina. Mrs. Hofland.
Dacre. Countess of Morley (Ed'r).
Daisy Burns. Julia Kavanagh.
Daltons. Chas. Lever.
Damsel of Darien. W. G. Simms.
Daniel Dennison. Mrs. Hofland.
Danish Fairy Legends & Tales. H. C. Andersen.
Dan Marble.
Darien; or, the Merchant Prince. Warburton.
Dark Lady of Doona. W. H. Maxwell.
Darnley. G. P. R. James.
Dashes at American Humor. Howard Paul.
Dashes at Life with Free Pencil. N. P. Willis.
Daughter of Night. S. W. Fullom.
Davenels.
David Copperfield. Chas. Dickens.
David Dumps. Thos. H. Bayly.
Day Dreams. Martha Allen.
Days of Bruce. Grace Aguilar.
Dead Boxer; an Irish Legend. Wm. Carleton.
Dean's Daughter. Mrs. Gore.
Debtor and Creditor. T. S. Arthur.
Decameron. (Fr. Ital.) Giov. Boccaccio.
Decision. Mrs. Hofland.
Decision; Profession is not Principle, &c.
De Clifford. R. P. Ward.
Deerbrook. Harriet Martineau.
Deerslayer. J. F. Cooper.
Deerstalkers. H. W. Herbert.
Deformed.
Delia's Doctors. Hannah G. Creamer.
De l'Orme. G. P. R. James.
Delphine. Mde. de Staël.
Demetrius the Imposter. P. Mérimée.
Denounced. J. Banim.
Dermot O'Brien. Wm. H. Herbert.
Deserted Wife. Emma D. E. N. Southworth.
Destiny. Miss Ferrier.

Desultory Man. G. P. R. James.
De Vere. R. P. Ward.
Devereux. E. L. Bulwer.
Devil's Pool. Geo. Sand.
Devoted.
Diamond and the Pearl. Mrs. Gore.
Diana of Meridor. Alex. Dumas.
Diary, a; and Strife and Peace. F. Bremer.
Diary of a Blasé. Capt. Marryat.
Diary of a Physician. S. Warren.
Diary of Lady Willoughby.
Dinarbas; a Continuation of "Rasselas."
Discarded Daughter. Mrs. Southworth.
Discipline. Mary Brunton.
Discipline of Life.
Disowned. Ed. L. Bulwer.
District School, as it Was. W. Burton.
Doctor Birch. W. M. Thackeray.
Dodd Family Abroad. Chas. Lever.
Doesticks: What he Says. Mort. N. Thompson.
Dolores. Harro Harring.
Dollars and Cents. Miss Warner.
Dombey and Son. Chas. Dickens.
Dominie's Legacy.
Dona Blanca of Navarre. F. N. Villorlada.
Don Quixote. (Fr. Span.) M. de Cervantes.
Doomed.
Dowager. Mrs. Gore.
Down-Easters, &c. John Neal.
Drama of Pokerville. J. M. Field.
Drayton; a Story of American Life.
Dream Chintz. Miss Planché.
Dream Land by Day Light. C. Chesebro'.
Dream Life. D. G. Mitchell.
Dream of Little Tuk. Hans C. Andersen.
Dreamer and the Worker. D. Jerrold.
Dreams & Rever. of a Quiet Man. T. S. Fay.
Duke and the Cousin. Mrs. Grey.
Duke of Monmouth. Gerald Griffin.
Dumb Love. Aug. Musäus.
Dunallan. Grace Kennedy.
Dutchman's Fireside. J. K. Paulding.
Duty and Inclination. Letitia E. Landon.
Earl's Daughter. W. Sewell (Ed'r.)
Earlswood; or, the Anglican Church. C. Anley.
Early Called. Mrs. Southey.
Earnestness. C. B. Tayler.
East and West. F. W. Thomas.
Eastbury. Ann H. Drury.
Eastford; or, Household Sketches. W. Brooke.
Easy Nat; or, the Apprentices. A. L. Stimson.
Easy Warren & his Con. Wm. T. Coggeshall.
Echoes of a Belle. By Ben Shadow.
Edgar Huntley. Chas. B. Brown.
Edith; or, the Quaker's Daughter.

Edward. J. Moore.
Edward Lascelles.
Effinghams; or, Home as I Found It.
Eighteen Hundred & Fifty-One. H. Mayhew.
Eighteen Hundred and Twelve. L. Rellstab.
Elder Sister. Marian James.
Elinor Fulton. Mrs. H. Lee.
Elinor Wyllys. Jas. F. Cooper (Ed'r.)
Elizabeth Benton.
Elkswatawa; or, the Prophet of the West.
Ella. (Aimwell Stories.) Wm. Simonds.
Ellen Linn; a Franconia Story. Jac. Abbott.
Ellen Middleton. Lady Geo. Fullerton.
Ellen Parry; or, Trials of the Heart.
Ellen Seymour. Mrs. Savile Shepherd.
Ellen Wareham. Ellen Pickering.
Ellie; or, the Human Comedy. Jno. E. Cooke.
Elliott Family. Chas. Burdett.
Elves, with other Tales and Sketches.
Emilia Wyndham. Mrs. Marsh.
Emma. Miss J. Austen.
Emma de Lissau.
Energy. Mrs. Hofland.
English at Home.
English Family Robinson. Mayne Reid.
English Life; or, Manners at Home.
*English Orphans. Mrs. Mary J. Holmes.
English Tales and Sketches. Mrs. N. Crosland.
Eoline; or, Magnolia Vale. Car. Lee Hentz.
Ephemera. G. A. Rice & S. H. Wainwright.
Epicurean. Thos. Moore.
Ernest Grey. Maria Maxwell.
Ernest Linwood. Caroline Lee Hentz.
Ernest Maltravers. Edw. L. Bulwer.
Errata; or, Works of Will Adams. J. Neal.
Escaped Nun, The; or, Dis. of Convent Life.
Essays and Tales in Prose. B. W. Proctor.
Ethan Allen; or, the King's Men. Melville.
Ethel Churchill; Two Brides. L. E. Landon.
Ethel; or, the Double Error. Marian James.
Ettore Vieramosca. Massimo Dazeglio.
Eugene Aram. Edw. L. Bulwer.
Eva; or, Isles of Life and Death. E. Maturin.
Evelina. Miss Burney.
Evelyn. Anna C. Mowatt.
Evening Book; or, Fireside Stories. J. Aiken.
Evenings at Donaldson Manor. Maria McIntosh.
Evenings at Woodlawn. Mrs. Ellet.
Eventide; a Series of Tales and Poems.
Exile of Erin; Sorrows of a Bashful Irishman.
Exiles; a Tale. Mrs. Robinson (Talvi.)
Expectant. Ellen Pickering.
Experience of Life. E. M. Sewell.
Experiences of a Barrister. W. Warner.
Fact and Fiction. L. Maria Child.

Fadette; a Domestic Story.
Fair Isabel. Eugene Sue.
Fairy Bower; or, History of a Month.
Fairy Legends and Traditions of Ireland.
Fairy Tales. Montalba.
Falcon Family; or, Y. Ireland. M. W. Savage.
Falkenburg; a Tale of the Rhine.
Falkland. Edw. L. Bulwer.
Falkner. Mrs. Shelley.
False Heir. G. P. R. James.
Fame and Fancy; or, Voltaire Improved.
Family Failings.
Family Secrets. Mrs. Ellis.
Fancies of a Whimsical Man.
Fanny Dale. T. S. Arthur.
Farmingdale. Caroline Thomas.
Fashion and Famine. Mrs. Ann S. Stephens.
Fashionable Dissipation. Metta V. Fuller.
Fatalist; or, Fortunes of Godolphin.
Fate. G. P. R. James.
Father and Son. Theo. Hook.
Father Bright-Hopes. J. T. Trowbridge.
Father Darcy. Mrs. Marsh.
Faust. G. W. M. Reynolds.
Fawn of the Pale Faces. J. P. Brace.
Fear of the World. Bros. Mayhew.
Felon's Track. M. Doheny.
Female Minister; or, a Son's Revenge.
Female Robinson Crusoe.
Fencing Master. Alex. Dumas.
Ferdinand Count Fathom. Tobias Smollett.
Fern Leaves fr. Fanny's Portf. Mrs. Farrington.
Fernande; or, Fallen Angel. Alex. Dumas.
Fernley Manor. Mrs. McDaniel.
Fielding; or, Society. R. P. Ward.
Fifteen Hundred and Seventy-Two. Merimee.
First and Second Marriages. Mrs. M. Leslie.
First Impressions. Mrs. Sarah Ellis.
First of the Knickerbockers. P. H. Myers.
Fitz George.
Fitzgerald and Hopkins. H. N. Moore.
Five Nights of St. Albans.
Five Years of Youth. H. Martineau.
Fleetwood; or, New Man of Feeling. Godwin.
Fleetwood; or, Stain of Birth. Epes Sargent.
Flitch of Bacon. W. H. Ainsworth.
Flora Lindsay. Mrs. Moodie.
Florence Betrayed. M. d'Azeglio.
Florence Egerton; or, Sunshine and Shadow.
Florence McCarthy. Lady Morgan.
Florence Sackville; or, Self-Depend. Burbury.
Florence, the Parish Orphan. Eliza B. Lee.
Flower Tables. Louisa M. Alcott.
Flower, Fruit, & Thorn Pieces. J. P. Richter.
Flower of the Family. Mrs. Prentiss.
Flowers that Never Fade.
Flush Times of Ala. & Miss. Jos. G. Baldwin.
Folchetto Malaspina. (Fr. Ital.)
Foragers. By W. G. Simms.
Forecastle Tom. Mary S. B. Dana.
Forest, the. J. V. Huntington.
Forest Days. G. P. R. James.
Foresters. Alex. Dumas.
Foresters; Tale of Domestic Life. J. Wilson.
Forest Life. Mrs. C. M. Kirkland.
Forest Tragedy & other Tales. Mrs. Lippincott.
Forgery. G. P. R. James.
Fortescue. James S. Knowles.
Fortune Hunter. Anna C. Mowatt.
Fortunes of Nigel. W. Scott.
Fortunes of Col. Torlogh O'Brien.
Fortunes of the Colville Family. F. E. Smedley.
Forty-Five Guardsmen. Alex. Dumas.
Foscarini; or, the Patrician of Venice.
Foster Brother. Leigh Hunt (Ed'r.)
Foster Brothers. Mrs. Emilie Carlen.
Fourth Experiment of Living.
Francesca Carrara. L. E. Landon.
Frank. Maria Edgeworth.
Frankenstein. Mrs. M. W. Shelley.
Frank Fairleigh.
Frank Freeman's Barber Shop. B. R. Hall.
Frank Mildmay; or, Naval Officer. F. Marryat.
Frank Netherton; or, the Talisman.
Frank Orby; or, One of the Eleven.
Friends and Fortune. A. H. Drury.
Freaks and Follies of Fabledom.
Freaks of Cupid.
Freaks of Fortune. J. B. Jones.
Fresh Leaves from West. Woods. M. V. Fuller.
Fright. Ellen Pickering.
Frolics of Puck.
Frontiersman; a Narrative of 1783.
Fudge Doings. D. G. Mitchell.
Full Proof of the Ministry. J. N. Norton.
Fun Jottings. N. P. Willis.
Gaieties and Gravities. Hor. Smith.
Gale Middleton. Horace Smith.
Galley-Slave. H. Zschokke.
Gambler's Wife. Mrs. Grey.
Game of Life. Leitch Ritchie.
Gammer Grethel. Brothers Grimm (Ed'rs.)
Gammer Gurton's Story Book.
Gaston de Blondveille. Mrs. A Radcliffe.
Gebel Teir.
Genevieve. A. de Lamartine.
Genevieve; or, Chev. of Maison Rouge. Dumas.
Gentleman in Black.
Gentleman of the Old School. G. P. R. James.
Geoffrey Moncton. Susanna Moodie.

George Balcombe. B. Tucker.
George Barnwell. T. S. Surr.
George Lovell. Jas. S. Knowles.
George Mason, the Young Backwoodsman.
George Wilson, a Foundation Scholar. Griffith.
George; or, Planter of Isle of France. Dumas.
George St. George Julian. H. Cockton.
Georgia Scenes. A. B. Longstreet.
Georgina Hammond. Mrs. Daniel.
Geral Milco.
Gertrude. Edited by Rev. Wm. Sewell.
Getting Along. A Book of Illustrations.
Ghost-Hunter, and his Family. J. Banim.
Ghost-Seer. (Fr. Ger.) F. Schiller.
Ghostly Colloquies.
Giafar al Barmeki. G. Spring, Jr.
Gideon Giles, the Roper. T. Miller.
Gilbert Gurney. Theod. Hook.
Gil Blas. A. R. Le Sage.
Gipsey. G. P. R. James.
Girlhood of Shakspeare's Heroines. Mrs. Clarke.
Glenwood; or, the Parish Boy.
Glimpses of Home Life. Emma C. Embury.
Godfrey Malvern. Thos. Miller.
Godolphin. Edw. L. Bulwer.
Golden Calf.
Golden Christmas. Wm. G. Simms.
Golden Sands of Mexico. W. Croome.
Gold-Maker's Village. H. Zschokke.
Gold Mines of the Gila. C. W. Webber.
Good Aunt. Fanny's Budget of Stories, &c.
Good Fellow. Paul de Kock.
Good Time Coming. T. S. Arthur.
Gossips & Sketches of Rivertown. Mrs Neal.
Gowrie; or, the King's Plot. G. P. R. James.
Grace Lee. Julia Kavanagh.
Grahame; or, Youth and Manhood.
Grandfather. Ellen Pickering.
Grantley Manor. Lady Geo. Fullerton.
Greatest Plague of Life. Brothers Mayhew.
Great Hoggarty Diamond. W. M. Thackeray.
Green Hand.
Green Mountain Boys. D. P. Thompson.
Greville; or, a Season in Paris. Mrs. Gore.
Greyslaer. C. F. Hoffman.
Groves of Blarney. Mrs. S. C. Hall.
Grummett's Log.
Guards, the.
Guarica, the Charib Bride. H. W. Herbert.
Guerilla Chief; or, a Romance of War.
Gulliver's Travels. Jonathan Swift.
Gurney Married. Theo. Hook.
Gustavus Lindorn. Em. F. Carlen.
Guy Mannering. W. Scott.
Guy Rivers. W. G. Simms.
Hagar; a Story of To-day. Alice Carey.
Hagar, the Martyr. Mrs. H. H. Stephens.
Half Sisters. C. E. Jewsbury.
Hampton Heights. C. Starbuck.
Handy Andy. Samuel Lover.
Hannah Corcoran. T. F. Caldicott.
Harcourts, the.
Hard Times. C. Dickens.
Harold, the Last of the Saxons. Bulwer.
Harper's Story Books. 5 v. J. Abbott.
Harrington. Maria Edgeworth.
Harry and Lucy. Maria Edgeworth.
Harry Austin.
Harry Burnham. H. A. Buckingham.
Harry Coverdale's Courts'p, & what came of it.
Harry Harson; or, the Benevolent Bachelor.
Harry Lorrequer. Chas. Lever.
Harry Muir; a Story of Scottish Life.
Harry O'Reardon. Mrs. S. C. Hall.
Harvestings. Sketches in Prose and Verse.
Hatchie, the Guardian Slave. W. T. Ashton.
Haunted Man & Ghost's Bargain. C. Dickens.
Haunted Merchant. C. F. Briggs (Ed'r.)
Haverhill. Jas. A. Jones.
Hawk Chief. John T. Irving, Jr.
Hawkstone. Rev. Wm. Sewell (Ed'r.)
Head of the Family.
Headlong Hall, and other Tales. G. Peacock.
Headsman. J. F. Cooper.
Heart, the. Martin F. Tupper.
Heart of Mabel Ware.
Heart Histories and Life Pictures. T.S.Arthur.
Hearts and Faces. J. T. Trowbridge.
Hearts and Homes. Mrs. Ellis.
Heartsease; or, the Brot'r's Wife. Miss Yonge.
Hearts Unveiled. Sarah E. Saymore.
Hector O'Halloran. W. H. Maxwell.
Heidelberg. G. P. R. James.
Heidenmauer. J. F. Cooper.
Heiress. T. S. Arthur.
Heiress. Ellen Pickering.
Heiress of Bruges. T. C. Grattan.
Heiress of Derwentwater. E. L. Blanchard.
Heir of Redcliffe. Miss C. M. Yonge.
Heir of Wast-Wayland. Mary Howitt.
Heirs of Randolph Abbey.
Helen. Maria Edgeworth.
Helen and Arthur. Car. Lee Hentz.
Helen Halsey. W. G. Simms.
Helen Mulgrave; or, Jesuit Executorship.
Heloise. Mrs. Robinson.
Henpecked Husband.
Henry Quatre. J. H. Mancur.
Henry Esmond. W. M. Thackeray.
Henry Masterton. G. P. R. James.

Henry Milner. Mrs. Sherwood.
Henry of Guise. G. P. R. James.
Henry of Ofterdingen. Fred. von Hardenberg.
Henry; or, Web & Woof of Life. Cambridge.
Henry Russell.
Henry Smeaton. G. P. R. James.
Herbert Tresham. J. M. Neale.
Herbert Wendall.
Heretic. (Fr. Russian.) Lajétchnikoff.
Hermann and Dorothea. J. W. von Goethe.
Hermit's Dell. From the Diary of a Penciler.
Hero, and other Tales.
Hester Somerset.
H—— Family. Frederika Bremer.
Hidden Path. Marion Harland.
High Life in New York.
Hill and the Valley. Harriet Martineau.
Hill-Side and Border Sketches. Maxwell.
History of a Flirt.
History of an Adopted Child. Miss Jewsbury.
History of John Marten. Mrs. Sherwood.
History of Tekeli. P. le Brun.
Hive of "The Bee-Hunter." T. B. Thorpe.
Hoary Head, and Valleys Below. J. Abbott.
Hoary Head, and McDonner. Jac. Abbott.
Hoboken. Theo. S. Fay.
Hobomok. Mrs. L. M. Child.
Holly Grange. Mde. E. de K——.
Home. Anna Leland.
Home. Catharine M. Sedgwick.
Home and its Influence. Adela Sidney.
Home as Found. J. F. Cooper.
Home Influence. Grace Aguilar.
Home in the Valley. Em. F. Carlen.
Home is Home.
Home Nar., fr. "Household Words." Dickens.
Home; or, the Iron Rule. Sarah Ellis.
Home Pictures. Mrs. M. A. Denison.
Home Scenes & Heart Studies. Grace Augilar.
Home Scenes & Home Influence. T. S. Arthur.
Home Scenes & Home Sounds. H. M. Stephens.
Homes Abroad. Harriet Martineau.
Homestead on the Hill-Side. Mrs. M. J. Holmes.
Homeward Bound; or, the Chase. Cooper.
Honey-Moon, &c. Various Authors.
Hope Campbell; or, Know Thyself.
Hope Leslie. Miss C. M. Sedgwick.
Horace Templeton. Chas. Lever.
Horse-Shoe Robinson. J. P. Kennedy.
Hour and the Man. Harriet Martineau.
Household of Sir Thomas More.
House of the Seven Gables. Nathl. Hawthorne.
House on the Rock. Miss Planché.
Howard Grey. A Story for Boys.
Huguenot. G. P. R. James.
Humor and Pathos. G. R. W. Baxter.
Humorist. Theod. Hook.
Humphrey Clinker. T. Smollett.
Hunchback of Notre Dame. Victor Hugo.
Hungarian Brothers. Anna M. Porter.
Hungarian Tales.
Hunters' Feast. Capt. Mayne Reid.
Hunting the Romantic. Jules Sandeau.
Hussar. G. R. Gleig.
Hypatia. Chas. Kingsley, Jr.
Hyperion. Hen. W. Longfellow.
Ida May. Mrs. Mary G. Pike.
Ida Norman. Mrs. E. Lincoln Phelps.
Image of his Father. Bros. Mayhew.
Improvisatore. (Fr. Danish.) H. C. Andersen.
Incognito. T. de Trueba.
India: Pearl of Pearl River. Mrs. Southworth.
Indiana. Geo. Sand.
Indian Cottage. B. de St. Pierre.
Infidel. Dr. Bird.
Inebriate's Hut. Mrs. E. D. E. N. Southworth.
Inez: A Tale of the Alamo.
Ingoldsby Legends. Rich. H. Barham.
Inheritance of Evil.
Initials; a Story of Modern Life.
Inklings. S. D. Pratt.
Inklings of Adventure. N. P. Willis.
Insubordination. T. S. Arthur.
Integrity. Mrs. Hofland.
Invalide. C. Spindler.
Io: A Tale of the Golden Fane. K. Barton.
Irrelagh, the Last of the Chiefs.
Irene, and other Tales. Genevieve G. Fairfield.
Irish Sketch-Book. W. M. Thackeray.
Iron Cousin. Mary C. Clarke.
Iron Mask. Alex. Dumas.
Ironthorpe; the Pioneer Preacher. Trowbridge.
Isa, a Pilgrimage. Caroline Chesebro'.
Isabel Carollton: A Personal Retrospect.
Isabel of Bavaria. Alex. Dumas.
Isabel; or, Influence.
Island Empire; or, the Exile of Napoleon I.
Island Home. F. J. Bowman.
Isora's Child. Mrs. Olcott.
Israel Potter. H. Melville.
Italian. Mrs. Radcliffe.
Ivanhoe. W. Scott.
Ivan Vejeeghen. T. Bulgarin:
Ivar; or, the Skjuts-Boy. Em. F. Carlen.
Jack Brag. Theod. Hook.
Jack Halyard, the Sailor Boy. W. S. Cardell.
Jack Hinton, the Guardsman. C. Lever.
Jack Malcolm's Log. Capt. Chamier.
Jack of the Mill. Wm. Howitt.
Jack Runnymede. D. Jerrold.

Jack Sheppard. W. H. Ainsworth.
Jack Tier; or, the Florida Reef. J. F. Cooper.
Jacob Faithful. Fran. Marryat.
Jacques. Geo. Sand.
Jacquerie, the. G. P. R. James.
James Montjoy. A. S. Roe.
James the Second. Wm. H. Ainsworth.
Jane Bouverie. Catherine Sinclair.
Jane Eyre. Miss Bronte.
Jane Seton. Jas. Grant.
Jane Talbot. Chas. B. Brown.
Janet Hamilton
Japhet in Search of a Father. F. Marryat.
Jasper Lyle. Mrs. Ward.
Jeames' Diary, & Rebec. & Rowena. Thackeray.
Jeanie Morrison; or, the Discipline of Life.
Jeremiah Parkes.
Jessie's Flirtations. Miss Curtis.
Jew, the. C. Spindler.
Joanna of Naples. Miss J. L. Park.
Joan, the Heroic Maiden. Alex. Dumas.
John Bull and Bro. Jonathan. J. K. Paulding.
John De Lancaster. Rich. Cumberland.
John; or, a Cousin and Two Counts. E. Carlen.
Jonathan Wild. Hen. Fielding.
Jonce Smiley, the Yankee Boy. H. H. Weld.
Joseph Andrews. Hen. Fielding.
Josephine. Grace Aguilar.
Joseph Rushbrook. Fran. Marryat.
Journal of a Poor Vicar. J. H. D. Zschokke.
Journeyman Joiner. Geo. Sand.
Julian; or, Scenes in Judea. Wm. Ware.
Julian; or, the Close of an Era. L. F. Bungener.
Julienne. Hugh de Normand.
Julius; and other Tales. (Fr. Ger.)
Juno Clifford.
Kaloolah. W. S. Mayo.
Kate Aylesford. Chas. J. Peterson.
Kate O'Donoghue. Chas. Lever.
Kate Stanton. A Page from Real Life.
Kate Walsingham. Ellen Pickering.
Kate Weston. Jennie DeWitt.
Katharine Ashton. Miss Sewell.
Katharine Walton. W. G. Simms.
Katie Stewart. A True Story.
Kavanagh. Hen. W. Longfellow.
Keeping House & House Keeping. S. J. Hale.
Keeping up Appearances. T. S. Arthur.
Kenilworth. W. Scott.
Kenneth. Miss C. M. Yonge.
Kenny's Mills. Mrs. H. C. Knight.
Kickleburys on the Rhine. M. A. Titmarsh.
King's Own. Fran. Marryat.
King's Highway. G. P. R. James.
King of the Hurons.
Kit Bam's Adventures. Mary C. Clark.
Kitty's Relations; & other Sketches. E. Leslie.
Klosterheim; or, the Mask. T. De Quincy.
Knick-Knacks from Editor's Table. L. G. Clark.
Knight of Gwynne. Chas. Lever.
Knight of Mauleon. Alex. Dumas.
Know Nothing (The)?
Koningsmarke. Jas. K. Paulding
Kruitzner; or, German's Tale. S. H. Lee.
La Hougue Bie de Hambie. J. Bulkeley.
Labor and Love. A Tale of English Life.
Laconia; or, Legends of the White Mountains.
Ladder of Gold. Robt. Bell.
Lady Alice; or, the New Una. Huntington.
Lady and the Priest. Mrs. Maberly.
Lady Bird. Lady G. Fullerton.
Lady Jane Grey. Thos. Miller.
Lady Killer. Rebecca Hicks.
Lady Lee's Widowhood. Capt. Hanley.
Lady Mary. Chas. B. Tayler.
Lady of Milan. Mrs. Thomson (Ed'r).
Lady of the Manor. Mrs. Sherwood.
Lady Una and her Queendom.
Lafitte, Pirate of the Gulf. J. H. Ingraham.
Lake of Killarney. Anna M. Porter.
Lake Shore. Emile Souvestre.
Lamplighter, the. Miss Maria Cummings.
Lancashire Witches. Wm. H. Ainsworth.
Land-Sharks and Sea-Gulls.
Laneton Parsonage. Rev. Wm. Sewell (Ed'r).
Lanmere. Mrs. Julia C. R. Dorr.
Last Days of Pompeii. E. L. Bulwer.
Last Leaf from Sunny Side. Mrs. E. G. Phelps.
Last of the Barons. E. L. Bulwer.
Last of the Lairds. J. Galt.
Last of the Mohicans. J. F. Cooper.
Last of the Plantagenets.
Last of his Name. Elbert Perce.
Later Years. Wm. Prime.
Latreaumont; or, Court Conspirator. E. Sue.
Launcelot Widge. Chas. Horton.
Laurie Todd. John Galt.
Lawyer. Mrs. L. C. Tuthill.
Lawyer's Story; or, The Orphan's Wrongs.
Leather Stocking and Silk. Jno. E. Cooke.
Leaves from a Family Journal. E. Souvestre.
Leaves from the Tree Igdrasyl. Martha Russell.
Legends and Records. C. B. Tayler.
Legends and Stories of Ireland. Sam. Lover.
Legends of a Log Cabin.
Legends of Mexico. Geo. Lippard.
Legends of Rubezahl. Musæus.
Legends of the Flowers. Susan Pindar.
Legends of the Revolution. Geo. Lippard.
Legends of the the West. Jas. Hall.

Leila; or, Siege of Granada. E. L. Bulwer.
Leila at Home. Ann F. Tytler.
Leila in England. Ann F. Tytler.
Leila; or, the Island. Ann F. Tytler.
Leonora. Maria Edgeworth.
Leontine. Mrs. Maberly.
Leslie Linkfield.
Lessons in Life. T. S. Arthur.
Letter-Bag of Great Western. Haliburton.
Letters from Rome. A. D. 138.
Levenworth. J. D. Nourse.
Lewie; or, the Bended Twig.
Lewis Arundel.
Liberia. Mrs. S. J. Hale (Ed'r).
Life and Adventures of an Arkansaw Doctor.
Life and Adventures of Geo. Wilson. Griffiths.
Life and Beauties of Fanny Fern.
Life, and its Aims.
Life at the South. W. L. G. Smith.
Life by the Fireside.
Life in Dalecarlia. F. Bremer.
Life in India; or, English at Calcutta.
Life in London.
Life in London. Pierce Egan.
Life in the Wilds. Harriet Martineau.
Life in the New World. Sealsfield.
Life in Varied Phases. Caroline H. Butler.
Life in the South. C. H. Wiley.
Life of a Sailor.
Life of Silas Barnstarke. T. Gwynne.
Life of Vicissitudes. G. P. R. James.
Life Scenes. F. A. Durivage.
Life's Discipline. Mrs. Edw. Robinson.
Life's Lessons.
Life's Lessons.
Light and Darkness. Mrs. Crowe.
Light and Darkness; or, the Shadow of Fate.
Light and Shade. Anna H. Drury.
Light Dragoon. G. R. Gleig.
Lights and Shadows of Scot. Life. J. Wilson.
Lights of Education.
Lily.
Lily Gordon, the Young Housekeeper.
Lily and the Totem.
Linda. Caroline Lee Hentz.
Linnie Lockwood. Cath. Crowe.
Linwoods, the. Cath. M. Sedgwick.
Lion's Skin and Lover Hunt. C. De Bernard.
Lionel Lincoln. J. F. Cooper.
Lionel Wakefield.
Little Ferns, for Fanny's Little Friends.
Little Nell, from the "Old Curiosity Shop."
Little Pedlington. Jno. Poole.
Little Savage. Fran. Marryat.
Little Wife. Mrs. Grey.
Live and Let Live. Cath. M. Sedgwick.
Locke Amsden. D. P. Thompson.
Lodore. Mrs. M. W. Shelley.
Lofoden. E. W. Landor.
Lofty and Lowly. Maria J. McIntosh.
Log of a Privateer's Man. Capt. Marryat.
Loiterings of Arthur O'Leary. C. Lever.
Look to the End. Mrs. Ellis.
Lone Dove.
Lone Star, a Tale of Texas. J. W. Dallam.
Long Look Ahead. A. S. Roe.
Lonz Powers; or, The Regulators. Jas. Weir.
Loom and the Lugger. Harriet Martineau.
Lord and Lady Harcourt. Catherine Sinclair.
Lord Roldan. Allan Cunningham.
Lorenzo Benoni. G. Ruffini.
Lorette; Louise, Daughter of a Nun.
Lorgnette. Don. G. Mitchell.
Lost Brooch.
Lost Heiress. Mrs. E. D. E. N. Southworth.
Lost Hunter; a Tale of Early Times.
Lost Ship; or, Atlantic Steamer. W. J. Neale.
Louisa Mildmay. Mrs. Marsh.
Louise Elton. Mrs. M. E. Herndon.
Louise la Vallière. Alex. Dumas.
Love and Ambition.
Love and Duty. Mrs. Marsh.
Love and Mesmerism. Horace Smith.
Love and Money. Mary Howitt.
Love, a Reality. Mrs. T. Geldart.
Love in High Life. T. S. Arthur.
Love Match. Hen. Cockton.
Love's Stratagem. Em. F. Carlen.
Love Token for Children. C. M. Sedgwick.
Lover upon Trial.
Lover and Husband. Mrs. Gore.
Lovers and Husbands. T. S. Arthur.
Luck of Barry Lyndon. W. M. Thackeray.
Lucretia. Edw. L. Bulwer.
Lucy Boston.
Luttrells; or, the Two Marriages. F. Williams.
Lydia; a Woman's Book. Mrs. H. Crosland.
Madaleine. Julia Kavanagh.
Magdalen, and Marcia. Mrs. Grey.
Magdalen, and other Tales. J. S. Knowles.
Magic Goblet. (Fr. Swed.) Emilie Carlen.
Magic of Kindness. Bros. Mayhew.
Magician's Show Box, and other Stories.
Magpie Castle, and other Tales. Theo. Hook.
Mahmoud.
Maid of Honor. Tale of 16th Century.
Maiden Aunt.
Major Jones's Courtship.
Major Jones's Sketches of Travel.
Making Haste to be Rich. T. S. Arthur.

Malleville; a Franconia Story. Jac. Abbott.
Mammon; or, Hards. of an Heiress. Mrs. Gore.
Manchester Strike. Harriet Martineau.
Man-at-Arms. G. P. R. James.
Man made of Money. Douglas Jerrold.
Manœuvering Mother.
Man of Fortune, and other Tales. Mrs. Gore.
Man of Honor; and, the Reclaimed.
Man of Many Friends.
Man-o'-War's Man.
Mansfield Park. Jane Austen.
Manuel Pereira. F. C. Adams.
Mapleton; or, More Work for the Maine Law.
Marco Paulo in Boston. Jac. Abbott.
Marco Paulo in Maine. Jac. Abbott.
Marco Paulo in New York. Jac. Abbott.
Marco Paulo in Vermont. Jac. Abbott.
Marco Paulo on the Erie Canal. Jac. Abbott.
Marco Paulo at the Springfield Armory. "
Marcus Warland. Car. Lee Hentz.
Mardens, the; and Daventrys. Miss Pardoe.
Mardi, and a Voyage Thither. H. Melville.
Margaret, a Tale of the Real and Ideal. Judd.
Margaret Cecil.
Margaret Hepburn.
Margaret; or, Prejudice at Home, &c.
Margaret; or, the Pearl. Chas. B. Tayler.
Margaret Percival. Rev. Wm. Sewell (Ed'r.)
Margaret Percival in America. W. Sewell.
Margaret Ravenscroft. Jas. A. St. John.
Marguerite de Valois. Alex. Dumas.
Marian; or, Young Maid's Fortunes. Mrs. Hall.
Mark Hurdlestone. Mrs. Moodie.
Mark Wilton, the Merch. Clerk. C. B. Tayler.
Marmaduke Herbert. Countess of Blessington.
Marmaduke Wyvil. Hen. W. Herbert.
Maroon. Wm. G. Simms.
Marriage. Susan Ferrier.
Marriage; a Lottery. Mrs. Grey.
Married and Single. T. S. Arthur.
Married Life. T. S. Arthur.
Marston; or, Memoirs of a Statesman. Croly.
Martin Chuzzlewit. C. Dickens.
Martin Faber; Story of a Crim'l. W. G. Simms.
Martin Merrivale. His x Mark. Trowbridge.
Martin, the Foundling. Eugene Sue.
Mary Barton.
Mary Bell; a Franconia Story. Jac. Abbott.
Mary de Clifford. Sir E. Brydges.
Mary Erskine; a Franconia Story. J. Abbott.
Mary Lawson. Eugene Sue.
Mary Maturin. Douglas Jerrold.
Mary of Burgundy. G. P. R. James.
Mary Schweidler; Amber Witch. W. Meinhold.
Master Builder. D. K. Lee.
Masterman Ready. Fran. Marryat.
Master's House; a Tale of Southern Life.
Matilda. Eugene Sue.
Matilda Montgomerie. Maj. Richardson.
Matricide. John K. Duer.
Matrimonial Shipwreck. Annette M. Maillard.
Matrimony; or, Love Affairs in our Village.
Matthew Wald. J. G. Lockhart.
Maurice Tiernay. Chas. Lever.
Maxwell. Theod. Hook.
May and December. Mrs. Hubback.
May-Day in New-York. Chas. A. Davis.
May Martin; or, Money Dig's. D. P. Thompson.
Mayor of Windgap. J. Banim.
Means and Ends. Cath. M. Sedgwick.
Mechanic. Mrs. L. C. Tuthill.
Melincourt. G. Peacock.
Mellichampe. W. G. Simms.
Melmoth, the Wanderer. R. C. Maturin.
Mem. of Fem. de Chambre. Lady Blessington.
Memoirs of a Nullifier. A. S. Johnson.
Memoirs of a Peeress. Lady C. Bury (Ed'r.)
Memoirs of a Physician. Alex. Dumas.
Memoirs of a Grandmother.
Men of Character. D. Jerrold.
Men's Wives. W. M. Thackeray.
Mephistopheles in England.
Mercedes of Castile. J. F. Cooper.
Merchant. Mrs. L. C. Tuthill.
Merchant's Clerk, and other Tales. S. Warren.
Merkland; or, Self-Sacrifice.
Merrimack; or, Life at the Loom. D. K. Lee.
Merry Mount; Romance of Mass.
Merry Tales of Three Wise Men of Gotham.
Messrs. Vanderput & Snock. Har. Martineau.
Michael Armstrong. Mrs. F. Trollope.
Midnight Sun. Frederika Bremer.
Midshipman Easy. Fran. Marryat.
Midshipman's Expedients and other Tales.
Midsummer Flowers. Mary Howitt.
Midsummer's Eve. Mrs. S. C. Hall.
Miles Tremenheere. A. M. Maillard.
Milford Malvoisin. F. E. Paget.
Mimic Life. Anna Cora Ritchie.
Ministering Children.
Minnie Hermon. T. W. Brown.
Minstrel Love. (Fr. Ger.) F. D. la M. Fouqué.
Miranda.
Miriam Coffin; or, Whale Fisherman.
Miriam; or, Power of Truth.
Mirror of Maidens. Mrs. Sherwood, Jr.
Miser; or, Convicts of Lisnamona. Carleton.
Miseries of Human Life.
Miseries of Marriage. Mrs. Gore.
Miserrimus.

Miser's Daughter. Wm. H. Ainsworth.
Missing Bride. Mrs. E. D. E. N. Southworth.
Mission; or, Scenes in Africa. Capt. Marryat.
Mississippi Scenes. J. B. Cobb.
Mistakes of a Life-time. W. Howard.
Mob Cap, and other Tales. Car. Lee Hentz.
Moby Dick; or, the Whale. H. Melville.
Moderation. Mrs. Hofland.
Modern Accomplishments. Catharine Sinclair.
Modern Chivalry. H. H. Brackenridge.
Modern Flirtations. Catherine Sinclair.
Modern Pilgrims. Geo. Wood.
Modern Society. Catherine Sinclair.
Modern Vassal. John Wilmer.
Monaldi. Wash. Allston.
Monastery. Walter Scott.
Money-Maker, & other Tales. J. C. Campbell.
Moneypenny. Cornelius Mathews.
Monikins. J. F. Cooper.
Monk. M. G. Lewis.
Monk's Revenge; or, Secret Enemy. S. Spring.
Mons. Violet. Fran. Marryat.
Moorland Cottage.
Montezuma, Last of the Aztecs. E. Maturin.
Montezuma, the Serf. Jas. H. Ingraham.
Moral Tales. Maria Edgeworth.
Moral Tales. Mad. de Genlis.
Moral Tales. Mad. Guizot.
Morals of Pleasure. (Stories for the Young.)
Mordaunt. John Moore.
Mordaunt Hall; or, Sept. Night. Mrs. Marsh.
Moredun; a Tale of 1210. W. Scott.
Morley Ernstein. G. P. R. James.
Morton Montagu. Charlotte B. Mortimer.
Morton's Hope. J. L. Motley.
Mosaic Workers. Geo. Sand.
Mosses from an Old Manse. Nath. Hawthorne.
Mother-in-Law. Maria A. Burlingham.
Mother-in-Law. Mrs. Southworth.
Mothers and Daughters. Mrs. Gore.
Mother's Recompense. Grace Aguilar.
Mother, the. T. S. Arthur.
Motley Book. Cornelius Mathews.
Mount Hope. C. N. Hollister.
Mrs. Brown's Let. to a Young Man. Thackeray.
Mr. Rutherford's Children. Misses Warner.
Mrs. Armytage. Mrs. Gore.
Mrs. Ben Darby. A. Maria Collins.
Mrs. Caudle's Curtain Lectures. D. Jerrold.
Mrs. Partington's Carpet Bag. S. P. Avery.
Mrs. Partington's Life & Say. B. P. Shillaber.
Mr. Sponge's Sporting Tour.
My Aunt Pontypool.
My Brother. Mrs. Ellis.
My Brother's Keeper. Miss A. B. Warner.
My Confession; the Story of a Woman's Life.
My Cousin Nicholas.
My First Season. Beatrice Reynolds.
My Life. Wm. H. Maxwell.
My Marine Memorandum Book. H. Jennings.
My Mother.
My Novel. E. B. Lytton.
My own Home and Fireside. Syr.
My Peninsular Medal.
My Scrapes & Escapes; or, Adven. of a Stud.
My Shooting-Box. Hen. W. Herbert.
My Sister Minnie. Mrs. Daniel.
My Uncle Hobson and I. Pascal Jones.
My Uncle, the Curate. M. W. Savage.
Myrtis; with other Etchings. Mrs. Sigourney.
Myrtle Wreath, the; or, Stray Leaves Recall'd.
Mystery, the; or, Forty Years Since.
Mysteries of Bedlam.
Mysteries of Berlin. C. B. Burkhardt.
Mysteries of City Life. Jas. Rees.
Mysteries of Paris. Eugene Sue.
Mysteries of the Backwoods. T. B. Thorpe.
Mysteries of the Heaths. Fred. Soulié
Mysteries of the Inquisition. V. de Fereal.
Mysteries of Udolpho. Mrs. Radcliffe.
Mysterious Picture.
Nag's Head; or, Two Months among Breakers.
Nan Darrell. Ellen Pickering.
Nanette and her Lovers. T. Gwynne.
Naomi. Mrs. Webb.
Naomi; or, Boston. Mrs. E. B. Lee.
Natalia; and other Tales. F. de la M. Fouqué.
Nathalie. Julia Kavanagh.
National Tales.
Nature and Human Nature. T. C. Haliburton.
Naval Sketch-Book.
Naval Stories. Wm. Leggett.
Neal Malone. Wm. H. Carleton.
Ned Musgrave. Theo. Hook.
Ned Myers. J. F. Cooper.
Neighbors. Frederika Bremer.
Neighbor's Children.
Nell Gwynne; or, the Court of the Stuarts.
Nellie of Truro.
Nevilles of Garretstown. Chas. Lever.
Newcomes. W. M. Thackeray.
New England Tale. Cath. M. Sedgwick.
New Forest. Horace Smith.
New Gil Blas. H. D. Inglis.
New Home. Mrs. C. M. Kirkland.
New Orleans Sketch-Book.
Newsboy. Mrs. E. Oakes Smith.
New Stories. C. Dickens.
Newton Forster. Fran. Marryat.
New York Aristocracy.

New York in Slices. G. G. Foster.
Nicholas Nickleby. Chas. Dickens.
Nick of the Woods. R. M. Bird.
Night and Morning. E. L. Bulwer.
Nights at Mess.
Nights in a Block-House. Hen. C. Watson.
Nights of the Round Table.
Nina; a Tale for the Twilight.
Nina; Seq. to "Presid't's Daughters." Bremer.
Nobody's Son.
No Fiction. And. Reed.
Norman Leslie. C. H. G.
Norman Leslie. Theo. Fay.
Norman's Bridge. Mrs. Marsh.
North and South.
Northanger Abbey. Jane Austen.
Northwood; or, Life North & South. S. J. Hale.
Norval Hastings.
Notre Dame de Paris. Victor Hugo.
Novellettes of a Traveller. H. J. Nott (Ed'r).
Now-a-days.
Now and Then. Sam. Warren.
Nubilia in Search of a Husband.
Nun, the. Mrs. Sherwood.
Nun, the. Chas. Spindler.
Nursery Basket.
Oakfield; or, Fellowship in the East. Arnold.
Oak Openings. J. F. Cooper.
O'Briens and O'Flahertys. Lady Morgan.
Ocean Queen. W. H. G. Kingston.
Odd Volume; a Collection of Tales.
O'Donoghue, the; a Tale of Ireland. Lever.
Ogilvies.
O'Halloran. Jas. McHenry.
Old Bell of Independence. Hen. C. Watson.
Old Brewery and the New Mission House.
Old Commodore. E. Howard.
Old Continental. J. K. Paulding.
Old Country House. Mrs. Grey.
Old Cro' Nest.
Old Curiosity Shop. Chas. Dickens.
Old Doctor.
Old Dominion. G. P. R. James.
Old Engagement. Julia Day.
Old English Baron. Clara Reeve.
Old Farm House. Car. H. Laing.
Old Friends.
Old Hicks, the Guide. Chas. W. Webber.
Old Homestead. Mrs. Ann S. Stephens.
Old House by the River. Wm. Prime.
Old Inn; or, Traveller's Entertainment.
Old Joliffe. Miss Planché.
Old Judge; or, Life in a Colony. Haliburton.
Old Karl, the Cooper. Elbert Perce.
Old London Bridge. C. H. Rodwell.

Old Maids.
Old Man's Bride. T. S. Arthur.
Old Oak Chest. G. P. R. James.
Olie; or, the Old West Room.
Olive.
Oliver Twist. C. Dickens.
One in a Thousand. G. P. R. James.
One Year; a Tale of Wedlock. Em. F. Carlen.
"Only." Miss Planché.
Only a Dandelion, &c. Mrs. Prentiss.
Only a Fiddler and O. T. H. C. Andersen.
Only Daughter.
Onslow; or, Protégé of an Enthusiast.
Onyx Ring. John Sterling.
Oriental Fairy Tales.
Ormond. Maria Edgeworth.
Oscar (Aimwell Stories). Wm. Simonds.
O'Sullivan's Love. Wm. Carleton.
Ottawah, Last Chief of the Red Indians.
Our Cousin Veronica. Mary E. Wormeley.
Our Folks at Home.
Our Guardian. Mrs. Daniel.
Our Honeymoon, and other Comicalities.
Our Island.
Our Neighborhood. Mrs. Southworth.
Our Parish; or, Annals of Pastor and People.
Our Street. W. M. Thackeray.
Our Village. Mary R. Mitford.
Our World; or, the Slaveholder's Daughter.
Outlaw.
Outward Bound. E. Howard.
Overing; or, the Heir of Wycherly.
Owl Creek Letters. Wm. Prime.
Pacha of Many Tales. Fran. Marryat.
Pageant; or, Pleasure & its Price. F. E. Paget.
Palais Royal. J. H. Mancur.
Panthea. Robt. Hunt.
Parent's Assistant. (For Youth.) Edgeworth.
Parish-Side.
Paris Sketch Book. W. M. Thackeray.
Parricide.
Parson's Daughter. Theod. Hook.
Partisan. W. G. Simms.
Partners for Life. Camilla Toulmin.
Passages from the History of a Wasted Life.
Pastor's Fireside. Jane Porter.
Pastourel. Fred. Soulié.
Path-Finder. J. F. Cooper.
Patient Waiting. Mrs. Alice B. Neal.
Patronage. Maria Edgeworth.
Paula Monti; or, Hotel Lambert. Eug. Sue.
Paul and Julia. Jno. C. Pitrat.
Paul and Virginia. J. H. B. de St. Pierre.
Paul Clifford. E. L. Bulwer.
Paul Pry's Delicate Attentions.

Paul Pry's Residence in Little Pedlington.
Paul Redding. T. B. Read.
Paul Ulric.
Peace Campaigns of a Cornet.
Pearl Fishing. Choice Stor. fr. House. Words.
Peasant and his Landlord. Baroness Knorring.
Peep at Number Five. Mrs. Phelps.
Peep at the Pilgrims in 1836. Mrs. Cheney.
Peeps from a Belfry. F. W. Shelton.
Peers and Parvenus. Mrs. Gore.
Peer's Daughter. Lady Bulwer.
Peg Woffington. Chas. Reade.
Pelayo; Story of the Goth. W. G. Simms.
Pelham. E. L. Bulwer.
Pencil Sketches. Miss Leslie.
Pendennis. W. M. Thackeray.
Pequinillo. G. P. R. James.
Percival Keene. Fran. Marryat.
Percy Effingham. Hen. Cockton.
Percy; or, the Old Love and the New.
Peregrine Pickle. Tobias Smollett.
Perils of Pearl Street.
Periscopics; or, Current Subjects. Wm. Elder.
Persuasion. Jane Austen.
Peter Ploddy, and other Oddities. J. C. Neal.
Peter Schlemihl. A. von Chamisso.
Peter Simple. Fran. Marryat.
Peter the Whaler. W. H. G. Kingston.
Peter Wilkins. R. Pultock.
Peveril of the Peak. Walter Scott.
Phantasmia.
Phantom Ship. Fran. Marryat.
Philanthropy; or, My Mother's Bible.
Phil Purcel. Wm. Carleton.
Philip Augustus. G. P. R. James.
Philip Colville. Grace Kennedy.
Philosopher's Stone. H. Balzac.
Philothea. Mrs. L. M. Child.
Phœnixiana.
Physiognomist.
Picciola. X. B. de Saintine.
Pickings from the New Orleans Picayune.
Pickwick Abroad. G. W. M. Reynolds.
Pickwick Club. C. Dickens.
Picnic Papers. Edited by Chas. Dickens.
Picnics; or, Tales of Ireland.
Pictures of Private Life. Mrs. S. Ellis.
Piérre; or, the Ambiguities. H. Melville.
Pilgrims of the Rhine. E. L. Bulwer.
Pilgrims of Walsingham. Agnes Strickland.
Pilot. J. F. Cooper.
Pin Money. Mrs. Gore.
Pioneers, J. F. Cooper.
Piquillo Alliaga. Eug. Scribe.
Pirate. Walter Scott.
Planter; or, 13 Years in the South.
Planter's Northern Bride. Car. Lee Hentz.
Planter's Victim; or, Incidents of Am. Slaver
Plebeians and Patricians.
Polly Peablossom's Wedding, and other Tale
Polish Orphan.
Poor Cousin. Ellen Pickering.
Poor Jack. Fran. Marryat.
Poor Rich Man, and Rich Poor Man. Sedgwicl
Popular Legends of Brittany.
Popular Tales. Maria Edgeworth.
Posthumous Papers.
Posthumous Records of a London Clergymai
Potiphar Papers (The). G. W. Curtis.
Pottleton Legacy. Alb. Smith.
Prairie. J. F. Cooper.
Prairie Bird. C. A. Murray.
Praise and Principle. Maria J. McIntosh.
Preacher and the King. L. Bungener.
Precaution. J. F. Cooper.
Preferment. Mrs. Gore.
President's Daughters. Frederika Bremer.
Pretension. Mrs. S. Ellis.
Pretty Plate. John Vincent.
Pride and Irresolution.
Pride and Prejudice. Miss Austen.
Pride of Life. Lady Scott.
Priest and the Huguenot. L. Bungener.
Prince and the Pedler. Ellen Pickering.
Prince Arthur and his Knights.
Princess; or, the Beguine. Lady Morgan.
Priors of Prague. W. J. Neale.
Prismatics. Rich. Haywarde.
Probus; or, Letters from Rome. W. Ware.
Prof. Julius Cæsar Hannibal's Scientif. Discou
Progress and Prejudice. Mrs. Gore.
Protestant. Miss Bray.
Provocations of Madame Palissy.
Puddleford and its People. H. H. Riley.
Punch's Prize Novelists. W. M. Thackeray.
Puritan and his Daughter. J. K. Paulding.
Purraul of Lum Sing.
Pynnshurst. Donald Mac Leod.
Quadroone, the. Jas. H. Ingraham.
Quarter Race in Kentucky. W. T. Porter.
Queechy. Miss Warner.
Queen Philippa's Golden Booke.
Queen of Denmark. Mrs. Gore.
Queen's Necklace. Alex. Dumas.
Queer Bonnets. Mrs. L. C. Tuthill.
Quentin Durward. Walter Scott.
Quiet Heart.
Quiet Husband. Ellen Pickering.
Quod Correspondence.
Quorndon Hounds. H. W. Herbert.

Rachel Gray. Julia Kavanagh.
Rag Bag. N. P. Willis.
Rag-Picker; or, Bound and Free.
Rambleton; Rom. of Life in N. Y. Sealsfield.
Random Recollections of an Old Doctor.
Random Shots & Southern Breezes. Tasistro.
Rangers. D. P. Thompson.
Ranthorpe. G. H. Lewes.
Raphael. A. de Lamartine.
Rasselas; a Tale. Sam. Johnson.
Rattlin, the Reefer. E. Howard.
Ravenscliffe. Mrs. Marsh.
Real Life.
Rebel; and other Tales. E. L. Bulwer.
Rebels. Mrs. Child.
Rectory of Valehead. R. W. Evans.
Recollections of a Chaperon. Lady Dacre.
Recollections of a Housekeeper. Gilman.
Recollections of a New England Bride. Gilman.
Recollections of a Policeman. Thos. Waters.
Recollections of a Southern Matron. Gilman.
Recollections of my Childhood. S. J. Clarke.
Records of a Good Man's Life. C. B. Tayler.
Rector of St. Bardolph's. F. W. Shelton.
Redburn. Herman Melville.
Red-Gauntlet. Walter Scott.
Red Rover. J. F. Cooper.
Red Skins. J. F. Cooper.
Redwood. Cath. M. Sedgwick.
Reel in the Bottle. Hen. T. Cheever.
Reflection. Mrs. Hofland.
Refugee in America. Mrs. Trollope.
Regent's Daughter. Alex. Dumas.
Regicide's Daughter. W. H. Carpenter.
Reginald Dalton. J. G. Lockhart.
Reginald Hastings. Eliot Warburton.
Reginald Lyle. Miss Pardoe.
Religion at Home. Mrs. Williams.
Rena; or, The Snow Bird. Mrs. C. Lee Hentz.
Retiring from Business. T. S. Arthur.
Retribution. Emma D. E. N. Southworth.
Reuben Apsley. Horace Smith.
Rueben Medlicott. M. W. Savage.
Reveries of a Bachelor. Don. G. Mitchell.
Reveries of an Old Maid.
Rhoda.
Rich Enough. Mrs. Lee.
Richard Edney. S. Judd.
Richard Hurdis. W. G. Simms.
Richard of York; or, White Rose of England.
Richelieu. G. P. R. James.
Riches have Wings. T. S. Arthur.
Rienzi. E. L. Bulwer.
Rifle Rangers. Mayne Reid.
Rising in the World. T. S. Arthur.
Rival Beauties. Miss Pardoe.
Robber. G. P. R. James.
Robber of the Rhine. Leitch Ritchie.
Robert Graham. Car. Lee Hentz.
Robert Macaire in Eng. G. W. M. Reynolds.
Robert Rueful. T. S. Fay.
Robin Day.
Robinson Crusoe. Dan. Defoe.
Rob of the Bowl. J. P. Kennedy.
Rob Roy. Walter Scott.
Roderick Random. Tobias Smollett.
Rodolphus; a Franconia Story. Jac. Abbott.
Roger Miller. George Orme.
Roland Cashel. Chas. Lever.
Roland Trevor; or, the Pilot of Human Life.
Rollo in London. Jac. Abbott.
Rollo in Paris. Jac. Abbott.
Rollo in Switzerland. Jac. Abbott.
Rollo on the Atlantic. Jac. Abbott.
Romance Dust from the Historic Placer.
Romance of American History. Jos. Banvard.
Romance of History. France. L. Ritchie.
Romance of History. India. H. Caunter.
Romance of History. Italy. C. Macfarlane
Romance of History. Spain. T. de Trueba.
Romance of Indian Life. Mary H. Eastman.
Romance of the Forest. Miss A. Radcliffe.
Romance of the Harem. Miss Pardoe.
Romance of the Revolution. O. B. Bunce, Ed'r.
Romance of Vienna. Mrs. Trollope.
Romance of War. Jas. Grant.
Roman Nights. Alex. Verri.
Roman Traitor. Hen. W. Herbert.
Rombert; a Tale of Carolina.
Rookwood. Wm. H. Ainsworth.
Rory O'More. Sam. Lover.
Rosamond. Maria Edgeworth.
Rose and the King. W. M. Thackeray.
Rose Clark. Mrs. Farrington.
Rose d'Albret. G. P. R. James.
Rose Douglas.
Rose of the Parsonage. R. Giseke.
Rose of Tistelon. (Fr. Swed.) Mrs. E. Carlen.
Rosine Laval. Mrs. Smith.
Round of Stories. C. Dickens.
Roxobel. Mrs. Sherwood.
Rum Plague. H. Zschokke.
Russell. G. P. R. James.
Russian Sketch-Book. Ivan Golovine.
Ruth.
Ruth Hall. Mrs. Farrington.
Safia. Roger de Beauvoir.
Sailor's Life and Sailor's Yarns.
Sainclair. Mad. de Genlis and Florian.
St. Antholins. Fran. Paget.

Saint Gildas. Julia Kavanagh.
St. Giles and St. James. Douglas Jerrold.
St. James's. Wm. H. Ainsworth.
Saint Leger; or, Threads of Life. Kimball.
St. Leon. W. Godwin.
St. Ronan's Well. Walter Scott.
Salander the Dragon. F. W. Shelton.
Salathiel; or, the Wandering Jew. G. Croly.
Salt Water Bubbles; or, Life on the Wave.
Sam Slick's Wise Saws and Modern Instances.
Saracen; or, Matilda and Malek Adhel.
Satanstoe; or, Littlepage Mans. J. F. Cooper.
Sayings and Doings. Theo. Hook.
Scarlet Letter. Nath. Hawthorne.
Scenes at Washington.
Scenes from the Life of an Actor. C. Hill.
Scenes in our Parish.
School for Fathers. T. Gwynne.
School for Husbands. Lady B. Lytton.
School of Fashion.
School of Life. Anna M. Howitt.
Scottish Chiefs. Jane Porter.
Scottish Orphans. Mrs. Blackford.
Scourge of the Ocean.
Scout. Wm. G. Simms.
Scrap-Book; Collection of Tales.
Sea-King. A Nautical Romance.
Sea Lions; or, Lost Sealers. J. F. Cooper.
Second Love. Musæus.
Secret Foe. Ellen Pickering.
Secret Passion. F. Williams.
Seed-Time and Harvest. T. S. Arthur.
Self-Denial. Mrs. Hofland.
Self. Mrs. Gore.
Self-Condemned.
Self-Control. Mary Brunton.
Self-Deception. Mrs. Ellis.
Sense and Sensibility. Jane Austen.
Separation, the. Mrs. Gore.
Sequel to "Old Joliffe." Mrs. Planché
Sequel to the Neighbour's Children.
Settlers in Canada. Fran. Marryat.
Seven Capital Sins. Anger. E. Sue.
" " " Avarice. "
" " " Envy. "
" " " Pride. "
" " " Voluptuousness. "
Seven Champions of Christendom.
Shabby Genteel Story. W. M. Thackeray.
Shady Side. Mrs. Hubbell.
Shakspeare and his Friends. F. Williams.
Shannondale. Mrs. Southworth.
She Lives in Hopes. Miss Hatfield.
Shepherd's Calendar. Jas. Hogg.
Sheppard Lee.
Shirley. Miss Bronte.
Shoshonee Valley. Tim. Flint.
Shoulder Knot. B. K. Tefft.
Sickness and Health of the People of Bleaburn.
Sidonia. Wm. Meinhold.
Siege of Vienna. Mde. C. de Pichler.
Simple Story. Mrs. Inchbald.
Single Blessedness.
Sin of Monsieur Antoine. Geo. Sand.
Sir Andrew Wylie. John Galt.
Sir Charles Grandison. S. Richardson.
Sir Edward Graham. Cath. Sinclair.
Sir Edw. Seaward's Narr. Miss J. Porter.
Sir Elidoc. F. de la M. Fouqué.
Sir Frizzle Pumpkin; and other Tales.
Sir Henry Morgan. E. Howard.
Sir Jasper Carew. Chas. Lever.
Sir Launcelot Greaves. T. Smollett.
Sir Roger de Coverley.
Sir Theodore Broughton. G. P. R. James.
Sister Agnes; or, the Captive Nun.
Sisters. H. Cockton.
Six Nights with the Washingtonians. Arthur.
Skeptic; a Tale. Mrs. E. L. Follen.
Sketch-Book of Fashion. Mrs. Gore.
Sketches. Mrs. L. H. Sigourney.
Sketches of a Seaport Town. H. F. Chorley.
Sketches from Flemish Life. H. Conscience.
Sketches of Every-Day Life, &c. C. Dickens.
Sketches of Married Life. Mrs. E. L. Follen.
Slave of the Lamp. Wm. North.
Smuggler. J. Banim.
Smuggler. G. P. R. James.
Snarleyyow; or, Dog Fiend. Fran. Marryat.
Snow Image. Nath Hawthorne.
Solomon Seesaw. J. P. Robertson.
Some Adventures of Capt. Suggs, &c.
Sorrows of Werter. (Fr. Ger.) J. W. Goethe.
Southward Ho! W. G. Simms.
Sowers, not Reapers. Harriet Martineau.
Spanglers and the Tingles. J. B. Jones.
Sparing to Spend. T. S. Arthur.
Specimens of the Novelists and Romancers.
Speculation. Miss Pardoe.
Spitfire. Capt. Chamier.
Spirit Rapper. O. A. Brownson.
Sporting Scenes.
Spy, the; a Tale of Neutral Ground. Cooper.
Squanders of Castle Squander. W. Carleton.
Squints through an Opera Glass. G. G. Foster.
Squire. Ellen Pickering.
Staff-Officer; or, Soldier of Fortune. O. Moore.
Standish, the Puritan. Eldred Grayson.
Stanhope Burleigh. The Jesuits in our Homes.
Stanley Buxton; or, Schoolfellows. J. Galt.

Stanley; or, Recollections of Man of World.
Stanley Thorn. H. Cockton.
Star Chamber. W. H. Ainsworth.
Star in the Desert. Miss Planché.
Step-Mother. G. P. R. James.
Steward. Hen. Cockton.
Stonehenge; or, Romans in Britain.
Stone-Mason of Saint Point. A. de Lamartine.
Stories for Parents. T. S. Arthur.
Stories for Young Housekeepers. T. S. Arthur.
Stories from "Blackwood."
Stories of Eng. & For. Life. W. & Mary Howitt.
Stories of the Sea. Fran. Marryat.
Stories of Waterloo. Wm. H. Maxwell.
Story of a Feather. Douglas Jerrold.
Story of a Royal Favorite. Mrs. Gore.
Story of a Life.
Story without a Name. G. P. R. James.
Straight Gate; or, Exclusion from Heaven.
Stray Subjects. F. A. Durivage & G. Burnham.
Stray Yankee in Texas. Phil. Paxton.
Streaks of Squatter Life. John S. Robb.
Strife for the Mastery.
String of Pearls. Arthur and Woodworth.
String of Pearls. G. P. R. James.
Struggles for Life; by a Dissenting Minister.
Stuart of Dunleath. Hon. Caroline Norton.
Student. E. L. Bulwer.
Stuyvesant; a Franconia Story. Jac. Abbott.
Subaltern's Log-Book.
Substance and Shadows.
Summer Land; a Southern Story.
Summer Stories of the South. T. A. Richards.
Summerfield; or, Life on a Farm. Day K. Lee.
Sunbeams and Shadows, &c. G. A. Hulse.
Sunny Side, the. Mrs. Lincoln Phelps.
Swallow-Barn. J. P. Kennedy.
Swamp Doctor. Madison Tensas.
Swamp Steed; or, the Days of Marion.
Swedes in Prague. Caroline Pichler.
Sweethearts and Wives. T. S. Arthur.
Sword and Distaff. Wm. G. Simms.
Sybil Lennard. Mrs. Grey.
Sybil; or, Two Nations. Benj. D'Israeli.
Sidney Clifton. Theodore S. Fay.
Sylvandire; or, Disputed Inheritance. Dumas.
Sylvester Sound, the Somnambulist. Cockton.
Talbot and Vernon.
Tales. Edgar A Poe.
Tales. (Fr. Ger.) L. Tieck.
Tales. H. Zschokke.
Tales and Ballads. Mrs. C. Gilman.
Tales and Fairy Stories. H. C. Andersen.
Tales and Sketches. Nath. Greene (Ed'r.)
Tales and Sketches. Cath. M. Sedgwick.
Tales and Sketches by a Schoolmaster. Legget.
Tales and Souvenirs of Residence in Europe.
Tales and Stories from History. A. Strickland.
Tales by the O'Hara Family. J. Banim.
Tales for Fifteen. Jane Morgan.
Tales for the Marines. Hen. A. Wise.
Tales for Mothers. (Fr. Fren.) J. N. Bouilly.
Tales from the German. N. Greene (Trans.)
Tales of a Physician. W. H. Harrison.
Tales of a Traveller. Washington Irving.
Tales of a Voyage in the Arctic Ocean.
Tales of Fashionable Life. M. Edgeworth.
Tales of Fashion & Reality. Misses Beauclerk.
Tales of Humor and Romance. Holcroft (Tr).
Tales of My Landlord. Walter Scott.
Tales of Old Times. G. Nieritz.
Tales of Peerage and Peasantry. Lady Dacre.
Tales of Travellers, for Wint. Even's. M. Hack.
Tales of Woman's Trials. Mrs. S. C. Hall.
Tales of the Border. Jas. Hall.
Tales of the Borders. Jno. M. Wilson.
Tales of the Caravanserai. J. B. Fraser.
Tales of the Crusaders. Walter Scott.
Tales of the Early Ages. Horace Smith.
Tales of the Garden of Kosciusko. Knapp.
Tales of the Genii. Sir. Chas. Morell.
Tales of the Glauber Spa. Sedgwick, &c.
Tales of the Good Woman. J. K. Paulding.
Tales of the Passions. G. P. R. James.
Tales of the Revolution. John. H. Mancur.
Tales of the Scottish Peasantry. H. Duncan.
Tales of the Sea. Capt. Marryat.
Tales of the Southern Border. C. W. Webber.
Tales of the Town. H. W. Bellairs.
Tales of the Wars of Montrose. J. Hogg.
Tales of the Woods and Fields. Mrs. Marsh.
Talpa; or, Chronicles of a Clay Farm.
Tancred; or, New Crusade. B. D'Israeli.
Tanglewood Tales, for Youth. N. Hawthorne.
Telemachus. Abbé Fénélon.
Temper and Temperament. Mrs. S. Ellis.
Tempest and Sunshine. Mrs. M Holmes.
Temptation. Eugene Sue.
Temptation of Wealth. Miss E. Carlen.
Ten Thousand a Year. Sam. Warren.
Tenant of Wildfell Hall. Miss Bronte.
Ten Nights in a Bar-Room. T. S. Arthur.
Teverino'. Geo. Sand.
Thaddeus of Warsaw. Jane Porter.
Thankfulness. C. B. Tayler.
Theatrical Apprenticeship of Sol. Smith.
Theobald. (Fr. Ger.) H. Stilling.
Thinks-I-to-Myself.
Thiodolf the Icelander. F. de la M. Fouqué.
Thirty Years Ago. W. Dunlap.

Thirty Years Since. G. P. R. James.
This, That, and the Other. Ellen P. Chandler.
Thorpe, a Quiet English Town. W. Mountford.
Thousand and One Phantoms. Alex. Dumas.
Three Courses and a Dessert. Geo. Cruikshank.
Three Eras of Woman's Life. E. E. Smith.
Three Experiments of Living. Mrs. H. Lee.
Three Guardsmen. Alex. Dumas.
Three Marriages. Mrs. Hubback.
Three Nights in a Life-Time.
Three Paths. Julia Kavanagh.
Three Perils of Woman. Jas. Hogg.
Three Sisters, and Three Fortunes. Lewes.
Three Spaniards. J. Walker.
Three Tales. Countess d'Arbouville.
Thurleston Tales.
Thyrnau, the Bohemian Conspirator. Palzoni.
Tell-Tale; or, Home Secrets. Mrs. Phelps.
Ticonderoga; or, the Black Eagle. James.
Time and Tide. A. S. Roe.
Time the Avenger. Mrs. Marsh.
To Love and to be Loved. A. S. Roe.
Tolla. Edmund About.
Tom Burke of Ours. Chas. Lever.
Tom Cringle's Log. Capt. Chamier.
Tom Jones. H. Fielding.
Tom Racquet, and his three Maiden Aunts.
Tor Hill. Horace Smith.
Totemwell. G. Payson.
Townley Clifton.
Traditionary Stories, &c. And. Picken.
Traits and Stories of Irish Peasantry. Lover.
Traits and Traditions of Portugal. Pardoe.
Traits and Trials. Letitia E. Landon.
Traits of American Life. Mrs. S. J. Hale.
Traits of Travel. T. C. Grattan.
Transfusion. W. Godwin, Jr.
Trap to Catch a Sunbeam. Miss Planché.
Travellers, the. Miss E. Savage.
Travels, Voyages, &c., of Gilbert Go-a-head.
Treasure Trove; or, £, *s. d.* S. Lover.
Trial and Self-Discipline. Miss S. Savage.
Trials & Confessions of an Amer. Housekeeper.
Trials of Margaret Lyndsay. John Wilson.
Trials of the Heart. Miss Bray.
Trippings in Author Land. Em. Chubbuck.
Trippings of Tom Pepper. C. F. Briggs.
Tristram Shandy. L. Sterne.
Triumphs of Time. Mrs. Marsh.
True Stories from Hist. and Biog. Hawthorne.
Truth; or, Persis Clareton. C. B. Tayler.
Tuileries. Mrs. Gore.
Turkish Captive. L. F. Lehmanowsky.
Turkish Evening Entertainments.
Twenty Years After. Alex. Dumas.
Twice Married; or, Connecticut Life.
Twice-told Tales. Nath. Hawthorne.
Twins, the. M. F. Tupper.
Two Admirals. J. F. Cooper.
Two Baronesses. Hans C. Andersen.
Two Brothers.
Two Dianas. Alex. Dumas.
Two Families.
Two Fathers. (Fr. Span.) A. Calpe.
Two Flirts; and other Tales.
Two Guardians. Miss C. M. Yonge.
Two Husbands; and other Tales. T. S. Arthur.
Two Lives; or, to Seem and to Be. McIntosh.
Two Loves; or, Eros and Anteros.
Two Old Men's Tales. Mrs. Marsh.
Two Rectors.
Two Sisters; or, Principle and Practice.
Two Wives; or, Lost and Won. T. S. Arthur.
Tylney Hall. Thos. Hood.
Ugly Effie; and other Tales. Car. Lee Hentz.
Unclaimed Daughter.
Uncle Horace. Mrs. S. C. Hall.
Uncle John. Mary Orme.
Uncle Robin in his Cabin. J. W. Page.
Uncle Sam's Emancipation. Mrs. H. B. Stowe.
Uncle Sam's Farm Fence. A. D. Milne.
Uncle Sam's Palace. Emma Wellmont.
Uncle Tom's Cabin Mrs. Harriet B. Stowe.
Uncle Tom in England.
Underground Mail-Agent.
Undine and Sintram. F. de la M. Fouqué.
Unfortunate Maid; or, Miser's Fate.
Unfortunate Man. Capt. Chamier.
Unloved One. Mrs. Hofland.
Unseen Hand; or, Episodes. S. J. Ram.
Up-Country Letters. L. W. Mansfield.
Up the River. F. W. Shelton.
Upper Ten Thousand. C. A. Bristed.
Ups and Downs. W. L. Stone.
Upward and Onward. Lucy E. Guernsey.
Use of Sunshine, the.
Valentine McClutchy, Irish Agent. Carleton.
Valentine Vox. H. Cockton.
Vale of Cedars. Grace Aguilar.
Valerie. Capt. Marryat.
Valerius. Jos. G. Lockhart.
Valley of Shenandoah.
Vanity Fair. W. M. Thackeray.
Vara; or, the Child of Adop. Mrs. Hornblower.
Vasconselos; a Romance of the New World.
Vathek; an Arabian Tale. W. Beckford.
Venetia. Benj. D'Israeli.
Veronica. J. H. D. Zschokke.
Vicar of Wakefield. Oliver Goldsmith.
Victim of Excitement. Car. Lee Hentz.

Victims of Society. Lady Blessington.
Village Belles.
Village Millionaire. Miss Lamont.
Village Notary. Baron Eötvos.
Village Tales.
Village Tales from Alsatia. Alex. Weill.
Villette. Miss Bronte.
Violet Woodville; or, the Danseuse.
Virginia and Magdalen. Mrs. Southworth.
Virginia Comedians.
Visionary. (Fr. Ger.) F. Schiller.
Visiting My Relations.
Vivian Grey. Benj. D'Israeli.
Volcano Diggings. A Tale of California Law.
Voyage to the Moon. G. Tucker.
Wacousta; or, the Prophecy. Maj. Richardson.
Wager of Battle. H. W. Herbert.
Waggeries and Vagaries. W. E. Burton.
Wagner, the Wehr-Wolf. G. W. M. Reynolds.
Waldemar. W. H. Harrison.
Wallace; a Franconia Story. Jac. Abbott.
Wallace, the Hero of Scotland. G. Alexander.
Walt and Valt; or, the Twins. J. P. Richter.
Waltham.
Wandering Jew. Eugene Sue.
Wanderings of a Germ. Tailor. P. D. Holthaus.
Warning to Wives.
War of Women; or, Riv. in Love. A. Dumas.
Warwick Woodlands. H. W. Herbert.
Watchman.
Water-Witch. J. F. Cooper.
Wau-nan-gee. Maj. Richardson.
Waverley; or, 'Tis Sixty Years Since. Scott.
Way Down East. Seba Smith.
Ways of Providence. T. S. Arthur.
Ways of the Hour. J. F. Cooper.
Wealth and Worth.
Wearyfoot Common. Leitch Ritchie.
We; by Us.
Week's Delight of Games and Stories.
Weldron Family; or, Vicissitudes of Fortune.
Wensley; a Story without a Moral.
Wept of Wish-ton-Wish. J. F. Cooper.
We're all Low People There. Sam. Phillips.
Western Clearings. Mrs. C. M. Kirkland.
Western Merchant; a Narrative.
Westward Ho! or, Amyas Leigh. C. Kingsley.
Westward Ho! Jas. K. Paulding.
What Not. Mrs. M. A. Denison.
What's to be Done?
Which? The Right or the Left?
Whim, and its Consequences. G. P. R. James.
Whimsical Women. Em. F. Carlen.
Whim-Whams. (Tales and Poems.)
Whiteboy; Story of Ireland, 1822. S. C. Hall.
White Jacket. Herman Melville.
White Slave; or, Archy Moore. R. Hildreth.
White Slave; or, Russian Peasant Girl.
Whom to Marry, and How to get Married.
Who shall be Heir? Ellen Pickering.
Wide, Wide World. Miss Warner.
Widow Bedott Papers.
Widow Rugby's Husband, and other Sketches.
Wieland; or, the Transforma'n. C. B. Brown.
Wife. T. S. Arthur.
Wife's Sister. Mrs. Hubback.
Wife, the, and Woman's Reward. Mrs. Norton.
Wigwam and the Cabin. W. G. Simms.
Wilderness and the War Path. Jas. Hall.
Wild Jack; or, the Stolen Child. Car. L. Hentz.
Wild Love. F. de la M. Fouqué.
Wild Sports of the West. W. H. Maxwell.
Wilhelm Meister. J. W. Goethe.
Willie and the Mortgage. Jac. Abbott.
Will Watch. W. J. Neale.
Wilmingtons. Mrs. Marsh.
Wiltshire Tales. Jno. Y. Akerman.
Windsor Castle. Wm. H. Ainsworth.
Wing-and-Wing; or, Le Feu Follett. Cooper.
Winkles, the; or, the Merry Monomaniacs.
Winnie and I.
Winter in Washington.
Wise Saws. T. C. Haliburton.
Wit and Humor. D. W. Valentine.
Wolfert's Roost and other Papers. W. Irving.
Wolfsden.
Woman an Enigma. Maria J. McIntosh.
Woman's Faith; a Tale of Southern Life.
Woman's Friendship. Grace Aguilar.
Woman's Trials. T. S. Arthur.
Woman's Whims. X. B. de Saintine.
Wonder Books for Boys and Girls. Hawthorne.
Wonderful Adventures of Captain Priest.
Wondrous Tale of Alroy, &c. Benj. D'Israeli.
Wood Leighton. Mrs. Howitt.
Woodcraft. Wm. G. Simms.
Woodhill. (Same as "Exiles.") Mrs. Robinson.
Woodman. G. P. R. James.
Woodreve Manor. Mrs. A. H. Dorsey.
Work; or, Plenty to Do. Marg. M. Brewster.
Work " " " 2d series. "
Woodstock. Walter Scott.
Wreath from Jessamine Lawn. Mrs. Livermore.
Writer's Clerk.
Wuthering Heights. Miss Bronte.
Wyandotte; or, Hutted Knoll. J. F. Cooper.
Wyoming; a Tale.
Yankee Notions; a Medley.
Yankee Tea Party. Hen. C. Watson.
Yeast; a Problem. Rev. Mr. Kingsley.

Yellow Mask. Chas. Dickens.
Yellow Plush Correspond. W. M. Thackeray.
Yemassee, the. W. G. Simms.
Yes and No. Eugene Sue.
You have heard of them.
Young Crusoe. Mrs. Hofland.
Young Duke. Benj. D'Israeli.
Young Husband. Mrs. Grey.
Young Kate; or, the Rescue.
Young Muscovite. Capt. Chamier.
Young Patroon.
Young Student. Mad. Guizot.
Young Voyageurs. Mayne Reid.
Youth of Jefferson. J. E. Cooke.
Youth of Shakspeare. F. Williams.
Zaidee. Margaret Oliphant.
Zanoni. E. L. Bulwer.
Zeluco. J. Moore.
Zenobia; or, Fall of Palmyra. W. Ware.
Zillah; Tale of the Holy City. Horace Smith.
Zoe; or, Quadroon's Triumph. Mrs. Livermore.
Zoe; History of Two Lives. M. J. Jewsbury.
Zohrab, the Hostage. J. Morier.

Part Second.

ARRANGED ACCORDING TO AUTHORS.

Abbott, Jac.

Malleville, Wallace, Mary Erskine, Mary Bell, Beechnut, Rodolphus, Ellen Linn, Stuyvesant, Caroline, Agnes, } Franconia Stories.
Bruno; or, Les. of Fidelity, Patience, &c.
Harper's Story Books. 5 vols.
Hoary Head, and the Valleys Below.
Hoary Head and McDonner.
Marco Paulo's Voy. and Trav. Vols. 1–6.
1. New York.
2. On the Erie Canal.
3. In Maine.
4. In Vermont.
5. In Boston.
6. The Springfield Armory.
Rollo on the Atlantic.
Rollo in London.
Rollo in Paris.
Rollo in Switzerland.
The Straight Gate; or, Exclus. fr. Heaven.
Willie and the Mortgage.

About, Edmond.

Tolla; a Tale of Modern Rome.

Adams, Chas.

Boys at Home.

Adams, F. C.

Manuel Pereira; or, the Rule of S. Carolina.

Aguilar, Grace.

Days of Bruce.
Home Influence.
Home Scenes and Heart Studies.
Josephine; or, the Edict and Escape.
Mother's Recompense.
Vale of Cedars.
Woman's Friendship.

Aiken, Jno.

The Evening Book; or, Fireside Stories.

Ainsworth, Wm. H.

Crichton.
Flitch of Bacon.
Jack Sheppard.
James II.; or, Revolution of 1688.
Lancashire Witches.
Miser's Daughter.
Old St. Paul's.
Rookwood.
St. James's; or, Court of Queen Anne.
The Star Chambers.
Tower of London.
Windsor Castle.

Akerman, Jno. Y.

Wiltshire Tales.

Alcott, Louisa M.
Flower Fables.
Alexander, Gabriel.
Wallace, the Hero of Scotland.
Allen, Martha.
Day-Dreams.
Allston, Washington.
Monaldi.
Andersen, Hans C.
Danish Fairy Legends and Tales.
Dream of Little Tuk.
Improvisatore.
Only a Fiddler; and O. T.
Tales and Fairy Stories.
Two Baronesses.
Anley, Charlotte.
Earlswood; or, the Anglican Church.
Arbouville, Countess d'.
Three Tales.
Arnold, D.
Oakfield; or, Fellowship in the East.
Arthur, T. S.
Cecilia Howard.
Debtor and Creditor.
Fanny Dale.
Good Time Coming.
Heart Histories and Life Pictures.
Heiress.
Home Scenes, and Home Influence.
Insubordination.
Keeping up Appearances.
Lessons in Life.
Love in High Life.
Making Haste to be Rich.
Married and Single.
Married Life.
Mother, The.
Old Man's Bride.
Retiring from Business.
Riches have Wings.
Rising in the World.
Seed Time and Harvest.
Six Nights with the Washingtonians.
Sparing to Spend.
Stories for Parents.
Stories for Young Housekeepers.
Sweethearts and Wives.
Two Husbands; and other Tales.
Two Wives; or, Lost and Won.
Ways of Providence.
Wife, the.
Woman's Trials.
Arthur, T. S., and Woodworth (F. C.)
String of Pearls.

Ashton, W. T.
Halthie, the Guardian Slave.
Austen, Jane.
Emma.
Mansfield Park.
Northanger Abbey.
Persuasion.
Pride and Prejudice.
Sense and Sensibility.
Avery, S. P.
Mrs. Partington's Carpet Bag.
Azeglio, M. d'.
Florence Betray.; or, Last Days of Repub.
Baldwin, Jos. G.
Flush Times of Alabama and Mississippi.
Balzac, Honoré de.
Philosopher's Stone.
Banim, J.
Bit o' Writin'; and other Tales.
Canvassing.
Denounced.
Ghost Hunter and his Family.
Mayor of Windgap.
Smuggler.
Tales by the O'Hara Family.
Banvard, Jos.
Romance of American History.
Barham, Rich. H.
Ingoldsby Legends.
Barnes, Jos.
Old Inn; or, Traveller's Entertainment.
Barrell, Geo., Jr.
Bubbles of Fiction.
Barton, K.
Io. A Tale of the Golden Fane.
Baxter, G. R. W.
Humor and Pathos.
Bayly, T. H.
David Dumps.
Beauclerk, C. F. and H. M.
Tales of Fashion and Reality.
Beauvoir, Roger de.
Safia.
Beckford, Wm.
Vathek; an Arabian Tale.
Bell, Robt.
Ladder of Gold.
Bellairs, S. W.
Tales of the Town.
Berger, E.
Charles Auchester. A Memorial.
Biglow, C. A.
Aurifodina; or, Adven. in Gold Regions.

Bird, Dr. R. M.
Calavar; a Romance of Mexico.
Infidel.
Nick of the Woods.
Blackford, Mrs.
Annals of the Family of McRoy.
Arthur Monteith.
Scottish Orphans.
Blanchard, E. L.
Heirs of Derwentwater.
Blessington, Countess of.
Confessions of an Elderly Gentleman.
Country Quarters.
Marmaduke Herbert.
Memoirs of a Femme de Chambre.
Victims of Society.
Boccaccio, Giovanni.
Decameron.
Bouilly, J. N.
Tales for Mothers.
Bowman, Jas. F.
The Island Home.
Brace, J. P.
Fawn of the Pale Faces.
Brackenridge, H. H.
Modern Chivalry.
Bray, Miss.
Protestant; Tale of Reign of Queen Mary.
Trials of the Heart.
Bremer, Frederika.
Brothers and Sisters.
Diary; and, Strife and Peace.
H—— Family.
Home; or, Family Cares & Family Joys.
Life in Dalecarlia.
Midnight Sun.
Neighbors.
Nina, (Sequel to "President's Daughters.")
President's Daughters.
Brewster, Marg. M.
Work; or, Plenty to Do.
The Same. 2d Series.
Briggs, C. F. [*Harry Franco.*]
Haunted Merchant.
Trippings of Tom Pepper.
Bristed, Chas. A.
Upper Ten Thousand.
Bronte, Miss. [*Currer Bell.*]
Jane Eyre.
Shirley.
Villette.
Bronte, Miss. [*Acton Bell.*] (*Sister to above.*)
Agnes Grey.
Tenant of Wildfell Hill.
Wuthering Heights.
Brooke, Wesley.
Eastford; or, Household Sketches.
Brougham, Jno.
Basket of Chips.
Brown, Chas. B.
Arthur Mervyn.
Edgar Huntly, the Sleep-Walker.
Jane Talbot.
Wieland; or, the Transformation.
Brown, T. W.
Minnie Hermon.
Brownson, O. A.
Charles Elwood.
Spirit-Rapper; an Autobiography.
Brunton, Mary.
Discipline.
Self-Control.
Brydges, Sir E.
Mary de Clifford.
Buckingham, Hen. A.
Harry Burnham; or, The Young Contin'l.
Bulgarin, Thaddeus.
Ivan Vejeehen; or, Life in Russia.
Bulwer, Lady.
Behind the Curtain.
Budget of the Bubble Family.
Cheveley.
Peer's Daughter.
School for Husbands.
Student.
Bulwer, Sir E. L.
Alice; or, the Mysteries.
Arasmanes; or, the Seeker.
Asmodeus at Large.
Calderon, the Courtier.
Caxtons, the.
Devereux.
Disowned.
Ernest Maltravers.
Eugene Aram.
Falkland.
Godolphin.
Harold, the Last of the Saxon Kings.
Last Days of Pompeii.
Last of the Barons.
Leila; or, Siege of Granada.
Lucretia.
My Novel; or, Varieties in English Life.
Night and Morning.
Paul Clifford.
Pelham.
Pilgrims of the Rhine.
Rebel; and other Tales.
Rienzi.
Zanoni.

Bulkeley, Jas.
La Hougue Bie de Hambie.
Bunce, O. B., Ed'r.
Romance of the Revolution.
Bungener, L. F.
Julian; or, The Close of an Era.
Preacher and the King.
Priest and the Huguenot.
Burbury, Mrs.
Florence Sackville; or, Self-Dependence.
Burdett, Chas.
Elliott Family; or, Trials of N. Y. Seam.
Burkhardt, C. B.
Mysteries of Berlin.
Burlingham, Maria A.
Mother-in-Law.
Burney, Frances. [Mad. D'Arblay.]
Camilla; or, Picture of Youth.
Cecilia.
Evelina.
Burton, Warren.
The District School, as it Was and Is.
Burton, W. E.
Waggeries and Vagaries.
Bury, Lady Charlotte.
Memoirs of a Peeress.
Butler, Caroline H.
Life in Varied Phases.
Butt, M. H.
Anti-Fanaticism; a Tale of the South.
Coldicott, T. F.
Hannah Corcoran; a Conv't fr. Romanism.
Calpe, A.
Two Fathers.
Cambridge, Wm. G.
Henri; or, the Web and Woof of Life.
Campbell, Jane C.
Money-Maker, and other Tales.
Campbell, Walter.
Old Forest Ranger.
Cardell, Wm. S.
Jack Halyard, the Sailor-Boy.
Carlen, Emilie.
Bride of Omberg.
Foster Brother.
Gustavus Lindorn.
Home in the Valley.
Ivar; or, the Skjuts-Boy. A Romance.
John; or, a Cousin and Two Counts.
Lover's Stratagem; or, The Two Suitors.
Magic Goblet.
One Year; a Tale of Wedlock.
Rose of Tistelon.
Temptation of Wealth.
Whimsical Woman.
Carleton, W. H.
Black Prophet.
Dead Boxer.
Miser; or, Convicts of Lisnamona.
Neal Malone.
O'Sullivan's Love.
Phil Purcell; and other Tales.
Squanderers of Castle Squander.
Valentine McClutchy, the Irish Agent.
Carey, Alice.
Clovernook; or, Recollections of the West.
The Same. Second Series.
Hagar; a Story of To-Day.
Carpenter, W. H.
Claiborne, the Rebel.
Regicide's Daughter.
Caruthers, Dr.
Cavaliers of Virginia.
Caunter, Hobart.
Romance of History. India.
Posthum. Records of a Lond. Clergyman.
Cervantes, Miguel de.
Don Quizote.
Chamberlayne, J. (Ed'r.)
Australian Captive.
Chamier, Capt.
Ben Brace.
Cruise of the Midge.
Spitfire.
Tom Cringle's Log.
Unfortunate Man.
Young Muscovite.
Chamisso, A. von.
Peter Schlemihl.
Chandler, Ellen L.
This, That, and the Other.
Chateaubriand, Viscount de.
Aben-Hamet, the Last of the Abencerages.
Cheever, Hen. T.
Reel in a Bot., for Jack in the Doldrums.
Cheney, Mrs. H. V.
Peep at the Pilgrims in 1836.
Chesebro', Caroline.
Beautiful Gate, and other Tales.
Dream Land by Day Light.
Isa, a Pilgrimage.
Child, L. Maria.
Fact and Fiction.
Hobomok; a Tale of Early Times.
Philothea.
Rebels; or, Boston before the Revolution.
Chorley, Hen. F.
Conti, the Discarded; and other Tales.
Sketches of a Sea-port Town.

Chubbuck, Emily. [*Fanny Forrester.*]
Alderbrook.
Trippings in Author Land.
Clark, L. G.
Knick-Knacks from Editor's Table.
Clark, Mary Cowden.
Girlhood of Shakspeare's Heroines.
Iron Cousin.
Kit Bain's Adventures.
Clark, Sarah J. [*Grace Greenwood.*]
Recollections of my Childhood.
Cobb, J. B.
Mississippi Scenes.
Cockton, Hen.
George St. George Julian.
Love Match.
Percy Effingham.
Sisters.
Stanley Thorn.
Steward.
Sylvester Sound, the Somnambulist.
Valentine Vox.
Coggeshall, Wm. T.
Easy Warren and his Cotemporaries.
Collins, A. Maria.
Mrs. Ben Darby.
Collins, M. W.
Basil; a Story of Modern Life.
Conscience, Hendrick.
Sketches from Flemish Life.
Cooke, Jno. Esten.
Leather Stocking and Silk.
Ellie; or, the Human Comedy.
Virginia Comedians.
Youth of Jefferson.
Cooper, Jas. Fennimore.
Afloat and Ashore.
Bravo, the.
Chain-Bearer; or, Littlepage Manuscripts.
Crater; or, Vulcan's Peak.
Deer-Slayer. (1)
Headsman.
Heidenmauer, The.
Home as Found.
Homeward Bound; or, the Chase.
Jack Tier; or, the Florida Reef.
Last of the Mohicans. (3)
Lionel Lincoln; or, Leaguer of Boston.
Mercedes of Castile.
Monikins, The.
Ned Myers.
Oak Openings; or, Bee-Hunter.
Pathfinder. (2)
Pilot.
Pioneers. (4)
Cooper, Jas. Fennimore.
Prairie. (5)
Precaution.
Red Rover.
Redskins, the; or, Indian and Injin.
Satanstoe.
Sea Lions; or, Lost Sealers.
Spy; a Tale of the Neutral Ground.
Two Admirals.
Water-Witch.
Ways of the Hour.
Wept of Wish-ton-Wish.
Wing-and-Wing.
Wyandotte; or, Hutted Knoll.
(*Ed'r.*) Elinor Wyllys.
[N. B.—Those of the above volumes marked (1), (2), (3), (4), (5), form the Series of the Leather-Stocking Tales.]
Creamer, Hannah G.
Delia's Doctors.
Croly, Geo.
Marston; the Memoirs of a Statesman.
Salathiel; or, the Wandering Jew.
Croome, W.
Golden Sands of Mexico.
Crosland, Mrs. H.
English Tales and Sketches.
Lydia; a Woman's Book.
Crowe, Mrs. Cath.
Light and Darkness.
Linny Lockwood.
Cruikshank, Geo.
Three Courses and a Dessert.
Cumberland, Rich.
John de Lancaster.
Cummings, Maria.
Lamplighter.
Cunningham, Allan.
Lord Roldan.
Curtis, Geo. W.
Potiphar Papers.
Curtis, Miss.
Jessie's Flirtations.
Dacre, Lady. (*Ed'r.*)
Recollections of a Chaperon.
Tales of the Peerage and Peasantry.
Dallam, J. W.
Lone Star of Texas.
Dana, Mary S. B.
Forecastle Tom.
Daniel, Mrs. Mackenzie.
Fernley Manor.
Georgina Hammond.
My Sister Minnie.
Our Guardian.
Daniel, Robt. M.
Cardinal's Daughter.

Davis, Chas. A. [*Jack Downing.*]
May-Day in New-York.
Day, Julia.
Old Engagement.
Dazelio, Massino.
Ettore Fieramosca.
De Bernard, Chas.
Lion's Skin, and the Lover Hunt.
De Foe, Daniel.
Captain Singleton.
Robinson Crusoe.
Roxana; or, The Fortunate Mistress.
Deming, Hen. C. (*Trans.*)
Mysteries of London.
Denison, Mrs. M. A.
Home Pictures.
What Not.
Desmond, D. G. (*Trans.*)
Folchetto Malaspina.
De Witt, Jennie.
Kate Weston.
Dickens, Chas.
Barnaby Rudge.
Battle of Life.
Bleak House.
Choice Stories from "Household Words."
Cricket on the Hearth.
Christmas Books.
Christmas Carol.
Christmas Stories.
David Copperfield.
Dombey and Son.
Hard Times.
Haunted Man, and the Ghost's Bargain.
Home Narratives from "Hous. Words."
Martin Chuzzlewit.
New Stories.
Nicholas Nickleby.
Old Curiosity Shop.
Oliver Twist.
Pearl Fishing, from "Household Words."
Pic-nic Papers.
Round of Stories by the Christmas Fire.
Pickwick-Club Papers.
Sketches of Every-Day Life and People.
Yellow Mask.
D'Israeli, Benj.
Coningsby; or, the New Generation.
Contarina Fleming.
Sybil; or, Two Nations.
Tancred.
Venetia.
Vivian Grey.
Wondrous Tale of Alroy.
Young Duke.
Doheny, Michael.
Felon's Track.
Dorr, Mrs. Julia C. R.
Lanmere.
D'Orsay, Countess.
Clouded Happiness.
Dorsay, Mrs. A. H.
Woodreve Manor; or, 6 Months in Town.
Douglas, R.
Adventures of a Medical Student.
Drury, Anna H.
Blue Ribbons.
Eastbury.
Friends and Fortune.
Light and Shade; or, the Young Artist.
Duer, John K.
Matricide.
Dumas, Alex.
Amaury.
Ascanio; the Sculptor's Apprentice.
Bragelonne, the Son of Athos.
Celebrated Crimes.
Chateau d'If.
Chevalier d'Harmental.
Conscript.
Count of Monte Christo.
Countess of Salisbury.
Diana of Meridor.
Fencing Master.
Fernande; or, the Fallen Angel.
Foresters.
Forty-Five Guardsmen.
Genevieve; or, Chev'l'r of Maison Rouge.
George; or, Planters of the Isle of France.
Iron Mask. (Sequel to "Bragelonne.")
Isabel of Bavaria.
Jack Malcolm's Log.
Joan; the Heroic Maiden.
Knight of Mauleon.
Louise la Vallière. (Sequel to Iron Mask.)
Marguerite de Valois.
Memoirs of a Physician.
Queen's Necklace.
Regent's Daughter.
Sylvandire; or, Disputed Inheritance.
Thousand and One Phantoms.
Three Guardsmen.
Twenty Years After. (Sequel to above.)
Two Dianas.
War of Women; or, Rivals in Love.
Duncan, Hen.
Tales of the Scottish Peasantry.
Dunlap, Wm.
Thirty Years Ago.

Dupuy, E. C.
The Conspirator.
Durivage, Fran. A.
Life Scenes, Sketched in Light, &c.
Durivage, F. A., and *Burnham, G.*
Stray Subjects.
Eastman, Mary H.
Aunt Phillis' Cabin.
Romance of Indian Life.
Edgeworth, Maria.
Tales and Novels. 20 vols. in 10.
Vol. 1. Castle Rackrent. Irish Bulls.
2, 3. Moral Tales.
4, 5. Popular Tales.
6–10. Tales of Fashionable Life.
11, 12. Belinda.
13. Leonora. Let. on Female Educa.
14–16. Patronage. Comic Dramas.
17. Harrington. Thoughts on Bores.
18. Ormond.
19, 20. Helen. Frank, Harry, and Lucy.
Parent's Assistant. (Tales.) Rosamond.
Egan, Pierce.
Life in London.
Elder, Wm.
Periscopics; or, Current Subjects.
Ellet, Mrs.
Evenings at Woodlawn.
Ellis, Mrs. Sarah. [*Miss Stickney.*]
Family Secrets.
First Impressions.
Hearts and Homes.
Home; or, the Iron Rule.
My Brother; or, the Man of Many Friends.
Look to the End; or, Bennets Abroad.
Pictures of Private Life.
Pretension.
Self-Deception.
Temper and Temperament.
Embury, Emma C.
Glimpses of Home Life.
Eötvos, Baron.
Village Notary.
Evans, R. W.
Rectory of Valehead.
Fairfield, Gen. G.
Irene; and other Tales.
Farrenc, Edm.
Carlotina and the Sanfadesti.
Farrington, Mrs. [*Fanny Fern.*]
Fern Leaves from Fanny's Portfolio.
do Second Series.
Little Ferns.
Rose Clark.
Ruth Hall.

Fay, Theo. S.
Countess Ida.
Dreams and Reveries of a Quiet Man.
Hoboken.
Norman Leslie.
Robert Rueful. Sydney Clifton.
Fénélon, F. de S. de L.
Telemachus.
Fereul, V. de.
Mysteries of the Inquisition.
Ferrier, Susan.
Destiny; or, Chief's Daughter.
Inheritance.
Marriage.
Field, J. M.
Drama of Pokerville.
Fielding, Hen.
Amelia.
Jonathan Wild.
Joseph Andrews.
Tom Jones.
Flint, Tom.
Shoshonee Valley.
Follen, Eliza L.
Skeptic; a Tale.
Sketches of Married Life.
Foster, G. G.
New York in Slices.
Squints through an Opera-Glass.
Fouqué, F. de la M.
Minstrel Love.
Natalia; and other Tales.
Sir Elidoc; an Old Breton Legend.
Thiodolf the Icelan.; & Aslauga's Knight.
Undine and Sintram, and his Companions.
Wild Love.
Fraser, Jas. B.
Tales of the Caravanserai.
Fuller, Metta V.
Fashionable Dissipation.
Fresh Leaves from Western Woods.
Fullerton, Lady G.
Ellen Middleton.
Grantley Manor.
Lady-Bird. A Tale.
Fullom, S. W.
Daughter of Night.
Galt, John.
Adam Blair.
Annals of the Parish.
Last of the Lairds.
Laurie Todd.
Sir Andrew Wylie.
Stanley Buxton; or, the Schoolfellows.

Gaskell, Mrs.
Cranford.
Mary Barton.
North and South.
Ruth.
Geldart, Mrs. T.
Love, a Reality; not Romance.
Genlis, Countess de.
Moral Tales.
Gilman, Caroline.
Recollections of a Housekeeper.
Recollections of a New England Bride.
Recollections of a Southern Matron.
Tales and Ballads.
Giseke, Robt.
The Rose of the Parsonage.
Gleig, Geo. R.
Country Curate.
Hussar.
Light Dragoon.
Godwin, Wm.
Caleb Williams.
Cloudesley.
Fleetwood; or, New Man of Feeling.
St. Leon; a Tale of the Sixteenth Cent.
Transfusion; or, Orphans of Unwalden.
Goethe, Johann W. von.
Hermann and Dorothea.
Sorrows of Werter.
Wilhelm Meister's Apprenticeship.
Goldsmith, Oliver.
Vicar of Wakefield.
Golovine, Ivan.
Russian Sketch-Book.
Gore, Mrs. Chas.
Abednego, the Money-Lender.
Agathonia.
Cabinet Minister.
Castles in the Air.
Cecil; or, Adventures of a Coxcomb.
Cecil a Peer. (Sequel to "Cecil.")
Courtier of Days of Chas. II., &c.
Dean's Daughter.
Diamond and the Pearl.
Dowager.
Greville.
Lovers and Husbands.
Mammon; or, the Hardships of an Heiress.
Man of Fortune, and other Tales.
Miseries of Marriage.
Mothers and Daughters.
Mrs. Armitage; or, Female Domination.
Peers and Parvenus.
Pin-Money.
Preferment; or, My Uncle, the Earl.

Gore, Mrs. Chas.
Progress and Prejudice.
Queen of Denmark.
Self.
Separation.
Sketch-Book of Fashion.
Story of a Royal Favorite.
Tuileries.
Grant, Jas.
Jane Seton; or, the King's Advocate.
Romance of War.
Grattan, Thos. C.
Agnes de Mansfeldt.
Chance Medley of Light Matters.
Heiress of Bruges.
Traits of Travel.
Grayson, Eldred.
Overing; or, the Heir of Wycherly.
Standish, the Puritan.
Greene, Nath. (Trans.)
Tales & Sketches. (Fr. Ital., Fren., & Ger.)
Tales from the German.
Gresley, W.
Clement Walton.
Grey, Mrs.
Bosom Friend.
Duke and the Cousin.
Gambler's Wife.
Little Wife.
Magdalen and Marcia; or, Rectory Guest.
Manœuvring Mother.
Marriage; a Lottery.
Old Country House.
Sybil Lennard; Record of Woman's Life.
Young Husband.
Griffin, Gerald.
Collegians.
Duke of Monmouth.
Griffith, Geo.
Life and Adventures of George Wilson.
Grimm, Brothers.
Gammer Grethel.
Guernsey, Lucy E.
Upward and Onward.
Guizot, Mad.
Moral Tales.
Young Student; or, Ralph and Victor.
Gurley, Robt. F.
Old Cro' Nest; or, Outlaws of the Hudson.
Gwynne, Talbot.
Life of Silas Barnstarke. A Story.
Nanette and her Lovers.
School for Fathers.
Hack, Maria.
Tales of Travellers for Winter Evenings.

Hale, Mrs. S. J.
Liberia; or, Mr. Peyton's Experiments.
Northwood; or, Life North and South.
Boarding Out.
Keeping House, and Housekeeping.
Traits of American Life.

Haliburton, Thos. C.
Clockmaker; or, Sayings, &c. of Sam Slick.
Letter-Bag of the Great Western.
Nature and Human Nature.
Old Judge; or, Life in a Colony.
Wise Saws; or, S. Slick in search a Wife.

Hall, B. R.
Frank Freeman's Barber Shop.

Hall, Jas.
Legends of the West.
Tales of the Border.
Wilderness and War-Path.

Hall, Mrs. S. C.
Groves of Blarney.
Harry O'Reardon.
Marian; or, a Young Maid's Fortunes.
Midsummer Eve.
Tales of Woman's Trials.
Uncle Horace.
Whiteboy; Story of Ireland in 1822.

Hamilton, Mrs. Eliz.
Cottagers of Glenburnie.

Hamilton. Thos. (*Capt.*)
Cyril Thornton.

Hanley, Capt.
Lady Lee's Widowhood.

Hardenberg, Friedrich von. [*Novalis.*]
Henry of Ofterdingen.

Harland, Marion.
Alone.
Hidden Path.

Harrison, W. H.
Tales of a Physician.
Waldemar.

Harro Harring.
Dolores.

Hatfield, Miss.
She Lives in Hopes; or, Caroline.

Hawthorne, Nath'l.
Blithedale Romance.
House of the Seven Gables.
Mosses from an Old Manse.
Scarlet Letter.
Snow Image; and other Twice Told Tales.
Tanglewood Tales for Girls and Boys.
True Stories from History and Biography.
Twice-Told Tales.
Wonder Book for Boys and Girls.

Hayden, Mrs. C. A.
Carrie Emerson; or, Life at Cliftonville.

Haywarde, Rich.
Prismatics.

Hentz, Caroline Lee.
Aunt Patty's Scrap-Bag.
Eoline; or Magnolia Vale.
Ernest Linwood.
Helen and Arthur.
Linda; or, Young Pilot of the Belle Creole.
Marcus Warland.
Mob Cap, and other Tales.
Planter's Northern Bride.
Rena; or, the Snow-Bird.
Robert Graham.
Ugly Effie, and other Tales.
Victim of Excitement, &c.
Wild Jack; or, the Stolen Child, &c.

Herbert, Hen. W.
Brothers.
Cromwell.
Deer-Stalkers.
Dermot O'Brien; a Tale of 1649.
Guarica, the Charib Bride.
Marmaduke Wyvil.
My Shooting-Box.
Quorndon Hounds.
Roman Traitor.
Wager of Battle.
Warwick Woodlands.

Hernden, Mrs. M. E.
Louise Elton; or, Things Seen and Heard.

Hicks, Rebecca.
Lady Killer.

Hildreth, Rich.
White Slave.

Hill, C.
Scenes from the Life of an Actor.

Hoffman, Chas. F.
Greyslaer.

Hofland, Mrs.
Czarina.
Dan Dennison & Cumberland Statesman.
Decision.
Energy.
Integrity.
Moderation.
Reflection.
Self-Denial.
Unloved One.
Young Crusoe.

Holmes, Mrs. Mary J.
English Orphans.
Tempest and Sunshine.

Hogg, Jas.
Shepherd's Calendar.
Tales of the Wars of Montrose.
Three Perils of Woman.
Holcroft, Rich. (*Trans.*)
Tales of Humor, &c., from Ger. Writers.
Hollister, C. H.
Mount Hope.
Holmes, Mrs. M. J.
Homestead on the Hill-side.
Holthaus, P. D.
Wanderings of a Journeyman Tailor.
Hood, Thos.
Tylney Hall.
Hook, Theo.
Fathers and Sons.
Gilbert Gurney.
Gurney Married.
Humorist.
Jack Brag.
Magpie Castle, and other Tales.
Maxwell.
Ned Musgrave.
Parson's Daughter.
Sayings and Doings.
Hope, Thos.
Anastasius; or, Memoirs of a Greek.
Horton, Chas.
Launcelot Widge.
Howard, Edw.
Jack Ashore.
Old Commodore.
Outward Bound.
Ratlin, the Reefer.
Sir Henry Morgan, the Buccaneer.
Howard, W.
Mistake of a Lifetime.
Howitt, Anna M.
School of Life.
Howitt, Mary.
Artist-Wife and other Tales.
Author's Daughter.
Heir of West-Wayland.
Love and Money.
Midsummer Flowers.
Wood Leighton.
Howitt, Wm.
Jack of the Hill.
Howitt, Wm. and *Mary.*
Stories of English and Foreign Life.
Hubback, Mrs.
May and December.
Three Marriages; or, Life at a Wat'g-pl'ce.
Wife's Sister; or, the Forbidden Marriage.

Hubbell, Mrs.
Shady Side; or Life in a Country Par- [sonage.
Hugo, Victor.
Bug Jargal.
Hunchback of Notre Dame.
Notre Dame de Paris.
Hulse, Georgie A.
Sunbeams and Shadows.
Hunt, Leigh.
Foster Brothers.
Hunt, Robt.
Panthea.
Huntington, Rev. J. V.
Alban: a Tale of the New World.
Forest.
Lady Alice; or, the New Una.
Inchbald, Mrs. Eliz.
Simple Story.
Inglis, Hen. D.
New Gil Blas; or, Penaflor.
Ingraham, J. H.
American Lounger.
Burton; or, the Sieges.
Captain Kyd.
Lafitte, the Pirate of the Gulf.
Montezuma, the Serf.
Quadroone.
Irving, John J., (Jr.)
Hawk Chief.
Irving, Washington.
Bracebridge Hall.
Crayon Sketches.
Tales of a Traveller.
Wolfert's Roost, and other Papers.
James, G. P. R.
Agincourt.
Agnes Sorel.
Aims and Obstacles.
Ancient Régime.
Arabella Stuart.
Arrah Neil.
Attila.
Beauchamp; or, the Error.
Castle of Ehrenstein.
Charles Tyrrell; or, the Bitter Blood.
Commissioner.
Convict.
Corse de Leon.
Darnley; or, Field of the Cloth of Gold.
De l'Orme.
Desultory Man.
False Heir.
Fate.
Forest Days.
Forgery.

James, G. P. R.
Gentlemen of the Old School.
Gipsey.
Gowrie; or King's Plot.
Heidelberg.
Henry Masterton.
Henry of Guise.
Henry Smeaton.
Huguenot.
Jacquerie, The.
King's Highway.
Life of Vicissitudes.
Man-at-Arms.
Mary of Burgundy.
Morley Ernstein.
Old Dominion; or, South'pton Massacre.
Old Oak Chest.
One in a Thousand.
Pequinillo: a Tale.
Philip Augustus.
Richelieu.
Robber.
Rose d'Albret.
Russell.
Sir Theo. Broughton; or, Laurel Water.
Smuggler.
Step-Mother.
Story without a Name.
String of Pearls.
Tales of the Passions.
Thirty Years Since; or, Ruined Family.
Ticonderoga; or, the Black Eagle.
Whim and its Consequences.
Woodman.

James, G. P. R., and *Field (M. B.)*
Adrian.

James, Marian.
Elder Sister.
Ethel; or, the Double Error.

Jennings, Hargrave.
My Marine Memorandum Book.

Jerrold, Douglas.
Chronicles of Clovernook.
Dreamer and the Worker.
Jack Runnymede.
Man Made of Money.
Mary Maturin; a Tale of Social Dictinct'ns.
Men of Character.
Mrs. Caudle's Curtain Lectures.
St. Giles and St. James.
Story of a Feather.

Jerrold, W. B.
Disgrace to the Family.

Jewsbury, Maria J.
Half-Sisters.
History of an Adopted Child.
Zoe: History of Two Lives.

Johnson, A. S.
Memoirs of a Nullifier.

Johnson, Sam.
Dinarbas: a Sequel to Rasselas.
Rasselas: a Tale.

Jones, J. A.
Haverhill.

Jones, J. B.
Freaks of Fortune.
Spanglers and the Tingles.

Jones, J. S.
Carpenter of Rouen.

Jones, Pascal.
My Uncle Hobson and I.

Judd, Sylvester.
Margaret: a Tale of the Real and Ideal.
Richard Edney; or, the Governor's Family.

Kavanagh, Julia.
Daisy Burns.
Grace Lee.
Madeleine.
Nathalie.
Rachel Gray.
Saint Gildas.
Three Paths: a Story for the Young.

Kennedy, Grace.
Decision; Profession is not Principle, &c.
Dunallan.
Philip Colville: a Covenanter's Story.

Kennedy, J. P.
Horse-Shoe Robinson.
Rob of the Bowl.
Swallow-Barn.

King, Mrs.
Busy Moments of an Idle Woman.

Kingsley, Rev. Chas., Jr.
Alton Locke: An Autobiography.
Hypatia; or, New Foes with an Old Face.
Westward Ho! or, Amyas Leigh.
Yeast: A Problem.

Kingston, Wm. H. G.
Albatross.
Ocean Queen; and Spirit of the Storm.
Peter the Whaler.

Kimball, R. B.
St. Leger; or, the Threads of Life.

Kirkland, Mrs. Caroline M.
Forest Life.
New Home; Who'll Follow?
Western Clearings.

Knapp, Sam. L.
Bachelors; and other Tales.
Tales of the Garden of Kosciusko.

Knight, Mrs. H. C.
Kenny's Mills; or, the Earnest Worker.

Knorring (Baroness).
Peasant and his Landlord.

Knowles, Jas. Sheridan.
Fortescue.
George Lovell.
Magdalen; and other Tales.

Kock, Paul de.
Goodfellow, The.

Kotzebue, Aug. von.
Sufferings of the Family of Ortenberg.

Laing, Car. H.
The Old Farm House.

Lajétchnikoff.
Heretic.

Lalor, Jno.
Money and Morals.

Lamartine, A. de.
Additional Memoirs of my Youth.
Confidences; or, Memoirs of my Youth.
Genevieve; Peasant Love and Sorrow.
Raphael.
Stone-Mason of Saint Point.

Lamont, Miss.
Village Millionaire.

Landon, Letitia E.
Duty and Inclination.
Ethel Churchill.
Francesca Carrara.
Traits and Trials.

Landor, E. W.
Lofoden; or, Exiles of Norway.

Le Brun, P.
History of Tekeli.

Lee, Eliza B.
Florence, the Parish Orphan.

Lee, D. K.
Master-Builder.
Merrimack; or, Life at the Loom.
Summerfield; or, Life on a Farm.

Lee, Mrs. Hannah.
Elinor Fulton.
Naomi; or, Boston a Hundred Years Ago.
Rich Enough.
Three Experiments of Living.

Lee, Sophia H.
Kruitzner; or, the German's Tale.

Lee, S. & H.
Canterbury Tales.

Leggett, Wm.
Naval Stories.
Tales & Sketch. by Country Schoolmaster.

Lehmanowsky, Louis F.
Turkish Captive.

Le Sage, A. R.
Gil Blas.

Leland, Anna.
Home.

Leslie, Miss E.
Althea Vernon.
Kitty's Relations.
Pencil Sketches; or, Outlines of Character.

Leslie, Mrs. M.
The First and Second Marriages.

Lever, Chas.
Charles O'Malley, the Irish Dragoon.
Confessions of Con Cregan.
Daltons; or, Three Roads in Life.
Dodd Family Abroad.
Harry Lorrequer.
Horace Templeton.
Jack Hinton, the Guardsman.
Kate O'Donoghue.
Knight of Gwynne.
Loiterings of Arthur O'Leary.
Maurice Tiernay, the Soldier of Fortune.
Nevilles of Garretstown.
O'Donoghue; Tale of Fifty Years Ago.
Roland Cashel.
Sir Jasper Carew.
Tom Burke of Ours.

Levis, Duke de.
Carbonaro, the; a Piedmontese Tale.

Lewes, G. H.
Ranthorpe.

Lewes, H.
Three Sisters, and Three Fortunes.

Linden, Augusta.
Children's Trials.

Lippard, Geo.
Blanche of Brandywine.
Legends of Mexico.
Legends of the Revolution.
Quaker City.

Lippincott, Mrs.
Forest Tragedy, and other Tales.

Little, Geo.
American Cruiser.

Livermore, Mrs. E. D.
Zoe; or, the Quadroone's Triumph.

Livermore, Mrs. Harriet.
Wreath from Jessamine Lawn.

Lockhart, John G.
Matthew Wald.
Reginald Dalton.
Valerius.
Longfellow, Hen. W.
Hyperion.
Kavanagh.
Longstreet, Aug. B.
Georgia Scenes.
Lover, Sam.
Barney O'Reirdon; and other Tales.
Handy Andy.
Legends and Stories of Ireland.
£. *s. d.*; or, Treasure Trove.
Rory O'More.
Traits and Stories of the Irish Peasantry.
Maberly, Mrs.
Lady and the Priest.
Leontine; or, Court of Louis Fifteenth.
Macfarlane, C.
Armenians.
Romance of History. Italy.
McHenry, Jas.
O'Halloran.
McIntosh, Maria J.
Aunt Kitty's Tales.
Charms and Counter Charms.
Conquest and Self-Conquest.
Cousins.
Evenings at Donaldson Manor.
Lofty and the Lowly. 2 v.
Praise and Principle.
Two Lives; or, to Seem and to Be.
Woman an Enigma.
Mackay, Mrs.
Family at Heatherdale.
Mackenzie, R. S.
Bits of Blarney.
Mac Leod, Donald.
Bloodstone.
Pynneshurst.
Maillard, Annette M.
Matrimonial Shipwrecks.
Miles Tremenheere; or, the Love Test.
Malory, T.
Prince Arthur and his Knights.
Mancur, John H.
Constantine; or, Debutante.
Henri Quatre; or, Days of the League.
Palais Royal.
Tales of the American Revolution.
Mansfield, L. W.
Up-Country Letters.
Manzoni, Allesandro.
The Betrothed; I Promessi Sposi.

Marryat, Fran. (Capt.)
Ardent Troughton.
Children of the New Forest.
Diary of a Blasé.
Frank Mildmay.
Jacob Faithful.
Japhet in Search of a Father.
Joseph Rushbrook; or, the Poacher.
King's Own.
Little Savage.
Log of a Privateer's Man.
Masterman Ready.
Midshipman Easy.
Mission.
Mons. Violet.
Newton Forster; Merchant Service.
Pacha of Many Tales.
Percival Keene.
Peter Simple.
Phantom Ship.
Poor Jack.
Settlers in Canada; Tale for the Young.
Snarleyyow; or, the Dog Fiend.
Stories of the Sea.
Valerie.
Marsh, Mrs.
Adelaide Lindsay.
Angela.
Castle Avon.
Emilia Wyndham.
Father Darcy.
Louisa Mildmay.
Love and Duty.
Mordaunt Hall.
Norman's Bridge.
Ravenscliffe.
Tales of the Woods and Fields.
Time the Avenger.
Triumphs of Time.
Two Old Men's Tales.
Wilmingtons.
Martineau, Harriet.
Berkeley, the Banker.
Charmed Sea.
Cousin Marshall.
Deerbrook.
Five Years of Youth.
Homes Abroad.
Hour and the Man.
Life in the Wilds.
Loom and the Lugger.
Manchester Strike.
Messrs. Vanderput and Snock.
Sowers, not Reapers.

Mathews, Cornelius.
Behemoth; Legend of Mound Builders.
Big Abel and Little Manhattan.
Chanticleer: A Thanksgiving Story.
Motley Book.
Moneypenny; or, Heart of the World.
Maturin, Edw.
Benjamin, the Jew of Granada.
Bianca: A Tale of Erin and Italy.
Eva; or, Isles of Life and Death.
Montezuma, the Last of the Aztecs.
Maturin, Robt. C.
Melmoth, the Wanderer.
Maxwell, Maria.
Ernest Grey; or, the Sins of Society.
Maxwell, W. H.
Bivouac; or, the Rival Suitors.
Brian O'Linn.
Captain O'Sullivan.
Dark Lady of Doona.
Hector O'Halloran.
Hill-Side and Border Sketches.
My Life.
Stories of Waterloo.
Wild Sports of the West.
Mayhew, Bros.
Fear of the World.
Greatest Plague of Life.
Image of his Father.
Magic of Kindness.
Mayhew, H., and Cruikshank, G.
1851; or, Mrs. Sandboy's Adventures.
Mayo, W. S.
Berber.
Kaloolah.
Romance Dust from the Historic Placer.
Meinhold, W.
Mary Schweidler, the Amber-Witch.
Sidonia.
Melville.
Ethan Allen; or, King's Men.
Melville, Herman.
Israel Potter. His Fifty Years' Exile.
Mardi, and Voyage Thither.
Moby Dick; or, the Whale.
Pierre; or, the Ambiguities.
Redburn.
White Jacket.
Mérimée, Prosper.
Demetrius, the Impostor.
Fifteen Hundred and Seventy-Two.
Milman, Capt. E. H.
Arthur Conway; or, Scenes in the Tropics.
Milne, A. D.
Uncle Sam's Farm Fence.
Mitchell, Donald G.
Dream Life: A Fable for the Seasons.
Fudge Doings.
Lorgnette.
Reveries of a Bachelor.
Miller, Thos.
Gideon Giles, the Roper.
Godfrey Malvern.
Lady Jane Grey.
Mitford, Mary R.
Atherton; and other Tales.
Belford Regis.
Our Village.
Montalba, A. K.
Fairy Tales.
Montgomery, Jorge.
Bernardo del Carpio.
Moodie, Mrs.
Flora Lindsay.
Geoffrey Moncton.
Mark Hurdlestone.
Moore, H. N.
Fitzgerald and Hopkins.
Moore, John (Dr).
Edward.
Mordaunt.
Zeluco.
Moore, Oliver.
Staff Officer; or, Soldier of Fortune.
Moore, Thos.
Epicurean.
More, Hannah.
Cœlebs in Search of a Wife.
Morell, Chas.
Tales of the Genii.
Morgan, Jane.
Tales for Fifteen.
Morgan, Lady.
Florence Macarthy.
O'Briens and the O'Flahertys.
Princess; or, the Beguine.
Morley, Countess of (Ed'r).
Dacre.
Morier, J.
Abel Allnut.
Ayesha, the Maid of Kars.
Hajji Baba in England.
Hajji Baba of Ispahan.
Zohrab, the Hostage.
Mortimer, Charlotte B.
Morton Montagu.
Motley, John L.
Morton's Hope.
Mountford, Wm.
Thorpe: a Quiet English Town.

Mowatt, Anna C.
Fortune Hunter.
Evelyn: a Tale of Domestic Life.
Mugge, Theo.
Afraja; or, Life and Love in Norway.
Murray, Chas. A.
Prairie Bird.
Musæus.
Dumb Love.
Legends of Rubezahl.
Myers, P. N.
First of the Knickerbockers.
King of the Hurons.
Young Patroon.
Myrthe, A. T.
Ambrosio de Letinez.
Neal, Mrs. Alice B.
All's not Gold that Glitters.
Contentment better than Wealth.
Gossips of Rivertown.
Patient Waiting no Loss.
Neal, John.
Down-Easters, &c., &c., &c.
Errata; or, Works of Will Adams.
Neal, Jos. C.
Charcoal Sketches.
Peter Ploddy, and other Oddities.
Neal, J. M.
Ayton Priory.
Herbert Tresham.
Neale, W. J.
Gentleman in Black.
Lost Ship; or, Atlantic Steamer.
Priors of Prague.
Will Watch.
Nieritz, Gustav.
Tales of Old Times.
Normand, Hugh de.
Julienne, the Daughter of the Hamlet.
North, Wm.
Slave of the Lamp.
Norton, Caroline E. S.
Stuart of Dunleath.
Wife; and Woman's Reward.
Norton, John N.
Boy Trained up a Clergyman.
Full Proof of the Ministry.
Nott, Hen. J.
Novelletes of a Traveller.
Nourse, J. D.
Levenworth.
Olcott, Mrs.
Isora's Child.
Oliphant, Margaret.
Zaidee.
Opie, Mrs. Amelia.
Works.
Orme, George.
Roger Miller; or, Heroism in Humb. Life.
Orme, Mary.
Uncle John; or, It's too Much Trouble.
Osborne, L.
Arthur Carryl.
Otis, Mrs. H. G.
Barclays of Boston.
Page, J. W.
Uncle Robin in his Cabin in Virginia.
Paget, C. F.
St. Antholins; or, Old Church and New.
Paget, F. E.
Milford and Malvoisin.
Pageant; or, Pleasure and its Price.
Pardoe, Miss.
Confessions of a Pretty Woman.
Mardens and the Daventrys.
Reginald Lyle.
Rival Beauties.
Romance of the Harem.
Speculation.
Traits and Traditions of Portugal.
Paulding, Jas. K.
Book of St. Nicholas.
Dutchman's Fireside.
John Bull and Brother Jonathan.
Köningsmarke.
Merry Tales. Three Wise Men of Gotham.
Old Continental.
Puritan and his Daughter.
Tales of the Good Woman.
Westward Ho!
Paxton, Phil.
Stray Yankee in Texas.
Payson, Geo.
Totemwell.
Peacock, Geo., and *Others.*
Atlantic Club-Book.
Headlong Hall, and other Tales.
Melincourt.
Peacocke, Jas. S.
The Creole Orphans.
Perce, Elbert.
Last of his Name
Old Karl, the Cooper.
Peterson, Chas. J.
Kate Aylesford: a Story of the Refugees.
Phelps, Mrs. Eliz. S.
Last Leaf from Sunny Side.
Peep at Number Five.
Sunny Side.
Tell Tale; or, Home Secrets.

Phelps, Mrs. L.
Ida Norman; or, Trials and their Uses.

Phillips, Sam.
Banking House: a Tale.
We're all Low People There.

Pichler, Mad. Caroline de.
Siege of Vienna.
Swedes in Prague.

Picken, And.
Traditionary Stories and Legendary Illus.

Pickering, Ellen.
Agnes Serle.
Ellen Wareham; or, Love and Duty.
Expectant.
Fright.
Grandfather.
Grumbler.
Heiress.
Kate Walsingham.
Nan Darrel.
Poor Cousin.
Prince and the Pedler.
Quiet Husband.
Secret Foe.
Squire.
Who shall be Heir.

Pike, Mrs. Mary G.
Ida May.

Pitrat, Jno. C.
Paul and Julia; or, the Church of Rome.

Planché, Miss.
Cloud with the Silver Lining.
Dream Chintz.
House on the Rock.
Old Joliffe.
Only.
Sequel to "Old Joliffe."
Star in the Desert.
Trap to Catch a Sunbeam.

Poe, Edgar A.
Tales.

Poole, Jno.
Little Pedlington and the Pedlingtonians.

Porter, Anna M.
Hungarian Brothers.
Lake of Killarney.

Porter, Jane.
Pastor's Fireside.
Scottish Chiefs.
Sir Edward Seaward's Narrative.
Thaddeus of Warsaw.

Porter, Wm. T.
Big Bear of Arkansas.
Quarter Race in Kentucky.

Pratt, S. D.
Inklings.

Prentiss, Mrs.
Flower of the Family.
Lily Gordon, the Young Housekeeper.
Only a Dandelion, and other Stories.

Prime, Wm.
Later Years.
Old House by the River.
Owl-Creek Letters.

Proctor, B. W.
Essays and Tales.

Pultock, Robt.
Peter Wilkins.

Quincy, M. de.
Klosterheim; or, the Mask.

Radcliffe, Mrs. Ann.
Gaston de Blondeville.
Mysteries of Udolpho.
Romance of the Forest.

Ram, S. J.
Unseen Hand; or, Episodes.

Randolph, J. T.
The Cabin & Parlor; or, Slaves & Masters.

Reach, Angus B.
Clement Lorimer; Book with Iron Clasp.

Reade, Chas.
Christie Johnson.
Clouds and Sunshine, and Art.
Peg Woffington: a Novel.

Reed, And.
No Fiction.

Reed, T. B.
Paul Redding; a Tale of the Brandywine.

Rees, J.
Mysteries of City Life.

Reeve, Clara.
Old English Baron.

Reid, Mayne.
English Family Robinson.
Hunter's Feast.
Rifle Rangers.
Young Voyageurs.

Rellstab, Louis.
Eighteen Hundred and Twelve.

Reynolds, Beatrice.
My First Season.
Faust: Romance of the Secret Tribunals.
Pickwick Abroad.
Robert Macaire in England.
Wagner, the Wehr-Wolf.

Richards, T. A.
Summer Stories of the South.

Richardson, Major.
Matilda Montgomerie.

Richardson, Major.
Wacousta; or, the Prophecy.
Wau-nan-gee; or, Massacre at Chicago.
Richardson, Sam.
Clarissa Harlowe.
Sir Charles Grandison.
Richter, J. P. F.
Flower, Fruit, and Thorn Pieces.
Walt and Vult; or, the Twins.
Ritchie, Leitch.
Game of Life.
Robber of the Rhine.
Romance of History. France.
Ritchie, A. C.
Mimic Life.
Wearyfoot Common.
Riley, H. H.
Puddleford and its People.
Robb, John.
Streaks of Squatter Life.
Robertson, J. P.
Solomon Seesaw.
Robinson, Mrs. Edw. [*Talvi.*]
Exiles.
Heloise; or, the Unrevealed Secret.
Life's Discipline.
Woodhill. (Same as "Exiles.")
Roche, Regina M.
Children of the Abbey.
Rodman, Miss Ella.
The Catanese; or, the Real and the Ideal.
Rodwell, C. H.
Old Lond. Bridge; or, Days of Hen. VIII.
Roe, A. S.
James Montjoy; or, I've been Thinking.
Long Look Ahead.
Time and Tide; or, Strive and Win.
To Love, and to be Loved.
Rowcroft, C.
Bush Rangers of Van Diemen's Land.
Ruffini, G.
Lorenzo Benoni.
Russell, Martha.
Leaves from the Tree Igdrasyl.
Saintine, X. B. de.
Picciola.
Woman's Whims.
St. John, James A.
Margaret Ravenscroft.
St. Pierre, J. H. B. de.
Indian Cottage.
Paul and Virginia.
Sand, Geo. [*Mad. Dudevant.*]
Consuelo.
Countess of Rudolstadt.
Sand, Geo. [*Mad. Dudevant.*]
Devil's Pool.
Indiana.
Jacques.
Journeyman Joiner.
Mosaic Workers.
Sin of Mons. Antoine.
Taverino.
Sandeau, Jules.
Hunting the Romantic.
Sargent, Epes.
Fleetwood; or, Stain of Birth.
Savage, Miss E.
Travellers.
Savage, M. W.
Bachelor of the Albany.
Falcon Family.
My Uncle, the Curate.
Reuben Medlicott; or, the Coming Man.
Savage, Sarah.
Trial and Self-Discipline.
Saymore, Sarah E.
Hearts Unveiled.
Schefer, Leopold.
Bishop's Wife.
Schiller, Frederic.
Ghost-Seer.
Visionary.
Schoolcraft, Hen. R.
Algic Researches. (Indian Tales.)
Scott, Lady.
Pride of Life.
Scott, Sir Walter.
Abbot. (Sequel to the Monastery.)
Anne of Geierstein.
Antiquary.
Chronicles of the Canongate.
1*st Series:* Higland Widow.
Two Drovers.
Surgeon's Daughter.
2*d Series:* St. Valentine's Day.
Fortunes of Nigel.
Guy Mannering.
Ivanhoe.
Kenilworth.
Monastery.
Peveril of the Peak.
Pirate.
Quentin Durward.
Red Gauntlet.
Rob Roy.
St. Ronan's Well.
Tales of the Crusaders.
Betrothed.
Talisman.

Scott, Sir Walter.
Tales of My Landlord,
1st Series: Black Dwarf.
Old Mortality.
2d Series: Heart of Mid Lothian.
3d Series: Bride of Lammermoor.
Legend of Montrose.
4th Series: Castle Dangerous.
Count Robert of Paris.
Waverley; or, 'T is Sixty Years Since.
Woodstock.

[*Scott, W.*]
Moredun: a Tale of the 1210.

Scribe, Eugene.
Piquillo Alliaga; Moors under Phil. III.

Sealsfield, Wm.
Life in the New World.
Rambleton; Romance of Fash. Life.

Sedgwick, Cath. M.
Boy of Mount Rhigi.
Clarence.
Home.
Hope Leslie; or, Early Times in Mass.
Linwoods.
Live and Let Live.
Love-Token for Children.
Means and Ends.
New-England Tale.
Poor Rich Man and the Rich Poor Man.
Redwood.
Tales and Sketches.
Travellers.
J. K. Paulding, &c. Tales of Glauber Spa.

Sedgwick, Mrs.
Alida; or, Town and Country.
Allen Prescott.

Sewell, Miss E. M.
Amy Herbert.
Clive Hall.
Earl's Daughter.
Experience of Life.
Gertrude.
Hawkstone.
Katharine Ashton.
Laneton Parsonage.
Margaret Percival.
Margaret Percival in America.

Shelley, Mrs. Mary W.
Falkner.
Frankenstein; or, Modern Prometheus.
Lodore.

Sherwood, Mrs.
Works. 16 v.
Vol. 1. History of Henry Milner.

Sherwood, Mrs.
2. Fairchild Family.
Orphans of Normandy.
Latter Days.
3. Little Henry and his Bearer.
Lucy and her Dhaye.
Memoirs of Sergeant Dale.
Susan Gray.
Lucy Clare.
Hedge of Thorns.
Recaptured Negro.
Susannah; or, Three Guardians.
Theophilus and Sophia.
Abdallah, Merchant of Bagdad.
4. Indian Pilgrims.
Broken Hyacinth.
Little Woodman.
Babes in the Woods of N. World.
Clara Stephens.
Golden Clew.
Katharine Seaward.
Mary Anne.
Iron Cage.
Little Beggars.
5. Infant's Progress.
Flowers of the Forest.
Juliana Oakley.
Ermina.
Emancipation.
6. Little Female Academy.
Little Momière.
Stranger at Home.
Père la Chaise.
English Mary.
My Uncle Timothy.
7. Nun.
Intimate Friends.
My Aunt Kate.
Emmeline.
Obedience.
Gipsey Babes.
Basket Maker.
Butterfly.
Alune.
Procrastination.
Mourning Queen.
8. Victoria.
Arzoomund.
Birthday Present.
Errand Boy.
Orphan Boy.
Two Sisters.
Julian Percival.
Edward Mansfield.
Infirmary.

Sherwood, Mrs.
Mrs. Catharine Crawley.
Joan; or, Trustworthy.
Young Forester.
Bitter Sweet.
Common Errors.
9–12. Lady of the Manor.
13. Mail Coach.
My Three Uncles.
Old Lady's Complaint.
Hours of Infancy.
Shepherd's Fountain.
Economy.
"Her Age."
Old Things and New Things.
Swiss Cottage.
Obstinacy Punished.
Infant's Grave.
Father's Eye.
Red Book.
Dudley Castle.
Happy Grandmother.
Blessed Family.
My Godmother.
Useful Little Girl.
Caroline Mordaunt.
Le Fevre.
Penny Tract.
Potter's Common.
China Manufactory.
Emily and her Brothers.
14. Monk of Cimies.
Rosary.
Roman Baths.
Saint Hospice.
Violet Leaf.
Convent of St. Clair.
15. History of Henry Milner, pt. 4.
Sabbaths on the Continent.
Idler.
16. History of John Martin.

Sherwood, Mrs., and others.
Mirror of Maidens.

Shelton, F. W.
Crystalline; a Romance.
Peeps fr. a Belfry; or, Parish Sketch-Book.
Rector of St. Bardolph's.
Salander and the Dragon.
Up the River.

Shepherd, Mrs. S.
Ellen Seymour.

Shillaber, B. P., Ed'r.
Mrs Partington's Life and Sayings.

Sidney, Adela.
Home and Its Influence.

Sigourney, Mrs. Lydia H.
Myrtis; & other Etchings and Sketchings.
Sketches.

Simms, Wm. G.
Border Beagles; Tales of Mississippi.
Carl Werner.
Castle Dismal; or, Bachelor's Christmas.
Confession; or, the Blind Heart.
Count Julian; or, Last Days of the Goths.
Damsel of Darien.
Forayers.
Golden Christmas.
Guy Rivers.
Helen Halsey; a Tale of the Borders.
Kath. Walton; or, Rebel of Dorchester.
Lily and the Totem.
Maroon; a Legend of the Carribees.
Martin Faber; Story of a Criminal.
Mellichampe.
Partisan.
Pelayo.
Richard Hurdis.
Scout; or, Black Riders of Congaree.
Southward Ho!
Sword and the Distaff.
Wigwam and the Cabin.
Woodcraft; or, Hawks about the Dovecote.
Yemassee.

Wm. Simonds. Aimwell Stories.
Clinton.
Oscar.
Ella.

Sinclair, Catherine.
Beatrice; or, the Unknown Relatives.
Jane Bouverie.
Lord and Lady Harcourt.
Modern Accomplishments.
Modern Flirtations.
Modern Society.
Sir Edward Graham.

Smedley, F. E.
Fortunes of the Colville Family.

Smith, Alb.
Christopher Tadpole.
Pottleton Legacy.

Smith, Eliz. E.
Three Eras of Woman's Life.

Smith, Mrs. E. Oakes.
Bertha and Lily.
Newsboy.

Smith, Horace.
Adam Brown.
Arthur Arundel.
Brambletye House.
Gaieties and Gravities.

Smith, Horace.
Gale Middleton.
Love and Mesmerism.
New Forest.
Reuben Apsley.
Rosine Laval.
Tales of the Early Ages.
Tor Hill.
Zillah; or, Tale of the Holy City.

Smith, Seba.
"Way Down East;" or, Yankee Life.

Smith, W. L. G.
Life at the South.

Smollett, Tobias.
Ferdinand Count Fathom.
Humphrey Clinker.
Peregrine Pickle.
Roderick Random.
Sir Launcelot Greaves.

Soulié, F.
Mysteries of the Heath.
Pastourel.

Southworth, Emma D. E. N.
Curse of Clifton.
Deserted Wife.
Discarded Daughter.
India: The Pearl of Pearl River.
Lost Heiress.
Missing Bride.
Mother-in-Law; or, the Isle of Rays.
Our Neighborhoods and New Settlements.
Retribution.
Shannondale.
Virginia and Magdalene.

Southworth, Mrs. S. N.
Inebriate's Hut.

Souvestre, Emile.
Attic Philosopher in Paris.
Lake Shore; or, Slave, Serf, & Apprentice.
Leaves from a Family Journal.

Spindler, Chas.
Archibald Werner; or, Brother's Revenge.
Invalide.
Jew.
Nun.
Countess of Morion.

Spring, G. (Jr.)
Giafar al Barmeki.

Spring, Sam.
Monk's Revenge.

Staël, Baroness de.
Corinne; or, Italy.
Delphine.

Starbuck, Caleb.
Hampton Heights.

Stephens, Mrs. H. H.
Hagar, the Martyr.
Home Scenes and Home Sounds.

Stephens, Mrs. Ann S.
Fashion and Famine.
Old Homestead.

Sterling, J.
Onyx Ring.

Sterne, Laurence.
Tristram Shandy.

Stilling, J. H. J.
Theobald; or, the Fanatic.

Stimson, A. L.
Easy Nat; or, Three Apprentices.

Stirling, Chas. F.
Buff and Blue.

Stoddard, R. H.
Adventures in Fairy Land.

Stone, Wm. L.
Ups and Downs.

Story, S. A., Jr.
Caste.

Stowe, Mrs. H. B.
Uncle Tom's Emancipation and Sketches.
Uncle Tom's Cabin.

Strickland, Agnes.
Pilgrims of Walsingham.
Tales and Stories from History.

Sue, Eugene.
Atar Gull; or, Slave's Revenge.
Commander of Malta.
Fair Isabel.
Latreaumont; or, Court Conspirators.
Martin, the Foundling.
Mary Lawson.
Matilda.
Mysteries of Paris.
Paula Monti; or, Hotel Lambert.
Seven Capital Sins. Avarice.
" " " Pride.
" " " Envy.
" " " Anger.
" " " Voluptuousness.
Temptation.
Wandering Jew.
Yes and No.

Surr, T. S.
George Barnwell.

Swift, Jonathan.
Gulliver's Travels.

Tautphœus, Baroness.
Cyrilla.
Initials.

Tasistro, Louis F.
Random Shots and Southern Breezes.

Tayler, Chas. B.
Angel's Song.
Earnestness.
Lady Mary; or, Not of this World.
Legends and Records, chiefly Historical.
Margaret; or, the Pearl.
Mark Wilton, the Merchant's Clerk.
Records of a Good Man's Life.
Thankfulness.
Truth; or, Persis Clareton.

Tefft, B. K.
Shoulder Knot.

Temme.
Anna Hammer. (Fr. Ger.)

Tensas, Madison.
Swamp Doctor.

Thackeray, W. M.
Book of Snobs.
Comic Tales. (Yellow Plush Corresp.)
Confessions of Fitz-Boodle.
Doctor Birch.
Great Hoggarty Diamond.
Henry Esmond.
Irish Sketch-Book.
Jeames' Diary, and Rebecca and Rowena.
Kicklebuys on the Rhine.
Luck of Barry Lyndon.
Men's Wives.
Mr. Brown's Let. to Y'ng Man about Town.
Newcomes.
Our Street.
Paris Sketch-Book.
Pendennis.
Punch Prize Novelists.
Rose and the Ring.
Shabby Genteel Story.
Vanity Fair.
Yellow Plush Correspondence.

Thomas, Caroline.
Farmingdale.

Thomas, F. W.
Clinton Bradshaw; Adven. of a Lawyer.
East and West.

Thompson, D. P.
Green Mountain Boys.
Locke Amsden.
May Martin; or, Money-Diggers.
The Rangers; or, the Tory's Daughter.

Thompson, Mort. U.
Doesticks: What he Says.

Thomas, Wm. J. (Ed'r.)
Ancient English Fictions.

Thomson, Mrs. Ed.
Lady of Milan.

Thorpe, T. B.
Hive of the "The Bee Hunter."
Mysteries of the Back Woods.

Tieck, Ludwig.
Tales from the German.

Toulmin, Camilla.
Partners for Life.

Traill, Cath. P.
Canadian Crusoes.

Trelawney, Capt.
Adventures of a Younger Son.

Trollope, Mrs. Frances.
Abbess.
Chas. Chesterfield.
Michael Armstrong.
Refugee in America.
Romance of Vienna.

Trowbridge, J. T.
Burrcliffe: Its Sunshine and Clouds.
Father Brighthopes.
Hearts and Faces, or Home-Life Unveiled.
Ironthorpe; the Pioneer Preacher.
Martin Merrivale, his X Mark.

Trueba, T. de.
Incognito.
Romance of History. Spain.

Tucker, B.
George Balcombe.

Tucker, G.
Voyage to the Moon.

Tupper, Martin F.
Crock of Gold.
Heart.
Twins.

Tuthill, Mrs. L. C.
Queer Bonnets; or, Truthfulness, &c.
Success in Life. The Artist.
" " The Lawyer.
" " The Mechanic.
" " The Merchant.

Tytler, Ann F.
Leila; or, the Island.
Leila at Home.
Leila in England.

Valentine, Dr. W.
Wit and Humor.

Valman, Karl.
Amadeus; or, a Night with the Spirit.

Van Lennep, J.
Adsonville; or, Marrying Out.

Van Palzoni, Mad.
Thyrnau, the Bohemian Conspirator.

Verri, Count Alex. de.
Roman Nights; or, Tomb of the Scipios.

Vigny, Alfred de.
Cinq-Mars.
Villoslada, F. N.
Donna Blanca of Navarre.
Vincent, John.
The Pretty Plate.
Walker, Geo.
Three Spaniards.
Walpole, Hor.
Castle of Otranto.
Warburton, Eliot.
Darien; or, the Merchant Prince.
Reginald Hastings.
Ware, Wm.
Julian; or, Scenes in Judea.
Probus: Let. from Rome in Third Cent.
Zenobia; or, Fall of Palmyra.
Ward, Mrs.
Jasper Lyle: a Tale of Kafirland.
Ward, R. P.
Chatsworth; or, Romance of a Week.
De Clifford; or, Constant Man.
De Vere; or, Man of Independence.
Fielding; or, Society, with other Tales.
Warner, Miss.
Casper.
Dollars and Cents.
Karl Krinken.
My Brother's Keeper.
Queechy.
Wide, Wide World.
Warner, Misses.
Mr. Rutherford's Children.
Warner, W.
Experiences of a Barrister.
Warren, Sam.
Diary of a Physician.
Merchant's Clerk, and other Tales.
Now and Then.
Ten Thousand a Year.
Waters, Thomas.
Recollections of a Policeman.
Watson, Hen. C.
Nights in a Block House.
Old Bell of Independence.
Yankee Tea Party; or, Boston in 1773.
Webb. Mrs. J. B.
Naomi; or, the Last Days of Jerusalem.
Webber, Chas. W.
Gold Mines of the Gila.
Old Hicks, the Guide.
Tales of the Southern Border.
Weill, Alex.
Village Tales from Alsatia.
Weir, Jas.
Lonz Powers; or, the Regulators.
Weld, H. H.
Butchers of Ghent.
Jonce Smiley.
Wellmont, Em.
Uncle Sam's Palace; or, Reigning King.
Wiley, C. H.
Life in the South.
Williams, F.
Luttrells; or, the Two Marriages.
Secret Passion.
Shakspeare and his Friends.
Youth of Shakspeare.
Williams, Mrs.
Religion at Home.
Willis, N. P.
Dashes at Life with a Free Pencil.
Fun-Jottings.
Inklings of Adventure.
Rag-Bag.
Wilmer, John.
Modern Vassal.
Wilmot, Mrs.
Blue-Stocking Hall.
Wilson, John.
Foresters.
Lights and Shadows of Scottish Life.
Trials of Margaret Lindsay.
Tales of the Borders.
Wise, Hen. A.
Tales for the Marines.
Wood, Geo.
Modern Pilgrims.
Worboise, Emma J.
Amy Wilton.
Wormeley, Eliz.
Amabel; a Family History.
Our Cousin Veronica.
Yonge, Miss C. M.
Beechcroft.
Castle Builders.
Heartsease; or, the Brother's Wife.
Heir of Redcliffe.
Kenneth.
Two Guardians.
Zschokke, John H. D.
Creole.
Galley Slave.
Gold-Maker's Village.
Journal of a Poor Vicar.
Rum-Plague: a Narrative.
Tales.
Veronica.

SUPPLEMENTAL CLASSIFIED INDEX.

The word in *italic* indicates its place in the preceding Alphabetical Arrangement.

THEOLOGY.

Bibles, and parts of the Bible.

Commentaries and Exegetical Works.

Prophecy.

Biblical and Early Church History.

290.

Compendium Ecclesiastical History. *Palmer,*
Eccles. Hist. of 1st and 2d Centuries. *Maurice.*
Christ. Kirche zum sechsten Jahr. *Hagenbach.*
Hippolytus and his Age. *Bunsen,*
Hist. of the Christ. Church and Rel. *Neander.*
Hist. of the Christ. Ch. to A.D. 590. *Robertson.*
Outlines of Eccles. Hist. to A. D. 1520. *Hoare,*
Hist. of the Church, 2d and 3d Cents. *Jeremie,*
St. Hippolytus and Ch. of Rome. *Wordsworth.*
Early Christianity in Arabia. *Wright.*

Devotional Works.

First Things. *Spring.*
Hist. of Prov. as Manifested in Scrip. *Carson,*
Three Gardens, Eden, Geths., and Par. *Adams,*
Friends of Christ in New Testament. *Adams.*
Lessons at the Cross. *Hartley,*
Christ our Passover. *Choules,*
The Glory of Christ. *Spring.*
The School of Christ. *Foote,*
Christ of History. *Young,*
Christ in History. *Turnbull.*
Anxious Enquirer after Salvation. *James,*
Discourses on Truth. *Thornwell,*
Theol. Papers, and other Essays. *De Quincy,*
Finger of God. *Cumming,*
Emblems, Divine and Moral. *Quarles,*
Thoughts to Help and to Cheer,
Home Truths. *Ryle,*
Little Earnest Book on a Great Sub. *Wilson,*
Half Hours with Old Humphrey. [*Binney.*
Is it possible to make the best of both Worlds?
Christ. Father's Pres. to his Children. *James,*
Religious Thoughts and Opinions. *Humboldt,*
Precious Stones, Aids to Reflection. *Willmott,*
Theologia Germanica,
Stunden der Andacht, &c. *Zschokke.*
Voices of Nature to her Foster-Child. *Cheever,*
Mornings with Jesus. *Jay,*
Closet Hours. *Palmer,*
Paulinæ; or, Devot's. of Apostle Paul. *Rives,*
Power of Religion in Retirement. *Murray,*
Christian Retirement; or, Spiritual Exercise,
Cause of Faith. *James,*
Christian Aspects of Faith and Duty. *Taylor,*
Christianity, the True Manliness. *Chapin,*
Seed Time and Harvest. *Tweedie,*,
Christian Thoughts on Life. *Giles,*
Benedictions; or, the Blessed Life. *Cumming,*
Daily Life. *Cumming,*
Christian Life. *Arnold,*
Graces and Powers of Christian Life. *Mayo,*
Charity and its Fruits. *Edwards,*
Our Campaign; or, Course of Life. *Reynolds,*
Nature, &c., of Christian Purity. *Foster,*
A Lamp to the Path. *Tweedie,*
Corner Stone. *Abbott,*
Religious Progress. *Williams,*
The *Saints:* An Example,
Christian Life; Social and Individual. *Bayne.*
Contrast between Good and Bad Men. *Spring,*
Christian Parlor Book.
Twelve Lects. before Glasgow Yo. Men's Assoc.
Wesley Offering. *Holmes,*
Voices of the Day. *Cumming,*

292.

Voices of the Night. *Cumming.*
Comfort for the Afflicted. *Greenleaf,*
Comforter. *Cumming,*
Mission of the Comforter. *Hare,* [*Barrett,*
Beauty for Ashes; or, Death of Little Child.
Thoughts on Death of Little Children. *Prime,*
Lights on the Dark River. *Lawrence,*
Sepulchres of the Departed. *Anspach,*
Church of the Redeemed. *Jarvis.*
The Better Land. *Thompson,*
My Father's House; or, Heaven. *Macdonald,*
The Heavenly Home. *Harbaugh,*
The Eternal Day. *Bonar.*
Happiness of the Blessed. *Mant,*
Attractions of the World to come. *Bryant,*
Powers of the World to come. *Cheever.*
Parables. *Krummacher,*
Thrilling Incidents and Narratives. *Belden,*
Parish and other Pencillings. *Murray,*
A Pastor's Sketches. *Spencer,*
Incidents in Life of a Pastor. *Wisner,*
The Last Gift; from a Pastor's Exp. *Gillette,*
Pastor's Gift. *Joy,*
A Pastor's Legacy. *Mason,*

Institutions and Ordinances.

Obligation of the Sabbath. *Brown,*
Sabbath Laws and Sabbath Duties. *Cox.*
Horæ Sabbaticæ. *Higgins.*
The Christian Sanctuary. *Taylor,*
Spots in our Feasts of Charity. *Thayer,*
Religion as seen through the Church,
The Christian World Unmasked. *Berridge.*
Readings for Every Day in Lent. *Taylor,*
Companion for the Altar. *Hobart,*
On the Lord's Supper. *Bickersteth,*

Sermons.

Consolation; in Dis. on Sel. Topics. *Alexander.*
Sermons and Writings, with Mem. *Broaddus,*
The Princeton Pulpit. *Duffield.*
Flint's Sermons,
Ser. in Order of Twelvemonth. *Frothingham,*
Harrington's Sermons,
Scenes in our Parish. *Holmes,*
The Church; Discourses. *Judd,*
Twenty-five Village Sermons. *Kingsley,*
Sermons on National Subjects. *Kingsley,*
The Truth and the Life. Sermons. *Mc Ilvaine.*
A Valedictory Offering. *Mc Ilvaine,*
Sermons on Facts, &c., in Sac. Hist. *Melvill.*
Melvill's Sermons.
Methodist Preacher. Containing 28 Sermons.
Parker's Sermons on Various Subjects,
Spencer's Sermons, with Life,
Stanford's Discourses deliv. on Public Occas.
Stone's Sermons,
Hulsean Lectures for 1845–46. *Trench,*
Twenty-three Sermons. *Whitefield,*

Miscellaneous and Collected Works.

Miscellaneous Pamphlets. *Hare.*
Inquiry into Ministerial Commis. *Windsor,*
Lectures on Pastoral Theology. *Vinet,*
Parochialia; or, Instruct. to Clergy. *Wilson,*

293.

Arminius' Works.
Wood's Works.
Beecher's Works,
Cumming's Minor Works. 2d series.
Edwards' Writings, with Memoir,
Watts' Works, with Memoir–

Missionary Enterprise.

Motives for Missions,
Gold and the Gospel,
Sermons before Gospel Propagation Society–
Christ'y rev'd in East among Armen. *Dwight,*
Account of his Gospel Labors. *Churchman.*
The Awaking. *Theremin,*
Reports of the Prot. Epis. Ch. Miss. Society.
Hist. of Missions of Meth. Epis. Ch. *Strickland,*
Hist. and Charac. of Amer. Revivals. *Colton,*
Cyclopædia of Missions. *Newcomb.*
Miss. and Missiona.'s Hist. viewed. *Kingsmill.*

Systematic Theology.

Outline of Study of Theology. *Schliermacher,*
Complete Body of Divinity. *Stackhouse.*
What is Christianity? *Short,*
The Way of Salvation. *Barnes,*
Defence of the same. *Barnes,*
Pure Gold; or, Truth in its Loveliness. *Holmes,*
True Theory of Christianity. *Grayson,*
Christian Doct. of Forgiveness of Sin. *Clarke,*
Philos. of Justice bet. God and Man. *Blood,*
Discourse of God's Sovereignty. *Coles,*

Church of Rome.

Canons and Decrees of the Council of Trent,
Catechism of the Council of Trent,
History of the Council of Trent. *Bungener,*
Du Pape. *Maistre,*
History of Latin Christianity. *Milman.*
The Papacy; its History, Dogmas, &c. *Wylie.*
Popery as it Was and Is. *Hogan,*
Popery Consid. as to its Claims, &c. *Weaver,*
The Contest with Rome. *Hare.*
Truth of God against the Papacy,
Idol Demol. by its own Priestcraft. *Knowles,*
Popery the Man of Sin. *Gault,*
Popery in Power; or, Sp't of Vatican. *Turnley.*
Persecutions of Popery. *Shoberl.*
Catholic and Prot. Nations Comp'd. *Roussel.*
Protestantism and Catholicism Comp. *Balmes.*

Mod. Jesuitism; or, Jesuits in 19th Cent. *Mich-*
Dealings with the Inquisition. *Achilli.* [*elsen.*
Americans Warned of Jesuitism. *Pitrat,*
Testimony of an Escaped Novice. *Bunkley,*
Archbishop; or, Romanism in U.S. *Bellisle,*
Romanism at Home. *Murray,*
"End of Controversy" Controver'd. *Hopkins,*

Reformation.

Reformers before the Reformation. *Ullman.*
History of the Reformation, v. 4, 5. *Aubigné.*
Articles of the Synod of Dort. *Scott,*
Christian Church during Reform'n. *Hardwick,*

294.

Internal Hist. of German Protestan. *Kalmis,*
History of the Protestant Church in Hungary,
Spanish Prots., Persecution by Ph. II. *Castro,*
L'Eglise pendant les Quatre Derniers Siecles.
Hist. of Prot. Reformat'n. in France. *Marsh,*
Histoire de Refugees Prot. de France. *Weiss.*
French Protestant Refugees. *Weiss,*
Huguenots in France and America,
Protestant in Ireland, 1853,

Church of England, &c.

Apology for Apost. Order and its Adv. *Hobart,*
Vindication of the Prot. Epis. Church. *How.*
Letters on the Prot. Epis. Church. *Sparks.*
On the Invalidity of Presb. Ordination. *Cooke.*
Exp. of Sev. Offices; adap. for Pub. Wor. *Boys.*
Exposition of the Creed. *Pearson.*
History of the Articles of Religion. *Hardwick.*
Horæ Liturgicæ. *Mant,*
A Church Dictionary. *Hook.*
Hist., Obj., and Proper Obser. of Lent. *Kip,*
Remarks on "Oxford Theology." *Livingston,*
England's Sacred Synods. *Joyce.*
Eng. Church Hist. to Reformation. *Martineau,*
Lectures on Causes, &c., of Brit. Ref. *Hopkins,*
Concise Hist. of Hampden Cont'sy. *Christmas,*
Official Calendar of the Church. *Boys.*
Official Hand-Book of Ch. and State. *Murray,*
Memoirs of Prot. Epis. Ch. in U. S. *White,*
Protestant Episcopal Church in U. S. *Colton,*
Novelties which Disturb our Peace. *Hopkins,*
Prot. Epis. Ch. in South Carolina. *Dalcho.*
Episcopal Methodism as it was. *Gorrie,*
Collections of the Prot. Episcopal Hist. Soc.

Presbyterians.

Westminster Shorter Catechism,
Form of Government of the Presb. Church,
Scotland and the Scottish Church. *Caswall,*
Hist. of Ch. of Scot. to James VI. *Spottiswoode.*
Old Redstone; or, Western Presb. *Smith.*

Congregationalism.

Footsteps of our Forefathers. *Miall,*
Dictionary of Cong. Usages, &c. *Cummings,*
Year-Book of Am. Cong. Union for 1854.
Protestant Separatists at Scrooby. *Hunter.*

Baptism and Communion.

Bapt. of Believers, and Close Com. *Baldwin.*
Open Com.—Restr'd Com. unscrip. *Whitney,*
Am. Bible Society and the Baptists. *Wyckoff,*
Concise History of Foreign Baptists. *Orchard,*

General Hist. of the Sabbatarian Chs. *Davis,*

Trinity.

Tracts Concerning Christianity. *Norton.*
God with Men. *Osgood,*
Ten Sermons on Religion. *Parker,*
Sermons on Theism, Atheism, &c. *Parker,*
Trinity in its Theolog. and other Asp. *Lazarus.*
Christ in Theol.; a Vind. of God in Christ.
[*Bushnell,*

MENTAL AND MORAL SCIENCE.

Moral and Metaphysical Philosophy. *Maurice*,
System of Moral Science. *Hickok*.
Outlines of Moral Science. *Alexander*,
Mundane Moral Government. *Doubleday*.
History of Moral Philos. in Eng. *Whewell*.
Systéme d'Etudes Philosophiques. *Ozaneaux*.
Elements of Intellectual Philosophy. *Wayland*,
Empirical Psychology. *Hickok*,
Elements of Psychology *Morell*,
Chapters on Mental Physiology. *Holland*.
Anatomy and Physiology of Mind. *Carlile*,
Philosophy of the Senses. *Wyld*,
The Senses and the Intellect. *Bain*.
Comment. on Medical and Moral Life. *Cooke*;
The Intellect, Emots. and Moral Nature. *Lyall*.
Active and Moral Powers of Man. *Stewart*,

Logic.

Elementary Treatise on Logic. *Wilson*,
Logique de Port Royal. *Arnauld*,
Subjective Logic. *Hegel*.
Meth. of Right. Conduct. the Reason. *Descartes*,
Theory of Reasoning. *Bailey*.
Historical Sketch of Logic. *Blakely*.

Metaphysics.

Institutes of Metaphysics. *Ferrier*,
Theory of the Infinite. *Calderwood*.
Inquiry into Speculat. and Socl. Science. *Vera*.
Philosophie de Kant. *Barni*.
Enquiry into Human Nature. *Macvicar*.
Philosophy of Human Nature. *Brewster*,
Philosophie Fondamentale, *Balmes*,
Positive Philosophy. *Comte*.
Cours de Philosophie Positive. *Comte*.
Catéchisme Positiviste. *Comte*,
Philosophy of the Sciences. *Comte*,
Discours sur l'Ensemble de Positivisme. *Comte*,
Premiers Essais de Philosophie. *Cousin*.
Lects. on the True, Beautl. and Good. *Cousin*,
Fragments Philosophiques. *Cousin*.
Fragments de Philosophie Cartésienne. *Cousin*,
Meditations; and Selections from *Descartes*,
Confucius, Four Books of.
Essays on Inductive Philosophy. *Powell*.
Principles of Psychology. *Spencer*.
Passions of the Human Soul. *Fourier*.
Discus. on Philos. and Literature. *Hamilton*:
On the Hist. of Ancient Philosophy. *Butler*,
History of Philosophy in Epitome. *Schwegler*,
Vies et Doctrines de Philosophes. *Diogine*,
History of Greek and Roman Philosophy,
Manual of the History of Philos. *Tenneman*,
History of Modern Philosophy. *Cousin*.
Histoire de la Philosophie Moderne. *Cousin*.

Education.

Instruction Publique. *Cousin*,
University Education. *Tappan*,
Hist. of Adult Educa. and Lity. Insts. *Hudson*,
Education; Nat. Volunt. and Free. *Fletcher*.
Bible in Common Schools. *Cheever*,
Pub. Educa. and Future Policy. *Shuttleworth*.
Introductory Lects. at the Op. of New College,
Introductory Lects. at the Op. of Owen's Coll.
Introduc. Disc. &c. before Bost. Conv. of Tea.
Lectures in Connect. with Educational Exhib.,
Lectures on Educa. before the Royal Institut.
Defense of Ignorance,
Useful Education. *Knox*.
Education and Progress. *Babbitt*,
School of the Future. *Zincke*,
School Economy. *Symons*,
Mother at Home. *Abbott*,
Child at Home. *Abbott*,
First Thoughts; or, Beginning to Think,
New England Primer,
Teacher and the Parent. *Northend*,
Calling and Responsibilities of a Governess,
National Education in Europe. *Barnard*.
Report on Education in Europe. *Bache*.
Hist. Phil. de l'Acad. de Prusse. *Bartholomess*.
Learned Socs. of the United Kingdom. *Hume*.
National System of Educat. in Ireland. *Trench*.
Legitimate System of National Educat. *Edisen*,
Reports on National Education in Ireland.
Hist. of the University of Cambridge. *Dyer*.
Five Years in an English University. *Bristed*,
On the Studies of Camb. Univer. *Sedgwick*.
History of the University of Oxford. *Chalmers*.
Recomnds. of Oxf. Univers. Commis. *Heywood*.
History of the Royal Society. *Thompson*.
Examina. Papers of King's College. *Browne*,
Minutes of the Council on Education. *Laurie*,
Amer. Edu. its Princ. and Elems. *Mannsfield*,
Catalogue of Offis. and Studs., Harvard Coll.,
Massachusetts System of Common Schools.
Reports on Public Schools in R. I. *Potter*.
Educational Documents of Connecticut. 1853.
Report of Super. of Com. Schools. N. Y. State.
Report of Regents of the N. Y. State Univers.
Com. School System of N. Y. State. *Randall*.
Instrucs. from the Regents of the N. Y. Univ.
Rept. of the Bd. of Educat. of N. Y. 1853 & 4.
Account of Free School Society of New York.
Journal of the Board of Education. 1854. N.Y.
Docs. of Brd. of Educat. of N. Y. 1842–52–54.
Docs. relative to the Free Academy; 1847–52
Manual of Board of Educat. of N.Y. 1852–4,
Manual of Discipline, of N. Y. Pub. Sch. Soc.
Hist. of Sch. of Ref. Prot. Dutch Ch. N.Y. *Dunshee*,
Rhode Island Educational Magazine.
Journal of Rhode Island Institute of Instruct.
Common School Journal. *Mann*.
Dedicat. of Antioch Coll. with Mann's Address,
Educatl. Systs. of Puritans and Jesuits. *Porter*,
Classl. Scholarsp. & Classl. Learng. *Donaldson*,
Reports of N. Y. Institut. for Deaf and Dumb.

Practical Ethics.

Nicomachean Ethics. *Aristotle*,

302.

Seoane's Spanish Dictionary, by Velasquez,
New Method of Learning Spanish. *Ollendorff*,
Gram. Port., à l'Usage des Fran. *Constancio*,

French.

Grammaire de Grammaires. *Girault*,
New Method of Learning French. *Fasquelle*,
Introduc. Course to the French Lang. *Ahn*,
Cours Complet de Langue fran. *Bescherelle*,
Manuel des Conjugaisons. *Bescherelle*,
French and English Dictionary. *Spiers*,
French and English Pronounc. Dict. *Surenne*,
Dict. of English and French Idioms. *Roemer*,
Aids to French Composition. *Howard*,
Confor. du Lan. fran. avec le grec. *Estienne*,
Philosophy of French Pronunciation. *Talbot*,
Polyglot Reader. *Roemer*,

Literary History.

Elements of Literature, *Ansley*,
Mémoires de Littérature,
History of Greek Literature,
Manual of Greek Literature. *Anthon*,
Language and Lit. of Ancient Greece. *Mure*,
History of Greek Classical Literature. *Brown*,
Histoire de la Littérature romaine. *Pierron*,
Hist. of Roman Classical Literature. *Brown*,
Storia della Litteratura italiana. *Tirabosch*,
Lit. of Ita. to the Death of Boccaccio. *Simpson*,
Hist. de la Littérature espagnole. *Bouterwek*,
Etu. sur l'Espg. et la Litté. espagn. *Charles*,
Histoire de la Littérature française. *Sayons*,
Etudes sur la Lit. fran. aux 19e Siécle. *Vinet*,
Histoire Littéraire de la Revolution. *Maron*,
Ma Bibliothèque française,
Literatu. and Rom. of Mod. Europe. *Howitt*,
German Literature. *Menzel*,
Guide to German Literature. *Moschzisker*,
Ecrivaines et Poétes de l'Allemagne. *Blaze*,
Encyclopädie der Deutschen Nat'l Lit. *Wolff*–
Hambu. Lit. Leben in 18 Jahrgung. *Wehl*,
Hist. de la Littérat. en Danemark. *Marmier*,
History of English Literature. *Spalding*,
Outlines of English Literature. *Shaw*,
Sketches of English Literature. *Balfour*,
Geschichte der Englische Literatur. *Kettner*,
Lectures on English Literature. *Reed*,
Litera. and Lit. Men of Great Britain. *Mills*,
Geschicte der Englischen Poesie. *Buchner*,
Lect. on Eng. Hist. and Tragic Poetry. *Reed*,
Poetical History of the Last Century. *Moir*,
Eng. Lit. of the Nineteenth Cent. *Cleveland*,
Catalogue of my English Library. *Stevens*,
Etudes de la Litte. des Anglo-Amer. *Chasles*,
Anglo-American Literatu. and Man. *Chasles*,
Essays on the Poets. *De Quincy*,
Poetics. An Essay on Poetry. *Dallas*,
Die Poesie und ihre Geschichte. *Rosenkrantz*,
Lectures on Dramatic Art and Lit. *Schlegel*,
Histoire de la Littérature Dramatiq. *Janin*,
Revue des Romans de plus Cel. Romanciers,
Essays on Philosophical Writers. *De Quincy*,
Satire and Satirists. *Hannay*,
Angling Literature of all Nations. *Blakey*,
Briefe von Schiller's Gattin. *Duncker*.

304.

Dis. on the 1st Decade of Livius. *Machiavelli*,
Mich. Angelo as a Philosophic Poet. *Taylor*,
Critical Essay on the Writings of T. Carlyle,
Goethe and Werther. *Kestnell*,
Wayland Smith. A Dissertation. *Depping*,
Analysis of Pope's Essay on Man. *Bell*,
On the New General Biographical Dictionary,

Bibliography.

Diction. Biblio. des Livres Rares, Preci., &c.,
London Catalogue of Books Pub. in 1816–51,
London Catalog. of Books Pub. from 1831–55,
Brit. Cat. of Books from Oct. '37 to Dec. '52,
Cyclopædia Bibliographia. *Darling*,
Catalogue of Books pub. in Germany in 1855,
Bibliothèque Americaine. *Ternaux*,
Amer. Booksellers' Trade List. *Blake*,
Supplement to Bibliotheca Amer. *Roorbach*,
Index to Periodical Literature. *Poole*,
Bibliographia Zoologiæ et Geologiæ. *Agassiz*,
Catalogue of Works on Methodism. *Decanver*,
Catalog. of Books on the Masonic Institution,
Ecrivains de la Compagnie Jesus. *Backer*,
Biblioteca de Obras Nacionales del Pineda,

Libraries.

Albany Young Men's Association. *Catalogue*,
American Bible Society. *Catalogue*,
American Institute Library. *Catalogue*,
Amherst College Library. *Catalogue*,
Andover Theological Seminary. *Catalogue*,
Astor Library. *Alphabetical Index*,
Astor Library Oriental Works. *Catalogue*,
Baltimore Mercantile Library. *Catalogue*,
Boston Mercantile Library. *Catalogue*,
Boston Public Library. *Catalogue*,
Brothers in Unity Society. *Catalogue*,
Cambridge High School. *Classed Catalogue*,
Cincinnati Mercantile Library. *Catalogue*,
Hamburg Commerz Bibliothek. *Katalog*,
London Library. *Catalogue*,
Massachusetts Historical Society. *Catalogue*,
New Haven Young Men's Institu. *Catalogue*,
New York Appren. and Demilt Li. *Catalogue*,
New York Soc. Lib. *Supplemental Catalogue*,
New York State Library. *Catalogue*,
Pancatuck Library Association. *Catalogue*,
Peabody Institute. *Catalogue*,
Philadelphia Library Co. *Catalogue*, vol. 3,
Philadelphia Mercantile Library. *Catalogue*,
Providence Atheneum Library. *Catalogue*,
San Francisco Mercantile Library. *Catalogue*,
St. Louis Mercantile Library. *Catalogue*,
Handbuch der Deutscher Biblio. *Petzholdt*,
Katechismus der Bibliothekenlehre. *Petzholdt*,
Bib. Sys. d. gesam. Wis. Kun. *Schliermacher*,
Bibliothekstechnik. *Seizinger*,
Catalogue of Library of Dr. Kloss,
New Cat. of Amer. and Eng. Books. *Appleton*,
Harper and Brothers' Book List, with Index,

Typography, &c.

Manual of Writ. and Print. Charac. *Wilme*,
General History of Printing. *Palmer*,

304.

Oriental Herald and Colo. Review (1824–29).
Panopolist and Missionary Mag. (1808–10).
People's and Howitt's Journal (1850).
People's Illustrated Jour. of Arts (1852).
Pioneer; or Califor. Monthly Mag. (1854–55).
Plough, Loom and Anvil (1848–55).
Practical Mechanic's Journal (1850–55).
Presbyterian Quarterly Review (1852–55).
Present (The) (1843–44).
Prospective Review (1848–54).
Putnam's Monthly (1853-55).
Quarterly Jour. of the Chem. So. (1849–55).
Quarterly Jour. of Micros. Science (1854–55).
Quar. Jour. of So. Meth. Epis. Ch. (1852–54).
Quarterly Review (1850–55).
Remembrancer (The) (1775–83).
Repertory of Patent Inventions (1850–55).
Retrospective Review (1853).
Revue Critique des Livres Nouv. (1850–54).
Revue de Nouveau Monde (1850).
Revue de Paris (1851–56).
Revue des Deux Mondes (1842; 1849–55).
Sacred Circle (1855).
Sailor's Magazine (1829; 1850–55).
Scalpel (1849–54).
Sharpe's London Magazine (1845-55).
Southern Literary Messenger (1850–52).
Southern Presbyterian Review (1852–54).
Southern Quarterly Review (1850–55).
Spirit of Missions (1850–55).
Sporting Magazine (1853–55).
Student (1850–55).
Student, or Oxford & Camb. Mis. (1750–51).
Tait's Edinburgh Magazine (1850–55).
Technologiste (1850-55).
Theological and Literary Journal (1852–55).
Theologische Studien und Kritiken (1854–55).
To Day; a Boston Literary Journal (1852).
Union Magazine (1850–52).
United S. Mag. & Dem. Rev. (1840; 1850–51).
Universalist Quarterly (1851–55).
Vegetarian Messenger (1855).
Wesleyan Methodist Magazine (1851–55).
Western Journal and Civilian (1855).
Westminster Review (1852–55).
Westminster and For. Quar. Rev. (1850–51).

Newspapers.

Allgemeine Zeitung (Aug'g) July '51–Dec. '55–
Atheneum Français (1852–55)–
Atheneum; a Weekly Journal (1850–53)–
The Atlas; a Lit. & Hist. Jour. (1831–32)–
The Broadway Journal (1845)–
Brother Jonathan (1842–43)–
Charivari, July '50–Dec. '52; Jan. '54–June '55
Critic; London Literary Journal (1853)–
Diogenes (1853)–
Economist, The (1853)–
Evening Post (1850–1854)–
Examiner (1851–53)–
Fliegende Blätter, Vols. 10, 12, 14, 16, 17, 20–
Gazette of the Union (1849)–
Great Gun (1844–45)–
Illustrated London News (1842–45, 1850–55)
Illustration; French (1850–51)–

305.

Illustrirte Zeitung (1850–55)–
Journal des Débats (1851–53)–
Journal of Commerce (1850–54)–
Kolnische Zeitung (July 1849–Dec. 1850)–
Maryland Jour. and Balt. Adv. (1792–93)–
Morning Courier & Enquirer (1850–54)–
National Journal (1823–25)–
National, May 16, 1849–Dec. 31, 1851–
New York Commercial Adv. (1850–54)–
New York Express (1854)–
New York Herald (1848–54)–
New York Municipal Gazette–
New York Times (Sept. '51–Dec. 1854)–
New York Tribune (1850—54)–
North Briton (1768–70)–
Parker's Journal (1850–51)–
Punch (1850–55)–
Spectator, Vols. 24–25–
Spirit of the Times (1845 and 1855)–
Times (July 1849, June 1854, Jan. Apr. '55)–
United States Economist (1853)–

Essays, Letters, Speeches, Miscellanies, &c.

Essays, Ecclesiastical and Social. *Conybeare.*
Essays and Reviews. *Brownson*,
Miscellaneous Essays and Reviews. *Barnes.*
Eight Essays on various subjects. *Maitland*,
Fruits of Leisure. *Helps*,
Miscellaneous Essays. *De Quincy*,
Star Papers. *Beecher*,
Essays and Miscellanies. *Aguilar*,
Winterslow Essays and Characters. *Hazlitt*,
Historical and Critical Essays. *De Quincy*,
Cambridge Essays (1855),
Oxford Essays (1856),
Essays from the London Times.
Essays and Marginalia. *Coleridge*,
Etudes sur Shakspeare, M. Stuart, &c. *Chasles*,
Narrative & Miscellaneous Papers. *De Quincy*,
Critical & Miscellaneous Essays. *Macaulay*,
Literary Criticisms & other Papers. *Wallace*,
Literary Papers. *Forbes*,
Contributions to Literature. *Gilman*,
Melanges Historiques et Littéraires. *Merimée*,
Literary Recreations & Miscellanies. *Whittier*,
Characteristics of Literature. *Tuckerman*,
Impressions Littéraires. *Ratisbone*,
Etudes Littéraires. *Planche*,
Nouvelles Causeries Littéraires. *Pontmartin*,
Nouvelles Etudes Historiques et Lit. *Fleury*,
Œuvres de Lit., et Fragments Lit. *Cousin*,
Tesoro della Prosa Italiana dai Primi Tempi.
Specimens of Newspaper Lit. *Buckingham*,
Philosophic & Æsthetic Letters. *Schiller*,
Sketches, Legal and Political. *Sheil*,
Small Books on Great Subjects. Vols. 19–22,
Journal of Proceedings of a Literary Conven.
Letters on Several Subjects. *Fitzosborne.*
Letters to a Young Man. *De Quincy*,
Lectures to Ladies on Practical Subjects,
Discourses on Various Subjects. *Bailly.*
Historical Dis. before Yale College. *Woolsey.*
Address to the Bost.Soc. of Nat. Hist. *Warren.*
Lectures before Yo. Men's Ch. As. '52, '53, '54,
Lectures of *Gavazzi.*

306.

Oration delivered Aug. 1, in Phil. *Adams.*
Oration & Poem before the Delta Phi Conven.
Address on Exploring Ex. to Pacific. *Reynolds.*
Sumner's Orations and Speeches,
Sumner's Recent Speeches and Addresses,
Hilliard's Speeches and Addresses.
Winthrop's Speeches and Addresses.
Parker's Speeches, Addresses, & Occa. Ser.,
Smith's Speeches in Congress.
Kossuth's Select Speeches.
Speeches of Gover's of N. Y. State, 1777–1825.
Giddings' Speeches in Congress.
Eulogy on Adams and Jefferson. *Webster.*
Selection of Eulogies on Adams and Jefferson.
Selected British Eloquence. *Goodrich.*
Peel's Speeches.
Macaulay's Speeches;
Wellington's Speeches in Parliament.
Miscellanies. *Martineau,*
Contributions to the Edin. Rev. *Brougham.*
Contributions to the Edinburgh Rev. *Jeffrey.*
Latter Day Pamphlets. *Carlyle,*
Story's Miscellaneous Writings.
Evelyn's Miscellaneous Writings.
Dramatic and Prose Miscellanies. *Beckett.*
Arthur Pym and Miscellanies. *Poe,*
Revolutionary Memorials, Poems, &c. *Case,*
Interviews, Memorable and Useful. *Cox,*
Illustrations of Genius. *Giles,*
Les Hom. et les Mœurs du XIX Siècle. *Chasles,*
Habits and Men. *Doran,*
Sparrowgrass Papers. *Cozzens,*
Mutterings and Musings of an Invalid,
The Rag Bag. *Willis,*
Wheat-Sheaf,
Olive Leaves. *Sigourney,*
Book of Romances, Lyrics and Songs. *Taylor,*
Diosma; a Perennial. *Gould,*
Learning and Working. *Maurice.*
Morning of Life,
Poetry of Life. *Ellis,*
Life; Painter of Variegated Characts. *Parker.*
Deck of the Crescent City. *Dix,*
Adventures of Huntrs. & Travls. & other Nar.,
Post Meridian. *Sigourney,*
History of the Hen Fever. *Burnham,*
Wide-Awake Gift & Know-Noth. Tok. for 1855,
Caspipina's Letters on various subjects. *Duche,*
Harvestings,
Hurry-Graphs. *Willis,*
Dies Boreales; or, Christr. und. Canvass. *Wilson,*
Noctes Ambrosianæ. *Wilson,*
The O'Doherty Papers. *Maginn,*
Silent Revolution—Steam & Electricity. *Garvey,*
Shoepac Recollections of American Life.
Solwan; or, Waters of Comfort. *Ibn Zafer,*
Notes: Theological, Political, &c. *Coleridge,*
Mercurius Rusticus. *Ryves.*
Mile Stones in our Life Journey. *Osgood,*
Méditations et Etudes Morales. *Guizot,*
Dealings with the Dead,
Kathayan Slave, and other Papers. *Judson,*
The Helping Hand. *Kirkland—*
New Bond of Love,
Sunshine on Daily Paths,
Home and Social Philosophy,

308.

Home Recreations, Perils and Adventures,
Book for the Home Circle. *Kirkland.*
Pleasant Pages for Young People. *Newcombe,*
Moral Amusement,
Evening Book. *Kirkland.*
Rural Hours. *Cooper,*
Summer Time in the Country. *Willmott,*
Rural Letters. *Willis,*
Country Margins. *Hammond,*
Country Year-Book. *Howitt,*
Rhyme and Reason of Country Life. *Cooper,*
Pictorial Calendar of the Seasons. *Howitt,*
Pencillings by the Way. *Willis,*
Rural Tales, Ballads and Songs. *Bloomfield—*
Readings for Railways. *Syme,*
Borderer's Tale Book. *Richardson.*
Recreation. A gift-book for Young Readers,
Ephemera. *Rice,*
Divers Choice Pieces of that Antiquary *Cotton,*
Truths Illustrated by Great Authors.
Chambers' Pocket Miscellany,
Chambers' Repository of Instructive Papers,
Chambers' Papers for the People.
Once upon a Time. *Knight,*
Rose Garden of Persia. *Costello.*
Collection of Familiar Quotations,
German Historical Anthology. *Bernays,*
Common-Place Book. *Southey.*
The Scrap Book. *Fields.*
Benthaminia. *Bentham,*
Selections from Writings of Landor. *Hillard,*
Common-Place Book of Thought. *Jameson,*
Horæ Vacivæ. *Elmes,*
Treasured Thoughts from fav. Authors. *May,*
Salad for the Social. *Saunders,*
Salad for the Solitary. *Saunders,*
Caprices et Zigzags. *Gautier,*
Table Talk, & Imaginary Conversations. *Hunt,*
Recollections of Table Talk of Sam. Rogers,
Table-Talk; or, Books, Men and Manners,
Table Traits; with Something on Them. *Doran,*
Thoughts and Apophthegms. *Whately,*
Greek Anthology,
Satires. *Boileau.*
Satyre Menippée. *Labitte,*
Poetic Works of Louis Napoleon [a Satire],
Wisdom & Wit of Sydney Smith. *Duyckinck,*
Cyclopedia of Anecdotes. *Arvine.*
Anecdotes for the Steamboat and Railroad,
Kaleidescope of Anecdts. & Aphors. *Sinclair.*
Boy's Own Book,
Physiology of the Opera,

Collected Works.

Fuller's Principal Works and Remains.
Selections fm. his Works, with Memoir. *Genin.*
Henry's Miscellaneous Works.
Mackintosh's Miscellaneous Works,
Ramsay's Works, with Life,
Reynolds' Literary Works,
Robertson's Historical Works.
Stewart's Collected Works.
Works of Jno. *Adams,* with Life and Notes.
Bancroft's Literary & Historical Miscellanies.
Calhoun's Works.

Poetical Works.

315.

Skelton's Poetical Works.
Smith's Poems,
Stagg's Poems,
Stoddard's Poems,
Trench's Poems,
Tuckerman's Poems,
Taylor's Poems of the Orient,
Winter's Poems,
Wolcott's Poetical Works,

Dramatic.

Before & Behind the Curtain. *Northall,*
Dramatic and Poetical Works. *Baillie.*
Dramas. *Calderon,*
Théatre. *Calderon,*
Adolphe, Anec.et Trag. de Wallstein. *Constant,*
Dramatic Works. *Goethe,*
The Very Age: A Comedy. *Gould,*
Saint's Tragedy: A Play. *Kingsley,*
Dramatic Works. *Knowles,*
Caius Gracchus. A Tragedy. *McCord,*
Modern Standard Drama. Vol. 13,
Comédies et Proverbes. *Musset,*
Historical Dramas. *Schiller,*
Dramatic Works, with Memoir. *Sheridan,*
Old New York. A Tragedy. *Smith,*
Modern Standard Drama. *Wemyss,*

Shakspeariana.

Dramatic Works. Lansdowne Ed. *Shakspeare.*
Dramatic Works. *Shakspeare,*
Dramatische Werke. *Shakspeare.*
Shakspeare's Scholar. *White.*
Miscellanies—The Shakes. Papers. *Maginn,*
Moral Play of Wit and Science. (*Shakspeare.*)
Shakspeare Society Papers. Vol. 1.
Works ent. at Stat's'.Offi. fr. 1577–87. (*Shaks.*)
Shakspeare's Works. After Collier;
Shakspeare's Works. Edited by Hudson,
Dictionary of Shaksperian Quotations,
Notes and Emendations to *Shakspeare,*
A Few Notes on Shakspeare. *Dyce.*
Text of Shakspeare Vind. from Collier. *Singer.*

Fables.

Æsop's Fables, by James.
Literary Fables. *Yriarte,*
Fables Choisies, avec Illustrats. *La Fontaine-*

Novels in Foreign Languages.

Amaury. *Dumas,*
Aus der Gegenwart. *König,*
Aventures de Télemaque. *Fénélon,*
Aventurier; ou le Barbe-Blue. *Sue,*
Attala; Réné; les Abencer. &c. *Chateaubriand,*
Bellezze delle Novelle. *Piranesi,*
Bohème Galante, la. *Nerval,*
Bourgeois de Molinchart. *Champfleury,*
Buveurs d'Eau, les. *Murger,*
Capitaine Paul. *Dumas,*
Caravane, la. *Hauff,*
Catherine Blum. *Dumas,*

318.

Causeries du Lundi. *Saint Beuve,*
Cecile. *Dumas,*
Charlotte Ackerman. *Müller.*
Chevalier de Maison Rouge. *Dumas,*
Colomba: suivi de la Mosaique, &c. *Mérimée,*
Compagnon du Foyer. *Surville,*
Comtesse de Charny. *Dumas,*
Comtesse de Rudolstadt. *Sand,*
Contes. *Musset,*
Contes d'Automne. *Champfleury,*
Contes Domestiques. *Champfleury,*
Contes et Nouvelles. *Pontmartin,*
Contes Eccentriques. *Nervil,*
Contes Fantastiques. *Nodier,*
Contes Nocturnes. *Hoffman,*
Contes Vieux et Nouveaux. *Champfleury,*
Conteur Génévois. *Mallet,*
Dame aux Camélias. *Dumas,*
Dernier Rendez-vous. *Murger,*
Derniers Paysans. *Souvestre,*
Ecolier Virtueux. *Proyart.*
Ekkehard. *Scheffel.*
Elisabeth; ou les Exiles de Sibérie. *Cottin.*
Feliz Independente del Mundo. *Almeyda.*
Femmes, les. *Karr,*
Fernand, Vaillance, Richard. *Sandeau,*
Fernande. *Dumas,*
Filles d'Eve. Les Trois Sœurs. *Houssaye,*
Frères Corses. *Dumas,*
Geneviève dans les Bois. *Beaulieu,*
Geneviève: Hist. d'une Servante. *Lamartine.*
Gesammelte Märchen. *Andersen.*
Georges. *Dumas.*
Guerre des Paysans. *Conscience,*
Histoire de Lydia Sommerville,
Histoires de Ménage. *Castille,*
Histoires Normandes. *Karr,*
Hommage à C. F. Derecourt. *Fontainbleau.*
Idiot. *Montepin,*
Impressions de Voyage. *Dumas.*
Isabel de Bavière. *Dumas,*
Jaques Ortis. *Dumas,*
Lampenputzer. *Cummings,*
Madame de Somerville. *Sandeau,*
Marguerite, ou Deux Amours. *Girardin,*
Marrianna. *Sandeau,*
Memorial de Famille. *Souvestre,*
Nouvelles. *Mérimée,*
Nouvelles Genevoises. *Töpffer,*
Novellen und Dichtungen. *Zschokke,*
Nuit du Midi. *Méry,*
Oheim Toms Hütte. *Stowe.*
Onkel Tom's Hütte. *Stowe.*
Originaux du XVII. Siècle. *Musset,*
Pauline et Pascal Bruno. *Dumas,*
Pays Latin. *Murger,*
Penelope Normande. *Karr,*
Pierrette. *Balzac.*
Presbytère. *Töpffer,*
Reine Margot. *Dumas,*
Roman d'une Femme. *Dumas,*
Rosa et Gertrude. *Topffer,*
Sacs et Parchemens. *Sandeau,*
Salons et Souterains. *Méry,*
Scènes de Compagne. *Murger,*
Scènes de la Bohême. *Murger,*

318.

Fine Arts.

319.

Music.

POLITICAL SCIENCE.

321.

Despotism in America. *Hildreth,*
Democracy Unveiled. *Fessenden,*
Politics for American Christians.
Madison Papers: purchased by Congress.
Political Writings. *Dickinson.*
Annals of Congress.
Reminiscences of Congress. *March,*
Sons of the Sires. A Hist. of the Am. Party.
Policy as op. to For. Im. & Popery. *Whitney,*
Repub. Landmarks; or For. Im. *Sanderson.*
Liberties of America. *Warner,*
Voice to America.
Thoughts on Policy of Retaliation. *Adams.*
American Negotiator. *Wright.*

Law.

Principles and Maxims of Jurisp. *Phillimore.*
Intro. to Study of Jurisprudence. *Thibaut.*
Caput "Si Pater" de Testament. *Costa–*
Lectures on Natural Law. *Tucker,*
Law of Nature & Na. Rel. to Divine Law. *Levi.*
The Organic Laws. *Sax.*
Gr. Charter, & Char. of the Forest. *Blackstone–*
Abridg. of Kent's Commentaries. *Johnson.*
Justinian; The Institutes of.
Blackstone's Com. abridged. *Warren.*
Law Dictionary and Glossary. *Burrill.*
Introduction to American Laws. *Walker.*
Elements of Laws in force in U. S. *Smith,*
Kent's Com. reduced to Questions. *Kinne.*
Digest of Ancient and Modern Laws. *Dew.*
Selection of Legal Maxims. *Broom.*
Romance of the Forum. *Burke.*

International Law.

Science of International Law. *Twiss.*
Copyright Law bet. Eng & France. *Burke.*
De Jure Belli et Pacis. Libri Tres. *Grotius.*
Commen. on International Law. *Phillimore.*
Influence of Christ. upon Inter. Law. *Kennedy,*
Rights of War and Peace, (abridged.) *Grotius.*
Dissertation on a Congress of Nations,

Civil Law.

Civil Law. *Domat.*
Essays on Uses and Trusts. *Sanders,*
On the Law relating to Trustees. *Hill.*
On the Law of Covenant for Title. *Rawle.*
Executors, Admr's., & Guard. Guide. *Wright,*
Law of Executors and Admr's. *Taylor,*
The Marriage Contract. *Raikes,*
Law of Marriage and Divorce. *Bishop.*
Treatise on the Law of Descents. *Reeve.*
Doctrine of Equity. *Adams.*
On Equity Jurisprudence. *Story.*
Treatise on Equity Jurisprudence. *Willard.*
Law of Suits by Attachment. *Drake.*
On Action of Ejectment. *Adams.*

Criminal Law.

History of Trial by Jury. *Forsyth.*
Essays on the Trial by Jury. *Spooner.*
On the Law of Evidence. *Greenleaf.*

322.

Digest of Laws of Ev. in Crim. Cases. *Roscoe.*
Forms of Proc. under N. Y. Prohib. Liq. Law.
Commen. on the Criminal Law. *Bishop.*

Real Estate Law.

On the Law of Covenants for Title. *Rawle.*
Digest of the Law of Real Property. *Cruise.*
Law of Real Property N. Y. State. *Lalor,*
American Law of Real Property. *Hilliard.*
Law of Landlord and Tenant. *Smith.*
Law of Mortgage. *Hilliard.*
Digest of Conv. and Test. Law. *Thornton.*

Commercial Law.

Com. Law, its Prin. and Adminis. *Levi–*
Leading Cases of Commercial Law. *Ross.*
Collection of Stat. on Shipping, Commerce, &c.
Laws of the Sea: or Seamen's Assist. *Butts,*
Compendium of Mercantile Law. *Smith.*
The Law of Contracts. *Parsons.*
Law of Contracts not under Seal. *Story.*
La Parf. Notaire; ou La Sci. des Not. *Massé–*
Manual for Notaries Public. *Roelker.*
Law of Fire and Life Insurance. *Angell.*
Cases relating to the Laws of Railways.
Patent Laws of all Nations. *Hughes.*
Einheim. und ansländ. Patent Gesetzg. *Stolle.*
Patent Office and Patent Laws. *Moore,*
On the Law of Patents in the U. S. *Curtis.*
Law Reports of Patent Cases. *Carpmael.*
Repertory of Patent Inventions, vols. 16–24.
Reports of Com. of Pat. 1844, '45, '49, 50–54.
Report of the Com. of Patents for 1850.
List of Pat. is. by U. S. from '90 to '47. *Burke.*
On Patent Cases. *Robb.*
Law of Pat. Familiarly Explained. *Carpmael.*
Patent Laws of the United States.
Invent. Assist. concerning Pat. Laws. *Dorr,*
Invent. Manual of Legal Principles. *Curtis.*
Die Inter. Pat. Gesetzgebung. *Kleinschrod.*
Laws of Exchange and Prom. Notes. *Tournay,*
On the Law of Bills of Exchange. *Story.*
On the Law of Promissory Notes. *Story.*
On the Laws of Insurance. *Phillips.*
Trea. on the Measure of Damages. *Sedgwick.*
Law of Partnerships in the U. S. *Troubat.*
On the Law of Partnerships. *Story.*
Law of Sales of Personal Property. *Story.*
Laws of Wages, Profits & Rent. *Tucker.*
On the Law of Agency. *Story.*
Law of Arbitration. *Caldwell.*
Mercantile and Bankrupt Law. *Davis.*
The Laws of Blockade. *Deane.*

Constitutional and Statute Law.

Cabinet Lawyer; a Digest of Laws of Eng.
Rise & Prog. of Eng. Constitution. *Creasy,*
Commen. on Universal Public Law. *Bowyer.*
Constitutions of the U. S. & Eng. *Tremenheere.*
Constitution of U. S. with Analysis. *Hickey,*
Exposition of the U. S. Constitution. *Story.*
Commentaries on American Law. *Kent.*
Lectures on Constitutional Law. *Tucker.*

322.

Documents of the Constitution. *Bowen.*
Constitutions of the Several States and U. S.
Col. of the Constitutions of 13 U. S. of Am.,
United States Statutes at Large.
United States Digest, vols. 6–16.
Supplement to the Same.
United States Digest in Com. Law and Adm.
Laws of the U. S. 1776–1833.
American State Papers & U. S. Public Doc.
Digested Sum. of Pri. Claims 1st to 31st Cong.
Journal of Debates on Mass. Constitution.
Official Report of Mass. Convention.
Revised Statutes of the State of New York.
Practices &c. of the U. S. Sup. Court. *Curtis.*
Acts of the General Court of Mass. 1854, '55.
Laws of New York Colony, 1691–1773–
Laws of N. Y. passed at 73d, 74th, 77th Ses.
Index to New York Legis. Doc., 1842–54.
Laws relating to the City of N. Y. *Davies.*
Statutes of the State of N. Y. *Blatchford.*
Code of Procedure of N. Y. State, Apr. 1849.
Code of Procedure of N. Y. State, Apr. 1852.
Reports of Comm. on the Code of Procedure.
Laws of New York on Canals.
New York Reports on Practice & Pleadings.
Estate & Rights of N. Y. City Cor. *Hoffman.*
By-Laws and Ordinances of the Mayor of N.Y.
Constitution and Government of Pa. *Franklin.*
Debates in California on the Const. *Browne.*
The *Code* Napoleon.
Cours de Code Civil. *Delincourt*–
Acts of Assem. pass'd in Barbadoes 1648–1718–
Am. Slave Code in Theory & Practice. *Goodell,*
Manual of N. Y. State Legislature for '54–5,
Constitutional Text Book.
The Legislative Guide. *Burleigh,*
Manual of Parliamentary Practice. *Jefferson,*
Yo. Am.; or, Book of Gov. & Laws. *Goodrich,*
New Clerk's Assistant. *Jenkins.*
Practical Forms and Precedents. *Gibbs.*
Rules of Order for Societies, &c. *Mathias.*
American Lawyer & Form Book. *Beadle.*
Secret Jour. of Acts and Proceed. of Congress.
Journals of Cong. Sep. 5, 1774–Nov. 3, 1788.
Debates & Pro. of U. S. Cong. 1st–17th Sess'n.
State Papers and U. S. Public Documents.
United States Public Docs., 32d & 33d Cong.
Congressional Globe, 31st to 33d Congress–
Messages of the Pres't of U. S.
Journal of Senate of N. Y. State, 74, 76, 77 Ses.
Journal of Assem. of N. Y. State, 74, 76, 77 Ses.
New York Docs. of Bd. of Aldermen & Assist.
New York Aldermen, Pro. of Bd. and Assist.
Proceedings and Docs. of Assistant Aldermen.
New York. Mayor Lee's Mess's to Com. Coun.
Message of Gov. of State of Florida, Nov., '52.
Offic. Lets. to Cong. dur. Am. Rev. *Washington.*
Correspondence of Am. Revolution. *Sparks.*
Reprint of his Let's to Jos. Reed. *Washington.*
Remarks on "Reprint of Letters," &c. *Sparks.*
Letters to Lord Mahon. *Sparks.*
Reply to the Strictures of Lord Mahon. *Sparks.*
Report of Superin. of Coast Survey, 1851–54–
Reports (Parl.), Printed Papers, 1837 & 1853–
Report on princ. Fisheries of Am. seas. *Sabine.*
Report of Regents of Smithso'n Inst. 1852–54.

323.

Criminal Law.

Message on Venal Code in Europe.
Complete Collection of State Trials to Geo. III–
Celebrated Trials of the Aristocracy. *Burke.*
Genuine Account of Trial of Eugene Aram.
Narratives from Crim. Trials in Scot. *Burton.*
Trial of Wm. Freeman for mur. of Van Nest.
Report of the Case of J. W. Webster. *Bemis.*
Full Report of the Trial of Matt. F. Ward.
American Print Works *vs.* C. W. Lawrence.
Howard Ins. Co. of N. Y. *ads.* S. Mathews.
New Eng. & N. Y. Law Reg. 1855. *Hayward,*
United States Law Magazine, vols. 1–4.
Procedures in de Zaak van P. Marcus.
New York City Hall Records.

Social Polity.

Introduction to Social Science. *Calvert,*
Knowledge is Power. *Knight,*
On Sanitary Condition of London. *Senior.*
Parliamentary Report on Large Towns–
Crime in England from 1801–48. *Plint,*
Rep. of Examin. in Poor Houses. *Chipman.*
Reformatory Schools for Children. *Carpenter,*
London Labor and London Poor. *Mayhew.*
Juvenile Delinquency. *Hill,*
Crime; Its Amount, Causes & Rem. *Hill.*
Sight of Land; an Es. on Rag. Schools. *Hall,*
The Rationale of Discipline. *Pillans.*
Mornings at Bow Street. *Wright,*
Irish Ethnology Socially & Pol. Con. *Ellis.*
Hist. de la Classe Ouvrière. *Robert du Var.*
Peasantry of England. *Perry,*
White Slaves of England. *Cobden,*
Report of Gov's of Alms-House, N. Y. 1853, '4.
Report on Poor and Insane of Rhode Island.
Etab. Philanthropiques des Etats Unis. *Bertal.*
Account of State Pris. in City N. Y. *Torrey.*
Concise Hist. of Eastern Penitentiary of Penn.
Report of the Prison Association of N. Y.
Fourth Annual Rep. of Gov. of *Alms House.*
Foreign Institutions for the Insane. *Earle.*
Reports (Parliamentary) on Friendly Soc.–
Annals & Anecdotes of Life Assnce. *Francis,*
Life Ass. Soc. and Savings Banks. *Scratchley.*
Deed of Settlement of the Rock Life Ass. Co.
Deed of Settlement of the Soc. for Life Ass.
Treaties on Life Annuities. *De Witt,*
Guide to Benefit Building Societies. *James,*
Laws of Benefit Building Societies. *Pratt,*
Civilisation et Barbarie. *Sarniente,*
Société et les Gouvernements de l'Europe.
The Agricultural Laborer. *Doyle.*
Meliora; or, better Times to Come. *Ingestre,*
Considerations of some Recent Social Theories,
Inquiry into Condition of Africans in U. S.

Political Economy.

Principles of Political Economy. *Bowen.*
Political Economy. *Stewart.*
Dictionnaire de l'Economie Politique.
Manual of Political Economy. *Smith,*
National System of Political Economy. *List.*
Treatise on Political Economy. *Opdyke,*

323.

Lectures on Political Economy. *Newman,*
Four Lectures on Political Economy. *Senior.*
Nine Letters to Dr. Adam Seybert. *Carey.*
Political Essays on Money, &c. *Webster.*
Monnaie du Crédit et de l'Impôt. *Puynode.*
Future Wealth of America. *Bonynge,*
Population and Capital. *Richards.*
Free Banking. An Essay. *Duncombe,*

Commerce and Trade.

Dangers and Duties of Mercan. Profn. *Hillard,*
Enterprises Industrielles Commerl. *Courcelle.*
Clavis Commercii; or, Key of Comm. *Hawkins.*
Mercantile Maritinal Guide. *Beedell.*
Naval and Military Resources of Eur. *Wraxall.*
The Merchant Shipping Acts. *Dowdeswell,*
Rural Economy of Eng. Irel. Scotl. *Lavergne.*
Customs Tariffs of all Nations. *Newdegate–*
Customs Guide for 1850–51, and '53. *Clements,*
Rates of Merchandise, with Duties and Draw-
Yearly Journal of Trade. *Pope.* [backs.
Comml. Prod's of Veget. Kingdom. *Symonds.*
Theory of Human Progression. *Dove.*
Tableau Hist. de l'Industrie et du Commerce.
Zolltariffe aller Länder; gesammelt v. Hubner.
Annuaire Général du Comm. 1813, 1847, '50.
Tableau du Comm. de la France, pour 1848–
Tableau des Mouvements du Cabotage, 1848–
Duties on Imports into France. *Yapp.*
Credit Syst. in France, Gt. Brit. U. S. *Carey–*
Documents of the European and N. Am. Rail'y,
Comm'l Tariffs and Regulations of France–
Comm'l Tariffs and Regulat'ns of Italian States–
Commercial Tariffs and Regulations of Spain–
Comm'l Tariffs and Regulations of Norway–
Comm'l Tariffs and Regulations of Denmark–
Comm'l Tariffs and Regulations of Portugal–
Comm'l Tariffs and Regulations of Holland–
Comm'l Tar. and Regul. of Germanic States–
Comm'l Tariffs and Regulations of Belgium–
Comm'l Tariffs and Regulations of Austria–
Comm'l Tariffs and Regula. of Hanse Towns–
Comm'l Tariffs, &c., of Russian Empire–
Comm'l Tariffs and Regulations of Greece–
Comm'l Tariffs, &c., of Ottoman Empire–
Comm'l Tariffs and Regulations West Indies–
Comm'l Tariffs and Reg. of India, Ceylon, &c.–
Comm'l Tariffs, &c., of African States–
Comm'l Tariffs and Regulations of Brazil–
Comm'l Tariffs, &c., of Europe and America–
Comm'l Tariffs, &c., of States of Mexico–
Commercial Tariffs, &c., of Spanish America–
Commercial Tariffs, &c., of U. S. of America–
Report of the Com. on Commerce with China–
Indian Tables of Weights, Measures, Money.
The Land Tax of India. *Baillie.*
Trade and Com. of Brit. N. Am. Col. *Andrews.*
Report on Commerce and Navig. for 1849–54.
Tables of Com. and Navig. of U. S. for 1851.
Steamboat Direct'y on West. Waters. *Lloyd.*
Laws of Trade on Internal Improv'ts. *Ellet.*
Report of Comm. on Har. and Riv. Improv'ts.
Public Documents relating to N. York Canals.
Report on the Fisheries of American Seas.
Report of Officers of Light House Board.

325.

Com. of Portugese Col. in S. Am. *Coutinho.*
Documents for Manufactures in the U. S.
Statist. Inform. on Industry of Mass. *De Witt.*
Indus. Resou. of So. and West. States. *De Bow.*
Cotton, its Growth, Trade, and Manu. *Dudley.*
Cotton and Commerce of India. *Chapman.*
Opium Trade in India and China. *Allen.*
Rise, Prog., &c., of Colonial Wools. *Southey.*
Coal Trade of British America. *Johnson.*
Report of Sec. of State on Commer'l Regul'ns.
Digest of Com. Rela'ns of U. S. w. For. Coun.
History of the Iron Trade. *Scrivinor.*
Com. Negot. bet. U. S. & Gt. Brit. *Tazewell.*
Treaty between Great Britain and U. S.,
Commercial and Banking Tables. *Bartlett–*
Commercial Tables. *Hartshorn–*
Elwood's Grain Tables. *Elwood,*
Postal Ref. its Neces. and Practicab'y. *Miles.*
La Science des Negocians. *La Porte.*
Universal Dict. of Weights & Meas. *Alexander.*
Practical Treatise on Business. *Freedley;*
Principles of Law of Marine Insur. *Hildyard.*
Merchant's Mag. and Com. Rev. Vols. 23–30.
De Bow's Commercial Review.
General Instructions to Consuls of U. S.
Réglements Cons. des Etats Maritimes. *Cussy.*
Origin, &c., of Consular Establish'nts. *Warden.*

Banking and Currency.

Practical Treatise on Banking. *Gilbart.*
Theory and Practice of Banking. *Macleod.*
Die Banker. *Hubner.*
Des Operations de Banque. *Courcelle.*
On Currency. *Carey.*
Short & Easy Method for Aver. Ac'ts. *Brooks.*
Tables of Ster. and Federal Exchange. *Oates.*
Interest and Average Tables. *Delisser.*
Equation Tables for Aver. Acc'ts. *Martin.*
Circumstances which det. Wages. *McCulloch.*
Essays on Int., Exch., Coins, &c. *McCulloch.*
Treat. on Subj. con. w. Econ. Pol. *McCulloch.*
Banker's Common-Place Book. *Homans.*
Banker's Almanac for 1851.
Banker's Magazine and Financial Register.
Banker's Magazine and Journal of Money.

Book-keeping.

Origin and Progress of Book-keeping. *Foster.*
Book-keeping by Sing. Dou. En. *Crittenden.*
Book-keeping by Sing. Dou. En. *Eastman,*
Double Entry Book-keeping. *Foster.*
Rudiments of Book-keeping. *Nixon,*
Book-keeping by Sing. & Dou. En. *McGregor,*
Practical System of Book-keeping. *Mayhew,*
First Lessons in Book-keeping. *Palmer,*

Statistics.

Eléments de Statistique. *Jonnés,*
Year-book of the Nations for 1855. *Burritt.*
Oxford University Calendar for 1856,
Catalogue of Oxford Gradu. from 1659–1770.
Newspaper Press Direct. of Gt. Brit. *Mitchell.*
Edinburgh and Leith Directory, 1852–55.

HISTORY AND GEOGRAPHY.

Universal Travels.

Collection of Early Voy. Trav. &c. *Hakluyt–*
Voyages to various Parts of World. *Coggeshall.*
Account of Several Late Voyages and Discov.
New Collection of Voyages, Disco. and Tra.
Purchas: His Pilgrimage, in 4 parts–
Voyages, Relations, et Mémoires Orig. *Ternaux.*
Collection of Voyages of Dutch East Ind. Co.
General Collection of Portug. and Span. Voy.
Voyages et Recits. *Yvan,*
Voyage Round the World. *Wilkes.*
Narrative of a Voy. Round the Wor. *Arago–*
Voyage Round the World. *Funnell.*
Narrative of a Jour. Round Wor. *Gerstaecker,*
Travels of Rolando round World. *Jaufaet,*
A Lady's Jour. Round the World. *Pfeiffer,*
Lady's Second Jour. Rou. World. *Pfeiffer,*
Erdumsegelung der Fregatte Eugenie. *Etzel.*
Voyage of H. M. S. Herald, 1845–51. *Seeman.*
Voyage of H. M. S. Rattlesnake. *Macgillivray.*
Four Years in a Gov. Explo. Ex. *Colvocoressis,*
Personal Narra. of First Voyage of Columbus.
Americus Vespucius and his Voys. *Santarem.*
Nar. of Expedition from Eng. in 1817. *Hackett.*
Voyage from Leith to Lapland. *Hurton.*
Les Voyageurs Nouveaux. *Marmier,*
Voyage from Holland to Am. 1632–44. *Vries–*
Pilg. in Europe and Am. 1821–23. *Beltrami.*
Voy. to Califor., Newfoundld., &c. *Auteroche.*
Notes of a Theological Student. *Hoppin,*
Recol. of Ramble fr. Sydney to Southampton.
Travels in Europe and the East. *Prime,*
Trav. in Ind., Abyssinia, and Egypt. *Valentia–*
Rambles and Scram. in N. & S. Am. *Sullivan.*
Traveler's Tour in N. & S. Am. in 1850. *Young.*
Australian and Calif. Gold Discov. *Stirling,*
Fünfzig Jahre in Beiden Hemisphären. *Nolte.*
Fifty Years in both Hemispheres. *Nolte,*
Thoughts and Things Home and Ab. *Burritt.*
World; Here and There,
Life Here and There. *Willis,*
Romance of Modern Travel,
Adventures of an Aide-de-Camp. *Grant.*
Traveler's Own Book,
Memorable Accidents, Unheard-of Transact'ns.
Progress of Maritime Discovery. *Clarke–*

Universal Geography.

Illustrated London Geography. *Guy.*
Manual of Geography. *Hughes,*
Hand-book of Universal Geography. *Callicot,*
Geographical View of the World. *Goldsmith,*
Cosmography. *Winslow,*
Tallis' Illustrated Atlas. *Martin–*
Atlas of the World. *Colton–*
Most Exact and Accurate Map of the World–
Mitchell's Universal Atlas–
Atlas Général. *Desnos–*
Modern Atlas. *Findlay.* [*Spruner–*
Atlas zur Geschichte Asien's Afrika's u. Am
Atlas Antiquus. *Spruner–*
Dict'y of Greek and Roman Geogra. *Smith.*
Classical Atlas to Illus. An. Geog. *Findlay.*
Geographia Classica and Atlas. *Butler.*
Classical Gazetteer. *Hazlitt,*
Manual of Geographical Science.
Dictionnaire Geographique et Statis. *Guibert.*
General Gazetteer *Johnston.*
The Imperial Gazetteer. *Blackie.*
Pronouncing Gazetteer. *Baldwin,*
Harper's Statis. Gazetteer of World. *Smith.*
Modern Geography and History. *Putz,*
Cosmographie en Moyen Age. *Santarem.*
Geographisches Jahrbuch, 1850–1. *Berghaus–*
Mittheilungen aus Geogr. Anst *Petermann–*
Jour. of Roy. Geog. Soc. vols. 11–23, index.
Bulletin de la Soc. de Geographie, vols. 1–7.
Bulletin of Amer. Geog. and Statist. Society.
Index to London Geogr. Journal. *Jackson.*

Physical Geography.

Physical Geography. *Barrington,*
Popular Physical Geology. *Jukes,*
Cosmos. *Humboldt,*
Kosmos. *Humboldt.*
Atlas to Humboldt's Kosmos. *Bromme–*
Physical Geography of the Sea. *Maury.*
Marine Atlas. *Norrie–*
De la Météorologie. *Foissac.*
Philosophy of the Weather. *Butler,*
Hand-book of the Law of Storms. *Birt.*
Mechanical Theory of Storms. *Bassnett.*
The Law of Storms. *Sedgwick.*
Meteorological Register f. 1843 to '54. *Army–*

Ethnography.

Analytical Ethnology. *Massy,*
Ancient Ethnography & Geograp. *Niebuhr.*
Ethnological Journal. Vol. 1.
Original Unity of the Human Race. *Caldwell,*
Unity of the Human Race. *Smyth,*
The Races of Men. *Knox,*
De l'Homme et des Races Humaines. *Holland,*
Natural Hist. of the Varieties of Man. *Latham.*
Histoire Générale des Races Humaines. *Salles,*
Types of Mankind. *Nott.*
Man and his Migrations. *Latham,*
Races of Men, their Geogr. Distr'n. *Pickering,*
The Celt, the Roman, and the Saxon. *Wright.*
The Earth, Planets, and Men. *Schouw,*
Ethnology of the British Colonies. *Latham,*
Native Races of the Russian Army. *Latham.*

Antiquities; Manners and Customs.

Encyclopedia of Antiquities. *Fosbroke.*
New Varieties of Gold and Sil. C'ns. *Eckfeldt*
Observazioni sopra i Sigilli Antichi. *Manni–*
Dialog. on Usefulness of Anc. Medals. *Addison*

330.

Scotland.

332.

Ireland.

London.

England, Miscellaneous.

333.

History of the County of Kent. *Ireland.*
Recollec. Manchester, 1792-1832. *Prentice,*
Manches. Worthies, their Founda's. *Edwards.*
Liverpool Described. *Thomson,*
The Erne; its Legends & Fly-Fishg. *Newland.*
Picturesque Tour of River Thames. *Murray.*
Excursion Companion from London. *Knight.*
The Wye and its Associations. *Ritchie.*
Hastings' Guide,
Original Bath Guide,
Oxford University and City Guide,
Parochial History of Cornwall. *Gilbert.*
Cornwall; its Mines and Miners,
Tour through Parts of Wales. *Sotheby–*
Shetland and the Shetlanders. *Sinclair,*
Sketches in the Isles of Scilly,

France.

Histoire de France. *Mennechet,*
History of France to 1850. *White,*
Histoire de la France au 16e Siècle. *Michelet.*
France, Ancienne et Moderne. *Patria,*
Lectures on The History of France. *Stephens.*
Rolla and His Race; or, Normans. *Warburton.*
French under the Merovingians. *Sismondi.*
Chronol. de l'Atlas Hist. de la France. *Duruy.*
Histoire des Protestants de France. *Félice,*
Civil Wars and Monarchy in France. *Ranke,*
Essai sur l'Histoire du Tiers Etat. *Thierry.*
Charles V. et son Abdication. *Pichot.*
Chronique du Temps de Chas. IX. *Mérimée,*
La Ligue et Henri IV. *Capefigue,*
La Reforme et Henri IV. *Capefigue,*
Histoire du France sous Louis XIII. *Bazin,*
Cent. dix Jours du Règne de Louis XVII.
Révolutions de Paris. [*Durdent.*
History of the French Revolution. *Jobson.*
Recueil de Piéces sur la Révolu. Française.
History of the French Revolution. *Thiers.*
Mémoires de la Révolu. Française. *Montlosier.*
Mémoires et Anecdotes à l'Histoire de la Rév.
Mémoires sur la Révolution Française. *Buzot.*
Apologie du Projets des Chefs de la Rév. Fran.
Histoire de la Révolution Française. *Blanc;*
Procès Célèbres de la Révolution.
Assassinats Commis sur 81 Prisonniers.
The Jansenists; Rise, Perse. &c. *Tregelles,*
Procedure Crim. Instruite au Chatelet de Paris.
Alliance des Jacobins de France avec le Min-
Journal. *Ramel.* [istre Anglais.
Actes des Apôtres.
Rapport fait des trouvés chez Robespierre, &c.
Saint Just et la Terreur. *Fleury,*
Guerres Maritim. sous la Répub. *La Gravière,*
Histoire des Crimes du 2d Décem. *Schœlcher.*
Divers Ecrits sur la Révolution de Juillet.
Guerre de la Vendée et des Chouans–
Histoire du Cabinet des Tuilleries.
Histoire du Consulat et de l'Empire. *Thiers.*
Histoire de la Restauration. *Capefigue,*
Restoration of Monarchy in France. *Lamartine,*
Histoire de la Restauration. *Lamartine;*
Louis Philippe et la Liste Civile. *Montalivet,*
France; its King, Court, and Govern't. *Cass.*
Les Constituants. *Lamartine,*

334.

Histoire d'un Coup d'Etat. *Belorimo.*
Histoire de Trente Heures, Fevrier, 1848,
Histoire de la Convention Nationale. *Barante,*
Histoire du Directoire. *Cassagnac.*
Histoire du Govern. Provisoire. *Reginault.*
The Bonaparte Plot. *Cassagnac.*
Causes de la Révolution Française. *Cassagnac:*
Rev'l of Fr. Emperorship Anticipated. *Faber,*
Louis Napoleon and his Times. *De Puy,*
Claret and Olives. *Reach,*
Letters of an Architect from France. *Woods–*
Pictures of Travel in South of France. *Dumas,*
Le Curé Manqué; or, Cust. of Fr. *Courcillon.*
New Paris Guide for 1854. *Galignani,*
Tableau de Paris. *Mercier,*
Etrangers à Paris.
Tableau de Paris. *Texier–*
Manual Complet du Voyageur dans Paris.
Paris Directory. [*Lebrun,*
The Ins and Outs of Paris. *De Margueritte,*
Battle Summer. *Mitchell,*
Lettres Parisiennes. *Girardin.*
Parisian Sights and French Principles. *Jarves,*
Faggot of French Sticks. *Head,*
Purple Tints of Paris. *St. John,*
Tri-colored Sketches in Paris,
La Vie de Paris. *Mornand,*
Mémoires d'un Bourgeois de Paris. *Véron.*
Paris after Waterloo. *Simpson,*
Celebrated Saloons and Parisian Letters. *Gay.*
La Bourse et la Vie. *Bernard,*
Police de Paris Dévoilée, par P. Manuel.

General Europe.

History of Europe. *Alison.*
Introduction to History of Europe. *Puffendorf.*
History of Modern Europe for Boys. *Edgar,*
History of Europe fr. Fall of Napoleon. *Alison.*
Atlas zur Geschichte der Staaten Eur. *Spruner–*
Europe and the Allies of the Past and To-day,
Campaign of Waterloo. *Jomini,*
Europe, Past and Present. *Ungerwitter,*
Hand-book for Travelers in Europe. *Park,*
Travelling Journals. *Arnold,*
Wild Oats, Sown Abroad,
Lights and Scenes in Europe in 1850. *Bullard,*
Paterfamilias's Diary of Everybody's Tour,
Foreign Reminiscences. *Holland,*
A Tennessean Abroad. *MacGavick,*
Scenes and Thoughts in Europe. *Calvert,*
Old Sights with New Eyes,
Europe in a Hurry. *Wilkes.*
Bell Smith Abroad. *Piatt,*
A Step fr. New World to the Old. *Tappan,*
Sunny Memories of Foreign Lands. *Stowe,*
Art, Scenery, and Philosophy in Eur. *Wallace.*
Glances at Eur. dur. Summer, 1851. *Greeley,*
My First Visit to Europe. *Dickinson,*
Pictures of Europe, framed in Ideas. *Bartol,*
Summer's Tour in Europe in 1851,
Men and Things as I saw them in Eur. *Murray,*
A Buckeye Abroad. *Cox,*
Cruise of the Yacht North Star. *Choules,*
Visit to Europe in 1851. *Silliman,*
Continental Tourist. *Roscoe.*

Spain and Portugal.

Modern Italy.

Switzerland.

Germany.

337.

Correspondence rel. to Affairs of Hung.1847–9–
Histoire de la Guerre de Hongrie. *Balleydier.*
Hungary and its Revo. with Mem. of Kossuth,
Kossuth and the Magyar Land. *Pridham,*
Hungary and Kossuth. *Tefft,*
Hungary in 1851. *Brace,*

Northern Europe.

Hand Book for Northern Europe.
Northern Mythology. *Thorpe,*
Guide to North. Archæology by Copenh. Soc.
Jour. to Iceland, Sweden & Norway. *Pfeiffer,*
Altnordisches Leben. *Weinhold.*
Religion of the Northmen. *Keyser,*
Travels on the Shores of the Baltic. *Hill.*
Histoire de Dannemarc. *Mallet,*
Sixteen Months on the Danish Isles. *Hamilton,*
Social and Pol. State of Denmark. *Laing.*
The Danes and the Swedes. *Scott,*
History of the Swedes. *Geijer.*
History of Sweden. *Fryxell,*
Sweden; its Religious State & Pros. *Lumsden.*
Pictures of Sweden. *Andersen.*
Life in Sweden; Ex. to Nor.& Den. *Bunbury,*
Brage Breaker with the Swedes. *Jerrold,*
Eight Weeks in Norway. *Andersen,*
Norway and its Glaciers in 1851. *Forbes.*
Norway and its Scenery, *Forster,*
Conquest of Finland by Russia. *Monteith,*
Nordufari; or, Rambles in Iceland. *Miles,*
Narrative of a Cruise among the Faroe Is. 1854.

Holland.

Rise of the Dutch Republic. *Motley.*
Geschichte der Deutschen Staaten. *Wirth.*
History of the Low Country Warres. *Strada-*

Russia and Poland.

Histoire de la Russie. *Lamartine.*
Court & Reign of Catharine II. *Smucker.*
Russia. *Custine,*
Russia as it Is. *Gurowski,*
Russia as it Is. *Morell,*
Russia and the Russians. *Cole,*
Guerres de la Rus. contre la Tur. *Saint Ange,*
Progress of Russia. *Urquhart,*
Productive Forces of Russia. *Tegoborski.*
Russian Em.; its Res., by a Looker-on fr.Am.
Pictures from St. Petersburg. *Jerrmann,*
The Russians in Bulgaria. *Moltke.*
Englishwoman in Russia,
Recollections of Rus. by a German Nobleman,
English Envoy at Court of Nicholas I. *Corner,*
The Knout and the Russians. *Lagny,*
The Russian Shores of the Black Sea. *Oliphant,*
Russia on the Borders of Asia. *Turnerelli,*
Travels in Siberia. *Hill.*
Exped. agst. Rus. Set. Siberia. *Whittingham,*
Autocracy in Poland and Russia. *Allen,*
Fall of Poland. *Saxton,*
Hist. and Literature of Poland. *Zaba,*
The Polish Question & Panslavism. *Krasinski.*
Tribes of the Caucasus. *Haxthausen,*
Transcaucasia; its Nat. & Races. *Haxthausen.*

338.

Modern Greece.

History of Greece from 1201–1451. *Finlay.*
Greece & Greeks of the Present Day. *About,*
A Picture of Greece in 1825. *Emerson,*
Athens and Peloponnesus. *Hettner,*

Mediterranean and Levant.

The Mediterranean. *Smyth.*
Shores and Isl. of Mediterranean. *Christmas,*
Summer Cruise in the Mediterranean. *Willis,*
Corsica, Picturesque and Hist. *Gregorovius,*
History of the Island of Minorca. *Armstrong.*
Six Semaines dans l'Ile de Sardaigne. *Delessert,*
Zephyrs from Italy and Sicily. *Gould,*
Sicily, a Pilgrimage. *Tuckerman,*
Pictures of Sicily.
Travels in Two Sicilies in 1777–80. *Swinburn.*
Hist. of the War of Sicilian Vespers. *Amari,*
Land and Sea in Bosphorus & Ægean. *Colton,*
Greece and the Golden Horn. *Olin,*
Picturesque Sketches of Gr. and Tur. *De Vere,*
Diary in Turkish and Greek Waters. *Carlisle,*
Lettres sur l'Adriat.et leMontenegro. *Marmier,*

Turkey and the East.

History of Turkey. *Lamartine,*
History of Turkey. *Porter.*
The Turkish Empire. *Besse,*
The Three Eras of Ottoman History. *Skene.*
Histoire de la Turquie. *Lamartine.*
History of Byzantine Em. 716–1453. *Finlay.*
Negot. for Peace of Dardanelles,1808–9. *Adair.*
Russo-Turkish Campaigns, 1828–9. *Chesney,*
Turkey, Past and Present. *Hutton,*
Turkey, Past and Present. *Morell,*
Predicted Downfall of Turkish Power. *Faber,*
Kismet; or, the Doom of Turkey. *MacFarlane,*
Letters on Turkey. *Ubicini,*
Lettres sur la Turquie. *Ubicini,*
Turkey and the Turks. *Smith,*
A Year with the Turks. *Smyth,*
Die Sclawen der Türkei. *Robert,*
European Turkey; its People, &c. *Knighton.*
The Turks in Europe. *St. John,*
La Turquie d'Europe. *Boué.*
The Sultan of Turkey. *Christmas,*
Hand-book for Travelers in Turkey,
Trip to Tur. & Guide to Constan. *Parnauvel,*
Stamboul and the Sea of Gems.

War in the East, 1853–55. *Klapka,*
The War in the Crimea. *Russell.*
Hist. de la Guerre de la Péninsule. *Foy.*
Guerre d'Orient. *Jouve.*
A Year of the War. *Gurowski.*
The Past Campaign; or, War in East. *Woods,*
Visit to Camp before Sebastopol. *McCormick,*
Lettres Ecrites d'Orient. *Frossard.*
Côté Religieux de Quest. Orient. *Ficquelmont.*
Military Tour in European Turkey. *Macintosh,*
The Czar and the Sultan. *Gilson,*
The Unholy Alliance. *Dix,*
Narrative of the Siege of Kars. *Sandwith,*
Campaign with the Turks in Asia. *Duncan,*

340.

Visit to India, China, and Japan. *Taylor,*
Acc't of East Ind. & Persia, 1672–81. *Fryer–*

India and Hindostan.

Administration of East India Company. *Kaye.*
India, Ancient and Modern. *Allen.*
History of British India. *MacFarlane,*
Hist. of India un. Báber & Humáyen. *Erskine.*
India; its Govern. und. Bureaucracy. *Dickinson,*
Modern India. *Campbell.*
India and the Hindoos. *Ward,*
Public Works in India. *Cotton,*
Memorials of Indian Government. *Tucker.*
The Land of the Veda. *Percival,*
India as it ought to be. *Hough.*
India as it may be. *Campbell.*
Travels in India and Kashmir. *Schonberg,*
Six Years in India. *Mackenzie,*
Thirty-five Years in the East. *Honigsberger.*
Travels in India. *Orlich.*
Journal of a Winter's Tour in India. *Egerton,*
Jour'l of Route across India to Eng. 1817–18.
Hints on Missions to India. *Winslow,*
British Conquests in India. *St. John,*
The Bhilsa Topes; or, Buddhist Monuments.
Polit. and Military Events in Brit. In. *Hough,*
The Brit. Army in India (1817–19). *Blacker–*
Sutlej Campaign of 1845–6. *Colvy,*
The Second Burmese War. *Laurie,*
Peace, War, and Adventure. *Chesterton,*
Ten Months among the Tents. *Hooper.*
Orig. Papers rel. to Distur. in Bengal, 1759–64.
Notes on North-Western India. *Raikes.*
Sindh, and Races in Valley of Indus. *Burton.*
Scinde; or, the Unhappy Valley. *Burton,*
Sir C. Napier's Adminis. of Scinde. *Napier.*
March thro' Scinde & Affghan. in 1842. *Allen.*
Hist. of the Reigning Family of Lahore. *Smyth.*
Goa and the Blue Mountains. *Burton.*
Theory and Practice of Caste. *Irving,*
Bengal as a Field of Missions. *Wylie.*
Tours in Up. In. & Himalaya Mount's. *Archer.*
Himalayan Journals. *Hooker.*

Five Years' Residence at Nepaul. *Smith,*
Jour. to Katmandu, Capit. of Nepaul. *Oliphant.*
Emb'y fr. Gov.Gen. of In. to C't Ava. *Crawford.*
Narrative of a Residence in Siam. *Neal,*
Thibet, Tartary and Mongolia. *Prinsep,*
Jour. thro' Tartary, Thibet, and China. *Huc,*
Western Himalaya and Thibet. *Thomson.*
Pictorial History of China and India. *Sears.*
Historical Rela. of Island of Ceylon. *Knox–*
Eight Years' Wanderings in Ceylon. *Baker.*
Eleven Years in Ceylon. *Forbes.*
Borneo and the Indian Archipelago. *Marryatt.*
Neue Reise-Beschreibung n. Ost Indien. *Dellon,*
Prison of Weltevreden at E.I. Archip'o. *Gibson,*
The Indian Archipelago. *St. John,*
Visit to Ind. Archipelago, in Mæander. *Keppel.*
Twenty Years in the Philippines. *La Gironière,*
Recollec. of Manilla and Philipp. *MacMicking,*
Voy. to New Guinea and Moluccas. *Forrest–*
Transport Voyage to the Mauritius and Back,

341.

China.

History of China,
Chine, Description Historique. *Pauthier.*
Insurrection in China. *Callery,*
Impres. of China & Present Revol. *Fishbourne,*
Journey through the Chinese Empire. *Huc,*
Voyage en Chine en 1847–50. *La Gravière,*
Three Years' Residence in China. *Power.*
Journey to the Tea Countries of China. *Fortune.*
China dur. the War and since the Peace *Davis.*
Lewchew and the Lewchewans. *Smith,*

Japan as it was and is. *Hildreth,*
Japan; Geogra. & Hist. Acc't of. *MacFarlane;*
Narrative of the Japan Expedition. *Hawks.*
Naval Expedition to Japan. *Perry–*
Japan and Around the World. *Spalding,*

Australia, &c.

Australia. *Fabian.*
Australia as it is. *Lancelott,*
Geography of Australian Colonies. *Evans,*
Australian Colonies. *Hughes,*
Three Colonies of Australia. *Sidney.*
Australia Visited and Re-visited. *Mossman.*
Cruise in the Australian Colonies. *Malone,*
Australia and her Gold Regions. *Jameson.*
Gold Colonies of Australia. *Earp,*
What I heard at the Aus'n Gold Fields. *Read.*
Boy's Adven. in Wilds of Australia. *Howitt.*
Adventures in Australia in 1852–3. *Jones,*
Floss; or, an Adventurer in Australia. *Hall,*
Two Exped. into So. Aust. in 1829–31. *Sturt.*
Emigrant's Guide to Australia. *Mackenzie,*
My Home in Tasmania. *Meredith,*
Land, Labor and Gold. *Howitt,*
Emigrant's Guide to Australia. *Capper,*
Practical Hints to Intending Emigrants.
Freedom & Independence for Australia. *Lang,*
Polit. Econ. & Represent'e Gov. in A. *Torrens.*
The Crown Lands of Australia. *Campbell.*
Victoria, late Australia Felix. *Westgarth.*
The Gold Era of Victoria. *Caldwell.*
Spring in the Canterbury Settlement. *Adams,*
Melbourne and the Chincha Islands. *Peck,*
Voyage to New South Wales. *White–*
New Zealand and its Inhabitants. *Taylor.*
New Zealand, its Cond., Prosp., & Res. *Fitton,*
Southern Districts of New Zealand. *Shortland.*
The Capital of New Zealand, &c. *Auckland.*

South Seas and Pacific.

Voyage to the South Seas, 1700–1. *Bulkeley.*
Voy. to South Sea, & R. Wor. 1708–11. *Cooke.*
Voyage to the South Sea in 1712–14. *Frezier–*
Life in the Sandwich Islands. *Cheever,*
Twenty-one Years in Sandwich Isl. *Bingham.*
Sandwich Islands Notes,
Island World of the Pacific. *Cheever,*
Tonga and the Friendly Islands. *Farmer,*
Cruise am. the Isl'ds of West. Pacific. *Erskine.*
Rovings in the Pacific.

342.

Terra Australis Cog.; or Voyages. *Callander.*
U. S. Expl. Exp. under Wilkes, &c. *Jenkins.*
Outline of the Revolution in Spanish America.

South America.

Travels in S. America in 1819–21. *Caldcleugh.*
Venezuela, Trin., Marg. & Tobago. *La Vaysse.*
Proceedings in Venezuela, 1819–20. *Chesterton.*
Campaigns in Venezuela & N. Gren. 1817–30.
Phys. & Pol. Geog. of N. Grenada. *Mosquera.*
Colombia; A Geograph. Account of Country.
Resi. & Travels in Colum. 1823–24. *Cochrane.*
Travels in Int. Prov. Columbia. *Hamilton.*
Voyage to Guiana, Brazil, & W. I. *Atkins.*
Voyage to Guiana. *Harcourt–*
Demerara after Fifteen Years of Freedom.
Voyage to the Demerary. *Bolingbroke–*
Notice Statistique sur la Guyane Française.
Histoire de Cayenne. *Bajon.*
Descrip. de la Colonie de Surinam. *Fermin.*
Life in Brazil. *Ewbank.*
Para; or Scenes & Adven. on Amaz. *Warren,*
Trav. on Amazon & Rio Negro. *Wallace.*
Brazil, the River Platte, &c. *Hadfield.*
Geral-Milco; or a Resi. in a Brazilian Valley.
Explor. of the Valley of Amazon. *Herndon.*
Les Hollandais au Brézil. *Netscher.*
Explor. of Valley of Amazon & Maps. *Gibbon.*
Brazil viewed thro' a Naval Glass *Wilberforce,*
Country & River of the Amazones. *Hamilton,*
History of Paraguay. *Charlevoix.*
Travels in Brazil. *Spix.*
Histoire de Brézil, 1800–1810. *Beauchamp.*
The Amaz. & Atlantic Slopes of Am. *Maury.*
Reise nach Brazilien. *Burmeister.*
Voyage à l'Equateur. *Condamine–*
Peruvian Antiquities. *Rivero.*
Voy. to Peru; by Conde of St. Malo, 1725–9,
Cuzco and Lima. *Markham,*
Voyage to Peru. *Brand.*
Seventeen Years' Travel in Peru. *Cieza–*
Sixteen Years in Chili & Peru. *Sutcliffe.*
Travels in Bolivia. *Bonelli,*
Voy. dans le Nord de la Bolivie. *Weddell.*
The Auracanians. *Smith,*
Jour. of a Residence in Chili in 1822. *Graham–*
Present State of Chili. *Bland.*
Travels in Chili and La Plata. *Miers.*
Jour. in Chili & the Argen. Prov. 1849. *Strain,*
Two Thou. Miles Ride thro' Arg. Pr. *Mac Cann,*
Letters from Paraguay. *Davie.*
Relation of R. M's. Voy. to Buenos Ayres, &c.
Views of Buenos Ayres & Monte Video. *Vidal–*
Bu. Ayres & Prairies of Rio de la Plata. *Parish.*
Dis. bet. Spain & Amer. Colonies. *Estrada,*
Les Consid. sur les Rep. de la Plata. *Brossard.*
Voy. to Pata. & Terra del Fuego. *Macdonald,*
Pata. and adjoining Parts of S. Amer. *Falkner–*
Rela. of Trav. concerning Patagonians. *Coyer,*
The Captive in Patagonia. *Bourne.*

West Indies.

De Insulis nuper Inventis. *Martyr–*
The West Indies as they are. *Bickell.*

342.

Four Years' Residence in the W. I., 1826–29.
Five Years' Residence in the W. I. *Day,*
Health Trip to the Tropics. *Willis,*
Voice from the West Indies. *Horsford.*
Extracts from Pa. of House of Com. rel to W. I.
History of Cuba. *Ballou,*
The Island of Cuba. *Humboldt,*
Cuba in 1851. *Jones.*
L'Ile de Cuba. *Daumont.*
Gan Eden; or, Pictures of Cuba,
The Free Flag of Cuba. *Hardemann,*
History of Jamaica. *Vernon.*
Civil and Natural Hist. of Jamaica. *Browne–*
Annals of Jamaica. *Bridges.*
Account of the Island of Jamaica. *Beckford.*
Jamaica in 1850. *Bigelow,*
Histoire de St. Domingue. *Charlevoix.*
Mémoires de la Revo. St. Domingue. *Lacroix.*
St. Domingo & Toussaint l'Ouverture. *Elliott,*
A Voyage to St. Domingo. *Stanislaus,*
Les Maladies, Plantes, &c., de St. Do. *Chevalier.*
History of the Caribby Is. Natural & Moral–
Caribbeanna, Relating chiefly to Barbadoes–
History of Barbadoes, 1605–1809. *Poyer–*
Voy. à la Martin. et Barbadoes. *Chanvalon–*
Antigua and the Antiguans.
St. Lucia, Historical, Statistical, &c. *Breen.*
Historical Account of St. Thomas, W. I. *Knox.*
Voyage aux Antilles. *Cassagnac.*
Navigation dans la Mer des Antilles. *Kerhallet.*
Histoire Naturelle et Morale des Iles Antilles.

Spanish America.

Concise Hist. of Spanish America. *Campbell.*
Essai Pol. sur le Roy. de Nouv. Esp. *Humboldt–*
Historia de la Conquista de Mexico. *Solis;*
Mexico and its Religion. *Wilson,*
Memoirs of the Mexican Revo. *Robinson:*
Mexican Illustrations. *Beaufoy.*
Map of the Valley of Mexico,
Residence and Tour in Mexico, 1826. *Lyon.*
Campaign in Northern Mexico. *Giddings,*
Jour. of a Reconnaissance in N. Mex. *Simpson.*
Travels and Adventures in Mexico. *Carpenter,*
Travels of Anna Bishop in Mexico in 1849,
Reisen in Mexico in 1845–48. *Heller.*
Visit to Mexico by the W. I. Is. *Robertson,*
Twelve Months Vol. in Mex., 1846–47. *Furber.*
Central America. *Baily.*
Notes on Central America. *Squier.*
Destiny of Nicaragua.
Nicaragua in 1852. *Reichardt.*
Nicaragua; its People, Scenery, &c. *Squier.*
Bosquejo de la Rep. de Costa Rica. *Molina.*
Costa Rica in 1853, '54. *Wagner.*
Waikna; Adventures on Musq. Shore. *Bard,*
Isthmus of Darien in 1852. *Gisborne.*
Isthmus of Darien, Ship Canal. *Cullen.*
The Isthmus of Panama. *Griswold,*
Story of Life on Isthmus Panama. *Fabens,*
Panama in 1855. *Tomes,*
The Isthmus of Tehuantepec. *Williams.*
Visit to Guatemala from Mexico. *Thompson,*
History of Yucatan. *Fancourt.*

347.

Hist. N. Y. State, vol. 1st, 1609–64. *Brodhead.*
History of New York. *Carpenter,*
History of New Amsterdam. *Davis,*
Documents relative to Col. Hist. of N.Y. State–
Documentary Hist of N. Y. *O'Callaghan–*
Antiquities of the State of N. Y. *Squier.*
Atlas of State of N. Y. and Counties. *Burr.*
Hist. of St. Lawrence & Franklin Cos. *Hough.*
History of Jefferson County. *Hough.*
Outline History of Orange County. *Eager.*
History of Herkimer County. *Benton.*
Annals of Albany. *Munsell,*
Chronicles of Cooperstown,
Out Doors at Idlewild. *Willis,*
Oxford Ac.Jub. held at Ox.N.Y. Aug. 1 & 2,'54.
Trappers of New York. *Simms,*
Hills, Lakes, and Forest Streams. *Hammond,*
Map of Railroads from Rome to Albany,
Trenton Falls. *Willis,*
New Mirror for Trav.; and Guide to Springs,
Harper's N. Y. and Erie Railroad Guide Book,
Guide to New Rochelle and its Vicinity,
New Mirror for Travelers. *Paulding,*
Stranger's Guide around N. Y. and Vicinity,
Pen and Ink Panorama of N.Y. City. *Mathews,*
Phelp's New York City Guide,
New York in a Nut Shell,
Manual de Neuva York. *Peña,*
New York as it is, in 1837,
What I saw in New York. *Ross,*
Visit of 1,000 Sab. Sch. Teach. of Mass. to N.Y.
History of the City of N. Y. *Valentine.*
New York, Past, Present and Future. *Belden,*
Sketch of the Resources of the City of N. Y.,
Catholic Church on N. Y. Island. *Bayley,*
Hist. of the Churches in City of N.Y. *Greenleaf,*
Collections of the N. Y. Historical Society.
Resources of the City of N. Y. Municipal Gov.
Proceedings of N. Y. Historical Society.
New Guide to Cities of N.Y. & Brook. *Francis,*
Hist'al. Sketches of Brook. & Neigh'd. *Bailey,*
Annals of Newtown, Queens Co., N.Y. *Riker.*
Hist. of Presb. Ch., Jamaica, L.I. *Macdonald,*

History of New Jersey. *Carpenter,*
Collections of the N. Jersey Historical Soc.
New Jersey Historical Society Proceedings.
Hist. of First Presb. Ch. in Newark. *Stearns.*
Early History of Perth Amboy. *Whitehead.*

Memoirs of the Historical Society of Penn.
Bulletin of the Historical Society of Penn.
Minutes of the Provincial Council of Penn.
Annals of Penn., 1609–82. *Hazard.*
Pamphlets on Harrisburgh Buckshot War.
Pictures of Philadelphia,
Philadelphia as it Is, in 1852. *Smith,*
Sketch of the History of Wyoming. *Chapman,*
History of Pittsburg. *Craig,*

DayStar of Am.Fr'dm; or,Tol.in Maryl'd. *Davis*
Message of Gov. of Maryland on Bound. Line.
Annals of Annapolis. *Ridgeley,*
Notes respecting the origin of Dist. Columbia.

348.

Morrison's Stranger's Guide to Washington,
United States Seat of Government. *Varnum.*
Report of Com. on Invasion of Wash. City.
History of Virginia. *Arthur,*
Hist. and Present State of Va. *Beverley.*
Discovery and Settlement of Va. *Stith.*
Early Set. & Indian Wars of West. Va. *DeHaas.*
Virginia Historical Register.
The Virginia Convention of 1776. *Grigsby.*
Sketches of Norfolk and its Vicinity. *Forrest.*
A Narrative of a Va. Exp. *Blackwater Chron.*
The Sum. of the Pestilence or Y. Fe. *Armstrong,*
White Sulphur Papers. *Pencil,*

Description of Carolina. *Archdale–*
Hist. Sketches of N. Car. 1584–1851. *Wheeler.*
History of South Carolina. *Simms,*
View of South Carolina. *Drayton.*
History of Georgia. *Arthur,*
Historical Collections of Georgia. *White.*
Gazetteer of the State of Georgia. *Sherwood,*
Conquest of Florida. *Irving,*
Notices of Florida and the Campaigns, *Cohen,*
Hist. of Ala., and Incidentally of Ga. & Miss.
History of Louisiana. *Bonner.* [*Pickett.*
History of Louisiana. *Pratz.*
Hist. of La., the Fr. & Span. Domin. *Gayarré.*
Louisiana as a French Colony. *Gayarré.*
Memoires Hist'ques sur la Louisane. *Dumont,*
Historical Collections of Louisiana. *French.*
Jackson and New Orleans. *Walker,*
The Manhattaner in New Orleans. *Hall,*
Report of the Land Office on Bastrop Grant.

Ohio Gazetteer. *Kilbourn,*
Transactions of Hist'l & Philosop. Soc. of Ohio.
Cincinnati in 1841. *List,*
Sketches & Statistics of Cincin. in 1851. *List,*
History of Kentucky. *Arthur,*
Sket. of Louisville and Environs. *McMurtrie.*
Pictorial Guide to the Mammoth Cave. *Martin,*
Annals of Tennessee. *Ramsay.*
History of Indiana till 1816. *Dillon.*
Indiana Gazetteer.
History of Illinois, 1812–47. *Ford,*
Letters from Illinois. *Birkbeck.*
Narrative of Riots at Alton. *Beecher,*
Traveling Map of Michigan. *Tanner,*

Wisconsin Gazetteer. *Hunt.*
Observations on the Wisconsin Territory,
Observations on Wisconsin Territory. *Smith,*
Iowa as it Is, in 1856. *Parker,*
Minnesota and its Resources. *Bond,*
Minnesota and the Far West. *Oliphant.*
Kansas Region. *Greene,*
Kansas and Nebraska. *Hale,*
Wild Scenes in Kansas and Nebraska. *Sage,*
Valley of the Gt. Salt Lake of Utah. *Stansbury.*
Utah and the Mormons. *Ferris,*
The Mormons at Home. *Ferris,*
History of the Mormons,
Female Life among the Mormons,

356.

Mem. Mrs. J. H. Scott, with her Poems. *Sawyer*,
Sontag, Henriette.—Life, with Inter. Sketches.
Memoir of Mary L. Ware. *Hall*,
The Teacher's Last Lesson. *Badger*,
Memoirs of Mrs. Sarah E. York. *Medberry*,

Correspondence.

Letters addressed to his Wife. *Adams*,
Private Letters. *Brooke*,
Bonaparte's Confid. Corresp. with his Brother,
Select Correspond. of Thos. Chalmers. *Hanna;*
Corres. of Chas. V. and his Ambas. *Bradford.*
Letters and Works of Chesterfield. *Mahon.*
Private Correspondence. *Colton.*
Correspondence Originale des Emigrés.

358.

Letters of Queen *Elizabeth.*
Letters of Qu. Elizabeth & James VI. *Camden-*
Correspondence. *Gray.*
Letters from Eng. Kings & Queens. *Hinman*,
Letters to a Female Friend, *Humboldt*,
Correspondence, 1774–1804. *Izard*,
James VI. of Scotland, Letters of.
Correspondence with Horace Walpole. *Mason.*
Correspondence with La Marck. *Mirabeau.*
Letters to his Music Publisher. *Moore*,
Corres. of Sir I. Newton & others. *Edleston.*
Correspondence of the Duchess *d'Orleans*,
Letters, *Russell*,
Letters, *Sévigné*,
Selections from the Letters of Southey.
Letters while Ambas. at the Hague. *Temple*,

MATHEMATICS.

Course of Pure Mathematics. *Francœur.*
Suite de Cours de Mathematiques. *Bezout.*
Introduction to Pract'l Mathematics. *Carlisle*,
Mathematical Sciences. *Young.*
Philosophy of Mathematics. *Comte.*
Logic and Utility of Mathematics. *Davies.*
Mathematical Recreations. *Robinson.*

Arithmetic.

Arithmetic. *Davies*,
Pract. and Commercial Arithmetic. *Docharty*,
Equational Arithmetic, applied. *Hipsley*,
Eléments d'Arithmétique. *Arnold*,

Algebra.

Algebra. *Dodd*,
Institutes of Algebra. *Docharty*,

First Lessons in Geom., Algeb., &c. *Kirkman*,

Geometry.

New Elements of Geometry. *Smith.*
Illustrated London Pract. Geometry. *Burn.*
Euclid, First Six Books of.

Trigonometry.

Treatise on Trigonometry. *Airy*,
Plane Trigonom. & its Application. *Perkins.*
Tables of Prime Numbers & Factors. *Hinkley.*
Trigonom., Plain and Spherical. *Hackley.*
Elements of Spherical Trigonometry. *Ham*,
Elem. of Differen. & Integ. Calculus. *Church.*
On the Dynamics of a Particle. *Tait*,
Quadrature of the Circle. *Parker.*

NATURAL SCIENCES.

Nature and Elements of the Material World.
Book of Nature. *Schoedler.*
Hist. of Earth & Animated Nature. *Goldsmith.*
Briefe über Humboldt's Kosmos.
Ansichten der Natur. *Humboldt.*
The Microscope. *Lardner*,
The Microscope & its Revelations. *Carpenter*,
On the Microscope. *Hannover.*
The Microscopist. *Wythes*,
The Microscope; its History, &c. *Hogg.*
Views of the Microscopic World. *Brochlesby.*
Sciences Naturelles au Moyen Age. *Ponchet.*
Principales Découv. Scient. Modernes. *Figuier*,

Natural History of Creation. *Kemp*,
Stray Leaves from Book of Nature. *De Vere*,
Natur Wissenschaften der letzten Funfzig jahre.
Philosophical Magazine. [*Klencke.*
Transactions of Amer. Philosophical Society–
Comptes Rendus des Séances de l'Acad. Fran.
Edinburgh New Philos. Journal. Vols. 49–57.
Scientific Researches. *Sturgeon.*
Royal Museum of Nat. Hist., Paris. *Deleuze.*
Catalogue of Cabinet of Nat. Hist. N. Y. State.
Proceedings of Amer. Assoc. of Scien. 1819–51.
Report of Brit. Assoc. 20, 21, 22, 23d. Meet'g.
Lectures on Natural Philosophy. *Mc Gauley.*

358.

Hand-bk. of Nat. Phil. and Astron. *Lardner*,
Elementary Physics. *Hunt*,
The Philosophy of Physics. *Brown*.
Philosophy of the Mechanics of Nature. *Allen*.
Familiar Letters on Physics of Earth. *Buff*,
Précis Elémentaire de Physique. *Archambault*,
The Harmonics of Physical Science. *Hinds*,
Analytical Physics. *Forfar*,
Lectures on a New Philos. of Physics. *Forfar*.
The Soul in Nature. *Oersted*,
Anal. View of Newton's Principia. *Brougham*.
Lectures on Polarized Light. *Pereira*,
Electricity in Theory and Practice. *La Rive*.
Electric Science; its History, &c. *Bakewell*,
Annals of Electricity, Magnetism & Chemistry.
Human Electricity. *Rutter*,
On Animal Electricity. *Jones*,
Magnetical Investigations. *Scoresby*.
Elements of Nat. Philos. Mechanics. *Bartlett*.
The World a Workshop. *Ewbank*,
Mechanics of Fluids, for Pract. Men. *Jamieson*.
Upward Forces of Fluids. *Genet*.
Theory of the Wind. *Wilkes*.

Astronomy.

Introduction to Astronomy. *Olmsted*.
The Solar System. *Hind*,
Popular Lecture on Astronomy. *Arago*.
Popular Astronomy. *Arago*.
Astronomie Populäre. *Arago*.
The Planetary System. *Nichol*.
Astronomy and General Physics. *Whewell*,
Astronomie Nouvelle. *Emmanuel*,
History of Physical Astronomy. *Grant*.
Dictionnaire d'Astronomie. *Guynemer*.
Researches in the Solar Realms. *Higgins*,
U. S. Astron. Exped. to South Amer. *Gillis*–
Astron. Observ. at Radcliffe Obser'y. *Johnson*.
Astronomical Observ. during the year 1846–
Annals of Georgetown Col. Astron. Observ'y.
Connaissance des Temps, ou des Mouvements
The Comets; a Descriptive Treatise. *Hind*,
Scientific Certainties of Planetary Life. *Simon*,
The *Universe* no Desert,
Plurality of Worlds;
Conversations on Plur. of Worlds. *Fontenelle*,
More Worlds than One. *Brewster*,
Plur. of Worlds. An Argument fr. Scripture,

Chemistry.

Elements of Chemistry. *Kane*.
First Principles of Chemistry. *Foster*,
Chemistry. *Pelouze*,
Hand-book of Chemistry. *Gmelin*.
Hand-book of Chemistry. *Abel*.
Principles of Chemistry. *Stöckhardt*,
Elementary Chemistry. *Scoffern*.
Elements of Chemistry. *Reginault*.
The Phases of Matter. *Kemp*,
Review of Chemistry for Students. *Murphy*,
Catechism of Chemical Philosophy. *Horsley*,
Manual of Chemical Physiology. *Lehman*.
Dict. Rais. des Denom. Chim. &c. *Chevallier*.
The Chemistry of Gold. *Scoffern*,
Six Lect. on Non-Metallic Elements. *Faraday*,

361.

Chemistry of Common Life. *Johnston*,
Chemistry of the Crystal Palace. *Griffiths*,
Instruction in Quantitative Analysis. *Fresenius*.
Outlines of Chemical Analysis. *Will*.
Manual of Qualitative Analysis. *Galloway*,
Aide-Mémoire p. l'Analyse Chimi. *Gerhardt*,
Analytical Chemist's Assistant. *Woehler*,
Comm'l Hand-b. of Chem. Analysis. *Normandy*.
Chemist. Vols. 1–3.
Chemical Gazette. Vol. 8.
Qnarterly Journal of Chem. Soc. Vols. 1, 4, 6,
Papers on Chemistry, &c.
Hand-book of Organic Chemistry. *Gregory*,
Chemical Works. *Neumann*.

Geology.

Elements of Geology. *St. John*,
Elementary Geology. *Hitchcock*,
Manual of Geology. *Phillips*,
Elements of Geology. *Gray*,
Elements of Geology. *Playfair*.
Manual of Elementary Geology. *Lyell*.
Principles of Geology. *Lyell*.
Geology of the Globe. *Hitchcock*.
Geology and Mineralogy. *Ansted*.
Siluria: Hist. of the Oldest Rocks. *Murchison*.
The Fossil Spirit. *Mill*,
Antediluvian Phytology. *Artis*–
Petrifactions and their Teachings. *Mantell*,
Fossil Remains. *Parkinson*–
Dissertation on Antiq. of the Earth. *Douglas*–
Schöpfungstage. *Klencke*,
On Coral Reefs and Islands. *Dana*.
Course of Creation. *Anderson*.
Two Records—Mosaic and Geological. *Miller*,
Creation and the Deluge: a New Theory.
Religion of Geol. and Connec. Sci. *Hitchcock*,
Six Days of Creation. *Rhind*,
Genesis and Geology. *Crofton*,
Geological Observer. *De La Beche*,
Quarterly Jour. of Lond. Geol. Soc. Vols. 2–6.
Records of the School of Mines and Science.
Geol. and Astron. Exped. to No. Russia. *Sauer*–
Physical Structure of Australia. *Jukes*.
Umrissen von Vulkanean au den Cordilleren.
Geology of the Bass Rock. *Miller*, [*Humboldt*–
Our Coal and Coal Pits,
Acadian Geology. *Dawson*,
Geological Map of U. S. & Brit. Prov. *Marcou*.
New York Geol. and Mineralogical Report–
Report of the Geological Survey of N. Jersey.
Reports on the Penn. Geol. Expl. *Rogers*.
Report on Geol. Survey of No. Ca. *Emmons*.
Geology of Lake Superior. *Foster*.
Mineral Region of Lake Superior, [*stonaugh*.
Geol. of Coun. bet. Missis. & Red Rivs. *Feather*-
Reps. of the Geol. Sur. of Missouri. *Swallow*.
Lead Mines of Missouri. *Schoolcraft*.
Report on Mines of Missouri. *Littin*.
Geol. Explo. of Iowa, Wis., & Illinois. *Owen*–

Mineralogy.

Elementary Introd. to Mineralogy. *Phillips*.
Popular Mineralogy. *Sowerby*,

361.

Manual of Mineralogy. *Dana,*
Pract. Mineralogy, Assay. & Min. *Overman,*

Botany.

Principles of Botany,
Class Book of Botany. *Balfour.*
Vegetation of Europe. *Henfrey,*
Société Linnéene de Paris. Hist. et Mémoires.
Hortus Americanus. *Barham.*
Wanderings among Wild Flowers. *Thomson,*
British Ferns and Allied Plants. *Moore,*
Brit. Species of Angiocarpous Lichens. *Roy. Soc.*
British Sea-Weeds. *Landsborough,*]*Pub.*
Sea-Weed Collector's Guide. *Cocks,*
Mahogany Tree.
Popular History of the Palms. *Seeman,*
Botanist's Word Book. *Macdonald.*
Lexicon of Ladies' Names w. Emblems. *Carter,*
Thesaurus Literaturæ Botanicæ. *Pritzel–*

Natural History.

Popular History of Mammalia. *White,*
Manual of Zoology. *Edwards,*
System of Natural History. *Smith,*
Natural History of Animals. *Jones,*
Illustrated Natural History *Wood,*
Sketches of Animal Life. *Wood,*
Economy of Animal Kingdom. *Swedenborg.*
Leaves fr. Note B'k of a Naturalist. *Broderip,*
Voyages d'un Naturaliste. *Descoutils.*
Hunter-Naturalist. *Webber.*
Natural Hist. of N. Y. State. Vol. 19–
Natural History of Carolina. *Catesby–*
Natural History of North Carolina. *Brickell.*
L'Hist. Nat. de la France Equinoxiale. *Barrere,*
Voy. to, and Nat. Hist. of Jamaica. *Sloane–*

364.

Naturalist's Sojourn in Jamaica. *Gosse,*
Historia Natural de Cuba. *Poey.*
Natural History of Barbadoes. *Hughes–*
Natural History of Guyana. *Bancroft.*
L'Instinct et l'Intellig. des Animaux. *Fée,*
The Passions of Animals. *Thomson.*
Habits and Instincts of Animals. *Lee,*
Romance of Natural History. *Webber.*
Readings in Zoology. *Comstock,*
Quadrupeds du Paraguay. *Azara.*
Natural History of the Sperm Whale. *Beale.*
The Camel; its Organiz. Hab. & Uses. *Marsh,*
Browne's Bird Fancier. *Saxton,*
Nat. Hist. of British Song Birds. *Bolton,*
Cage and Chamber Birds. *Bechstein,*

Instruc. Practiques en la Pisciculture. *Coste,*
Treatise on Artificial Fish-Breeding. *Fry,*

Anatomy of the Invertebrata. *Siebold.*
Life of North American Insects. *Jaeger.*
Episodes of Insect Life.

Mollusks.

The Ocean. *Gosse,*
The Aquarium; or, Won. of Deep Sea. *Gosse,*
Tenby; a Sea-side Holiday. *Gosse.*
Glaucus; or, Wonders of the Shore. *Kingsley,*
Introduction to Conchology. *Johnston.*
British Mollusca. *Alden.*
Popular History of Mollusca. *Roberts,*
Synopsis of the Mollusca of Gt. Brit. *Leach.*
Catalogue of Shells in Cabinet of J. C. Jay–
Monograph on Sub Cass Cirripedia. *Ray* Soc.
British Nudibranchiate Mollusca. *Ray* Soc.
Drops of Water, and their Inhabitants. *Catlow,*

MEDICAL SCIENCE.

Anatomy and Physiology.

Manual of Human Anatomy. *Knox,*
Text Book of Anatomy and Dissection. *Handy,*
Lectures on Histology. *Quekett.*
Anatomy of the Human Body. *Bell.*
Anatomy, Physiology, and Hygiene *Lambert,*
Human Body, & its Con. with Man. *Wilkinson,*
Physiological Anatomy. *Todd.*
Principles of Physio. General & Comparative.
Human Physiology. *Hooker.* [*Carpenter.*
Principles of Human Physiology. *Carpenter.*
Analysis of Physiology. *Reese,*
Every Day Wonders,
Functions of the Nervous System. *Smith.*
Automatic Powers of the Brain. *Rogers,*
Brain in Relation to the Mind. *Swan.*
The Functions of the Lungs. *Fitch.*
On the Blood. *Bernard,*
Essays on Life, Sleep, Pain, &c. *Dickson,*
Sleep Physiologically Considered. *Fosgate,*
Sudden Death. *Granville.*
What to Observe at the Bedside & After Death,
Decline of Life in Health & Disease. *Van Oven.*
Effect of Occupation on Longevity. *Wynne.*
Human Longevity. *Flourens,*
Causes of Death from Old Age. *Bostwick.*
Art of Prolonging Life. *Hufeland,*
Report on Food and Diet. *Gould.*
Fruits and Farinacea the Food of Man. *Smith,*
Tea and Coffee. *Alcott,*
Adulteration of Food and Drink. *Byrn,*
Report on Public Hygiene. *Wynne.*
Compendium of Hygiene. *Mills,*
The Laws of Life. *Blackwell,*
Laws of Health. *Beale,*
Philosophy of Health. *Coles,*
Preservation of Health. *Corning.*

367.

Present Age, and Inner Life. *Davis.*
Philosophy of Intellectual Psychology. *Dods,*
Phreno-Geology. *Grimes,*
Neurological System of Anthro'gy. *Buchanan.*
Mental Alchemy. *Williams,*
Esoteric Anthropology. *Nichols,*
Book of Human Nature. *Sunderland,*
Theory of Pneumatology. *Stilling,*
The Human Trinity. *Lazarus,*
Magnétisme et Magneto-Thérapie. *Szapary.*
Magnétisme. *Cahagnet,*
Letters on Animal Magnetism. *Gregory,*
Researches on Magnetism. *Reichenbach,*
Credulity and Superstition. *Blakeman,*
Credulity, as Illustrated by Impo'n. *Macdonald,*
Popular Superstitions. *Mayo,*
Hallucinations. *Boisemont.*
History of Magic. *Ennemoser,*
Lessons from Hist. of Med. Delu'ns. *Hooker,*
Extraordinary Popular Delusions. *Mackay,*
Irish Popular Superstitions. *Wilde,*
Manuel des Sorciers. *Fontenelle,*
Narrative of Sorcery and Magic. *Wright.*
The Night Side of Nature. *Crowe,*
Fiends, Ghosts, and Sprites. *Radcliffe,*

368.

Phantom World. *Calmet,*
The Spirit World. *Ross,*
Voices from the Spirit Land. *White,*
Spiritualism. *Edmonds.*
Spiritualism. *Britain.*
Light from the Spirit World. *Hammond,*
History of Recent Develop'ts in Spir. Manifes.
Modern Spiritualism, its Facts, &c. *Capron,*
Phenomena of Modern Spiritualism. *Hayden,*
Spiritual Vampirism. *Webber,*
The Celestial Telegraph. *Cahagnet,*
"*To Daimonion;*" or Spiritual Medium,
Investigation of Spirit Manifestations. *Hare.*
Spiritual Visitors,
Philosophy of Mysterious Agents. *Rogers.*
Modern Mysteries Explained. *Mahan,*
Mysteries; Glimpses of Supernatural. *Elliott,*
Review of Spiritual Manifestations. *Beecher,*
Spiritual Telegraph,
Spirit Rappings.
Spirit Rappings Unveiled. *Mattison,*
The Rappers, their Mysteries and Fallacies,
Table Moving Explained. *Birt,*
Modern Mys.; or, Table Tipping. *Mac Walter,*

TECHNOLOGY.

Technical Dictionary. *Crabb,*
Outlines of Mechanical Philosophy. *Coues,*
Principles of Mechanical Philosophy. *Tate.*
*Cyclopedia of Useful Arts. *Tomlinson.*
Dictionary of Terms Used in Art. *Weale,*
Curiosities of Industry. *Dodd.*
Plough, Loom, and Anvil.
The Useful Arts. *Martin,*
Industry of the U. S. in Machinery Manufac.
Journal of Design and Manufactures.
Transactions of American Institute.
Reports of the American Institute.
The Patentee's Manual. *Johnson.*
Information concerning Patent Office.

Surveying.

Practical Surveyor's Guide. *Duncan,*
Manual for Practical Surveyors. *Beans,*
Treatise on Land Surveying. *Gillespie.*

Navigation.

Rudimentary Treatise on Navig'n. *Greenwood,*
Machinery used in Navigation. *Tredgold–*
Naval Dry Docks of the U. States. *Stuart–*
Plan for Shortening the Passage to London.
Explanations and Sailing Directions. *Maury–*
Nautical Magazine.
Nautical Almanac for 1854–55.
American *Ephemeris* and Nautical Alma. 1855.

Naval Architecture.

Marine and Naval Architecture. *Griffiths–*
Naval Architecture. *Montague.*
History of Naval Architecture. *Fincham.*
Descrip. Geom. & Appli. to Ship Buil. *Woolley.*
Prin. to Regulate the Form of Ships. *Bland,*
The Sailing Boat. *Folkard,*
Naval and Mail Steamers of the U. S. *Stuart–*
Report on Life Boat Models–
Metallic Life Boat Corporation. *Francis.*

Mechanical Arts.

Elements of Mechanism. *Baker,*
The Mechanic's Manual. *Byrne,*
Mechanics; their Principles and Appli. *Byrne.*
Lécons de Mécanique Pratique. *Morin.*
Calculator's Constant Companion. *Byrne,*
Practical Model Calculator. *Byrne.*
Dictio. of Machines, Mechanics, &c. *Appleton.*
Engineer and Machinist's Assist. *Byrne–*
Artizan and Engineer's Hand-book. *Byrne.*
Mechanic's & Engineer's Book of Refe. *Haslett,*
Engineer's & Mechanic's Comp. *Templeton,*
Text Book for Architects, Engineers, &c. *Ryde.*
Book of Industrial Design. *Johnson–*
Collection of Drawings of Am. Machinery–
Dynamics, Construction of Mach'y, &c. *Warr.*
The Indicator and Dynamometer. *Main.*
Technologiste.

368.

Practical Mechanic's Journal–
Artist and Tradesman's Companion. *Byrne,*
Cabinet Maker & Upholsterer's Comp. *Stokes,*
Marble Worker's Manual,
Jeweller's Hand-Book. *Kerr,*
Designs of Silver and Gold Work. *Scott–*
Tanning, Curry. and Leather Dress. *Morfit.*
Paper Hanger's Companion. *Arrowsmith,*
Clock and Watch Making. *Reid.*
Clock and Watch Making. *Denison,*
Moulder's & Founder's Pocket Guide. *Overman,*
Miller and Millwright's Assist. *Hughes.*
Mechanics for Millwright & Machin. *Overman,*
Turning & Mechanical Manipulat. *Holtzappfel.*
Turner's Companion,
Illustrations of Paper Manufacture–
Plates to Masonry & Stone Cutting. *Dobson–*
Elements of Practical Hydraulics. *Downing.*
Treatise on Hydraulics. *Aubuisson.*
Hydraulic Tables and Tide Tables. *Beardmore,*
On the Power of Water. *Glynn,*
On Hydraulic Machines. *Ewbank.*
Tuner's Guide for the Piano Forte, Organ, &c.,

Architecture.

Rudiments of Architecture. *Gwilt.*
Rudiments of Architecture. *Benjamin.*
Rudiments of the Art of Building. *Bullock,*
Rudimentary Architecture. *Bury,*
Hand-Book of Architecture. *Furgussen,*
The Architect. *Ranlett–*
Builder's Pocket Companion. *Smeaton,*
American House Carpenter. *Hatfield.*
Builder, The–
History in Ruins; or, Sketch of Arch. *Godwin,*
The Model Architect. *Sloan–*
Architettura Antica. *Canina–*
Architectural Studies in France. *Petit.*
Elements of Architectural Criticism. *Gwilt.*
Stones of Venice. *Ruskin.*
Origin, &c. of Window Tracery. *Freeman.*
Hints on Public Architecture. *Owen–*
New York Crystal Palace. *Carstensen–*
Art of Painting on Glass. *Gessert,*
School Architecture. *Barnard.*
City Architecture. *Field.*
Stair Builder's Guide. *De Graff.*
On Smokeless Fireplaces, Chimneys, *Arnott.*
A Home for All. *Fowler,*
Domestic Architecture in England. *Turner,*
Some Account of Domestic Architect. in Eng.
Rural Homes. *Wheeler,*
Healthy Homes, & how to make them. *Bardwell.*
Homes for the People, *Wheeler,*
American Cottage Builder. *Bullock,*
Plans &c., of Cottage Villas. *Pattison–*
Village and Farm Cottages. *Cleaveland.*
Architecture of Country Houses. *Downing.*
Cottage Building for Laboring Classes. *Allen,*
Prize Model Cottages. *Goddard–*
Construction, &c. of Lighthouses. *Stevenson,*
Rustic Adorn. for Homes of Taste. *Hibberd,*
Painter, Gilder, and Varnisher's Companion,
Treatise on Lightning Conductors. *Lyon,*
Designs for Monum. & Mural Tablets. *Smith–*

370.

Civil Engineering.

Elem'y Course of Civil Engineering. *Mahan.*
Complete Course of Civil Engin'g. *Gregory.*
Useful Information for Engineers. *Fairbairn.*
Manual of Topographical Drawing. *Smith.*
Theory of Bridge Construction. *Haupt.*
Practice of Embanking Lands. *Wiggins,*
Struct. & Statistics of Plank Roads. *Kingsford.*
Report of N. Y. State Engineer on Canals.
Civil Engineer and Architect's Journal–
Field-book for Railroad Engineers. *Henck,*
Useful Formula for Railroad Making. *Borden.*
History of English Railways. *Francis.*
Our Iron Roads; their Hist. &c. *Williams.*
Report on R.R. from Miss. R. to Pacific Ocean
Guide du Mécanicien des Machines Locomot.
The Locomotive Engine. *Colburn,*
Hand-book for Locomotive Engineers. *Norris,*
Tab. for Find. Mean Heights of Cr. Sec. *Sym.*
Railroad Accidents; their Causes. *With,*
Railway and Electric Communication. *White,*
On Steam and Locomotion. *Sewell,*
Catechisme du Mécanicien à Vapeur. *Paris.*
Marine Steam Engine. *Main.*
On Steam and Steam Engines. *Templeton,*
Marine Engines and Steam Vessels. *Murray,*
On the Screw Propeller. *Bourne–*
On Screw Prop. & Steam Engines. *Nystrom.*
Hist. of Prop. & Steam Navig. *Macfarlane,*
The Electric Telegraph. *Highton,*
Book of the Telegraph,
Electro Magnetic Telegraph. *Turnbull.*
Hist. Sketch of Electric Telegraph. *Jones.*
The Brachial Telegraph. *Jenks.*
Electricity & the Electric Telegraph. *Wilson,*
Warming and Ventilating. *Tredgold.*
On Economy of Fuel. *Ryder.*

Chemical Technology.

Chemical Technology. *Ronalds.*
Recent Improve. in Chemical Arts. *Booth.*
Photography. *Heath.*
Practice of Photography. *De La Motte,*
Photography. *Croucher,*
Manual of Photog. Chemistry. *Hardwick,*
Guide to Taking Photog. Portraits. *Rintoul,*
Traité de Photog. sur Papier. *Blanquart.*
Photography on Paper and Glass. *Heath.*
Daguerrian Journal–
Elements of Electro-Metallurgy. *Smee,*
Manual of Electro-Metallurgy. *Napier,*
Manipulations Hydroplastiques. *Roseleur.*
Art of Manufacturing Soaps. *Kurten,*
Manual of the Art of Dyeing. *Napier,*
Chemistry applied to Dyeing. *Napier,*
Dyer's Instructor, and Art of Padding. *Smith,*
The Art of Perfumery. *Piesse,*
Pyrotechnist's Companion. *Mortimer,*
Pyrotechny; or, Recreative Firewks. *Mortimer,*
Directions for Testing Cane Juice. *Shier,*
Complete Practical Brewer. *Byrn,*
Practical Distiller. *Byrn,*
Hand-book of Wines. *McMullen,*
Statistics of Coal. *Taylor.*
Treatise on Metallurgy. *Overman.*

370.

Manual of Metallurgy. *Phillips,*
Manufacture of Steel. *Overman,*
Practical Metal Worker's Assistant. *Byrne.*
Brass and Iron Founder's Guide. *Larkin,*
Cast & Wro't Iron applied to Build. *Fairbarn.*
Reports of Experiments on Metals for Cannon–
Gold Mining and Assaying. *Phillips,*
Working & Ventila. of Gold Mines. *Hedley.*
Lectures on Gold, for Emigrants to Australia,
Assay of Gold and Silver Wares. *Ryland,*
Mining Manual and Alk. for 1851. *English,*

Agriculture.

Elements of Agriculture. *Waring,*
Elements of Scientific Agriculture. *Norton,*
Skinner's Elements of Agriculture. *Saxton,*
Farmer's Vade Mecum. *Pedder,*
Complete Farmer & Rural Econ. *Fessenden,*
The Progressive Farmer. *Nash,*
Farmer's Every-day Book. *Blake.*
Lessons in Modern Farming. *Blake,*
Transactions of the Michigan Agri. Society.
Journal of Transactions of the Va. Agr. Soc.
Report of the Sec. of Mass. Board of Agricul.
Transactions of Wisconsin Agricul. Society.
Transactions of N. Y. State Agricul. Society.
Transactions of Highl'd & Ag. Soc. of Scotland.
Year Book of Agriculture, 1855–56. *Wells.*
Natural History of Agriculture of N. York–
Monthly Journal of Agriculture. *Skinner.*
Journal of Agriculture.
Cultivator.
English Agriculture in 1850–51. *Caird.*
Walks & Talks of an Am. Far. in Eng. *Olmsted,*
Southern Agriculture. *Beatty,*
On Science and Practical Agricul. *Johnston,*
Rural Essays. *Downing.*
Farm and Fireside. *Blake,*
Agricultural Engineering. *Andrews,*
Farm Implements. *Thomas,*
Essay on Manures. *Dana,*
Dana's Essay on Manures. *Saxton,*
Essay on Calcareous Manures. *Ruffin,*
Of Clay Lands and Loamy Soils. *Donaldson,*
Richardson's Pests of the Farm. *Saxton,*
Culture and Com of Cotton in India. *Royle.*
Richardson on the Horse. *Saxton,*
Stable Practice,
Horses and Hounds. By "Scrutator,"
Treatise on Proper Condition for Horses,
Milburn on the Cow. *Saxton,*
Richardson on the Hog. *Saxton,*
Greyhound, Art of Rearing, Breeding, &c., the,
The Poultry Book. *Wingfield–*
Poultry Yard. *Martin,*
Illustrated Book of Domestic Poultry. *Doyle.*
Richardson on Domestic Fowls. *Saxton,*
Of Ornamental Domestic Poultry. *Dixon,*
Richardson on the Honey Bee. *Saxton,*
Honey Bee,
On the Hive and Honey Bee. *Langstroth,*
Easy Method of Managing Bees. *Weeks,*

Horticulture.

Magazine of Horticulture.

371.

Horticulturist.
Transactions of Horticultural Soc. of London–
Rural Annual and Horticultural Directory,
Gardener's Text Book. *Schenck,*
American Kitchen Gardener. *Fessenden,*
Fessenden's Amer. Kitchen Gardener. *Saxton,*
Fruit, Flower, & Veget. Gard'r's Comp. *Neill,*
Hand-book to Fruit & Veget. Garden. *Glenny.*
Every Lady her own Gardener.
Companion for the Orchard. *Phillips.*
American Fruit-Grower's Guide. *Elliot,*
The Fruit Garden. *Darby,*
Concise Description of Selec. Apples. *Ronalds–*
The Cold Grapery. *Chorlton,*
Manual for Cultivation of Strawberry. *Pardee,*
Every Lady her own Flower Gardener. *Saxton,*
The *Flower* Garden,
American Rose Culturist. *Saxton,*
American Rose Culturist,
Essay on Trees in Landscape. *Kennion–*
Parks and Pleasure Grounds. *Smith,*
On Planting Ornamental Trees. *Standish,*

Manufactures.

Cotton Spinner and Manager's Guide. *Baird,*
Manager's Ass't; or, Treat. on Cotton Manuf.
Practical Cotton Spinner. *Scott.* [*Snell,*
Preparation of Long Line, Flax Cot. &c. *Ryan.*
Manufactures imp. de Tapisseries des Gobelins. [*Lacordaire.*

Domestic Arts.

Art of Ornamental Hair Work,
Ladies' Guide to Crochet, &c. *Stephens,*
Complete Guide to Ornamental Leather Work,
Home Cookery; or, Tried Receipts. *Chadwick,*
Ladies' New Book of Cookery. *Hale,*
New System of Domestic Cookery,
Pantropheon; or, History of Food. *Soyer.*
New Household Receipt Book. Hale,
Book of One Hundred Beverages. *Bernhard,*
Cyclopedia of 6,000 Receipts. *Cooley.*
Three Thousand Receipts. *Wright.*
Five Thousand Receipts. *Mackenzie.*

Military Arts.

Livre de Guerre. *Perrot.*
Manual of Bayonet Exercises. *McClellan,*
Regulations for Uniform & Dress of U. S. A.–
Aide-Mémoire to the Military Sciences.
Theory and Pract. of Naval Gunnery. *Jeffers.*
Catechism on Regimental Stand. Ord. *Walshe.*
Treatise on Camp and March. *Grafton,*
Infantry Tactics. *Scott,*
Rifle and Light Infantry Tactics. *Hardee,*
Projectile Weapons & Explo. Comp. *Scoffern,*
Summary of the Art of War. *Jomini,*
Manual of Field Operations. *Jervis,*
Past and Present State of Fire Arms. *Chesney.*
Eclaireur, The. A Military Journal.
French Naval & Military Dictionary. *Burn,*

Encyclopædic.

Encyclopedia Britannica. Vols. 1–10–

372.

Iconographic Encyclopedia–
English Encyclopedia–
Universal Lexicon, with Supplement. *Pierer.*
Smithsonian Contribu. to Knowl. Vols. 2–7–
Catechism of Familiar Things. *Willement,*
Enquire within for Everything,
Elements of General Knowledge. *Kett.*
Hand-book of Lit. and Fine Arts. *Ripley,*
Year-Book of Facts for 1851–6. *Timbs,*
Annual of Scientific Discov. for '51–55. *Wells,*
Circle of the Sciences. *Orr.*
Familiar Science. *Wells.*
Familiar Science. *Peterson,*
Journal of Franklin Institute.
Polytechnisches Journal.
Quarterly Journal of Science and Art.
Mechanics' Magazine.
Notes and Queries–
School Journal and Vermont Agriculturist.

372.

Volksbibliothek. *Meyer,*
Every-day Book of History, &c. *Munsell,*
Cyclopædia of Indus. of All Nations. *Knight.*
Year Book of Facts for Gt. Exhib. 1851. *Timbs,*
The World in its Workshop. *Ward,*
Report on the Great Exhibition. *Johnson.*
Official Catalogue of the Great Exhibition.
Gt. Exhibition; its Pal. & Con'ts. *Stephenson,*
Exposition Univer. 1851. Commission Franç.
Exhibition of Works of Indus. of All Nat. 1851.
Lectures on Results of Gt. Exhibition of 1851,
The Gt. Exhibition & Lond. in 1851. *Lardner,*
Report on 11th French Exposition of Industry–
Report of Commissioners for Exhib. of 1851.
A Day in the Crystal Palace. *Richards,*
World of Science, Art, & Industry. *Silliman–*
Science & Mechanism Illust. in N. Y. Exhibit.–
Art & Industry as represented in Crystal Pal,
Exposition Universelle de Paris, 1855. *Tresca,*

ADDITIONS

MADE TO

AUGUST 1, 1856.

[*** The following are included in the foregoing CLASSIFIED INDEX.]

Abbie Nott and other Knots	12o.	Phil.	1856
Abbott, J. S. C.—History of Hernando Cortez	16o.	N. Y.	1855
——— —— Napoleon at St. Helena	8vo.	N. Y.	1855
——— Jacob.—The Way to Do Good	12o.	N. Y.	1852
About, E.—Greece and the Greeks of the Present Day	12o.	Edin.	1855
——— —— Tolla	16o.	Paris.	1855
Acts and Resolves of the General Court of Mass., 1854–55	8o.	Bost.	1854–55
Adams' Edin. Geographical Word Expositor	16o.	Lond.	1856
——— Wm.—Three Gardens—Eden, Gethsemane, and Paradise	12o.	N. Y.	1856
Ainsworth's Magazine. Vol. 26	8vo.	Lond.	1854
Airy, G. B.—Treatise on Trigonometry	12o.	Lond.	1855
*Albany Directory and City Register for 1856	12o.	Albany.	1856
Alison, A.—History of Europe from 1815–52. Vols. 4 and 5.	8vo.	Edin.	1855
Allen, R. L.—Analysis of the Fountains at Saratoga Springs	16o.	S. Springs.	1853
*Allgemeine Zeitung. Oct.—Dec. 1854	4to.	Augsburg.	1854
——— ——— April—Dec. 1855. 3 v.	4to.	Augsburg.	1855
Alvary, Eman.—Latin Prosody	16o.	Dublin.	1829
American Journal of Insanity. Vols. 1, 2, 5, and 6	8vo.	Utica.	1844–50
——— ——— Medical Sciences. Vol. 29. [*Continued*]	8vo.	Phil.	1855
——— ——— Science and Arts. S. Series. Vol. 19	8vo.	N. Hav.	1855
Ampére, J. S.—Promenade en Amérique. 2 v.	8vo.	Paris.	1855
Analecta Latina Majora	8vo.	Lond.	s. a.
Anderson, Eustace.—Chamouni and Mont Blanc	16o.	Lond.	1856
——— John.—History of Edinburgh to 1850	8vo.	Edin.	1856
Angel in the House—The Betrothal	12o.	Bost.	1850
Annalen der Physik und Chemie. Vols. 94–96. [*Continued*]	8vo.	Leipzig.	1855
Annals of Electricity and Magnetism, by Sturgeon. Vol. 3	8vo.	Lond.	1838–9
——— and Magazine of Natural History. Vols. 15, 16. [*Continued*]	8vo.	Lond.	1855
Anne, Duchess of Brittany; Memoirs by L. S. Costello	12o.	Lond.	1855
*Annuaire des Deux Mondes, 1854–55	8vo.	Paris.	1855
*Annual Register for 1852–54. 3 v.	8vo.	Lond.	1853–55
Ansted, D. T., Tennant and Mitchell—Geology, Mineralogy, &c.	8vo.	Lond.	1855
*Appleton's Cyclopædia of Biography	8o.	N. Y.	1856
Arago, F.—Popular Astronomy (Fr. Fren.) Vol. 1	8vo.	Lond.	1855
——— — Populäre Astronomie. Vol. 2	8vo.	Leipzig.	1856
——— — Sammtliche Werke. Vol. 5	8vo.	Leipzig.	1856
Archambault, P. J.—Précis Elémentaire de Physique	12o.	Paris.	1855
Armstrong, Geo. B.—Summer of the Pestilence; or, Yel. F. in Norfolk,	16o.	Phil.	1856

*Babbitt, E. D.—Education and Progress	16o. Cincin.	1856
Baily, F.—Tour in Unsettled parts of N. America in 1796–7	8vo. Lond.	1856
Bain, Alex.—The Senses and the Intellect	8vo. Lond.	1855
Baker, S. W.—Eight Years' Wanderings in Ceylon	8vo. Lond.	1855
Ballads of Ireland.—Collected and edited by E. Hayes. 2 v.	12o. Lond.	1855
Banker's Magazine. Vol. 15. [*Continued*]	8vo. Lond.	1855
——— ——— By J. S. Homans. Vol. 9	8vo. N. Y.	1854–55
Barber, G. D.—Ancient Oral Records of the Cimri	12o. Lond.	1855
Barham, R. H.—Ingoldsby Legends. 2 v.	12o. Phil.	1856
Barnes, Albert.—The Way of Salvation	12o. Phil.	1855
Barnwell, R. G.—Life and Times of John DeWitt	12o. N. Y.	1856
Beaulieu, Mme. M. de.—Geneviève dans les Bois	16o. Paris.	1821
Beauvallet, Léon—Rachel and the New World	12o. N. Y.	1856
Beecher, Catherine E.—Physiology and Calisthenics	16o. N. Y.	1856
Belcher, Edw.—The Last of the Arctic Voyages, 1852–54. 2 v.	8vo. Lond.	1855
Bellot, Jos. René ; Memoirs and Journals of. 2 v.	8vo. Lond.	1855
Bentley's Miscellany.—Vols. 37, 38. [*Continued*]	8vo. Lond.	1855
Benton, N. S.—History of Herkimer County	8vo. Albany.	1856
——— Thos. H.—Thirty Years' View of Amer. Government. Vol. 2,	8vo. N. Y.	1856
Bernays, A.—German Historical Anthology	12o. Lond.	1835
Besser, L.—Die Naturgeschichte der Arbeit	8vo. Leipzig.	1855
Biblical Repertory and Princeton Review. Vol. 27. [*Continued*]	8vo. Phil.	1855
*Bibliotheca de Obras Nacionales del Pineda	8vo. Bogota.	1853
Bibliotheca Sacra and American Biblical Repository. Vol. 12	8vo. Andover.	1855
Bickersteth, Edw.—On the Lord's Supper	16o. Phil.	1841
Biernatzki.—Hallig, or Sheepfold in the Waters (Fr. Ger.)	12o. Bost.	1856
Binney, Thos.—Study for Young Men ; or, Sketch of T. F. Buxton	16o. Bost.	1851
Biographical Magazine. Vol. 7	8vo. Lond.	1855
Bird, Dr.—The Hawks of Hawk Hollow. 2 v.	12o. Phil.	1835
Bishop, J. P.—Commentaries on the Criminal Law. Vol. 1	8vo. Bost.	1856
Blackwood's Edinburgh Magazine. Vols. 74, 75, 77. [*Continued*]	8vo. N. Y.	1853–55
——— ——— ——— Vols. 77, 78. [*Continued*]	8vo. Edin.	1855
*——— ——— ——— General Index to vols. 1–50	8vo. Edin.	1855
Blackstone, Wm.—Commentaries, abridged by Sam. Warren	8vo. Lond.	1855
*Blake, A. V. (Compiler)—American Bookseller's Trade List	4to. Claremont.	1847
Blakely, John.—Theology of Inventions	12o. N. Y.	1855
Blakey, Robt.—Sketches of the Angling Literature of all Nations	16o. Lond.	1856
Bledsoe, A. T.—Essay on Liberty and Slavery	12o. Phil.	1856
*Blue-Book for 1855–56	8vo. Wash.	1855
Bœuf's French Grammar	12o. N. Y.	1837
Bond, Hen.—Genealogies of Watertown, Mass	8vo. Bost.	1855
Bowden, Jas.—History of the Society of Friends in America. 2 v.	8vo. Lond.	1850
Bonelli, L. H.—Travels in Bolivia. 2 v.	12o. Lond.	1854
Bouton, Nath.—History of Concord from 1725 to 1853	8vo. Concord.	1856
Bowen, Fran.—Principles of Political Economy	8vo. Bost.	1856
Boyer's French Dictionary	8vo. Bost.	1827
*Bradstreete, Mrs. Anne.—The Tenth Muse	12o. Lond.	1650
Brandes, Karl—Sir John Franklin	8vo. Berlin.	1854
Brehm, A. E.—Reiseskitzzen aus Nord-Ost Afrika, 1847–52. 3 v.	8vo. Jena.	1855
Bremer, Fred.—Hertha	12o. N. Y.	1856

Brewerton, G. D.—The War in Kansas	12o. N. Y.	1856
*British Almanac for 1834, 44, 50, 55, 56. 5 v. . .	12o. Lond.	s. a.
——— Quarterly Review. Vols. 21, 22. [*Continued*] . .	8vo. Lond.	1855
*Bromme, Traugott (Heraus.)—Atlas to Humboldt's Kosmos, .	Fol. Stuttgart.	s. a.
Brooklyn (L. I.) Directory for 1856–57	8vo. Brooklyn.	1856
Brougham, Hen.—Contributions to the Edinburgh Review. 3 v.	8vo. Lond.	1856
——— —— and Routh, E. S.—Analyt. View of Newton's Principia,	8vo. Lond.	1855
——— John.—The Bunsby Papers. Second Series. . .	12o. N. Y.	1856
Broughton, Lord.—Travels in Albania in 1809–10. 2 v. .	8vo. Lond.	1855
Brown, Geo.—Personal Adventures in South Africa . .	16o. Lond.	1855
——— Goold.—English Grammar	12o. N. Y.	1830
Brownson's Quarterly Review. Third Series. Vol. 3. [*Continued*]	8vo. Bost.	1855
Buckingham, Duke of.—Court and Cabinet of Geo. III. Vols. 3 & 4	8vo. Lond.	1855
——— Jas. Silk.—Autobiography. 2 v. . . .	12o. Lond.	1855
Buchner, Alex.—Geschichte der Englischen Poesie. 2 v. . .	8vo. Darmstadt.	1855
*Builder (The) for 1848–49. 2 v.	Fol. Lond.	1848–49
*Bulletin of the American Art Union for 1850 and 1851. 2 v. .	4to. N. Y.	1850–53
*——— Historical Society of Pennsylvania. Vol. 1. .	8vo. Phil.	1845–7
——— de la Société de la Géographie. Vols. 6, 8, & 9. [*Continued*]	8vo. Paris.	1853–5
Bunbury, S.—Life in Sweden; Excursions to Norway and Den. 2 v.	12o. Lond.	1853
Bunsen, C. C. J.—Die Zeichen der Zeit. 2 v. . . .	12o. Leipzig.	1855
Burk, Mrs. Wm.—Mediæval Popes, Emperors, and Kings. 4 v. .	8vo. Lond.	1854–56
Burritt, Elihu.—Year Book of the Nations for 1855 . .	12o. Lond.	1855
Burton, R. F.—Pilgrimage to El Medinah and Meccah. 3 v. .	8vo. Lond.	1855
Butler, T. B.—Philosophy of the Weather and Guide to its Changes	12o. N. Y.	1855
——— Wm. A.—On the History of Ancient Philosophy. 2 v. .	8vo. Camb. (E.)	1856
Byrne, Oliver.—The Mechanics' Manual . . .	32o. N. Y.	1855
Caddell, Cecilia M.—Missions in Japan and Paraguay . .	12o. Lond.	1856
Calderwood, Hen.—Philosophy of the Infinite	8vo. Edin.	1854
Caldwell, Robt.—The Gold Era of Victoria	8vo. Lond.	1855
Calvert, Geo. H.—Introduction to Social Science . . .	12o. N. Y.	1856
——— Gen. Harry.—Journals and Correspondence . .	8vo. Lond.	1853
Cambridge Essays, contributed by Members of the University	8vo. Lond.	1855
Camden.—A Tale of the South. 2 v.	12o. Phil.	1830
Campbell, Wm.—The Crown Lands of Australia	8vo. Glasgow.	1855
Capefigue, B. H. R.—Louis XVI.	12o. Paris.	1856
Carcil, A. F.—Refutation of Spinoza, by Leibnitz	16o. Edin.	1855
Carleton, Wm.—Willy Reilly, and his dear Coleen Bawn . .	12o. Bost.	1856
Carpenter, Wm. B.—The Microscope and its Revelations . .	16o. Lond.	1856
Carter, R. B.—Influence of Education and Training on Nervous Syst.	12o. Lond.	1855
Cary, Alice.—Married, not Mated	12o. N. Y.	1856
——— Thos. G.—Memoir of Thomas Handasyd Perkins . .	8vo. Bost.	1856
Cass, Lewis.—France, its King, Court, and Government .	8vo. N. Y.	1840
Castille, Hippolyte.—Histoires de Ménage: Scènes de la Vie réele	16o. Paris.	1856
*Catalogue of Amherst College Library	8vo. Amherst.	1855
*——— Books in the Astor Library, on Oriental Linguistics	8vo. N. Y.	1854
*——— published in Germany in 1855. 2 v. .	12o. s. a.	and C.
*——— belonging to the Phila. Library Co. Vol 3. .	8vo. Phil.	1856
——— Graduates from the Univ. of Oxford from 1659—1770	8vo. Oxford.	1772

*Catalogue de Livres en Vente par H. Bossange. 1er Suppt. .	8vo.	Paris.	1847
*———— The same. 3e Supplément . . .	8vo.	Paris.	1850
*———— of the San Francisco Mercantile Library . .	8vo.	San Fran.	1854
Cervantes, M. de.—Don Quijote de la Mancha . . .	12o.	N. Y.	1853
Chambers' Journal. Vol. 20	8vo.	Lond.	1854
———— The Same. N. S. Vols. 2—4. [*Continued*]	8vo.	Lond.	1854–55
*Chapin, Jno. R.—Historical Picture Gallery. Vol. 5 . .	4to.	Bost.	1856
*Charivari (Le), June, 1854—June, 1855. 2 v. . . .	Fol.	Paris.	1854–55
Cheever, Geo. B.—On the Life, Genius, and Insanity of Cowper	12o.	N. Y.	1856
———— H. T.—Life and Trials of a Youthful Christian .	12o.	N. Y.	1851
Chesebro', Caroline.—Philly and Kit; or, Life and Raiment .	12o.	N. Y.	1856
Chevreul, M. E.—Harmony and Contrast of Colors . .	12o.	Lond.	1855
Christian Examiner. Vols. 58, 59. [*Continued*] . . .	8vo.	Bost.	1855
———— Observer. N. S. Vol. 18. [*Continued*] . .	12o.	N. Y.	1851
———— Review. Vol. 20. [*Continued*]	8vo.	N. Y.	1855
Christian Retirement: or, Spiritual Exercises of the Heart .	12o.	N. Y.	1851
Church of England Quarterly Review. Vol. 57—58. [*Continued*]	8vo.	Lond.	1855
———— Review and Ecclesiastical Register. Vol. 4 . .	8vo.	N. Hav.	1851–52
Cheni, J. H.—Sea Nile, the Desert and Nigritia . . .	8vo.	Lond.	1853
*Cincinnati Directory, City Guide, and Business Mirror . .	8vo.	Cincin.	1856
Clara; or, Slave Life in Europe	12o.	N. Y.	1856
Clark, J. H.—Sight and Hearing; How Preserved and Lost .	12o.	N. Y.	1856
Clarke, E. D.—Travels in Europe, Asia, and Africa. 2 v. .	12o.	N. Y.	1813
Clay, Henry; Last Seven Years of the Life of, by Colton . .	8vo.	N. Y.	1856
Clyde, Jas.—Romaic and Modern Greek Compared . .	8vo.	Edin.	1855
Code of Procedure of N. Y. State, as amended April 1, 1849 .	8vo.	Albany.	1849
Coggeshall, Geo.—Hist. of Amer. Privateers & Let. of Marque, 1812–14,	8vo.	N. Y.	1856
Colburn's United Service Magazine for 1855. Parts 1 and 2. .	8vo.	Lond.	1855
Colenso, J. W.—Ten Weeks in Natal	16o.	Camb. (E.)	1855
Coley, Jas.—Sutlej Campaign of 1845–6	16o.	Lond.	1856
Collection of Familiar Quotations	16o.	Camb.	1856
*Collections of the Maine Historical Society. Vol. 3 . .	8vo.	Portland.	1853
*———— Massachusetts Historical Soc. Fourth Ser. Vol. 2	8vo.	Bost.	1854
*———— New Hampshire Historical Soc. Vols. 3 and 4.	8vo.	Concord.	1832
*———— New York Historical Society. Vols. 4 and 5 .	8vo.	N. Y.	1829–30
*———— The Same. Second Series. Vol. 2. Part 1	8vo.	N. Y.	1848
*Colton's Atlas of the World. Vol. 2.	Fol.	N. Y.	1856
Colton, Calvin.—Last Seven Years of the Life of Henry Clay .	8vo.	N. Y.	1856
Comte, Auguste.—Appel aux Conservateurs . . .	8vo.	Paris.	1855
*Comptes Rendus des Séances de l'Acad. des Sciences. Vols. 38–40	4to.	Paris.	1854–55
Conant, Mrs. H. C.—The Earnest Man; or, Life of Judson .	12o.	Bost.	1856
Condorcet, J. A. N. C.	8vo.	Tubingen.	1796
Cone, Spencer H.; Some Account of the Life of, . . .	12o.	N. Y.	1856
Contrast; By R. Maria Roche. 2 v.	12o.	N. Y.	1828
Conversations on Harmony	8vo.	Lond.	1855
Conybeare, W. J.—Essays, Ecclesiastical and Social . .	8vo.	Lond.	1855
Cooke, Parsons.—The Divine Law of Beneficence . . .	16o.	N. Y.	s. a.
*Correio Braziliense, ou Armazem Literario. 10 v. . .	8vo.	Lond.	1808–13
Cortez, Hernando; History of, by J. S. C. Abbott . . .	16o.	N. Y.	1855
Coste, ———— Instructions Pratiques sur la Pisciculture .	12o.	Paris.	1856

Costello, Louisa S.—Memoirs of Anne, Duchess of Brittany . 12o. Lond. 1855
Courcelle, Seneuil, J. G.—Enterprises Industrielles, Commerciales, &c. 8vo. Paris. 1855
——— ——— Des Operations de Banque . . 8vo. Paris. 1853
Coxe, A. Cleveland.—Impressions of England . . . 12o. N. Y. 1856
Cozzens, Fred.—Sparrow Grass Papers . . . . 12o. N. Y. 1856
Cresswell, Mrs. F.—Memoirs of Elizabeth Fry . . . 8vo. Lond. 1856
Crittenden, S. W.—Book-keeping by Single and Double Entry . 8vo. Phil. 1855
Cullen, Edw.—Isthmus of Darien Ship Canal . . . 8vo. Lond. 1853
Cumberland, Rich.—Memoirs of himself . . . . 8vo. Phil. 1856

*Darley, F. O. C.—Illustrations of Rip Van Winkle . . 4to. N. Y. 1848
*——— ——— Legend of Sleepy Hollow, Illustrated . . 4to. N. Y. 1849
Daisy Chain (The), or Aspiration. By Miss Yonge. 2 v. . 12o. N. Y. 1856
Dalzel, And.—Græca Majora. 2 v. . . . . . . 8vo. Bost. 1832
——— ——— ——— Minora . . . . . . 8vo. Camb. 1821
Davis, H., and Laurent E.—Mercantile and Bankrupt Law of France 12o. Lond. 1855
Davis, G. L. L.—Day Star of Am. Freedom; or Toleration in Maryland 12o. N. Y. 1855
Davy, Humphrey;—Sketch of, by Henry Mayhew . . 16o. N. Y. 1856
Dawson, J. W.—Acadian Geology; or, Structure of Nova Scotia . 16o. Edinb. 1855
Dealings with the Dead. 2 v. . . . . . . 12o. Bost. 1856
Deane, Jas. R.—The Law of Blockade . . . . . 8vo. Lond. 1855
*Debates and Proceedings of U. S. Congress, 1st to 17th Session. 40 v. 8vo. Wash. 1837–55
De Bow's Review. Vol. 19. [*Continued.*] . . . . 8vo. N. Orleans. 1855
Delamotte, P. H.—Practice of Photography . . . 12o. Lond. 1855
Democratic Review. Vol. 19. [Title Wanting.] . . . 8vo. N. Y. 1852
Dennistoun, J.—Memoirs of R. Strange and A. Lumisden. 2 v. 12o. Lond. 1855
De Quincey, Thos.—Memorials and other Papers. 2 v. . . 12o. Bost. 1856
Despotism; or the Last Days of the American Republic . . 12o. N. Y. 1856
Destiny of Nicaragua . . . . 8vo. Bost. 1856
Deutsche Vierteljahrs Schrift. Vols. 34 & 35. [*Continued.*] . 8vo. Stutt. 1854–55
Deutsches Museum. Vols. 8, 9. . . . . . . 8vo. Leipzig. 1854–55
Delvincourt (Mons.) Cours de Code Civil. 2 v. . . . . 4to. Paris. 1824
DeWitt, Tran.—Statistical Information relating to Industry in Mass. 8vo. Bost. 1856
——— Jno.—Life and Times, by Barnwell . . . 12o. N. Y. 1856
——— ——— Treatise on Life Annuities. [Bound with above]
*Digested Summary & List of Private Claims—1st to 31st Cong. 3 v. 4to. Wash. 1853
Dixon, E. H.—Scenes in the Practice of a New York Surgeon . 12o. N. Y. 1855
*Documents relating to the Colonial History of N. Y. State. Vol. 6. 4to. Albany. 1855
Donaldson, John.—Agricultural Biography from 1480 . . 8vo. Lond. 1854
——— J. W.—Classical Scholarship and Classical Learning . 12o. Camb. (E.) 1856
Dowdeswell, Geo. M.—The Merchant Shipping Acts . . . 12o. Lond. 1856
Dorr, Benj.—Notes of Travel in Egypt, the Holy Land, &c. . 12o. Phil. 1856
Downing, Saml.—Elements of Practical Hydraulics . . . 8vo. Lond. 1855
Doyle, J. B.—Towns in Ulster. Hand-Book to North Ireland . 12o. Dublin. 1854
——— M.—The Agricultural Laborer in his Moral Condition, &c. . 8vo. Lond. 1855
Drummond, Wm.—Poetical Works . . . . . 16o. Lond. 1856
Dublin Review. Vols. 37–39. [*Continued.*] . . . . 8vo. Lond. 1854–55
——— University Magazine. Vols. 43, 45, 46. [*Continued.*] . 8vo. Dublin. 1854–55
Dumas Alex., Fils.—La Vie à Vingt Ans . . . . 16o. Paris. 1856
Duncan, Chas.—Campaign with the Turks in Asia. 2 v. . 12o. Lond. 1855

Duncker, H.—Briefe von Schillers Gattin	12o.	Leipzig.	1856
——— Max.—Geschichte der Altherthums. Vol. 2. . .	8vo.	Berlin.	1855
Duyckinck, E. A.—Memoir of Sydney Smith, with Wit and Wisdom	12o.	N. Y.	1856
Dwight, M. A.—Introduction to the Study of Art . . .	12o.	N. Y.	1856
Ecarté; or, the Saloons of Paris. 2 v.	12o.	N. Y.	1829
Eclectic Magazine Vols. 30, 34–36. [*Continued.*]	8vo.	N. Y.	1853–55
——— Review. N. S. Vols. 9, 10. [*Continued.*] . ,	8vo.	Lond.	1855
Edinburgh New Philosophical Journal. N. S. Vol. 1. [*Continued.*]	8vo.	Edin.	1855–56
——— Review. Vols. 101, 102. [*Continued.*] . . .	8vo.	Lond.	1855
Edison, J. S.—Legitimate System of National Education . .	8vo.	Lond.	1855
Edwards, Edw.—Manchester Worthies and their Foundations .	8vo.	Manchester.	1855
——— Milne—Manual of Zoology	16o.	Lond.	1856
Emmons, Eben.—Report on the Geological Survey of North Carolina	8vo.	Raleigh.	1852
*Encyclopedia Britannica. Eighth Edition. Vols. 1–10, . .	4to.	Bost.	1853–56
Enquire within upon Everything	12o.	Lond.	1856
*Epitome Historiæ Sacræ . . , ...	18o.	N. Y.	1832
Erk, L.—Deutsche Volkslieder mit ihren Meloden . .	8vo.	Berlin.	1856
Erskine, Wm.—History of India under Báber and Humáyun. 2 v. .	8vo.	Lond.	1854
Essay on Intuitive Morals	8vo.	Lond.	1855
Etiquette for Ladies and Gentlemen	12o.	Lond.	s. a.
Etzel, A.—Erdumsegelung der Fregatte Eugenie, 1851–53. 2 v. .	8vo.	Berlin.	1856
Ewbank, Thos.—Life in Brazil	8vo.	N. Y.	1856
European Magazine. Vol. 68.	8vo.	Lond.	1815
Everest, R.—Journey through the United States and Canada .	8vo.	Lond.	1855
Evans, Jas.—Geography of the Australian Colonies. . .	12o.	Sydney.	1854
Excelsior. Vols. 2–4. [*Continued*]	8vo.	Lond.	1854–55
*Exhibition of Art Industry in Paris, 1855	4to.	Lond.	no date
Fairbairn, Wm.—Useful Information for Engineers . . .	8vo.	Lond.	1856
Faraday, M.—Experimental Researches on Electricity. Vols. 1 & 3	8vo.	Lond.	1849–55
Farmer, Sarah S.—Tonga and the Friendly Islands . .	12o.	Lond.	1855
Fergusson, Jas.—Illustrated Hand-book of Architecture. 2 v. .	8vo.	Lond.	1855
Ferris, Jas.—The States and Territories of the Great West .	12o.	N. Y.	1856
——— Mrs. B. G.—The Mormons at Home	12o.	N. Y.	1856
Finch, Margaret.—The Englishwoman in America . .	8vo.	Lond.	1856
Fishbourne, Capt.—Impressions of China, and the present Revolution	12o.	Lond.	1855
Fitton, E. B.—New Zealand; its Condition, Prospects and Resources	16o.	Lond.	1856
Five Hundred Mistakes in Speaking, Pronouncing & Writing, corrected	12o.	N. Y.	1856
Fontainebleau: Hommage à C. T. Devecourt	12o.	Paris.	1855
Forbes, Edw.—Literary Papers	12o.	Lond.	1855
——— J. D.—Tours of Mont Blanc and Monte Rosa . .	16o.	Edin.	1855
——— Major.—Eleven Years in Ceylon. 2 v.	8vo.	Lond.	1841
*Force, Peter.—American Archives—4th Ser. 6 v. . . .	Fol.	Wash.	1837–46
*——— ——— The Same—5th Ser. Vols. 1–3.	Fol.	Wash.	1848–53
Fowler, Henry.—The American Pulpit	8vo.	N. Y.	1856
Francis' Metallic Life-Boat Corporation . . . , .	8vo.	N. Y.	1853
Franklin, Sir John; Narrative of, by Sir John Ross . .	8vo.	Lond.	1855
*Franz, Ad.—Der Preussische Staat. Vol. 1.	8vo.	Leipzig.	1854
Fraser's Magazine. Vols. 51, 52. [*Continued*]	8vo.	Lond.	1855

Freer, M. W.—Life of Jeanne d'Albret, Queen of Navarre. 2 v.	12o. Lond.	1855
Fremont, J. C.—Life, Explorations and Public Services	12o. Bost.	1856
Frontier Lands of the Christian and Turk. 2 v.	8vo. Lond.	1853
Frossard, Emilie—Lettres Ecrites d'Orient	12o. Toulouse.	1855
Fry, Elizabeth; Memoirs of, by Mrs. Cresswell	8vo. Lond.	1856
Gabriel Vane: His Fortune and his Friends	12o. N. Y.	1856
Gajani, Gulielmo—The Roman Exile	12o. Bost.	1856
Gallenga, Antonio—History of Piedmont. 3 v.	12o. Lond.	1855
Garth, Saml.—The Dispensary	8vo. Lond.	no Title
Gasparin, A.—Ecoles du Doute et l'Ecole de la Foi	8vo. Geneve.	1853
General Instructions to the Consuls and Agents of the United States	8vo. Wash.	1855
Gentleman's Magazine. Vols. 43, 44. [*Continued*]	8vo. Lond.	1855
George III., Court & Cabinets of, by Duke of Buckingham. Vols. 3 & 4.	8vo. Lond.	1855
George IV.—Life and Reign, by Wallace. 3 v.	16o. Lond.	1831
Gerard, Jules—Adventures of a Lion Killer. (Fr. Fren.)	12o. N. Y.	1856
Gerhard, Edw.—Griechische Mythologie. Vol. 2.	8vo. Berlin.	1855
Gerhardt, M. R. B.—Taschenbuch der Munz-Maas-und Gervichtskunde	16o. Berlin.	1798
Gilman, Saml.—Contributions to Literature	12o. Bost.	1856
Goethe, J. W.—Sämmtliche Werke. 6 v.	8vo. Stuttgart.	1854–55
Goldsmith, J.—A Geographical View of the World	12o. Bost.	1827
Goodrich, Chas. A.—History of the United States	8vo. Hart.	1829
Gosse, P. H.—The Aquarium; or, Wonders of the Deep Sea	12o. Lond.	1854
—— —— The Ocean	12o. Phil.	1856
—— —— Tenby; A Sea-side Holiday	8vo. Lond.	1856
Granville, A. B.—Sudden Death	8vo. Lond.	1854
Greenhow, Robt.—History of Oregon and California	8vo. Bost.	1845
Grey, Mrs.—Young Prima Donna	12o. Lond.	1854
Grigsby, H. B.—The Virginia Convention of 1776	8vo. Richmd.	1855
Gross, J. B.—Heathen Religion and its Popular Development	12o. Bost.	1856
Grote, Geo.—History of Greece. Vol. 12.	8vo. Lond.	1856
Guthrie, Wm.—The Christian's Great Interest	12o. N. Y.	1856
—— Thos.—The Gospel in Ezekiel	12o. N. Y.	1856
Guyon, R. D.—Gen. Guyon on the Battle Fields of Hungary and Asia	8vo. Lond.	1856
Guyot, Arnold—The Earth and Man	12o. Bost.	1851
Gwynne, John—The Military Memoirs of the Great Civil Wars	4to. Edin.	1822
Hagenbach, K. R.—Christliche Kirche bis zum Sechsten Jahrhundert	8vo. Leipzig.	1855
*Hain, John—Statistik des Osterreichischen Kaiserstaates. 2 v.	8vo. Vienna.	1852–53
Hale, Nathan—Life by S. W. Stuart	12o. Hartford.	1856
Hall, B. H.—Collection of College Words and Customs	12o. Camb.	1856
—— G. J.—Sought and Saved; a Prize Essay on Ragged Schools	16o. Lond.	1855
Hallig, (The) or Sheepfold in the Waters, by Biernatzki	12o. Bost.	1856
Hambleton, J. P.—Biographical Sketch of Henry A. Wise	8vo. Richmond.	1856
Hand-book for Northern Europe. 2 v.	12o. Lond.	1849
Vol. 1. Denmark, Norway and Sweden.		
2. Finland and Russia.		
*—— Travelers in Turkey	12o. Lond.	1854
—— —— France.	12o. Lond.	1854
Handelmann, H.—Geschichte der Amerikanische Kolonisation. Vol. 1.	8vo. Kiel.	1856

Hare, J. C.—Miscellaneous Pamphlets . . . . . 8vo. Camb. (E.) 1855
Hardwich, T. F.—Manual of Photographic Chemistry . . 16o. Lond. 1855
Hardwick, Chas.—Christian Church during the Reformation . 12o. Camb. (E.) 1856
Hardwick's Annual Biography for 1856 . . . . . 16o. Lond. 1856
Harpers' New Monthly Magazine. Vols. 4, 7, 10, 11. . . 8vo. N. Y. 1851–55
Haslett, Chas.—Mechanic's, Machinist's and Engineer's Book of Refer. 12o. N. Y. 1856
Hastings' Guide . . . . 12o. Hastings. s. a.
Hauff, W.—La Caravane. (De l'Allemand.) . . . . 16o. Paris. 1855
Hawks, F. S. (Comp.)—Narrative of the Japan Expedition, 1852–54 8vo. N. Y. 1856
——— of Hawk Hollow. By Dr. Bird. 2 v. . . . . 12o. Phil. 1835
Hawkins, John—Clavis Commercii; or, the Key of Commerce . 4to. Lond. 1718
Haxthausen, A.—Tribes of the Caucasus . . . . 12o. Lond. 1855
——— ——— Transcaucasia; its Nations and Races . . 8vo. Lond. 1854
Haym, R.—Wm. von Humboldt; Lebensbild . . . . 8vo. Berlin. 1856
Heath, A. S. & A. H.—Photography on Paper and Glass . 8vo. N. Y. 1855
Heathman, W. G.—Switzerland in 1854–55 . . . . . 8vo. Lond. 1855
Hegel, G. W. F.—Subjective Logic. (Fr. Ger.) . . . . 12o. Lond. 1855
Helps, Arthur—The Spanish Conquest in America 2 v. . . 8vo. Lond. 1855
——— ——— The Same. 2 v. . . . . 12o. N. Y. 1855
Hertha; By Frederika Bremer . . . . 12o. N. Y. 1856
Herzen, Alex.—My Exile . . . . 12o. Lond. 1855
Hettner, H.—Geschichte der Englischen Literatur, 1660–1770 . 8vo. Braunsch. 1856
Hibbard, S.—Rustic Adornments for Homes of Taste . . 12o. Lond. 1856
Higgins, Godfrey—Horæ Sabbaticæ . . . . 8vo. Lond. 1851
Heighway, O. W. T.—The Relatives of Leila Ada . . 16o. N. Y. 1856
Hillard, G. S.—First Class Reader . . . . 12o. Bost. 1856
Histoire de Lydia Sommerville. [de l'Ang.] . . . . 16o. Paris. 1822
Hobart, J. H.—Apology for Apostolic Order and its Advocates . 12o. N. Y. 1844
——— ——— Companion for the Altar . . . . . 12o. N. Y. 1837
Hodge, Chas.—Commentary on the Epistle to the Ephesians . 8vo. N. Y. 1856
Hogan, J. S.—Canada; A Prize Essay . . . . . 8vo. Montreal. 1855
*Hogarth, Wm.—Works . . . . Fol. Lond. 1822
Holden's Dollar Magazine. Vols. 1, 5, and 6 . . . . 8vo. N. Y. 1848–50
Holland, J., and Everett, J.—Memoir of James Montgomery. 2 v 12o. Lond. 1854
Holstein, H. L. V. D.—Memoirs of Gilbert M. La Fayette. (Fr. Fren.) 12o. N. Y. 1824
Home Missionary. Vols. 24, 27, 28. [*Continued.*] . . . . 8vo. N. Y. 1851–56
——— Mission Record. Vols. 1–4 in one vol. . . . . Fol. N. Y. 1849–53
Hood, Thos.—Humorous Poems . . . . 12o. Bost. 1856
Hooper, W. H.—Ten Months among the Tents of the Tuski . 8vo. Lond. 1853
Hopkins, J. H.—Lectures on Causes and Results of Brit. Reformation 12o. N. Y. 1848
——— Sam.—Youth of the Old Dominion . . . . 12o. Bost. 1856
Horses and Hounds. A Practical Treatise, by "Scrutator" . 12o. Lond. 1855
Horsford, John—A Voice from the West Indies . . . 12o. Lond. 1856
Horsley, John—Catechism of Chemical Philosophy . . 12o. Lond. 1856
Horticulturist. N. S. Vol. 5. [*Continued*] . . . . 8vo. Phil. 1855
Household Words. Vols. 10 and 11. [*Continued*] . . . . 8vo. Lond. 1854–5
Houssaye, Arsène—Le Violon de Franjolé . . . . 12o. Paris. 1855
*Hubner, Otto—Die Banken . . . . 8vo. Leipzig. 1854
——— ——— Jahrbuch fur Volkswirthschaft u. Statistik . 8vo. Leipzig. 1856
Hughes, E. J.—Patent Laws of All Nations . . . . 8vo. Manchester. 1854

Huguenot Exiles; or the Times of Louis XIV. . . . 12o. N. Y. 1856
Hume's History of England. See *Plates.*
Humboldt, Alex.—The Island of Cuba (Fr. Span.) . . 12o. N. Y. 1856
——— Wm.; Lebensbild u. Charakteristik, von Haym . . 8vo. Berlin. 1856
Hunt, Freeman—Worth and Wealth; or, Maxims for Men of Business. 12o. N. Y. 1856
—— H. K.—Glances and Glimpses 50 Yrs. Social and 20 Prof. Life 12o. Bost. 1856
Hunt's Merchant's Magazine. Vols. 29, 32, 33. [*Continued*] . 8vo. N. Y. 1853–5
Hutchinson, T. J.—The Niger, Tshadda, and Binuë Expedition . 12o. Lond. 1855
Hyder Shah, and Tippoo Sultaun, History of . . . 8vo. Lond. 1855

Illustrated Magazine of Art. Vol. 4 . . . . . 8vo. N. Y. 1854
*Illustrirte Zeitung. Vol. 24 . . . . . . Fol. Leipzig. 1855
Ilsley, Chas. P.—Forest and Shore; or, Legends of the Pine Tree State 12o. Bost. 1856
Imray, Keith—Popular Cyclopædia of Domestic Medicine . 8vo. N. Y. 1856
*Index to the Documents of the Legislature of N. Y. 1842–54 . 8vo. Albany. 1855
Indian Commercial Tables of Weights, Measures, and Money . 8vo. Calcutta. 1852
Ingoldsby Legends, by R. H. Barham. 2 vols. . . . 12o. Phil. 1856
*Instructions from the Regents of the Uni. to Colleges, Academies, &c. 8vo. Albany. 1853
*Interiano, Paolo—Ristretto delle Histori Genovesi . . . 4to. Lucca. 1551
Irish Quarterly Review. Vols 4 and 5 . . . . . 8vo. Dublin. 1854–55
*Irving, Wash.—Life of George Washington. Vols. 1 and 2 . 4to. N. Y. 1855
——— —— The Same. Vol. 3 . . . . . 8vo. N. Y. 1856

Jacobs, Fred.—The Greek Reader . . . . . . 8vo. N. Y. 1829
——— F.—Hellas; or, the Home, History, &c., of the Greeks . 16o. Lond. 1855
James, G. P. R.—The Old Dominion; or, Southampton Massacre . 8vo. N. Y. 1856
——— J. A.—Anxious Enquirer after Salvation . . 16o. N. Y. 1838
Janin, Jules—Histoire de la Littérature Dramatique. 4 vols. . 12o. Paris. 1855
Jarves, J. S.—Italian Sights and Papal Principles . . 12o. N. Y. 1856
——— —— Parisian Sights and French Principles. 2nd ser. . 12o. N. Y. 1855
Jeanne d'Albret, Queen of Navarre, Life of, by M. W. Freer. 2 vols. 12o. Lond. 1855
Jokai, M.—Hungarian Sketches in Peace and War . . . 16o. Edin. 1855
Journal of Classical and Sacred Philology. Vol. 1 . . 8vo. Camb. (E.) 1854
——— des Economistes. 2nd Ger. Vols. 3 and 4 . . . 8vo. Paris. 1854
——— of the Franklin Institute, N. S. Vols. 29, 30 . . 8vo. Phil. 1855
——— —— ——— ——— —— Vol. 54 . . . 8vo. Phil. 1852
——— —— Psychological Medicine. Vol. 8 . . . 8vo. Lond. 1855
——— —— Public Health and Sanitary Review. Vol. 1 . . 8vo. Lond. 1855
——— —— Sacred Literature. Vol. 7 . . . . . 8vo. Lond. 1854–5
——— —— Society of Arts. Vol. 3 . . . . . 8vo. Lond. 1854–5
——— —— Statistical Society of London. Vols. 17 and 18 . 8vo. Lond. 1854–5
——— —— Transactions of the Va. Agric. Society to 1853. Vol 1 8vo. Rich. 1853
John Halifax, Gentleman . . . . . . 8vo. N. Y. 1856
Johnson, A. B.—Physiology of the Senses . . . . 12o. N. Y. 1856
Joyce, Jas. W.—England's Sacred Synods . . . . 8vo. Lond. 1855
Judson, Adoniram—Sketch of, by Mrs. Conant . . . 12o. Bost. 1856

Kahnis, C. F. A.—Internal History of German Protestantism . 16o. Edin. 1856
Kaye, J. W.—Life and Correspondence of Charles, Lord Metcalfe. 2 vols. 12o. Lond. 1854
Kemp, T. L.—The Phasis of Matter; or, Modern Chemistry. 2 vols. 12o. Lond. 1855

Kennard, A. S.—Eastern Experiences in Egypt and the Holy Land 12o. Lond. 1855
Kennedy, C. M.—Influence of Christianity upon International Law 12o Camb. (E.) 1856
Kenrick, John—Phenicia . . . . 8vo. Lond. 1855
Kingsley, Chas.—The Heroes; Greek Fairy Tales for Children . 16o. Bost. 1856
——— —— Poems . . . . 12o. Bost. 1856
Kinzie, Mrs. J. H.—Waubun, the "Early Day" in the North-west 8vo. N. Y. 1856
Kitto, John—Memoirs of, by J. E. Ryland. 2 v. . . . . 12o. N. Y. 1856
Klapka, George—War in the East. 1853 to 1855 . . 12o. Lond. 1855
Kleinschrod, C. T.—Die Internationale Patentgesetzgebung . 8vo. Erlangen. 1855
Knickerbocker (The). Vols. 41, 42, 45, 46 . . . . 8vo. N. Y. 1853–5
Knight, Chas.—Knowledge is Power . . . . . 12o. Bost. 1856
——— —— The Same . . . . . . 12o. Lond. 1855
Knowles, Jas. Sheridan—Dramatic Works. 2 v. . . . 16o. Lond. 1856
Kohl, J. G.—Reisen in Canada u. New York u. Pennsylvania . 8vo. Stuttgart. 1856
König, Theod.—Aus der Gegenwart. 2 vols. . . . 12o. Leipzig. 1855
Krasinski, V.—The Polish Question and Panslavism . . 8vo. Lond. 1855
Krusenstern, Adam G.; Memoir (Fr. Ger.) . . . . 8vo. Lond. 1856
Kugler, F.—Hand-buch der Kunstgeschichte. Vol. 1 . . 8vo. Stuttgart. 1856
*——— —— Schriften und Studien zur Kunstgeschichte. 3 v. 8vo. Stuttgart. 1853–4
Kurnberger, Ferd.—Amerikanisches Kulterbild . . . 12o. Frankfort. 1856

Labarte, Jules—Hand-book of the Arts of the Middle Ages . 8vo. Lond. 1855
Lacordaire, A. L.—Manufactures imp. de Tapisseries des Gobelins 8vo. Paris. 1853
Lamartine, Alphonse—Histoire de la Russie . . . . 8vo. Paris. 1855
——— —— Histoire de la Turquie. Vols. 3 and 4 . 8vo. Paris. 1855
——— —— Memoirs of Celebrated Characters. 2 vols. . 12o. Lond. 1854
Landor, Walter Savage—Selections from the Writings of . 12o. Bost. 1856
La Porte, Mons.—La Science des Négocians . . . . 12o. Paris. 1792
Lardner, Dionysius—The Microscope . . . . . 12o. Lond. 1856
Larpent, G.—See *Porter, Jas.*
Laurie, J.—Homœopathic Domestic Medicine . . . 8vo. N. Y. 1848
——— S. S.—Minutes of the Commissioners of Council on Education 12o. Edin. 1856
Lavergne, L. de—Rural Economy of England, Ireland, and Scotland 8vo. Edin. 1855
Lectures before the London Young Men's Association, 1854–6. 2 vols. 12o. Lond. 1855–6
——— on Education, before the Royal Institute . . 12o. Lond. 1855
——— to Ladies on Practical Subjects . . . . 12o. Camb. (E.) 1856
Lehmann C. G.—Manual of Chemical Physiology. (Fr. Ger.) . 8vo. Phil. 1856
Leibnitz, G. G.—Refutation of Spinoza. See *Carcil.*
Le Quesne, Chas.—Constitutional History of Jersey . . 8vo. Lond. 1856
Leslie, C. R.—Hand-book for Young Painters . . . 12o. Lond. 1855
Lesseps, T.—The Isthmus of Suez Question . . . 8vo. Lond. 1855
Lever, Chas.—The Martins of Cro' Martin . . . . 8vo. N. Y. 1856
*Levi, L.—Commercial Law, its Principles and Administration. Vol. 2. 4to. Lond. 1851–2
——— —— Law of Nature and Nations related to Divine Law . 8vo. Lond. 1855
Lewis, G. C.—Inquiry into Credibility of Early Roman History. 2 v. 8vo. Lond. 1855
L'Homond, C. F.—Viri Illustres Urbis Romæ . . . 16o. N. Y. 1828
Liddell, H. G.—History of Rome to the Empire . . . 8vo. Lond. 1855
——— —— and Scott, R.—Greek-English Lexicon . . . 8vo. N. Y. 1851
List, Fred.—National System of Political Economy . . 8vo. Phil. 1856
Literary and Scientific Register and Almanac for 1856 . . 32o. Lond. s. a.

Littell's Living Age. Vols. 31, 32, 34-36, 38, 44, 46, 47. 8vo. Bost. 1851–5
Litton, A.—Report on Mines of Missouri. Bound with *Swallow's Reports.*
Livingston's Monthly Law Magazine. Vol. 2. . . . . 8vo. N. Y. 1854
Livingston, Vanbrugh—Remarks on the "Oxford Theology" . 16o. N. Y. 1841
Livy, Titus—Historiarum Liber Primus . . . . 12o. Camb. 1831
Lloyd's Steamboat Directory and Disasters on Western Waters . 8vo. Cincin. 1856
*Lodge, Edw.—Peerage and Baronetage of the British Empire . 8vo. Lond. 1856
*London Catalogue of Books published in Great Britain, 1816–1851 8vo. Lond. 1851
*——— —— The Same from 1831–1855 . . . . 8vo Lond. 1855
——— Edinburgh and Dublin Phil. Magazine, 4th Ses. Vol. 9. . 8vo. Lond. 1855
——— Quarterly Review. Vols. 3–5. . . . . . 8vo. Lond. 1854–56
Louth, Geo. T.—The Wanderer in Arabia. 2 v. . . . 12o. Lond. 1855
Lumsden, James—Sweden ; its Religious State and Prospects . 16o. Lond. 1855
Lyall, Wm.—Intellect, the Emotions and the Moral Nature . . 8vo. Edin. 1855
Lyra Germania. (Fr. Ger.) . . . . 12o. N. Y. 1856

*Ma Bibliothéque Francaise . . . . 12o. Paris. 1855
Macaulay, T. B.—History of England. Vols. 3 & 4. . . 8vo. Phil. 1836
——— —— The Same . . . . 8vo. Lond. 1855
McClellan, G. B.—Manual of Bayonet Exercise . . . 12o. Phil. 1856
McCosh, James, & Dickie, G.-Typical Forms & Special Ends in Creation 8vo. N. Y. 1856
McCullagh, W. T.—Memoirs of Robert Lalor Sheil. 2 v. . . 12o. Lond. 1855
McDonald, Mary N.—Poems . . . . . . 8vo. N. Y. 1844
Macintosh, Maj. Gen.—Military Tour in European Turkey. 2 v. . 12o. Lond. 1854
Mackie, J. M.—Life of Schamyl . . . . . . 12o. Bost. 1856
Macleod, H. D.—Theory and Practice of Banking. 2 v. . . 8vo. Lond. 1855
Macvicar, J. G.—Philosophy of the Beautiful . . . 12o. Edin. 1855
Magazine of Horticulture. Vol. 21. . . . . . . 8vo. Bost. 1855
Maginn, Wm.—Miscellanies. Vol. 3. The Shakspeare Papers . 12o. N. Y. 1856
Magruder, A. B. & Orvis, E. E.—Debate on Endless Punishment . 12o. Richmond. 1855
Mair's Introduction to Latin Syntax . . . . . 12o. N. Y. 1828
Mant, Rich.—Happiness of the Blessed . . . . . 12o. N. Y. 1847
——— —— Horæ Liturgicæ . . . . . . 12o. N. Y. 1847
Manual of British Rural Sports, by Stonehenge . . . 12o. Lond. 1856
Marble Worker's Manual. (Fr. Fren.) . . . . . 15o. N. Y. 1856
Margaret Maitland of Sunnyside. By Mrs. Oliphant . . 12o. N. Y. 1856
Markham, C. R.—Cuzco and Lima . . . . . 12o. Lond. 1856
Marmier, X.—Hist. de la Littérature en Danemarck et Suède . 8vo. Paris. 1839
——— A.—History of the Maritime Ports of Ireland . . 8vo. Lond. 1855
Maron, Eugène—Histoire Littéraire de la Révolution . . 12o. Paris. 1856
Marryat, F. S.—Borneo and the Indian Archipelago . . 8vo. Lond. 1848
Marsden, J. B.—History of Christian Churches and Sects. 2 v. . 8vo. Lond. 1856
Marsh, Geo. P.—The Camel; its Organization, Habits and Uses 12o. Bost. 1856
Marston, John—Works. 3 v. . . . . . . 16o. Lond. 1856
Martin, W. C. L.—The Poultry Yard . . . . . 16o. Lond. 1855
Martins of Cro' Martin, by Chas. Lever . . . . 8vo. N. Y. 1856
Martyr, Pet.—De Insulis nuper Inventis . . . . 4to. Basle. 1821
Marx, A. B.—Music in the 19th Century, and its Culture . . 8vo. Lond. s. a.
Maryland Journal and Baltimore Advertiser. Vols. 19 & 20. . Fol. Balt. 1792–93
Massé, A. G.—Le Parfait Notaire, ou la Science des Notaires. 3 v. . 4to. Paris. 1821

Mason, G. H.—Life with the Zulus of Natal . . . . 12o. Lond. 1855
Mason, John M.—Memoirs of, by J. Van Vechten . . . 8vo. N. Y. 1856
Massey, Rich. T.—Analytical Ethnology . . . 16o. Lond. 1855
Mather, Cotton—Magnalia Christi Americana . . . 12o. Lond. 1702
——— Increase—Remarkable Providences in Amer. Colonization 16o. Lond. 1855
Maurice, F. D.—Learning and Working . . . . . 12o. Camb. (E.) 1855
Maury, M. F.—Explanations and Sailing Directions . . 4to. Wash. 1851
——— —— Explanations to Wind & Current Chart, & Sailing Direc. 4to. Phil. 1855
——— —— Physical Geography of the Sea . . . . 8vo. N. Y. 1856
Mayhew, Henry—The Wonders of Science ; or, Young Humphrey Davy 16o. N. Y. 1856
——— Ira—Practical System of Bookkeeping . . . 12o. N. Y. 1851
Mechanics' Magazine. Vol. 62. . . . . . . 8vo. Lond. 1855
Melish, John—Geographical Description of the U. States . . 8vo. Phil. 1822
Mellville, Herman—The Piazza Tales . . . . . 12o. N. Y. 1856
Melvill, Henry—Sermons on Facts and Reference in Sacred Story. 2 v. 8vo. N. Y. 1844–46
*Memoirs of the Historical Society of Pennsylvania. Vols. 3 & 4. . 8vo. Phil. 1834–50
Men of the Time and Women of the Time . . . . 12o. Lond. 1856
Mercersburg Quarterly Review. Vol. 7 . . . . . 8vo. Chambers. 1855
Merimée, Prosper—Colomba . . . . 16o. Bost. 1856
——— —— Melanges Historiques et Littéraires . . 12o. Paris. 1855
Message from the President of the U. S. to 34th Cong. 1st Ses. 3 v. 8vo. Wash. 1855
——————— 31st Cong. 2d Ses. . 8vo. Wash. 1850
——————— 32d Cong. 2d Ses. Part 1. 8vo. Wash. 1852
——————— On Penal Codes in Europe 8vo. Wash. 1854
——————— On Enlistments & Cen. Am. 8vo. Wash. 1856
Meurice, Paul—Scénes du Foyer—La Famille Aubry . . 16o. Paris. 1856
Michelsen, E. H.—Jesuitism ; or Jesuits in the 19th Century . 82o. Lond. 1855
Milman, Henry H.—History of Latin Christianity. Vols. 4–6. . 8vo. Lond. 1855
*Miners' and Business Men's Directory of Tuolumne, California . 8vo. Columbia. 1856
Minerva. Vol. 3. . . . . 8vo. Geneva. 1854
Mining Magazine. Vols. 1–5. . . . . . . 8vo. N. Y. 1853–55
Mirror of Fashion . . . . 4to. N. Y. 1853–55
Missionary Herald. Vols. 48, 51. . . . . . . 8vo. N. Y. 1852–55
Modern Story Teller . . . . 12o. N. Y. 1856
Moffat, Jas. C.—Introduction to the Study of Æsthetics . . 12o. Cincin. 1856
*Mohl, M.—Aus den Gewerbswissenschaftlichen
Moore, Thos.—Memoirs, Journals, &c., by Lord John Russell. 6 v. 12o. Lond. 1853–4
Montalembert, Comte de.—De l'Avenir Politique de l'Angleterre . 8vo. Paris. 1856
Monteith, Gen. (Edw.)—Conquest of Finland by Russians, 1808–9 12o. Lond. 1854
——— W.—Kars and Erzeroum ; Campaigns of Paskiewitsch 8vo. Lond. 1856
Montépin, Xavier—L'Idiot. 2 v. . . . . 12o. Paris. 1852
Montgomery, Jas.—Memoirs by J. Holland and G. Everett. 2 v. 12o. Lond. 1854
Mortimer, G. W.—Pyrotechnist's Companion . . . . 12o. Phil. 1852
Motley, J. L.—Rise of the Dutch Republic. 3 v. . . 8vo. N. Y. 1856
Mr. Sponge's Sporting Tour. Edited by Frank Forrester . . 8vo. N. Y. 1856
Müffling, Baron—Missions to Constantinople and St. Petersburg 16o. Lond. 1855
Mundt, Theo.—Krim-Girai, Khan of the Crimea. (Fr. Ger.) . 12o. Lond. 1856
Murger, Henry.—Scénes de Campagne—Adeline Protal . 16o. Paris. 1856
——— —— Le Dernier Rendezvous . . . . . 16o. Paris. 1856
Myers, Fred.—Lectures on Great Men . . . . . 8vo. Lond. 1856

Narrative of a Cruise among the Faroe Islands in 1854	8vo.	Lond.	1856
National Magazine. Vols. 6, 7.	8vo.	N. Y.	1855
——— —— and Republican Review. Vol 1.	8vo.	Wash.	1839
Nautical Magazine. Vol. 24.	8vo.	Lond.	1855
Neale, F. A.—Narrative of a Residence in Siam	12o.	Lond.	1852
New Age of Gold; or, Life, &c., of R. D. Romaine, by himself	12o.	Bost.	1856
Newark (N. J.) Directory, for 1856–57	12o.	Newark.	1856
New Brunswick Review. Vol. 1.	8vo	N. Y.	1854-55
*Newdegate, C. N.—Customs, Tariffs of All Nations	4to.	Lond.	1855
New Englander. Vol. 13.	8vo.	N. Haven.	1855
—— England Historical and Genealogical Register. Vol 9.	8vo.	Bost.	1855
—— Monthly Magazine. Vols. 102–105.	8vo.	Lond.	1855
—— Quarterly Review. Vol. 4	8vo.	Lond.	1855
—— System of Domestic Cookery	12o.	N. Y.	1817
Newton's London Journal of Arts and Sciences, N. S. Vols. 1 & 2	8vo.	Lond.	1855
*New York City Directory for 1828–9, 1830–33, 1833–36, 1837–40. 9 v.	12o.	N. Y.	1828–39
*——————— for 1856–57	8vo.	N. Y.	1856
————— Hall Recorder. Vols. 1–4.	8vo.	N. Y.	1816–19
———— Municipal Gazette. Vol. 2.	4to.	N. Y.	1855
———— Quarterly. Vols. 2 & 3.	8vo.	N. Y.	1853–55
Nerval, Gérard—La Bohème Galante	12o.	Paris.	1855
Nichols, T. L.—Religions of the World	8vo.	Cincin.	1855
Noble, L. L.—Course of Empire and other Pictures of T. Cole	12o.	N. Y.	1853
North American Review. Vols. 80, 81.	8vo.	Bost.	1855
—— British Review. Vols. 22–24.	8vo.	Edin.	1854–55
Notes and Queries. Vols. 9–12.	4to.	Lond.	1854–55
Notice Statisque sur la Guyane Française	8vo.	Paris.	1843
Old Dominion; or Southampton Massacre, by G. P. R. James.	8vo.	N. Y.	1856
Oldknow, Joseph.—A Month in Portugal	16o.	Lond.	1855
Oliphant, L.—Minnesota and the Far West	8vo.	Edin.	1855
Olyphant, Mrs.—Margaret Maitland of Sunnyside	12o.	N. Y.	1856
Olmsted, F. L.—Journey in the Seaboard Slave States	12o.	N. Y.	1856
Original Bath Guide	12o.	Bath.	s. a.
Ossoli, Margaret Fuller—At Home and Abroad	12o.	Bost.	1856
Overbeck, J.—Pompeji	8vo.	Leipzig.	1856
Ovid, P. N.—Metamorphoses. Notes by Nimellius	8vo.	Lond.	1837
Owen, D. D.—Geolog. Explo. of Iowa, Wisconsin and Illinois	8vo.	Wash.	1844
—— Hugh—Here and There in Portugal	12o.	Lond.	1856
Oxford Academy Jubilee held at Oxford, N. Y., Aug. 1 & 2, 1854	8vo.	N. Y.	1856
——— Essays, 1856	8vo.	Oxford.	1856
——— University Calendar, 1856	12o.	Oxford.	1856
————— and City Guide	12o.	Oxford.	1821
Pfeiffer, Ida—Lady's Second Voyage round the World	12o.	N. Y.	1856
Paine, Thos.—The Age of Reason	12o.	N. Y.	1856
Palmer, Wm.—Compendious Ecclesiastical History	12o.	N. Y.	1846
Pamphlets. Vols. 36–39.	8vo.	Various.	
Parker, R. G.—Lessons in Reading and Elocution	12o.	N. Y.	1852
Parkman, Frances—Vassall Morton. A Novel	12o.	Bost.	1856

Parnauvel, O. T.—Trip to Turkey, and Guide to Constantinople	16o. Lond.	1855
Parish, W.—Buenos Ayres, and the Prairie of the Rio de la Plata .	8vo. Lond.	1852
Pestalozzi, H.; Life and System of, by Karl Raumer. (Fr. Ger.)	8vo. Lond.	1855
Paterfamilias's Diary of Everybody's Tour	16o. Lond.	1856
Patmore, P. G.—My Friends and Acquaintances. 3 v. . .	12o. Lond.	1854
Peabody, A. P.—Conversation, its Faults and Graces . .	16o. Bost.	1856
Pension Laws of the U. S., 1776–1833. Compiled by R. Mayo, .	8vo. Wash.	1833
Pereira, Jonathan—Lectures on Polarized Light . .	16o. Lond.	1854
Percival, Peter—The Land of the Veda	12o. Lond.	1854
Perkins, Thomas Handasyd; Memoir of, by Cary . .	8vo. Bost.	1856
Pertz, G. H.—Das Leben der Ministers von Stein. Vol. 5. . .	8vo. Berlin.	1854
Peterborough, Earl of; Memoirs by Capt. Warburton. 2 v. .	12o. Lond.	1853
*Petermann, A.—Mittheilungen aus Perthes Geographischer Anstalt	4to. Gotha.	1855
*Petzholdt, Julius—Katechismus der Bibliothekenlehre .	16o. Leipzig.	1856
Peyster, J. Watts de—Life of Leonard Forstensen . . .	8vo. Poughk.	1855
Phelps, S. D.—Sunlight and Hearthlight: Poems . .	12o. N. Y.	1856
Phillimore, J. G.—Principles and Maxims of Jurisprudence .	8vo. Lond.	1856
——— Robt.—Commentaries on International Law. Vols. 1 and 2	8vo. Lond.	1854–55
Phillippsohn, L.—Religious Idea in Judaism, Christianity, &c. .	8vo. Lond.	1855
Phillips, John.—Manual of Geology	12o. Lond.	1855
——— M. L.—Worlds beyond the Earth	12o. Lond.	1855
Phipps, E.—Political and Literary Life of R. P. Ward. 2 v. .	8vo. Lond.	1850
Physiology of Marriage	16o. Bost.	1856
Piazza Tales (The). By Herman Melville . . .	12o. N. Y.	1855
Pickard, Mrs.—The Kidnapped and Ransomed; or, Peter Still & Wife.	12o. Syracuse.	1856
Pioneer; or, California Monthly Magazine. Vols. 2 and 3 .	8vo. San Fran.	1854–5
Plain Talk and Friendly Advice to Domestics	12o. Bost.	1855
Planche, Gustave.—Etudes Littéraires	12o. Paris.	1855
——— ——— L'Ecole Française, 1831–52. Peinture et Sculp. 2 v.	12o. Paris.	1855
Planché, Miss.—Sunbeam Stories	16o. Bost.	1856
——— ——— Sibert's Wold	12o. Bost.	1856
*Plates to Illustrate Hume's History of England	4to. Lond.	s. a.
Plough, Loom, and Anvil. Vol. 7	8vo. N. Y.	1854–55
Plu-ri-bus-tah. By M. U. Thompson	12o. N. Y.	1856
Poe, Edgar A.—Works; vol. 4. Arthur Gordon Pym, & Miscellanies.	12o. N. Y.	1856
Pollen, John H.—Five Years at St. Saviour's, Leeds . .	12o. Oxford.	1851
Polytechnisches Journal. Von Dingler. Vols. 134–137. [*Continued*]	8vo. Stuttgart.	1854–5
Pontmartin, A. de.—Contes et Nouvelles . . .	16o. Paris.	1856
*Pope, Chas.—Yearly Journal of Trade, 1856	8vo. Lond.	1856
Porter, Jas.—History of Turkey; continued by Sargent. 2 v.	8vo. Lond.	1854
——— S. L.—Five Years in Damascus. 2 v.	12o. Lond.	1855
Pote, R. G.—Nineveh, its Ancient History and Modern Explorers	16o. Lond.	s. a.
Powell, Baden.—Essays on Inductive Philos., Unity of Worlds, &c.	8vo. Lond.	1855
Practical Arithmetic, prepared for Mrs. Okill's School . .	12o. N. Y.	1828
——— Mechanics' Journal. Vol. 7	4to. N. Y.	1854
Preces Paulinæ; or, Devotions of the Apostle Paul . .	16o. Lond.	1855
Presbyterian Quarterly Review. Vol. 3	8vo. Phil.	1855
Piesse, G. W. S.—The Art of Perfumery	12o. Phila.	1855
*Proceedings of the New Jersey Historical Society. Vols. 1–7. 2 v.	8vo. Newark.	1847–55
*——— New York Historical Society for 1849 .	8vo. N. Y.	1849

Prospective Review. Vol. 10	8vo. Lond.	1854
*Proyart, Abbé—L'Ecolier Vertueux	16o. Lyons.	1822
Prus, Mme.—Residence in Algeria	8vo. Lond.	1852
Punch. Vol. 29	4to. Lond.	1855
Putnam's Monthly. Vols. 5 and 6	8vo. N. Y.	1855
Putter, J. S.—Development of the German Political Constitution. 3 v.	8vo. Lond.	1790
Quarles, Fran.—Enchiridion—Institutions Divine and Moral	16o. Lond.	1856
Quarterly Journal of the Chemical Society of London. Vols. 7 and 8	8vo. Lond.	1854–55
——— of Microscopical Science. Vols. 2 and 3	8vo. Lond.	1854–55
——— Review. Vols. 96, 97	8vo. Lond.	1854–55
Rachel and the New World. By L. Beauvallet	12o. N. Y.	1856
Raikes, Thos.—Journal from 1831–1847. Vols. 1 and 2	12o. Lond.	1856
Raising the Veil; or, Scenes in the Courts	12o. Bost.	1856
*Raleigh, Walter—History of the World	Fol. Lond.	1614
Raphall, M. J.—Post Biblical History of the Jews. 2 v.	12o. Phil.	1855
Rasgos Historicos de Magnanimad, Valor, y Nobleza	12o. N. Y	1835
Rates of Merchandise, with Duties and Drawbacks	8vo. Lond.	1782
Ratisbonne, Louis—Impressions Littéraires	12o. Paris.	1855
Raumer, F. (Edr.)—Historisches Taschenbuch	12o. Leipzig.	1856
——— K.—Life and System of Pestalozzi. (Fr. Ger.)	8vo. Lond.	1855
Rawle, Wm. H.—On the Law of Covenants for Title	8vo. Phil.	1852
Receipts and Expend. of U. S. Gov. for half year end. June 30, 1843.	8vo. Wash.	1854
——— for year ending June 30, 1849	8vo. Wash.	s. a.
Recollections of Russia by a German Nobleman	12o. Edin.	1855
——— Table Talk of Samuel Rogers; and Porsoniana	12o. N. Y.	1856
Reichensperger, A.—Vermischte Schriften über Christliche Kunst	8vo. Leipzig.	1856
Religion as seen through the Church	12o. N. Y.	1845
Renwick, Jas.—Outlines of Natural Philosophy. 2 v.	8vo. N. Y.	1826
Repertory of Patent Inventions. Vols. 25, 26	8vo. Lond.	1855
Report in relation to Cholera in New York in 1849	8vo. N. Y.	1849
——— of the Commission of Indian Affairs for 1854	8vo. Wash.	1855
——— Commissioner of Land Office on Bastrop Grant (La.)	8vo. Wash.	1852
——— Patents for 1850. Part 2	8vo. Wash.	1851
——— Commissioner on Harbor and River Improvements	8vo. Wash.	1848
——— Geological Survey of New Jersey, 1854	8vo. N. Bruns.	1855
——— (32d) of the N. Y. Institution for the Deaf and Dumb	8vo. Albany.	1851
——— of the Secretary of the Treasury on Finances	8vo. Wash.	1855
——— 24th Meeting of British Association	8vo. Lond.	1855
——— (Parliamentary) on Printing	Fol. Lond.	1855
——— on State of Large Towns	Fol. Lond.	1844–45
*Reports of Experiments on the Strength, &c., of Metals for Cannon	4to. Phil.	1856
——— (Nos. 1 to 20) of Comm. of Nat. Education in Ireland. 11 v.	8vo. Dublin.	1851–54
——— (1 and 3) of the Secretary of the Board of Agriculture, Mass.	8vo. Bost.	1854–56
——— of the Commissioners on the Code of Procedure	8vo. Albany.	1849
Revue Critique des Livres Nouveaux. 3 v.	8vo. Paris.	1850–54
——— des Deux Mondes. Vol. 29	8vo. Paris.	1842
——— The same. N. S. Vols. 5, 6, 8—12	8vo. Paris.	1854–55
——— du Nouveau Monde. Vols. 1–4	8vo. N. Y.	1850

Title	Size. Place.	Date
Revue de Paris. Vols. 23–29	8vo. Paris.	1854–56
*Richardson, C. J.—Studies of Ornamental Design	Fol. Lond.	1848
Rintoul, A. N.—Guide to Painting Photographic Portraits	16o. Lond.	s. a.
Roche, R. Marie—Contrast. 2 v.	12o. N. Y.	1828
Rogers, Sam.—Table Talk. See *Recollections.*		
Romaine, R. D.; Life &c., of. By Himself	12o. Bost.	1856
Rosenkranz, Karl—Die Poesie und ihre Geschichte	8vo. Konigsberg.	1855
Roseleur, A.—Manipulations Hydroplastiques	8vo. Paris.	1855
Ross, G.—Leading Cases in Criminal Law of England and Scotland. 2 v.	8vo. Phil.	1854–5
—— John—Sir John Franklin. A Narrative	8vo. Lond.	1855
Roussel, N.—Catholic Nations and Protestant Compared	8vo. Lond.	1855
*Royal Blue Book—April, 1856.	12o. Lond.	1856
Rural Annual and Horticultural Directory	12o. Rochester.	1856
*Ruskin, John—Modern Painters. Vol. 3. Of Many Things	8vo. Lond.	1856
—— —— The same	12o. N. Y.	1856
*—— —— Modern Painters. Vol. 4. Of Mountain Scenery	8vo. Lond.	1856
Russell, John (Edr.)—Memoirs, Journal, &c., of Thos. Moore. 6 v.	12o. Lond.	1853–4
—— Wm.—Sequel to the Primary Reader	16o. Bost.	s. a.
—— W. H.—The War in the Crimea to the Death of Lord Raglan	12o. Lond.	1855
Ryland, J. E.—Memoirs of John Kitto. 2 v.	12o. N. Y.	1856
Ryle, Thos.—American Liberty and Government Questioned	12o. Lond.	1855
Sacred Circle. Vol. 1	8vo. N. Y.	1855
Sailor's Magazine. Vol. 1	8vo. N. Y.	1828–29
—— Vol 25, 27	8vo. N. Y.	1852–55
Saint Beuve, C. A.—Causeries du Lundi. Vol. 4	12o. Paris.	1852
Sand, Geo.—Histoire de Ma Vie. Vols. 5–13	16o. Paris.	1855
Sandeau, Jules—Sacs et Parchemins	16o. Paris.	1856
Sanderson, J. P.—Repub. Landmarks; Amer. Statesmen on Immigra'n.	8vo. Phil.	1856
Sandwith, H.—Narrative of the Siege of Kars	12o. Lond.	1856
Sargent, Epes—Standard Speaker	12o. Phil.	1855
Saunders, Fred.—Salad for the Social	12o. N. Y.	1856
Savage, John—'98 and '48; or, Rev'y Hist. and Literature of Ireland	12o. N. Y.	1856
Say, J. B.—Political Economy. (Fr. Fren.)	8vo. Phil.	1832
Scalpel (The).—Vols. 1 and 2, 5 and 6	8vo. N. Y.	1849–54
Schamyl; Life of. By Mackie	12o. Bost.	1856
Scheffel, J. V.—Ekkehard. Gesch. aus dem Zehnten Jahrhundert	12o. Frankfort.	1855
Schiller, Fried.—Sämmtliche Werke. 2 v.	8vo. Stuttgart.	1855
Schoolcraft, Hen. R.—Myth of Hiawatha and other Legends	12o. Phil.	1856
Schreber, Moritz—Illustrated Medical In-door Gymnastics. (Fr. Ger.)	8vo. Lond.	1856
Schulz, O. A.—Addressbuch für den Deutschen Buchandel, 1855	8vo. Leipzig.	s. a.
*Schulze, Ernst—Gothisches Glossar.	4to. Magdeburg.	s. a.
Schwegler, A.—History of Philosophy in Epitome. (Fr. Ger.)	12o. N. Y.	1856
Scoffern, John—Elementary Chemistry of the Imponderable Agents	8vo. Lond.	1855
Scott, Chas. H.—The Danes and the Swedes	12o. Lond.	1856
—— David B.—History of the U. States, for Schools	12o. N. Y.	1852
Seeman, Berthold—Popular History of the Palms	12o. Lond.	1856
Selections from the best Spanish Poets	16o. N. Y.	1856
Sharpe's London Magazine, N. S. Vol. 7	8vo. Lond.	1855
Sheil, Richard Lalor; Memoirs by W. T. McCullagh. 2 v.	12o. Lond.	1855

Sheil, Richard Lalor; Sketches, Legal and Political. 2 v.	12o. Lond.	1855
Sheldon, D. W.—Sin and Redemption	12o. N. Y.	1856
Shoepac Recollections. A Wayside Glimpse of American Life	12o. N. Y.	1856
Short, Thos. V.—What is Christianity?	12o. N. Y.	1844
Sibert's Wold. By Miss Planché	16o. Bost.	1836
Siebold, C. W.—Anatomy of the Invertebrata. (Fr. Ger.) Vol. 1	8vo. Bost.	1854
Simmonds, P. L.—Commercial Products of the Vegetable Kingdom	8vo. Lond.	1854
Simms, W. G.—Charlemont	12o. N. Y.	1856
——— —— Beauchampe	12o. N. Y.	1856
——— —— Eutaw.	12o. N. Y.	1856
Senior, John—Reports on the Sanatory Condition of London	8vo. Lond.	1854
Sketches and Adventures in Madeira, Portugal and Spain	12o. N. Y.	1856
——— in the Isles of Scilly	12o. Lond.	s. a.
Smith, Edw., & Dallas, W. S.—System of Natural History. 2 v.	8vo. Lond.	1855
—— Horace—Walter Colyton; A Tale of 1688. 2 v.	12o. N. Y.	1830
—— J. W.—Law of Landlord and Tenant	8vo. Phil.	1856
—— Sydney—Wit and Wisdom of, with Memoir	12o. N. Y.	1856
Smyth, G. C.—History of the Reigning Family of Lahore	8vo. Calcutta.	1847
Song of Milkan Watha	12o. Cincin.	1856
Soper, E.—The Practical Stenographer	12o. Lond.	1856
Southern Presbyterian Review Vol. 1.	8vo. Colum.	1834
——— Quarterly Review. Vol. 11.	8vo. Charleston.	1855
Southey, Robert—Selections from the Letters of. 4 v. Vols. 1 & 2	12o. Lond.	1856
Southgate, H.—Tour through Armenia, Kurdistan, &c.	8vo. Lond.	1840
Souvestre, E.—Brittany and La Vendée—Tales and Sketches	12o. Edin.	1855
——— —— Le Memorial de Famille	12o. Paris.	1854
Sparrow Grass Papers. [By Fred. Cozzens.]	12o. N. Y.	1856
Spencer, Herbert—Principles of Psychology	8vo. Lond.	1855
——— J. A.—History of the Reformation in England	16o. N. Y.	1846
Spirit of Missions. Vol. 20	8vo. N. Y.	1855
Sporting Magazine for 1855. 2 v.	8vo. Lond.	1855
*Spruner, Karl—Atlas Antiquus	Fol. Gotha.	1855
*——— Atlas zur Geschichte Asien's, Africa's, America's	Fol. Gotha.	1855
*——— Atlas zur Geschichte der Staaten Europa's	Fol. Gotha.	1854
Stanley, A. P.—Sinai and Palestine	8vo. Lond.	1856
Stein, Freihern; Leben, von Pertz	8vo. Berlin.	1854
Stuart, Dugald—Works. Vol. 9. Political Economy. Vol. 2.	8vo. Edin.	1856
Stockton, Robert F.; Sketch of the Life of	8vo. N. Y.	1856
Stuart, J. W.—Life of Nathan Hale, the Martyr Spy	12o. Hartford.	1856
Student. Vols. 9–11.	8vo. N. Y.	1854–55
Sunbeam Stories. By Miss Planché	16o. Bost.	1856
Sumner, Chas—Recent Speeches and Addresses	12o. Bost.	1856
Sutherland, P. C.—Voyage in Baffin's Bay and Barrow's Straits. 2 v.	8vo. Lond.	1852
Swallow, G. C.—Reports (1st & 2d) of the Geological Survey of Mo.	8vo. Jeff. City.	1855
Szabad, Emeric—Hungary, Past and Present	12o. Edin.	1854
Szeredy, J.—Asiatic Chiefs. 2 v.	12o. Lond.	1856
Table of Post Offices in the United States, Jan. 1, 1851.	8vo. Wash.	1851
Table Talk on Books, Men and Manners. Edited by C. Evelyn	12o. N. Y.	1853
Tait, P. G., & Steele, W. J.—On the Dynamics of a Particle	12o. Camb. (E.)	1856

Tait's Edinburgh Magazine. Vol. 22	8vo.	Edin.	1855
Tangletown Letters	12o.	Buffalo.	1856
Tappan, Henry P.—Elements of Logic	12o.	N. Y.	1856
Taylor, Richard—New Zealand and its Inhabitants	8vo.	Lond.	1855
Technologiste (Le). Vols. 13, 16	8vo.	Paris.	1851–55
Tegoborski, M. L.—Productive Forces of Russia. 2 v.	8vo.	Lond.	1855
Tennyson, Alfred—Poetical Works	24o.	Bost.	1856
Theologia Germanica. (Fr. Ger.)	12o.	Andover.	1856
Theological and Literary Journal. Vols. 4 & 7	8vo.	N. Y.	1851–55
Theologische Studien und Kritiken	8vo.	Gotha.	1855
Thibaut, A. F. J.—Introduction to Study of Jurisprudence. (Fr. Ger.)	8vo.	Lond.	1855
Thompson, M. U.—Plu-ri-bus-tah	12o.	N. Y.	1856
*Thom's Irish Almanac and Official Directory for 1856	8vo.	Dublin.	1856
Thomson, Jas.—The Seasons	12o.	N. Y.	1819
——— H. B.—Military Forces and Institutions of Great Britain	8vo.	Lond.	1855
Thrupp. Jos. F.—Ancient Jerusalem	8vo.	Camb. (E.)	1855
Timbs, Jas.—Curiosities of London	12o.	Lond.	1855
*Times (The)—January–April, 1855.	Fol.	Lond.	1855
To-Day: a Boston Literary Journal. Vols. 1 & 2	8vo.	Bost.	1852
Torrens, R.—Political Economy and Representative Gov. in Australia	8vo.	Lond.	1855
Transactions of the American Institute for 1851–52. 2 v.	8vo.	Albany.	1852–53
——— ——— Michigan State Agricultural Soc. 1849–53. 5 v.	8vo.	Lansing.	1850–54
Trench, R. C.—Calderon; his Life and Genius	12o.	N. Y.	1856
——— ——— Poems	12o.	N. Y.	1856
——— W.—Letter on the National System of Education in Ireland	8vo.	Dublin.	1855
Tresca, Mons.—Exposition Universelle de Paris en 1855	16o.	Paris.	1855
*Trübner's Bibliographical Guide to American Literature	8vo.	Lond.	1855
Tschudi, F.—Sketches of Nature in the Alps	12o.	Lond.	1856
Tulloch, John—Theism	12o.	N. Y.	1856
Turner, S. H.—Biographical Notices of distinguished Jewish Rabbis	12o.	N. Y.	1847
Turnerelli, E. T.—Russia on the Borders of Asia. 2 v.	12o.	Lond.	1854
Tuthill, Mrs. S. C.—Reality; or, the Millionaire's Daughter	12o.	N. Y.	1856
Tweedie, W. K.—Man and his Money. Its Use and Abuse	12o.	Lond.	1855
Twiss, T.—Two Lectures on the Science of International Law	8vo.	Lond.	1856
Ubicini, A.—Letters on Turkey. (Fr. Fren.)	12o.	Lond.	1856
Ullmann, C.—Reformers before the Reformation. (Fr. Ger.) Vols. 1 & 2	8vo.	Edin.	1855
United States Magazine and Democratic Review. Vol. 8	8vo.	Wash.	1840
*——— ——— Public Documents, 32d and 33d Congress. 162 v.	8vo.	Wash.	1851–54
Universalist Quarterly. Vol. 12	8vo.	Bost.	1855
Valentine, D. T.—Manual of the Corporation of New York City	12o.	N. Y.	1856
Van Oven, B.—Decline of Life in Health and Disease	8vo.	Lond.	1853
Van Vechten, Jacob—Memoirs of John M. Mason	8vo.	N. Y.	1856
Vassall Morton. By Francis Parkman	12o.	Bost.	1856
Vaughan, R. A.—Hours with the Mystics. 2 v.	16o.	Lond.	1856
Vegetarian Messenger. Vol. 6	8vo.	Lond.	1855
Vera, A.—Inquiry into Speculative Social Science	8vo.	Lond.	1856
Vicars, Hedley, Memorials of	12o.	N. Y.	1855
Victory Won; or the last Days of G. R.	16o.	N. Y.	1856

Visit of 1,000 Sabbath School Teachers of Mass. in New York .	12o.	Bost.	1855
Volney, C. F.—Ruins; or Revolutions of Empires . . .	12o.	Albany.	1822
Wagner, M., und Scherzer, C.—Costa Rica in 1853–54 . .	8vo.	Leipzig.	1856
Walford, Edw.—Hardwick's Annual Biography for 1856 . .	16o.	Lond.	1856
Walker, J. B.—Sacred Philosophy	12o.	Bost.	1855
Wallace,——Life and Reign of George the Fourth. 3 v. . .	16o.	Lond.	1856
——— David A.—Theology of New England . . .	12o.	Bost.	1856
——— H. Binney—Literary Criticisms and other Papers .	12o.	Phil.	1856
Walter Colyton; A Tale of 1688; by Horace Smith. 2 v. .	12o.	N. Y.	1830
Warburton, Capt.—Memoir of the Earl of Peterborough. 2 v. .	12o.	Lond.	1853
Ward, R. P.—Political and Literary Life, by E. Phipps. 2 v. .	8vo.	Lond.	1850
Warren, J. C.—Address to the Boston Society of Natural History	8vo.	Bost.	1853
——— Sam. (Edr.) Blackstone's Commentaries abridged .	8vo.	Lond.	1855
Watson, John—The Medical Profession in Ancient Times .	8vo.	N. Y.	1856
——— W. C. (Edr.)—Men and Times of the Revolution . .	8vo.	N. Y.	1856
Wehl, F.—Hamburgs Literaturleben in 18 Jahrhundert . .	12o.	Leipsig.	1856
Weinhold, Karl—Altnordisches Leben	8vo.	Berlin.	1856
Weld, C. R.—Vacation Tour in the United States and Canada .	12o.	Lond.	1855
Wellington, Duke of—Memoir of, by J. M. Wilson . . .	8vo.	Lond.	s. a.
Wells, David A.—Familiar Science	8vo.	Phil.	1856
——— ——— Year Book of Agriculture, 1855–56 . . .	8vo.	Phil.	1856
Wesleyan Methodist Magazine. Vols. 77, 78 . . .	8vo.	Lond.	1854–55
Western Journal and Civilian. N. S. Vol. 8. . . .	8vo.	St. Louis.	1855
Westminster Review. N. S. Vols. 7 and 8. . . .	8vo.	Lond.	1855
Whately, Archbishop—Thoughts and Apophthegms . .	12o.	Phil.	1856
——— ——— Scripture Revelations concerning Good & Evil Angels	12o.	Phil.	1856
Wheeler, J. T.—Life and Travels of Herodotus. 2 v. . .	12o.	Lond.	1855
White, B., Jr.—The Green Mountain Girls	12o.	N. Y.	1856
Whitehead, Wm. A.—Contributions to the Early Hist. of Perth Amboy	8vo.	N. Y.	1856
Whitney, S. W.—Open Communion; or, Restricted Com. Unscriptural	16o.	N. Y.	1853
——— I. R.—American Policy as opposed to Foreign Influence	12o.	N. Y.	1856
Whittier, J. G.—The Panorama, and other Poems . .	16o.	Bost.	1856
Whittingham, B.—Expedition against Russian Settlements in Siberia	12o.	Lond.	1856
Widow of Kent; or, the History of Mrs. Parley. 2 v. . .	12o.	N. Y.	1810
Wilberforce, Edw.—Brazil viewed through a Naval Glass .	12o.	Lond.	1856
Wilkes, Chas.—Theory of the Wind	8vo.	N. Y.	1856
*Wilkinson, Gardner—Hand-book for Travelers in Egypt .	12o.	Lond.	1846
Williams, J.W. H.—Unsoundness of Mind in Legal and Medical Consid.	8vo.	Lond.	1856
*Willmore, G., and Beedell, E.—Mercantile and Maritime Guide .	8vo.	Glasgow.	1857
Willy Reilly and his dear Coleen Bawn; by Carleton . .	12o.	Bost.	1856
Wilson, J. L.—Western Africa; its History and Prospects. .	12o.	N. Y.	1856
——— J. M.—Memoir of the Duke of Wellington. 2 v. .	8vo.	Lond.	s. a.
——— W. D.—Elementary Treatise on Logic . . .	12o.	N. Y.	1856
Winslow, Miron—Hints on Missions to India . . .	16o.	N. Y.	1856
Wise, Henry A.—Biographical Sketch of, by J. P. Hambleton .	8vo.	Richmond.	1856
With, Emile—Railroad Accidents, their Causes, &c. (Fr. Fren.)	12o.	Bost.	1856
Woods, N. A.—The Past Campaign; or, the War in the East. 2 v.	12o.	Lond.	1855
Woolsey, T. D.—Historical Discourse before the Graduates of Yale	8vo.	N. Haven.	1850
Wordsworth, Chas.—St. Hippolyte and the Ch. of Rome in Third Cent.	8vo.	Lond.	1853

Wraxall, Lascelles—Naval and Military Resources of Europe .	8vo. Lond.	1856
Wright, Henry G.—Headaches, their Causes and their Cure .	16o. Lond.	1856
——— Thos.—Early Christianity in Arabia . . .	8vo. Lond.	1855
Wrightson, Rich. H.—History of Modern Italy to 1850 . .	12o. Lond.	1855
Wylie, J. A.—Pilgrimage from the Alps to the Tiber . .	12o. Edin.	1856
——— M.—Bengal as a Field of Missions	8vo. Lond.	1854
Wynne, Jas.—Effect of Occupation on Longevity. . . .	12o. N. Y.	1856
——— —— Report to American Med. Asso. on Hygiene. .	8vo. Phil.	1850
——— —— ——— British Government on Cholera in U. States	8vo. Lond.	1851
——— —— Vital Statistics of the United States . .	8vo. N. Y.	1856
Yapp, G. W.—Duties on Imports into France . . .	8vo. Lond.	1855
Yonge, C. D.—Dictionary of [Latin] Epithets . . .	8vo. Lond.	1856
——— Miss—The Daisy Chain; or, Aspirations. 2 v. . .	12o. N. Y.	1856
Youatt, Wm.—The Horse; revised by "Cecil" . . .	12o. Lond.	1855
Young, John.—The Christ of History	12o. N. Y.	1856
——— J. R., Twisden, J. F., & Jardine, Alex. Mathematical Science	12o. Lond.	1854
——— Prima Donna. By Mrs. Grey	8vo. Lond.	1854
Zaba, N. F.—History and Literature of Poland . . .	16o. Lond.	1855

www.ingramcontent.com/pod-product-compliance
Lightning Source LLC
LaVergne TN
LVHW011204110826
845150LV00006B/1319